'Zoppi and Schmidt, themselves Jungian analysts of international reputation on the subject of trauma, have assembled a set of papers crammed with the insights and expertise of a group of esteemed authors. Originally formulated as a lecture series, the book offers sharp focus on experiences of analyst and patient in consulting room encounters. The reader will find exploration of unconscious unmetabolized states of early overwhelm that may be somatically, behaviourally or inter-subjectively expressed. Fresh post-Jungian perspectives are teamed with clinical acumen. I can recommend it to anyone working in a clinical context or seeking to immerse themselves in a diversity of academic and clinical reflections on this topic, which is of fundamental importance in understanding psychic gridlock and psychic development.'

Susanna Wright, *Former Co-editor in Chief of the* Journal of Analytical Psychology, *Training and Supervising Analyst for SAP and BJAA and a member of the IAAP Executive Committee*

'Trauma and PTSD are the dominating ailments of our age which plague the victim and torment the analyst. Finally, we have a volume, based on a unique, international dialogue between Italian, British, Austrian, Colombian, Chinese, Latvian, Russian, Serbian and American analysts that firmly embraces *The Complexity of Trauma* in depth. The collection brings together well-known shamans of trauma, like Donald Kalsched, as well as lesser known but vibrant voices from the Jungian world. The interconnection between high level theory, from across the full psychoanalytic spectrum, with engaging clinical cases is especially rewarding. This volume is one you will want to read again and again.'

Henry Abramovitch, *Founding President, Israel Institute of Jungian Psychology in honour of Erich Neumann, Professor Emeritus, Tel Aviv University Medical School*

'*The Complexity of Trauma*, co-edited by Luisa Zoppi and Martin Schmidt, contains a collection of highly informative, thought-provoking and wide-ranging articles on trauma; a topic that sadly, for many tragic reasons, has become more and more relevant for us Jungian analysts in today's world. The chapters in the book cover a wide range of perspectives, which together contribute to a highly valuable analytical psychological understanding of trauma. The combination of poignant clinical studies and unique, innovative theoretical contributions makes this book an indispensable addition to the libraries of training institutes and of Jungian analysts, psychoanalysts and other professionals in the psychological field.'

Misser Berg, Jungian Analyst, President of the IAAP,
former President of DSAP and former Director
of Training at the Jung Institute in Copenhagen

'Arising from a response to the traumas induced by the COVID-19 pandemic, this remarkable collection of essays by a broad range of international experts in analytical psychology is a true gift to therapeutic communities around the world. A 21st century understanding of complexes, their role in trauma and subsequent healing will advance the field on multiple fronts. Chapters explore a wide range of topics from psychodynamics including mythic and symbolic understanding, to the history of the field, and on to contributions from the neurosciences, and socio-cultural phenomena associated with the study of trauma and subsequent recovery. These are all integrated within a Jungian-based model which makes *The Complexity of Trauma* a rare and insightful volume. Editors and authors Luisa Zoppi and Martin Schmidt have done us all a great service in their thoughtful choices and excellent presentation assembled in this volume.'

Joe Cambray, PhD, IAAP, Past President/CEO,
Pacifica Graduate Institute

'The book *The Complexity of Trauma* is born, as the two Editors write in their Introduction, from significant and multiple exchanges among expert Jungian psychoanalysts working in different parts of the world, who contributed to a course of higher education promoted by the Italian Association for Analytical Psychology (AIPA). This course, coordinated by Luisa Zoppi (Rome) in 2021, was a fruitful occasion for many international colleagues to meet and discuss theoretical and clinical approaches to the theme of trauma and post-traumatic developments from the latest perspectives of Analytical Psychology. This book, collecting together innovative insights and deep reflections which arose from those exchanges, presents itself as an updated review of the many theoretical issues which help clinicians to understand symptoms and states of mind derived from developmental trauma in different conditions and at different ages and how to treat them. Furthermore, clinical strategies and techniques are discussed, which are relevant in analytical assessment and psychotherapy of traumatized patients in childhood, adolescence and adulthood. For instance, special consideration is devoted to new therapeutic techniques, that analysts can introduce in their work, aiming at treating very early relational traumas, which are neither remembered nor symbolically representable.'

Alessandra De Coro, *Former Professor at 'Sapienza' University Rome, Training Analyst and former President of AIPA, IAAP EC member from 2010 to 2016, and Liaison Person for Kazakhstan*

'The editors of this collection of outstanding articles, Luisa Zoppi and Martin Schmidt, have managed to gather an exquisite array of perspectives on the ubiquitous and challenging topic of working with trauma. This book offers the reader a clinical smorgasbord, from a Jungian perspective, on a topic that lies at the very heart of analytic and psychotherapeutic work, regardless of one's clinical orientation. Donald Kalsched's article on early relational trauma and his understanding of the Self-care System sets the stage for links to the earlier contributions of such eminent authors as Fordham, Winnicott and Bion on this very topic. Daniela Eulert-Fuchs' article on her clinical work with a young boy provides the reader with a vivid and penetrating example of the clinical maze of navigating one's way through the impervious intensity of the constellated counter transferential affects in order to get a clearer grasp and understanding of root causes of the trauma. The spectrum of the remaining articles includes the exploration of the topic of trauma from a neurobiological perspective, dissociation and the link to trans-generational trauma, cultural trauma and work with migrants, and the role of memory and creativity in healing trauma. This book is unique in its broad perspective and an absolute must for clinicians seriously interested in delving into and deepening their understanding of the complexity of the wounds underlying trauma. I highly recommend this book and consider it a must for clinicians.'

Tom Kelly, *Past President of IAAP (2013–2016), current Chair of the Ethics Committee of IAAP, in clinical practice in Montreal, Canada*

'This book emerged from an online course on trauma and complexes. Masterly edited by Luisa Zoppi and Martin Schmidt, it fascinates in its range of topics. Earlier work by Michael Fordham, Fairbairn and Bion are covered as well as Donald Kalsched's original ideas. It includes topics such as early relational trauma, dissociative processes, transgenerational trauma, social trauma, neurobiological findings and creative methods of healing. This is an eminently clinical book with the emphasis on transference and countertransference in the clinical encounter, unconscious communication and not avoiding sexualised transference, hatred and violence. Contributors share the richness of their experience and give moving insights into their work, including social and cultural aspects. The last section is dedicated to creative methods of healing. Professor Heyong Shen offers a poetic Oriental approach and introduces the reader to the Chinese "Psychology of the Heart". This book is a treasure trove!'

Arthur Niesser, *Medical doctor and Jungian Analyst, Member of AJA (London) and the C.G. Jung Institut Stuttgart (Germany), current co-editor of the* Journal of Analytical Psychology

'This book is so timely given that we are all living through such a difficult time of collective and personal trauma with war and destructiveness all around us. It should be read. In their book, Zoppi and Schmidt have gathered together a group of international authors expert in different aspects of trauma ranging from the impact of early relational trauma to the cultural aspects of trauma evident in different parts of the world. The book offers readers a contemporary Jungian approach that acknowledges the fractured complexes observable in patients suffering from trauma, the different types of dissociation that can develop and more generally an understanding of the kinds of defences we are likely to encounter with our patients. This is a volume that will be valuable to therapists, analysts and those in training for many years to come.'

Jan Wiener, *Jungian Supervising Analyst, former Vice-President of the IAAP, Society of Analytical Psychology, London*

'In *The Complexity of Trauma*, the editors, Luisa Zoppi and Martin Schmidt, have gathered and curated a wonderful selection of papers on trauma written by eminent scholars and clinicians (including Donald Kalsched) from the field of Analytical Psychology. The breadth and depth of the papers is inspiring – providing a contemporary exploration of trauma (individual, collective, cultural and transgenerational) and the treatment of trauma from a Jungian perspective. The close relationship between trauma and complex theory is examined by several of the authors. Points of intersection between trauma and dissociation, somatic experience, eroticized transference, affect, neuroscience and creativity are also explored. This volume is an essential read for practicing Jungian clinicians and students of Analytical Psychology. Highly recommended.'

Mark Winborn, PhD, *Jungian Psychoanalyst, Clinical Psychologist, author of* Interpretation in Jungian Analysis: Art and Technique *and* Jungian Psychoanalysis: A Contemporary Introduction

The Complexity of Trauma

This important volume offers a broad and in-depth overview of how to understand and treat trauma from a Jungian perspective, written by internationally recognized experts in the field of Jungian and traditional psychoanalysis.

It applies C.G. Jung's concept of the 'complex' and his understanding of splitting processes of the psyche to trauma. Traversing a range of pertinent themes including archetypal defences, primary narcissistic wounding, somatic symptoms, symbolic representation and processing, transference and types of memory, the book features a variety of voices from different theoretical perspectives, with each contributor offering clinical examples and lessons from their experiences working with patients. Chapters cover a wide range of clinical phenomena including early relational trauma, dissociative states, the Self-care System, unconscious communication, embodied countertransference, eroticization, PTSD, creativity and cultural/social issues.

The Complexity of Trauma is key reading for psychoanalysts and therapists as well as for researchers, students and trainees in schools of psychodynamic psychotherapy and those interested in working with trauma.

Luisa Zoppi is a Clinical Psychologist and Jungian Training Analyst (Italian Association of Analytical Psychology [AIPA]). Since 2015, she has been teaching Theory of Complexes, Transcendent Function and Dynamics of the Individuation Process at AIPA. Since August 2019, she has been a member of the Executive Committee of the International Association for Analytical Psychology (IAAP).

Martin Schmidt is a Jungian Training Analyst (Society of Analytical Psychology in London) who lectures and supervises widely around the world. He has worked for over 20 years as a psychologist in psychiatric rehabilitation, was former Honorary Secretary of the IAAP and its Regional Organiser for Central Europe.

The Complexity of Trauma

Jungian and Psychoanalytic Approaches
to the Treatment of Trauma

Edited by Luisa Zoppi and Martin Schmidt

Routledge
Taylor & Francis Group

LONDON AND NEW YORK

Designed cover image: Livia Del Duca

First published 2025
by Routledge
4 Park Square, Milton Park, Abingdon, Oxon OX14 4RN

and by Routledge
605 Third Avenue, New York, NY 10158

Routledge is an imprint of the Taylor & Francis Group, an informa business

British Library Cataloguing-in-Publication Data
A catalogue record for this book is available from the British Library

Library of Congress Cataloging-in-Publication Data
Names: Zoppi, Luisa, editor. | Schmidt, Martin (Jungian training analyst), editor.
Title: The complexity of trauma : Jungian and psychoanalytic approaches to the treatment of trauma / edited by Luisa Zoppi and Martin Schmidt.
Description: Abingdon, Oxon ; New York, NY : Routledge, 2025. | Includes bibliographical references and indexes. |
Identifiers: LCCN 2024015541 (print) | LCCN 2024015542 (ebook) |
ISBN 9781032286976 (hardback) | ISBN 9781032287003 (paperback) |
ISBN 9781003298076 (ebook)
Subjects: MESH: Stress Disorders, Traumatic--therapy |
Psychoanalysis--methods | Jungian Theory
Classification: LCC RC552.T7 C655 2025 (print) | LCC RC552.T7 (ebook) |
NLM WM 172.5 | DDC 616.85/21--dc23/eng/20240506
LC record available at https://lccn.loc.gov/2024015541
LC ebook record available at https://lccn.loc.gov/2024015542

ISBN: 978-1-032-28697-6 (hbk)
ISBN: 978-1-032-28700-3 (pbk)
ISBN: 978-1-003-29807-6 (ebk)

DOI: 10.4324/9781003298076

Typeset in Times New Roman
by SPi Technologies India Pvt Ltd (Straive)

We would like to dedicate this book to the memory of our dear friend and colleague, Dr Daniela Eulert-Fuchs. We have been blessed with the gift of her beautiful chapter which she wrote while struggling with a terminal illness. It serves as a fitting legacy to her brilliant career. She illuminated the lives of so many people. We feel honoured that she has graced this book with her insights and experience. She lives on in these pages and in our hearts.

We also dedicate this book to our families who have supported us in every step particularly Gianfranco, Livia, Fulvia, Nataša, Amelia, Esmé and Speck. We also hope that the book will be a source of inspiration and guidance for those who have suffered trauma and the wounded healers who try to support them.

Contents

PART IV
Poetic and Creative Methods   283

Contributors

Editors

Martin Schmidt, MBPsS, Jungian Training Analyst of the Society of Analytical Psychology (SAP) London. He has worked as a psychologist and psychotherapist in psychiatric rehabilitation for over 20 years. He teaches and supervises widely both in the UK and in over 20 countries around the world. From 2016–2019, he was the Honorary Secretary of the International Association of Analytical Psychology (IAAP) and its Regional Organiser for Central Europe. He continues to serve as IAAP Liaison for Serbia. For over seven years, he was a visiting supervisor/lecturer on the IAAP Russian Revival programme in Moscow and St Petersburg. He has published numerous papers in the *International Journal of Analytical Psychology* (JAP), the *Russian Journal of Analytical Psychology*, *Studi Junghiani* (Italy), the *Chinese Journal of Analytical Psychology* and *Cahiers de Psychoanalyses* (France). His paper 'Psychic skin: Psychotic defences, borderline process and delusions' (Feb 2012, Vol 57, no 1) won the Fordham prize for best clinical paper in the *JAP* in 2012 and was nominated for the Gradiva Award by the National Association for the Advancement of Psychoanalysis in New York in 2013.

Luisa Zoppi, Clinical Psychologist, Jungian Training Analyst of AIPA. She has worked for many years in the field of empirical research on Psychosomatics, at Sapienza University in Rome, where she has regularly given lectures on Referential Activity. She has been published in a number of journals and collected books. Besides her scientific work on Psychosomatics, she has also published: 'Chilled to the bone: Embodied countertransference and unspoken traumatic memories' in the *Journal of Analytical Psychology* (2017). More recently, her article '*Blade Runner* und die Welt des echten Lebens' was published in the German *Journal of Analytical Psychology*, *Analytische Psychologie* (Heft 199, 54, 1/2023). Since 2015, she has been teaching 'The theory of complexes and the dynamics of the individuation process' at AIPA. Since August 2019, she has been a member of the Executive Committee of IAAP. She works as an analyst in private practice in Rome.

Contributors

Fabrizio Alfani, Psychiatrist, Training Analyst of AIPA, member of IAAP. His main interests concern the treatment of trauma and the study of dissociation, as well as the investigation of similarities between analytical psychology and advancements in contemporary psychoanalysis. Fabrizio has served on the Editorial Board of the Italian Jungian Journal *Studi Junghiani*. He has been published in several Italian journals and, in 2020, in the collected book *Continuità e discontinuità dei processi dissociativi* (Germani M. and Maulucci M., Eds., Frammenti di Psiche. Franco Angeli, 2020). He lives and practices in Modena (Italy).

Mariella Battipaglia, Psychiatrist, teacher, Supervisor and Training Analyst of AIPA, Rome, IAAP member, specialist in Relational Psychosomatics, teacher and co-founder of the Training Institute of Integrated Relational Therapy (ITRI-Rome). She works as a teacher, analyst, coordinator and supervisor of multidisciplinary medical-psychotherapy teams. She is a member of the Training Committee of the AIPA Training School. She has written many articles that have been published in Jungian and psychoanalytic journals. She has been involved in various international psychiatric research projects and has contributed to numerous publications. Other publications constitute contributions to books. She has been a speaker at both national and international seminars and conferences.

Patrizia Brogna, Clinical Psychologist and Psychotherapist at the Prevention and Early Interventions Unit, Mental Health Department – Roma 1. She has extensive experience in the treatment of PTSD and also psychosis from a phenomenological perspective. Patrizia teaches on the Treatment of Disorders of Affect Regulation at LUMSA University (Rome), on the Treatment of Borderline Personality Disorders at IIPP (Palermo) and is also Professor of Treatment of Dysregulation of Affects in Adolescence at Consorzio Universitatio Humanitas, Rome. Her main interest of investigation is the nature of self-experience in complex trauma and PTSD. She also works as a psychotherapist at a Public Mental Health Service in Rome.

Chiara Caprì, Psychiatrist, Jungian Analyst at the Italian Centre of Analytical Psychology (CIPA). She has worked for the European Project I.C.A.R.E.: 'Integration and Community care for Asylum and Refugees in Emergency' at a Public Health Centre for refugees. Since 2019, she has been working as a psychiatrist for the European project 'Freedom of Choice'. This project explores the psychological traits of children of Mafia families in the South of Italy. Currently she is working with adolescents at the Early Interventions Centre, Mental Health Department – Rome 1. She is the author of books about the Sicilian mafia (2010, 2011, 2012) focusing on investigating the psychological aspects of adolescents affiliated with it.

Eduardo Carvallo, Venezuelan Psychiatrist, Humanistic Psychotherapist, Jungian Analyst, IAAP member. For years, he has been investigating the auto-regulation and auto-organization processes of the psyche and their application to clinical work. Currently, he is interested in studying archetypal patterns in psychic functioning, trauma and the relationship between indigenous cultures, shamanism, psychology and spirituality. Eduardo is a member of the International Association of Expressive Sandwork (IAES), co-founder of the Colombian Society of Jungian Analysts (SCAJ), co-founder of the Venezuelan Society of Jungian Analysts (SVAJ) and co-founder and current president of the Latin American Committee for Analytical Psychology (CLAPA).

Giancarlo Costanza, Child and Adolescent Psychiatrist since 1986 and chief consultant in a CAMHS unit of the Italian NHS. As a Jungian Analyst belonging to AIPA, he practices in Catania. Giancarlo Costanza regularly gives lectures for the AIPA Training School and is particularly interested in neurodevelopmental disorders, personality disorders, and trauma, as well as the entwining of shadow and power in the helping professions. He is currently a member of the Editorial Board of the Italian Jungian journal *Studi Junghiani*. He also serves in the scientific committee for CME of AIPA (Milano).

Giovanna Curatola graduated in Medicine and is Full Professor of Biological Chemistry. She taught Biochemistry and Neurochemistry at the Faculties of Medicine, Surgery and Biology of the Polytechnic University of Marche. She is a psychotherapist (Honorary Member) at AIPA. She is a teacher in several psychotherapy Schools. She was a member of the Scientific Committee of the AIPA Training School.

Gianluigi Di Cesare, Psychiatrist and Jungian Analyst, member of AIPA and IAAP. He is the Director of the Prevention and Early Interventions Unit, Mental Health Department – Roma 1. He teaches Evolutionary Factors in Antisocial Development at the Psychology Department, University LUMSA,

Rome. His main scientific and professional interests are trauma, dissociation, transference-countertransference relationships and the setting and early intervention in psychosis.

Daniela Eulert-Fuchs, MD, GP, was a paediatrician and neuropediatrician. She had a psychoanalytic practice for adults, infants, children and adolescents in Vienna, Austria. She was Training and Supervising Analyst for the Austrian Association of Analytical Psychology (ÖGAP). She also worked for the IAAP router programme. Active for many years in different psychotherapeutic and psychosomatic clinics and institutions, she had specialized in work with infants and their caregivers and helped to set up the Crying-Baby Ambulance. Daniela had a keen interest in exploring transference-countertransference dynamics as well as the influence of the analytical attitude in the analytic encounter.

George Hogenson, PhD, LCSW (USA), is former Vice-President of the International Association for Analytical Psychology and is member of the editorial board of the *Journal of Analytical Psychology*. He is the author of *Jung's Struggle with Freud* (1994) and numerous articles on analytical psychology. He is in private practice in Chicago and Oak Park Illinois.

Donald Kalsched, PhD, Clinical Psychologist and Jungian Psychoanalyst with a private practice in Brunswick, Maine. He is Senior Faculty Member and Training Analyst with the Inter-Regional Society of Jungian Analysts and serves on the Board of the Maine Jung Center. He lectures and teaches nationally and internationally on the subject of early childhood trauma and its treatment, and has led master classes for clinical supervisors in many clinical settings. His celebrated book *The Inner world of trauma: Archetypal defenses of the personal spirit* (Routledge 1996) explores the interface between contemporary psychoanalytic theory and Jungian thought as it relates to practical clinical work with the survivors of early childhood trauma. His second book, *Trauma and the soul: A psycho-spiritual approach to human development and its interruption* (Routledge, 2013) explores some of the mystical dimensions of clinical work with trauma survivors. He is currently working on a third major book which will explore the practical aspects of working more directly with feelings and defenses-against-feelings in the clinical situation.

Emilija Kiehl, MSc, Jungian Analyst practising in London. She is Training and Supervising Analyst for the British Jungian Analytic Association and Senior Member of the British Psychotherapy Foundation. She is a former vice-president, current Honorary Secretary and editor of several publications by IAAP. She was a book review editor for *Spring Journal* and current journal review editor for the *Journal of Analytical Psychology*. Her published translations include works by Noam Chomsky, Harold Pinter, Arthur Miller, John Updike and others. She lectures, teaches and supervises in the UK and abroad.

Lara Lagutina, Training Analyst of the Society of Analytical Psychology (SAP) London and Clinical Psychologist, with specialist training in working with trauma and a particular interest in relational trauma and early states of mind. She is on the editorial board of the *Journal of Analytical Psychology* and is Programme Director for the Analytic Training at the SAP. She teaches and supervises internationally. Her paper, 'Meeting the orphan: Early relational trauma, synchronicity and the psychoid' (2021), was nominated for the Gradiva Award. She works in full-time private practice in London.

Emanuela Mundo, Psychiatrist and Jungian Analyst at AIPA. She practices in Milan and teaches 'Psychoanalysis and Neuroscience' at Sapienza University, Rome. Emanuela is Training Analyst for AIPA and a member of IAAP. She has worked for years at the Centre for Addiction and Mental Health and the Department of Psychiatry, University of Toronto (Canada), and then at several psychiatric and psychotherapeutic institutions in Italy. She has specialized in psychotherapeutic work with trauma victims and transgender people, and she has published in several international scientific journals. She is also one of the Editors of the Adult Symptom Section (Axis S) of the Psychodynamic Diagnostic Manual, Second Edition (PDM-2).

Julia Ovchinnikova, PhD, Jungian Analyst and Supervisor. The main area of her research is personality crisis, with a particular interest in identity and midlife crises, multicultural therapy and symbolic function. She works in private practice in London, supervises and teaches nationally and internationally, including seminars at AJA and the SAP (London), Master's Programme 'Psychoanalytic Psychotherapy' at the HSE University (Moscow), and supervises at The Singapore University of Social Sciences (Singapore). Julia also runs a project 'ProPsy-Emigration' which aims to help people who have relocated to a new culture.

Roberta Perri, Neurologist, Neuropsychologist and Jungian Analyst at AIPA and IAAP. For over 20 years, she has been in charge of the Cognitive Disorders and Dementia Centre at the IRCCS Santa Lucia Foundation,

Rome. She has extensively published on Clinical Neuropsychology and Cognitive Neuroscience in international journals such as *Neuropsychologia, Cortex, Journal of Neurology* and in collected books. She is in private practice in Rome.

Heyong Shen, PhD, Professor of Psychology (City University of Macao, and South China Normal University, Guangzhou), Jungian analyst (member of the IAAP), Sandplay therapist (member of the International Society of Sandplay Therapy), President of the China Society for Analytical Psychology (CSAP) and the China Society for Sandplay Therapy (CSST), speaker at the Eranos East and West Round Table Conferences (1997, 2007, 2019 and 2022), main organizer of the International Conference of Analytical Psychology and Chinese Culture (1998–2023), chief editor of the Chinese translation of the Collected Works of C.G. Jung and founding member of the Garden of the Heart & Soul project. He is author of *Psychology of the heart* (Fay Lecture), *C.G. Jung and Chinese culture* and *The heart of Chinese culture psychology*, as well as numerous articles on the interface between analytical psychology and Chinese culture.

Preface

George Hogenson

In his War Memoir, Wilfred Bion recounts:

> [A]s I and a runner named Sweeting crouched together in one spot, a shell seemed to burst on top of us, and I heard a groan from Sweeting. The left side of his tunic seemed covered in blood, and as I looked, I discovered that the whole of his left side had been torn away so that the middle of the trunk lay exposed. But he was not dead. He was quite a young boy and was terrified, as he did not quite realize what had happened. He tried to see what had happened, but I would not let him. I pretended to bandage him, but of course the field dressing was far too small and simply didn't come near to covering the cavity. He kept saying "I'm done for, sir! I'm done for", hoping against hope I would contradict him. This I did, telling him it was nothing—but his eyes were already glazing over, and it was clear that death was even then upon him. He kept trying to cough, but the wind only came out of his side. He kept asking me why he couldn't cough.
> (Bion, 1997: 131)

Bion's daughter, Parthenope, remarked in her 'Aftermath', appended to the memoir, that when speaking of these events and others from the war, Bion expressed 'hardly any emotion or intellectual elaboration' (Bion, 1997: 307). As Robert Hinshelwood observes in his study of Bion, Bion likely suffered from 'war neurosis', or post-traumatic stress disorder (Hinshelwood, 2022: 2). Bion's experience was not unique, either in the Great War or the history of war. Two thousand five hundred years earlier, Herodotus, in his history of the Greco/Persian war, gave what is probably the first account of PTSD:

> In this fight at Marathon there were slain of the Barbarians about six thousand four hundred men, and of the Athenians a hundred and ninety and two. Such was the number which fell on both sides; and it happened also that a marvel occurred there of this kind: an Athenian, Epizelus the

son of Cuphagoras, while fighting in the close combat and proving himself a good man, *was deprived of the sight of his eyes, neither having
received a blow in any part of his body nor having been hit with a missile,
and for the rest of his life from this time he continued to be blind*: and I was
informed that he used to tell about that which had happened to him a tale
of this kind, namely that it seemed to him that a tall man in full armor
stood against him, whose beard overshadowed his whole shield, and this
apparition passed him by, but killed his comrade who stood next to him.
Thus, as I was informed, Epizelus told the tale.

(Herodotus, 1890, Book 6:117, emphasis added)

These accounts, and many others like them, give us clues to the profound
impact of trauma, whether in war or experiences ranging from the sexual
abuse of children by trusted figures, too often associated with religious or
spiritual settings, or as is now often the case in the United States while shop-
ping in the neighbourhood grocery store. Wilfred Bion, who would go on to
investigate the profound depths of the psyche and focus increasingly on the
role of affect in the workings of the unconscious, was nevertheless left, when
speaking of his wartime experience, with the flat affect that may never leave
the survivor of trauma. On the other hand, Epizelus, at Marathon, recounts
another aspect of trauma, the appearance of the agent of his experience in
the form of an 'apparition' or 'phantom' (Φάσμα). This phantom warrior
who passes by Epizelus, and kills his friend, nevertheless rendering Epizelus
blind for the rest of his life, stands in curious juxtaposition to the beneficent
phantasm 'Orpha' identified by Ferenczi in his Clinical Diary (Ferenczi,
1932) as a protective figure in a case of severe trauma. These phantom figures take us directly into the world of C.G. Jung, where the imaginal complexity of the deep, collective unconscious assumes a central role in the lived
experience of the individual.

I have known and worked with Luisa Zoppi and Martin Schmidt for many
years, and it is truly a pleasure to offer some comments on this essential
volume. Luisa and Martin are uniquely qualified to bring together this
group of authors whose insights into trauma marshal materials that are
deeply informed clinically while looking beyond the individual's experience
and treatment to shed light on the deeper dimensions of this increasingly
common experience throughout the world. Trauma is a singularly complex
problem that can ramify throughout the life of the victim as well as the culture within which it becomes manifest. Wilfred Bion, who figures promi-
nently in these essays, went from war trauma to becoming one of the most
consequential psychoanalysts of the 20th century. Epizelus' encounter with

the phantom warrior was immortalized not only by Herodotus but on the Stoa Poikile (or painted porch) on the North side of the Athenian agora. It is increasingly important for clinicians of all clinical persuasions to grapple with this complexity. The chapters in this collection contribute to this process and provide avenues for further investigation and clinical practice, in this instance with the unique insights provided by Jung's analytical psychology. The chapters reward careful reading and continued reflection.

References

Bion, W.R. (1997) *War Memoirs, 1917–1919*. London: Karnac Books.

Ferenczi, S. (1932 [1988]) *The Clinical Diary of Sandor Ferenczi*. J. Dupont (ed.), M. Balint and N.Z. Jackson (trans.) Cambridge, MA: Harvard University Press.

Herodotus (1890) *The History of Herodotus – Vol II*. G.C. Macaulay (trans.) Urbana, IL: Project Gutenberg.

Hinshelwood, R.D. (2022) *W.R. Bion as a Clinician*. New York: Routledge.

Acknowledgements

There are a number of people we would like to thank, without whom this book would not have been possible. First of all, we are very grateful to Alexis O'Brien and Katie Randall from Routledge. Alexis helped us to get the project off the ground and Katie has guided us throughout the process. Friends and family have also helped us along the way, not least Livia Del Duca who designed the artwork for the cover and formatted the entire book. Gianfranco and Nataša have been a constant source of support (both practical and emotional). Other colleagues have been a font of inspiration and always there for us in our hour of need including Antonio de Rienzo, Elisabetta Bertolotti, Michela Di Trani, Rupert Tower, Patrizia Di Gioia and Federico Lucidi. Luisa would also like to personally thank her English teacher Sophie West whose help has been invaluable. Last, but not least, we would like to thank all of our patients, without whom this book would never have come to fruition.

Permission Credits

The painting by William Blake in Chapter 2 is reproduced under permission from Tate Images.

The watercolours by Francesco Finocchiaro in Chapter 13 are reproduced by kind permission of the author.

The drawing by Livia Del Duca on the cover is reproduced by kind permission of the author.

Introduction

Luisa Zoppi and Martin Schmidt

In December 2020, during the COVID pandemic, the training analysts of the Italian Analytical Association (AIPA) were asked if they were willing to organize online Higher Education Courses for analysts. The aim of AIPA's request was to keep Italian Jungian analysts up-to-date with the latest developments in analytical psychology and psychoanalysis, despite the rigid restrictions of the pandemic in Italy. Before the pandemic, Luisa Zoppi had been teaching the theory of Complexes to AIPA's trainee analysts and had found it increasingly important in understanding her patients. She realized that understanding trauma from the perspective of the theory of Complexes deeply enriched her work. She felt that AIPA would benefit from a course based on this topic which she hoped would be provided by a mixture of both eminent Italian and international colleagues who had expertise in this area. So, quickly, and maybe foolishly, Luisa set to work and was surprised at how easy it was to write the outline of the course. It was as if it had already been written! Her first thought was to invite Donald Kalsched as his ideas on working with trauma have been seminal in the Jungian world. She was delighted by how readily other analysts and experts in the field accepted the invitation to speak.

Therefore, in February 2021, the online course *Feeling-Toned Complexes and Treatment of Trauma* began. Despite the online setting, many colleagues enthusiastically took part in the meetings and a shared space was quickly created. The course turned out to be a great success and received very positive feedback. Many colleagues expressed their gratitude for the depth and structure of the programme. Martin Schmidt, one of the many highly valued international speakers, made a suggestion that he lived to regret! He remarked that, as Luisa had assembled such a rich and varied group of clinicians for the course (and that it had been so well received), why not turn the course lectures into a book? She agreed, but only if he would co-edit it with her. The rest is history.

DOI: 10.4324/9781003298076-1

The course in Rome was a celebration and expansion of Kalsched's invaluable contribution to understanding trauma and, in particular, early relational trauma, meaning that which occurs before ego and language have developed. Trauma is widely understood as an experience that overwhelms the mind, a devastating burst of excessive psychic excitation which disrupts the capacity for emotional containment, thinking and understanding. Building on the work of Michael Fordham, Kalsched recognized that if trauma impacts at an early age, then Fordham's (1974) "defences of the Self" are activated, interrupting the de-integration/re-integration cycle and preventing a healthy internal world from forming. As Fordham warns, here a: "persistent over-reaction of the defence-system may start to take place, leading to an accumulation of violence and hostility which is split off from any libidinal and loving communication with the object that may take place" (Fordham, 1976: 90–91). This emphasis on the dynamics of hatred and violence in working with trauma patients has become crucial in understanding the nature of the transference and countertransference in the clinical encounter. This is a leitmotif throughout this book.

Kalsched and Fordham have built upon the work of earlier psychoanalysts such as Fairbairn and Bion who understood that the child is often unable to channel this aggression towards those responsible for the trauma. Instead, the violence and hatred are directed against oneself driven by that which Bion (1967: 107) refers to as a sadistic or "ego-destructive superego", Fairbairn (1952: 136) an "inner saboteur" and Kalsched (2017: 478) the "dark angel".

Kalsched proposed that powerful archetypal agencies representing the early opposing affects of love and hate are recruited by a "Self-care System" (SCS) of defence, and that this system either violently attacks the links between the patient's child-like vulnerability and his ego or seeks to numb it through encapsulation and illusion. As we know, early trauma is defended against, first, by dissociation and then, later, by repression. The SCS is a dissociative system which tries to prevent the infant's mind from becoming overwhelmed by anxiety and trauma-linked memories. Kalsched describes how the SCS, in traumatized patients, can become a significant resistance to healing. This is because, in the course of therapy, traumatic memories and affects begin to return which triggers the defensive SCS. It tries to prevent further violation to the patient's psyche by preventing certain painful emotions from becoming conscious, dissociating them and blocking them from associating with the ego. Kalsched portrays this as a violent attack by the child's instinctive (archetypal) aggression against its own vulnerable emotional life.

All the authors in this book are Jungian analysts, or scholars influenced by Jung, who have been inspired in different ways by Kalsched's original ideas. Jung believed that trauma can cause the psyche to fracture. In this way, trauma can produce autonomous complexes: "Complexes are in fact 'splinter psyches'. The aetiology of their origin is frequently a so-called trauma, an emotional shock or some such thing, that splits off a bit of the psyche" (Jung, 1934, para. 204). These trauma-related complexes, which act as if they have a life of their own, are charged with fury and hatred. West (2016) describes how early trauma-related patterns of interaction become installed in implicit memory (as opposed to explicit cognitive memory) and are relived in the therapeutic relationship as a trauma-related complex is constellated. Here, the therapist becomes the re-traumatizing other and unwittingly triggers the trauma.

For Kalsched, the SCS is a "compartmentalization system" that includes normal complex-formation within its structure but goes beyond it with regard to the severity of trauma that it defends against. In addition to what Jung described as normal ego-complexes, the SCS deals with more "primitive" emotions that are a part of early infancy and early traumatic neglect or impingement. As a result of the power of these archaic affects, the defences necessary to control them are also extreme, hence the preponderance of aggression and violence in the defences of the SCS.

These dissociative defences come at a cost. Although defensive compartmentalization allows these patients to function in the outer world, they often suffer from feelings of "fraudulence". They struggle with low self-esteem, intense feelings of shame and various self-destructive behaviours where their unconscious anger cuts them off from a painful reality that they must avoid at all costs.

Our book expands upon these ideas and approaches the complexity of trauma from diverse perspectives. We start with Luisa Zoppi who, in Chapter 1: "Feeling-Toned Complexes and the Treatment of Trauma: A Jungian Perspective", lays the foundation for the book. She explores the current debate in Jungian analysis with regard to complexes and their place in analytical psychology. Luisa accompanies us to the dynamic period at the Burghölzli in which Jung lived, where together with many other passionate young doctors, he was enthusiastically involved in empirical research on the Word Association Test, under the guidance of Bleuler. From these studies, she shows how Jung acquired his first insights into the nature of complexes. He was able to investigate the crucial role of autonomous complexes in psychic functioning, with the help of new instruments and measurements (e.g., electrocardiography, plethysmographic spirometry – the measure of breathing rate and depth – and a more accurate recording of the psychogalvanic-reflex) as well as seeing dissociation as a normal part of psychic life. Luisa points out that Jung, from early on, understood that trauma is the main factor in the origin of autonomous complexes. Now, the complex is a cornerstone concept in Analytical Psychology: it is the smallest unit of psychic structure and can become *autonomous* when there is a trauma (Jung, 1934). Interestingly, although trauma is an important concept in analytical psychology and not least in the theory of complexes (see Jung, 1934, para. 204), it has largely been underestimated in Jungian thinking until more recently. Luisa describes how the remarkable work of Donald Kalsched (1996) on trauma has been seminal in furthering the debate on the role of complex theory in Jungian analysis. She provides a powerful clinical vignette to illustrate how the psyche can function when facing trauma, and how analysis can serve to integrate split-off complexes throughout the analytic journey, framed by compassion.

In Chapter 2: "Trauma and the Inner World: The Self-care System as a Resistance to Healing", we hear from Donald Kalsched himself. He illustrates the working of the SCS through a powerful and moving case example where an enactment is described in which the violent energies of the patient's SCS enter the transference field and are partly transformed. Such transformation is heralded by the emergence of a "lost child" in the material and the significance of this "child" in Jung's theory is discussed. Donald also uses William Blake's illustration (from the Tate Gallery in London) of "Good and Evil Angels Fight for Possession of a Child", as a self-portrait of the psyche's dissociative defensive operations perpetrated by the two Angels representing archetypal affects and dynamic structures of the collective unconscious. The Dark Angel represents violence and the negative affects of hatred, malice, domination, shame and attack. By contrast, the Bright Angel represents illusion and all the soothing images and fantasies associated with hope, comfort and safety, including primitive love and compassion. Both are portrayed as necessary forces of dissociation, when trauma is extreme in early life, each trying, in his own way, to keep the child away from the painful feelings in reality that have been impossible to entertain consciously. Each trying, through dissociation, to keep the child unconscious of its vulnerable feelings.

The next three chapters concern the topic of early relational trauma.

We believe that Chapter 3: "Countertransference in Working with Early Relational Trauma: In Dialogue with the Body", will become a seminal piece of work for years to come. In this excellent clinical exposition,

Daniela Eulert-Fuchs poignantly demonstrates how early trauma is not remembered or symbolically represented, but repeated, in ordinary life and the analytic relationship. This is especially the case with early relational trauma where, in contrast to conventional analytic techniques, the work is less about insight and interpretation than about creating an analytic stance which allows for the experiencing of that which could never be thought and felt. In this clinically oriented and beautifully constructed chapter, which focuses on three very moving cases, the author attempts to show how the analyst, by participating in primary process dynamics, gains access to the patient's split-off traumatic experience. This requires not only acceptance of long periods of not knowing, but also of bodily and psychic states that are often accompanied by hopelessness. Daniela writes about this with compassion, tenderness, resilience, technical brilliance and grace which are rare qualities in an analyst. These states, she posits, must be experienced each time anew and are regarded as the analyst's contribution to making the unthinkable thinkable. She calls this "reverie of the shared body" and compares it to pre-verbal exchanges that are recreated in the analytic field. This reverie encompasses not only essential communicative but also therapeutic elements that are, as the vignettes show, both represented and symbolically processed, eventually contributing to a transformed understanding of self and world.

Chapter 4, by Mariella Battipaglia and Giovanna Curatola, entitled: "The Body Roots of Traumatic Experiences: From Unsymbolized Body Memory to Bodily Reverie", reflects on how bodily phenomena in analytic work are connected to difficulties in symbolization and mind-body dissociation. They argue that perceptions and body sensations (proprioception, balance and enteroception) provide information about the actual external world, while somatic and visceral body (the internal physical world) information is linked with past memories. They illustrate how these early memories are susceptible to dissociative defences which affect the analytical relationship and emerge in enactments, transference-countertransference dynamics, dreams and reverie, including bodily ones. They expertly demonstrate how the symbol-poietic potential of these early experiences enables the transformation of preverbal and pre-symbolic elements into images and words that can access consciousness and help create a meaningful narrative. They show how contemporary neuroscience and Jungian theory acknowledge the central role of affectivity and its corporeal roots in the organization of psychic functioning. Using the concept of the *unremoved unconscious* (Mancia, 2006), they argue that certain experiences of early relations with primary objects remain dissociated from explicit autobiographical memory and are instead maintained in preverbal implicit affective memory. In the clinical vignette, bodily phenomena are understood as an aid to negotiate the threat of potentially overpowering unconscious contents. They carefully illustrate how regressive sensory experiences, especially somatic reverie, used as a listening tool in the analytical field, can help restore the integration of affective dissociated elements. Their aim is to bridge different viewpoints, including Jungian and neuroscientific perspectives, to highlight how cognitive-affective neurosciences, analytical psychology and post-Bionian thinking can be of help in exploring bodily phenomena that arise during trauma treatment. They concur with Addison (2019) who suggests that Jung's concept of the psychoid offers a model of an "analytical attitude" that can guide the analyst when using receptive psycho-physical listening that contains and processes emerging phenomena, whilst paying attention to the unknowable.

In Chapter 5, "Working with Early Relational Trauma and Borderline States: The Role of Unconscious Communication", Lara Lagutina sensitively explores disruptions in the earliest developmental processes that can leave a long-term imprint in the form of splitting of the ego, reliance on dissociation and persistence of borderline states of mind – part of the sequelae of early relational trauma. In her fine examination of the dynamic processes involved, she draws upon the works of Jung, Winnicott, Bion, Bick, Anzieu and others in understanding the function and development of psychic skin as well as Lutenberg's formulation of the structural void based on dissociation. She provides us with an extended and deeply thoughtful clinical example which illustrates the analytic process with a patient who suffered birth trauma. This is brought to life by some verbatim material of the actual exchanges between analyst and patient. Lara expertly explains the role of unconscious communication, based on symbiotic relatedness or "unconscious identity", in working with states of persistent self-hatred, terror, aloneness and suicidal despair.

The next four chapters focus on dissociative processes in trauma.

Chapter 6, by Gianluigi Di Cesare and Patrizia Brogna on "PTSD: Feeling-Toned Complexes and the Twilight of Self-Awareness" explores normal and pathological psychic functioning from the perspective of the theory of complexes, emphasizing how the psyche is structurally dissociable. They describe the psyche as composed of a set of functional units aggregated according to a specific affective tone (a so-called feeling-toned complex) and coordinated by a main complex, the Ego complex. They demonstrate that when there is a traumatic experience the Ego complex fails in its function of psychic integration. A very impressive and challenging clinical case of a female patient is presented. They describe how the impact of a recent trauma produced symptoms of PTSD which was initially diagnosed by their colleagues as psychosis. However, their understanding of the entire clinical picture including the girl's narrative, allowed them to make a more accurate diagnosis for this young patient, which completely changed the therapeutic intervention as well as her prognosis. The authors focus on how PTSD can be understood through the lens of complexes and the theories of selfhood from a phenomenological psychopathology pathway. They argue that the lack of integration of the Ego complex can be better understood as a lack of unitary self-experience with the "basic or minimal self". They also suggest that the psychic energy that leads the complexes to affective tonality can be better understood if considered a stream of consciousness of unitary self-awareness. Furthermore, they expertly frame a dialogue between phenomenological, neurobiological and Jungian aspects in understanding the particular configuration of the dynamics of the psyche in Post-Traumatic Stress Disorder (PTSD).

In Chapter 7: "Trauma and Dissociation: A Psychodynamic Perspective", Emanuela Mundo explores what constitutes a traumatic event for a particular patient (with reference to Jungian Complex theory) and the consequences of this on subjective experience. She describes how dissociation is a complex and variable phenomenon, which may include cognitive, psychic and/or somatic symptoms happening around the time of the original trauma, or when a situation arises that resembles one when the original trauma occurred, as well as when the traumatic experience is recalled (e.g., during a psychotherapy session). In light of recent research, she expertly examines dissociative manifestations (from conversion symptoms to Dissociative Identity Disorder) and their neurobiological and psychic implications. She also describes a very interesting phenomenon which occurs after acute traumatization called the "kindling response". In kindling, a sensitized system may react as if the original trauma (single or multiple) is occurring when, in reality, an almost neutral stimulus is present. In other words, psychological kindling is the changed pattern of neuronal responses to internal stimuli, clinically giving rise to flashbacks, nightmares and dissociation as a defence response. Emanuela goes on to address dissociative phenomena from the perspective of both the patients who have been exposed to one or more traumatic experiences and the perspective of the therapist, who is exposed to the patient's dissociation. She refers to this as "vicarious" traumatization and/or "vicarious" dissociation. As well as considering the inter-subjective spectrum of dissociative phenomena occurring in both patient and therapist, she assesses their implications for the clinical setting and the management of dynamic psychotherapy.

In Chapter 8: "Eroticized Trauma and its Manifestations in the Transference", Martin Schmidt explores how trauma in childhood can become eroticized as a means of converting overwhelming painful and helpless feelings from early life into those which can be pleasurable and under one's control in adult sexual activity. He examines manifestations of this phenomenon in consensual adult sadomasochistic activity as expressed in BDSM. BDSM refers to a variety of erotic practices including bondage, discipline, dominance and submission, sadomasochism and other related interpersonal dynamics. He demonstrates, through the use of striking clinical examples, how trauma-related complexes, which arise in childhood as a consequence of sexual abuse, can be transformed, through eroticization, into behaviours which revision the trauma in a new way. This psychodrama can then find life in the dynamics of erotic and eroticized transference in the clinical encounter. Particular consideration is given to the difference between eroticized and erotic transference/countertransference and how this conceptual distinction can support our understanding of how to work with trauma. The chapter has been informed by the seminal work of Blum on the concept of erotized (eroticized) transference (1973). The author references classical psychoanalytic ideas on trauma and the erotic which are contrasted with Jungian and post-Jungian contributions.

In Chapter 9, "The Black Sun of a Transgenerational Trauma: Dissociative Processes, Affects and the Symbolic Function", Fabrizio Alfani describes a very powerful clinical case of a man who grew up in a family overshadowed by the death of his paternal uncle before his birth. The patient, although he knew about his uncle's demise, had no awareness of the extent of the impact that this event had had on his psychic life. On a number of occasions, the boundaries of the analytic work were challenged as the analyst struggled to maintain an analytic attitude. Fabrizio sensitively describes how he allowed the affects connected to the patient's loss to be thought about and then communicated. This constituted a very important breakthrough for the patient since it progressively enabled reducing the dissociative states produced by his transgenerational trauma. The clinical process is delineated through a series of very impressive dreams and a drawing of a Black Sun. The emergence of this image marked a turning point in the analysis, as it represented an internal saboteur by whom the patient felt persecuted. The extremely interesting clinical material is accompanied by theoretical reflections on dissociation which Fabrizio understands as a possible consequence of the lack of affective attunements with the primary caregiver during early childhood. This failure is seen as a hindrance to the development of higher psychic functions.

The next four chapters address sociological as well as analytic aspects of trauma.

In Chapter 10, Emilija Kiehl continues her interesting reflections on the issue of "Social Trauma" that began with a paper published in the *Journal of Analytical Psychology* (2016). Its title, "You were not born here, so you are classless, you are free!", came from a statement that a patient made to her in relation to their different social status in British society. In that article, she explored the impact of the British socio-economic class system on the sense of self. Emilija recounts that a British colleague told her that it was good that someone finally approached this topic as it is a taboo one in Britain. She calls upon the epidemiologists Wilkinson and Pickett, who claim that: "Many people tend to be evasive about class and status differences, and some deny not only their importance but occasionally even their existence" (2018: 202). Emilija pointedly notes that, in recent years, some explorations of the psychological impact of racism have tentatively entered the psychoanalytic and psychotherapeutic discourse, but the effects of income inequality on sense of self-worth still remain largely unexplored. She then presents two meaningful clinical vignettes in which her patients struggle with the transgenerational trauma of being born working class, whilst attempting to make a class transition which, for one of them, was extremely challenging. She poignantly observes that, despite their social achievements, they had remained stuck in a "no man's land", a lost territory between the social class of their parents and that of the new status they had entered or were struggling to enter.

Gianluigi Di Cesare and Chiara Caprì, in Chapter 11: "New Evolutionary Perspectives between Trauma and Resilience: Dysregulated and *Con-fused*", outline possible new ways of understanding juvenile distress. They reflect on a current phenomenon, first and foremost amongst adolescents, which seems increasingly traumatophilic. By this, the authors mean that every new event is experienced, by both adolescents and their families, as being potentially traumatic and that this brings with it the loss of symbolic containment, essential for the structuring of personality. Gianluigi and Chiara see adolescents as trapped by claustrophilic families, where their path for separation and individuation is often hampered by the intrusive care of parents, for whom *the other* becomes an enemy and a persecutor. The authors observe that adolescents can fluctuate between internalizing and externalizing behaviours when expressing their difficulties. They succinctly address the notion that the absence of symbolic capacity seems to prevent adolescents from experiencing resilience. Furthermore, they suggest that now we are witnessing a loss of imaginative capacity in adolescents, despite the fact that they are often immersed in a virtual reality, and that this can lead them to seek an identity in their symptoms. As a consequence, their identity remains fragile and unpredictable.

In Chapter 12, Julia Ovchinnikova engagingly writes about "Working with Cultural Trauma: The Archetype of the Wounded Healer in a Multicultural Analytic Couple". The author's aim is to highlight the constellation of the Wounded Healer archetype and its application to cultural trauma as it doesn't get the attention it deserves. Reflecting on her experience of being a Jungian analyst from Russia living in London for many years, the author suggests that an analyst from another culture can be seen as a particular, unconscious as well as conscious, choice by a patient with cultural trauma. Encounters between an analyst and a patient from different cultures can evoke the whole history of cultural complexes and wounds for them. Julia thinks that the unconscious impact of both the patient's and the analyst's history finds expression in a specific dynamic in the transference and in the activation of the Wounded Healer archetype. She succinctly describes five phases of this dynamic, illustrating each with reference to meaningful clinical vignettes. As Julia suggests, the choice of an analyst from another culture may serve to ease unbearable feelings provoked by trauma associated with a particular culture and facilitate the start of therapy. At the beginning of the analysis, she describes how frequently the analyst is seen as a "healer" who is free from cultural and other wounds. As the work progresses, the analyst and the patient may then become able to acknowledge their cultural wounds. This precipitates a final phase, where they may become able to recognize that both can hurt, and be healing, to the other.

In Chapter 13: "A Jungian Approach to Working with the Trauma of Migrants: Waves, Tempests, Harbours", Giancarlo Costanza discusses his work with migrants as chief consultant of a Child and Adolescent Mental Health Service in Catania, Sicily. He sensitively describes the difficulties in working analytically with young people who arrive as refugees from Africa and China. Giancarlo is able to provide us with an insight into the inner world of these adolescents who have often suffered many traumas including the loss of home, loved ones and their own mental health. He has felt it necessary to adapt his technique to address the specific challenges presented by this group of young people. Giancarlo describes how he uses toys and dream images in sessions as symbolic means of understanding his patients. Drawing on the dynamics of the archetype of the wounded healer, he reveals the dangers of the analyst too easily hiding behind a position of "healer" when this may render the patient stuck in a position of "wounded".

The final three chapters approach working with trauma from the perspective of focussing on creative methods.

In Chapter 14: "Myths, Trauma and the Neurobiological Psyche", Roberta Perri provides a phenomenological reading of the trauma described in the myth of Daphne, in Ovid's *Metamorphoses*. The premise of this chapter is that myths accurately represent human behaviour. She uses Daphne as a "clinical" case and argues that Ovid seems to understand the neurobiology of the human psyche by looking for signs in Daphne of that which, we now consider in neurophysiology, as "threats to survival". In examining the consequences of relational violence, the author reveals how Ovid's attentive gaze is able to describe the state of apparent psychic death which is aimed at protecting the trauma survivor's vital core. She describes how the poet helps us to see that the trauma victim requires the right conditions for rebirth through the recovery of symbolization processes. This myth reveals a plot in which the narrated phenomena are similar to those we can observe in the consulting room. Roberta also explains how neuroscience can frame the phenomena pictured in the myth through the neurobiology of the human psyche.

In Chapter 15: "The Role of Memory and Creativity in the Healing Process of Trauma", Eduardo Carvallo describes his work with trauma victims in Colombia. He sees creativity as rooted in the Self, nourished by its regulatory, constructive and healing dynamics, which promote the structuring of the psyche. He describes how he uses Expressive Sandwork technique (ES) to help his patients. This technique was founded by Eva Pattis-Zoja, a Jungian analyst, in response to the needs of earthquake victims in China in 2008. Eduardo observes that one of the frequent responses to trauma is the repression of the memory of the traumatic event, from which distorted versions of oneself, of one's environment and of life itself can originate. He argues that reconstructing biographical memory (in individual cases) or historical memory (in collective cases) allows reframing the experience in a new way, activating the natural mechanisms of assimilation, elaboration and reconstruction of the event. Using two very moving case examples of a 6-year-old boy (who was a victim of severe neglect/abuse) and a 24-year-old woman (who was kidnapped and raped), he compassionately demonstrates how, by using creative expression tools as well as his skills as a psychiatrist and Jungian analyst, he facilitated the reconstruction of the memory of the trauma and elaboration of new symbolic scenarios which gave the traumatic event new meaning. This allowed for the relaxation of the dynamics that keep the psyche paralysed, and the redirection of the regulatory mechanisms that permitted the process of individuation to resume.

In the final chapter: "Understanding Trauma and Mourning from the Knowledge of the Heart", Professor Heyong Shen offers a poetic Oriental approach to treating trauma, based on both Jungian analysis and the Chinese "Psychology of the Heart". He beautifully explores symbolic images and Chinese characters which reveal the meaning of trauma, suffering and mourning. Heyong realized that it is through the profound depths of suffering and the expansive realms of knowledge that lies the path to self-knowledge and the knowledge of the heart. In 2006, Professor Shen and his colleagues set up a project named Garden of the Heart & Soul in Chinese orphanages, which uses Jungian psychology, Sand-play Therapy and the psychology of the heart to support the psychological development of orphans. This was later expanded to help victims of earthquakes and natural disasters (2008). Many people refer to his work as healing by "Ci-bei" (loving-grief-compassion therapy). He argues that Jung's intuitive method, the wisdom of the I Ching and the psychology of the heart can offer us many insights and guidance. He feels that suffering and mourning are the key to understanding the knowledge of the heart and the meaning of trauma.

References

Addison, A. (2019) *Jung's Psychoid Concept Contextualised*. London: Routledge.

Bion, W.R. (1967) "Attacks on linking", in *Second Thoughts: Selected Papers on Psychoanalysis*. London: Maresfield Library.

Blum, H.P. (1973) "The concept of erotized transference", *Journal of the American Psychoanalytic Association*, 21(1): 61–76.

Fairbairn, W.R.D. (1952) *Psycho-Analytic studies of the personality*. London: Routledge and Kegan Paul.

Fordham, M. (1974) "Defences of the Self", *Journal of Analytical Psychology*, 19(2): 192–199.

Fordham, M. (1976) *The Self and Autism – Library of Analytical Psychology, vol. 3*. London: Heinemann.

Jung, C.G. (1934) *A Review of the Complex Theory*. CW8. London: Routledge & Kegan Paul.

Kalsched, D. (1996) *The Inner World of Trauma: Archetypal Defences of the Personal Spirit*. New York: Routledge.

Kalsched, D. (2017) "Trauma, innocence and the core complex of dissociation", *Journal of Analytical Psychology*, 62(4): 474–500.

Kiehl, E. (2016) "'You were not born here, so you are classless, you are free!' Social class and cultural complex in analysis", *The Journal of Analytical Psychology*, 61(4): 465–480.

Mancia, M. (2006) "Implicit memory and early unrepressed unconscious: Their role in the therapeutic process (how the neurosciences can contribute to psychoanalysis)", *International Journal of Psychoanalysis*, 87(Pt 1): 83–103.

West, M. (2016) *Into the Darkest Places: Early Relational Trauma and Borderline States of Mind*. London: Karnac Books.

Wilkinson, R. and Pickett, K. (2018) *The Inner Level*. London: Penguin Books Ltd.

Chapter 1

Feeling-Toned Complexes and the Treatment of Trauma

A Jungian Perspective

Luisa Zoppi

The Complex as a Challenging Concept

Perhaps Jung's encounter with *complexes* was one of the experiences he was referring to when he declared "Nothing but unexpected things kept happening to me" (Jung, 1963: 418). In fact, he came to conceptualize the existence of complexes by chance, thanks to being assigned the replication of the word association test by Bleuler, at the Burghölzli Psychiatric Clinic in Zurich.[1]

From the Macmillan Online Dictionary (2022) we see that the noun *complex* can refer to "an emotional problem caused by unreasonable fears or worries". David Sedgwick has observed that the commonly used expression "having a complex" has become part of the vernacular and refers to "being emotionally sensitive about a particular topic" (Sedgwick, 2001: 31), while Anthony Stevens notes that the concept of the complex "is often thought – quite erroneously – [as being] essentially pathological" (Stevens, 2002: 74). In 1904, Jung and Riklin published a study of *The Associations of Normal Subjects*, where they "put forward the concept of the 'feeling-toned complex'" (Jung and Riklin, 1904, para. 478), and some years later, in 1911, Jung stated that a complex was just the normal grouping of various ideas, linked together by "an emotional tone common to all" (Jung, 1911a, para. 1350). From his psychiatric observations, he became more interested in the ways complexes affect psychic life. They were seen as "splinter psyches" (Jung, 1934, para. 204), namely a manifestation of "the psyche's tendency to split" (Jung, 1936, para. 253), which is a fundamental normal phenomenon (Jung, 1936), when the psyche finds itself under traumatic influences or certain incompatible tendencies (Jung, 1936, para. 253). Thus, *autonomous* complexes are fragments that, under these conditions, have "detached themselves from consciousness to such an extent that they not only appear foreign but lead an autonomous life of their own" (Jung, 1936, para. 253). Referring *to split-off* complexes – which are autonomous – simply as complexes, led to the

DOI: 10.4324/9781003298076-2

common misunderstanding that they are essentially pathological, as Sedgwick (2001) and Stevens (2002) both concurred. Both in our daily life and clinical work, if someone has an excessive and apparently inexplicable reaction to a certain situation, he can be understood as driven by a complex, without any reference to the *split-off* or *autonomous* nature of that complex, as we will see later in this chapter.

The Word Association Tests (WAT) and the Roots of the Theory of Complexes

In October 1900, Jung took a post as assistant physician at Burghölzli and in 1902 he discussed his doctoral dissertation, which became his first published work, *On the Psychology and Pathology of So-called Occult Phenomena* (1902), where he mentioned *cryptomnesia*.[2] Here Jung considered this phenomenon as "an everyday occurrence (that) is intimately bound up with normal psychic processes" (Jung, 1902, para. 139).

The years at Burghölzli were an apprenticeship for Jung (see *Memories, Dreams, Reflections*, 1963), and his experience under the direction of Bleuler was extremely important in grounding his later thinking. In fact, in the Foreword to *The Psychology of Dementia Praecox* (1907), Jung claimed that he had been very much inspired by reflections that had "matured in almost daily conversation with my respected chief, Professor Bleuler" (Jung, 1907, para. 1079). As Hogenson observes, Bleuler, while being devoted to investigating psychic functioning more deeply, was also concerned with "the scientific basis of psychiatry [and this] prompted him to assign genuinely experimental projects to his staff" (Hogenson, 2004: 39; Colman, 2015). As we know, he had suggested that Jung reproduce the associative experiment, following the procedure that had already been developed by the Wundt group at the University of Leipzig (1879). In the meanwhile, Jung had been very impressed by Freud's book *Die Traumdeutung* (1900), although he had no ideas of his own on the matter, as he declared in a long interview with Richard Evans (1964). He simply reproduced the same experimental association method of Wundt, studied the results and, in his words, "had the idea that one should go once more over it, so I made these association tests, and I found out that *the important thing in them has been missed*" (Evans, 1964: 42, italics added). He then continued, in his conversation with Evans: "it is not interesting to see that there is a reaction – a certain reaction – to a stimulus word; that is more or less uninteresting. But the interesting thing is why people could *not* react to certain stimulus words, or only react in an entirely inadequate way" (Evans, 1964: 42).

So Jung, curious about the data from the previous WATs, that had perhaps too quickly been "taken by the German school as 'irrelevant answers'" (Jung, 1907, para. 16), started to explore further. "It was then that I discovered the feeling-toned complexes, which had always been registered before as failures to react" (Jung, 1934, para. 196). These were phenomena such as prolonged reaction times to the word stimulus, comments, laughing, inability to give a word association and a wide range of emotional reactions. While he was studying the WAT, as he mentioned in 1907 (Jung, 1907, para. 92), Jung came across Freud's ideas in his work *Zur Psychopathologie des Alltagslebens* (1901), and this also helped him come to different conclusions about the results from the WAT. So, "instead of brushing these [results] to one side ..., he applied the interpretative method and formulated the *theory of complexes*" (Editorial note, CW2: 322, italics added). Following Freud, he quickly understood that what the psyche does is never by chance, and always has a meaning.

Under the direction of Bleuler, it was a dynamic period at Burghölzli, full of emerging new ideas and the courage to present them in a way which, at the time, led to a striking advance in the use of experimental techniques (Editorial note, CW2). As already stated, Bleuler himself had an insatiable curiosity for advancements in psychology and psychopathology (Hogenson, 2004). Furthermore, he was a pioneer in introducing psychoanalysis into his hospital. As reported by Dalzell (2007), Bleuler and his colleagues even started interpreting their own dreams together. Moreover, he put enormous energy and enthusiasm into supporting his young assistants. Indeed, Bleuler used to sponsor them for further education, consequently Jung was sent to Paris to study with Janet in the winter of 1902–1903.

The experience Jung gained during his time with Janet, although brief, would later have a very important influence on the development of his thinking – through the idea of the dissociability of the psyche – as Hogenson (2004) and others observe (see also Haule, 1983; Charet, 2000; Astor, 2001; Saban, 2016). Additionally, Bleuler was well known for his support of an empirical approach to psychiatry and, as a result, under his direction (from 1898 to 1927) numerous young doctors, enthusiastic about empirical research, came to the Burghölzli to study the WAT. These included Ludwig Binswanger, Karl Abraham, Franz Riklin and others such as the Americans Abraham Brill, Charles Ricksher and Frederick Peterson. Inspired by the research on the WAT at Burghölzli, they were then able to explore new horizons in the investigation of psychopathology.

This dynamic period is known as the *golden age* of the Burghölzli (Kallivayalil, 2016) and allowed Peterson and Jung to see that "it is not intellectual factors but *the emotions that play the chief part in determining these associations*" (Peterson and Jung, 1907, para. 1079, italics added) thus making big strides towards the formulation of the theory of complexes. For Jung, affects are at the core of complexes, since "every affective event becomes a complex" (Jung, 1907, para. 140). Jung didn't invent the Association Experiment, however, he perfected it on a technical level[3] by introducing new instruments and measurements. Besides electrocardiography and plethysmographic spirometry (the measure of breathing rate and depth), he now used a more accurate recording of the psycho-galvanic-reflex, and was then able to further focus on affects and acknowledge the role that they play in daily life. The role of affects in perception and thinking had already been highlighted by Bleuler, to whom Jung is indebted for having suggested that "attention like all our actions is always directed by an affect" (Bleuler, 1906: 30) and that "attention is an aspect of affectivity and does nothing more than what we know affectivity does, i.e., it facilitates certain associations and inhibits others" (quoted in Jung, 1907, footnote nr.7). All these influences helped him formulate his views on the functioning of the human psyche and what we now see as networks of clustered feeling-states, better known as complexes.

The progress Jung and the others made in applying the WAT to clinical psychiatry and in understanding the possible diagnostic value of such a simple experiment was rooted in the important work of associationists Theodor Ziehen and Robert Sommer. The former was the first to write about feeling-toned complexes and to apply the association experiments to children (Ziehen, 1898a, 1898b), while Sommer had used the findings from the WAT as an aid to psychiatric diagnostics (1894) and for advancements in Criminal Psychology (1904).

"What Then, Scientifically Speaking, is a Feeling-toned Complex?" (Jung, 1934, para.201)

In his paper for the Australasian Medical Congress (1911a), Jung stated that his theoretical views on neuroses and psychoses, especially dementia praecox, were also rooted in the psychological outcomes of the association experiments. As a result of the WAT studies, he came to conceive the complex as the functional unit of the psyche (Jung, 1907). Later, he expounded, "Complexes are in truth the living units of the unconscious psyche, and it is only through them that we are able to deduce its existence and its constitution" (Jung, 1934, para. 210). If we look more attentively at psychic material, we inevitably find that almost every association belongs to a complex (Jung, 1907), through the link of a shared emotional tone.

The question remains, as Jung formulated in 1934, "What then, scientifically speaking, is a 'feeling-toned complex'?" (Jung, 1934, para. 201). Currently we understand feeling-toned complexes[4] – simply known as *complexes* – as clusters of information, where images with feelings and physiological responses are linked together through an affect and, consequently, they have behavioural responses, since they *affect* the body. It was in 1907, reflecting on the results of the WAT in his *Psychology of Dementia Praecox*, that Jung suggested that "the cement binding complexes together is some definite affect" (Jung, 1907, para. 56). The measurement of heart frequency, blood pressure, respiratory rhythm and reactivity of the skin had proved that complexes are connected to *and through* an affect. Interestingly, the neuronal correlates of affects activating complexes have in recent times been confirmed by several functional brain imaging studies applied to the WAT (Roesler and van Uffelen, 2018). Among these are the important works performed by Kehyayan et al. (2013), Petchkovsky et al. (2013), Petchkovsky (2017) and Escamilla et al. (2018), that provide empirical evidence for the role that the affective core of complexes can have in bodily functioning. Feeling-toned complexes are understood to be the foundation stone of both conscious and unconscious psychic structure (Sedgwick, 2001). Dieckmann (1991) suggests seeing them as ecotypes, in the system of the human psyche, as occurs in ecological systems in nature.

In an ideal *healthy* psyche, the ego complex[5] and the Self keep the cohesion of the system (Dieckmann, 1991) while complexes are harmoniously connected in a wider psychological network made up of individual and cultural complexes. They constitute the *fabric* of the psyche. However, we only experience the *feeling-toned* complex when it impacts our physical and psychological life, namely when it gains a certain degree of autonomy from consciousness (as will be discussed later). The issue of the autonomy of a complex captured Jung's attention from the beginning of his psychiatric observations[6] and he had also been impressed by Freud's work on lapses of speech (1901) and other parapraxes (Jung, 1905).

It is interesting to note the similarities between the concept of the complex and that of *Emotion Schemas*, as conceived in recent developments in psychoanalysis by Wilma Bucci in her Multiple Code Theory (1997, 2015) of psychic functioning. According to Bucci, Emotion Schemas organize personal experience as they are *clusters of memories* (Bucci, Maskit and Murphy, 2015), which develop from the very beginning of life. These clusters of memories activate sensory, visceral and motor processes in relation to specific people and situations and constitute the affective core of the emotion schema (Bucci, 2009). According to Bucci, an emotion schema is also characterized, as it is for complexes, by "experiences of arousal – heart beating faster (and) blood pressure rising" (Bucci, 2009: 34) in response to specific stimuli.[7] This is exactly what happens with the activation of complexes, as documented in the WAT, and the activation of corresponding neuronal circuits, as seen in fMRI studies. Thus, we can recognize some similarities between complexes and Emotion Schemas, since they are both image-action schemata and are linked more to the functioning of the visceral processing systems (or emotional processing) than to cognition (Bucci, Zoppi and Solano, 2001). Therefore, Emotion Schemas, like complexes, have a certain degree of autonomy from consciousness.

Archetypes and Complexes, a Natural Bond?

Despite the centrality that the concept of the complex has in analytical psychology, it's important to stress that Jung never defined them with "sharp and conclusive terms" (Jacobi, 1959: 29). Jolande Jacobi, in her major work *Complex/Archetype/Symbol* (1959), addressed the issue of the nature of complexes, which she saw as rooted in the archetypal core of the functioning of the psyche. For Jacobi, complexes "belong to the basic structure of the psyche" (Jacobi, 1959: 25) because they have an archetypal core.

As Christian Roesler suggests (2022), Jung came to delineate his hypothesis of archetypal patterns of behaviour through his works on the WAT. Reflecting on the results from the association experiments, Jung discovered the existence of corresponding interindividual core complexes (Roesler, 2022), as "there is ... only a limited number of continually repeating thematic cores" (Roesler, 2022: 75). Moreover, in these regularly repeating thematic cores of complexes, an archetype can be found "which directs individuals' experience and which produces supra-individual similarity" (Roesler, 2022: 75). Although the archetype is one of the most recognized of Jung's concepts, it is also the most misunderstood, as Hogenson has highlighted (2004). I agree with Hogenson that because "*Jung did not have a theory of archetypes*" (Hogenson, 2004: 33, italics in original), he missed a coherent conceptualization of them, which could explain the confusion that frequently characterizes the debate on this topic (Hogenson, 2004).

The debate on the concept of the archetype has traditionally focused on the following questions: are they innate or acquired? Do they belong to "some transcendent realm of Platonic ideas" (Hogenson, 2019: 685), eventually leading to a *taxonomy of archetypes* as if their form is given "a priori"? In his overview of the debate on archetypes, Roesler reminds us that, besides considering them as a *numinous factor* "with seeming foreknowl-edge" (Jung, 1954a, para.411), Jung "was strongly influenced by the ... emerging behavioral science in biology" (Roesler, 2022: 55) which led him to understand archetypes also as an "*inherited mode of psychic functioning*, a 'pattern of behaviour'" (Jung, 1948, para. 1228, italics added) that help us organize images in order to process life experiences according to specific *gestalten*. Interestingly, decades after Jung's intuitions, studies on newborn observations (see Morton and Johnson, 1991, on the innate face detection device, known as CONSPEC) suggest that we are programmed to process experience, and thus organize behaviour, according to specific responses to certain forms of reality, thus ensuring survival of the species. The newborn's behaviour is designed to look for, and then allow, the essential encounter with the caregiver with the help of the smile reflex,[8] an instinctual action aimed at eliciting a caring response in the other. Moreover, the mother (car-egiver), on her side, is physiologically ready to respond to her baby smiling. Both are "programmed" to meet each other. These outcomes from infant observations have provided support to the argument, from some post-Jungians, that archetypes are genetically imprinted (see on this debate Stevens, 2002 and Roesler, 2022).

However, more recently, this understanding has been challenged by new perspectives from theories of human development (Martin-Vallas, 2013;, 2015; Roesler, 2019) based on evolutionary biology, as well as from the advancements in complex-systems science and in epigenesis (Gottlieb, 2007). From this perspective, archetypes, and any other human phenomena, *cannot be reduced* to their biological aspect. In his many writings on this topic, Hogenson strongly argues from this perspective (Hogenson 1998, 2001, 2004, 2009, 2019) suggesting that archetypes can now be regarded as "the emergent properties of the dynamic developmental system of brain, environment, and narrative" (Hogenson, 2001: 607). As Martin-Vallas illus-trates, using the well-known example of the bird building his nest (see Jung, 1948), "the bird is reliant on favourable conditions without which he would be unable to find either the place or the material essentials for the construc-tion, nor possibly the stimuli which will trigger his instinctual project" (Martin-Vallas, 2013: 280). The same argument has been addressed by Roesler (2022), when discussing CONSPEC. He observes that this genetic predisposition in the newborn relies on the presence of a caregiver, in order to develop a significant relationship with her. However, the question for us here concerns the understanding of archetypal dynamics in complex sys-tems, where we can think of brain structures as modelled through experi-ence, that is, through interaction with the environment (Kandell et al., 2023).

Trauma Can Split *Off* a Complex

As already stated, complexes constitute the fabric of the psyche. In an ideal "healthy" psyche they are constantly interconnected, through affective links, to form a harmonious network. But, in real life, unbearable affects *can* unexpectedly and powerfully tear apart the fabric of the psyche. The harmony of the network gets lost. We can imagine that it was exactly this *lack of harmony* in the answers to the WAT that captured Jung's attention at the beginning of his work as a researcher. What he was observing were interferences, phenomena that he would later understand to be the consequences that split-off complexes can have on mental functioning. Years later, reflecting on autonomous complexes, Jung wrote that their origin is to be found *"frequently* (in) a so-called trauma, an emotional shock or some such thing, that splits off a bit of the psyche" (Jung, 1934, para. 204, italics added). The adverb "frequently" here draws attention to that which Jung had already mentioned in his work *The Theory of Psychoanalysis* (1912), when observing that there isn't always a causal relationship between trauma and psychopathology so that, *in itself,* "trauma … has no absolute aetiological significance" (Jung, 1912, para. 217). However, in order to understand the actual impact of the event on a subject, we need to consider his personal history and look for the *inner predisposition* that makes trauma so devastating. To avoid any possible misunderstanding about the nature of the *inner predisposition* to trauma, Jung states: "This inner predisposition is not to be understood as that obscure, hereditary disposition of which we know so little, but as a psychological development which reaches its climax, and becomes manifest, at the traumatic moment" (Jung, 1912, para. 217).

The concept of affect dis-regulation (Taylor, Bagby and Parker, 1997) concerns a defect in psychological development which leads to an inability to effectively regulate affects when coping with difficult experiences. Such a dis-regulation comes from disturbances or failures in the early relationship between a child and its caregiver. According to Taylor, this explains the weakness of the ego[9] and the subsequent "heightened susceptibility to disease" (Taylor, in Taylor, Bagby and Parker, 1997: 219) under particular circumstances. It can be argued that the paradigm of the dis-regulation of affects can help us better understand the idea of the *inner predisposition* for the individual to suffer from trauma and then develop a disease that manifests itself "at the traumatic moment" (Jung, 1912).

The individual's likelihood to suffer from traumatic experiences can result from failures in early attachment relationships, such as prolonged neglect, physical abuse and intrusive care. These experiences frequently have consequences not only on psychological but also physical health as extensive data from the CDC-Kaiser Permanente Study on ACEs[10] has shown (see Felitti et al., 1998; Felitti, 2002; Lanius, Vermetten and Pain, 2010).

There are however resilient people, whose stories give us a deeper understanding concerning the *inner predisposition* that Jung highlighted in 1912. The idea of an inner predisposition to suffer trauma clearly emphasizes that trauma, per se, does not have a given aetiological significance. These reflections open up an additional discourse (which is not the aim of this chapter) concerning the concept of *resilience*, which has recently become more central to work with trauma survivors (see Cyrulnik, 2009). What Jung says about the inner predisposition to react to trauma in a certain, subjective way, pre-empts what was later understood by researchers in the field of psychosomatics as well as of *trauma theory*.[11] It was in 1979 that Horowitz, together with Wilner and Alvarez, challenged what early researchers in psychosomatics had been thinking for decades – that the traumatic event has the same pathogenic power for each person – by addressing the issue of the empirical measure of subjective distress related to specific life events. The *Impact of the Event Scale* (IES, Horowitz, Wilner and Alvarez, 1979) and the revised version of it (IES-R, Weiss and Marmar, 1997), are the most widely used measures within trauma literature (Beck et al., 2008) and help explore the relationships between trauma and psychosomatic disease. The current perspective on this investigates how different people experience trauma, that is, the impact a particular event has for different people on both their mental and physical health. This depends largely on their psychological make-up (derived mainly from their psychological history) at the exact moment of the trauma.

As already mentioned, Jung understood that trauma can split a complex off (Jung, 1934). This sometimes happens when life throws us challenges where we face "the apparent impossibility of affirming the whole of one's nature" (Jung, 1934, para. 204). These can be experiences of acute trauma: a singular traumatic event, brief and focused such as an isolated incident of physical or sexual abuse; or other dramatic events and chronic experiences that can become cumulative trauma.

Donald Kalsched (1996, 2013) suggests that archetypal defences allow the individual to continue functioning in real life when the world collapses (Ferenczi, 1932). He conceives the existence of a *self-care system*, an "archaic and typical (archetypical) ... structure ... devoted to defense" (Kalsched, 2013: 12) and offers us a very moving case example to understand how the archetypal defence system works. This is a story that was told by Edinger during a conference given at the Los Angeles Jung Institute in 1986, and is attributed to Esther Harding. It concerns a six-year-old girl and her encounter with the *unbearable*.

"The little girl and the angel":

The mother sent her young daughter to her father's study one morning to deliver an important note, written on a piece of paper. The little girl went off to deliver the note. Shortly thereafter, the daughter came back in tears and said "I'm sorry mother, the angel won't let me go in". Whereupon the mother sent the daughter back a second time, with the same result only this time more tears and distress. At this point the mother became irritated at her youngster's imaginative excess, so she took her little girl by the hand and the two of them marched the message over to the father. As they entered the father's study, the mother saw her husband slumped in his chair, his drink spilled on the floor, dead from a heart attack.

(Kalsched, 2013: 28)

As is clear from this story, the functioning of the self-care system implies some degree of dissociation of the psyche. As Wilkinson observes (2006), in line with Kalsched's intuition, "in order to avoid psychic pain…(the) mind that is fundamentally associative becomes dissociative as a defensive measure" (Wilkinson, 2006: 32). Life shows us that the splitting of the affect from the image, from the memory it belongs to, is one of the most effective ways for a person to protect himself from an experience that is too much for the conscious psyche to bear.

A Brief Note on Dissociation

Jung had observed dissociation as a psychic mechanism early on with his first patients, and it became evident to him in the case of the patient who was a medium and whom he described in his dissertation (Jung, 1902). As already mentioned, in his first published work (1902) Jung considered *cryptomnesia* as a phenomenon emerging from normal psychic functioning, which helped him also to understand dissociation as a normal psychic process. It was in 1911, when writing "On the doctrine of complexes", that he challenged the role that dissociation, through autonomous complexes, plays in the origin of neuroses and dementia praecox. Furthermore, based on the observations of the phenomenon of disturbances in the WAT, he could affirm that "more or less autonomous complexes occur everywhere, even in so-called normals" (Jung, 1911a, para. 1354). Jung's ideas on the role of dissociation in normal psychic functioning also found support in works by Janet, Flournoy and Morton Prince, whose book *The Dissociation of a Personality* he really appreciated (Jung, 1911b).

Moreover, his ideas regarding the mechanism of dissociation had probably been strengthened by a conversation he had with William James during the Clark Lectures, in 1909. As he wrote in a letter to Mrs Virginia Pine in 1949 (Jung, 1973), he was very impressed by James' reflections on the case of Mrs. Piper, a famous medium that the latter was studying as a case of dissociation. It is very likely that this exchange of ideas with James further confirmed the hypothesis that he had been developing from the beginning of his clinical work, which saw dissociation as a phenomenon typical of normal psychic functioning. This was also supported by the experience he had with Janet in 1902.[12] As the American psychologist Samuel Kohs wrote in *The American Journal of Psychology* in 1914, "We are all, in a slight manner, however, examples of split-off personalities" (Kohs, 1914: 533). This splitting functioning of the psyche is at the core of recent advancements in trauma theories.

In victims of trauma, be it a single event or a complex trauma, we can frequently see that affects are split from the memory of the event(s) they belong to. In these cases, we can often observe that, despite the inability of the person to recall the connected affect, there are vivid and even extremely detailed memories of the dynamics of the traumatic event. Interestingly, a detailed memory of what happened is often linked to a particular smell, an olfactory memory. In fact, often for trauma victims, the most powerful memories are the olfactory ones – rooted in the most primitive form of memory in mammals, from the reptilian brain.[13] Anna, a patient who, as a child, was sexually abused by her uncle for years, had vague memories of what had happened and was desensitized to the connected affects. However, despite being numb to the experience, she had one clear memory which was the smell of her uncle. Her most vivid memory of what had happened was the cologne her uncle wore immediately before abusing her.

In the 1990s, I spent several years working in empirical research on the psychophysiological consequences of trauma, together with Professor Luigi Solano at the Department of Psychology at Sapienza University Rome (Bucci, Zoppi and Solano, 2001; Solano, 2001; Solano et al., 2001). I still remember how interested we were to find that alexithymia was regularly the most powerful data from the groups in question. There were, for example, people who had suffered a powerful earthquake in Italy (in Umbria) in 1997. Often, they were able to describe – sometimes in exact detail – the facts of what had happened, but without any affect connected to the experience. In some cases, they were only able to convey an olfactory memory, as Anna did. This was the smell of the air full of the dust of the ruined buildings immediately after the earthquake. Here alexithymia, which we can now see as the splitting of affects from words represented, in many cases, a normal response to trauma.

It is a common experience that, in the encounter with severe trauma survivors, we find ourselves, as researchers, as analysts, as well as ordinary people, faced with a crucial question. It is the question that, for me, is at the core of Kalsched's work: "What is there in the *inhuman* which may save the *human*?". The splitting off from consciousness of the "inhuman" part of our experience can allow life to go on, as Schmidt (2012) has impressively described in its more pathological manifestations. The autonomy of the split-off complex is perfectly highlighted by one of Jung's most famous quotes: "Everyone knows nowadays that people *have complexes*. What is not so well known, though far more important theoretically, is that complexes *can have* us" (Jung, 1934, para. 200, italics added). This was what happened to Laura, when I met her, some years ago.[14]

"Who Are the Children?"

When I opened the door at our first session, there stood a young woman in her 40s, without make-up, with long, curly, black hair and a lost, frightened look in her blue eyes. Her glance struck me. An almost imperceptible shiver ran through me. Bewildered, I asked myself "What is going on?". However, in the intersubjective shared field – the analytic field – that had already been created (de Rienzo, 2021; Zoppi, 2017, 2023), the meaning of such an early bodily countertransference experience was still not known to me. Often, with traumatized patients, we experience powerful feelings of threat, rage and compassion, which we feel because they are missing in the patient's conscious experience (Kalsched, personal communication, 2013). Inside Laura's inner world there was an immediate threat to life, as I came to understand later.

She started talking in a self-composed way, but the tone of her faint voice conveyed deep suffering. Laura explained why she had come to me for help. She had become very anxious with obsessive thoughts about accidentally hurting children, while playing with them, even though this had never actually happened. These thoughts became increasingly disturbing for her and now it was a huge effort for her to concentrate on work. She also had great difficulties falling asleep and during the night would be woken by sudden doubts of inadvertently having hurt a child during the day. What troubled her most, moreover, was that she was no longer able to play her flute. She felt blocked from doing something that she had loved to do in her free time. As she talked, I thought that she must be a teacher in a kindergarten and imagined her surrounded by children. Then, when I asked her about her job, she replied that she was a manager, was single and had no children. I was astonished and asked myself *"Who are the children?"*.

Although split from consciousness, the autonomous complexes persistently disturb consciousness and affect our physical well-being. They affect our lives. The body keeps score of trauma, as van der Kolk (2014) claims in the title of his remarkable book. From a Jungian perspective, the WAT studies show that the *body keeps score of split-off complexes*. In fact, they disturb our psychic life, as they often *possess* and disturb us through lapsus or ridiculous behaviour (Jung, 1957), or they *obsess* our conscious life with repetitive, apparently meaningless, thoughts. They also affect our physiological functioning, as highlighted by neuroscientific studies (Roesler and van Uffelen, 2018). Jung clearly stated that autonomous complexes "appear and disappear according to their own laws (and) they can temporarily obsess consciousness" (Jung, 1934, para. 253). In the lectures that he gave at the Tavistock Clinic (1935), we find his most impressive account of the autonomous nature of a split-off complex, one that behaves *as an animated foreign body* in one's consciousness. Returning to Laura, in her daily life, she was being disturbed by obsessive thoughts, which she experienced as meaningless *animated foreign ideas*, which at that time she could hardly manage.

From the very beginning of our work, I could observe the high degree of autonomy of the split-off complex, the nature of which I then couldn't see. For a long time, Laura continued to tell me, always with a faint voice that I had to strain to hear, the story of an ordinary childhood in an ordinary family. In contrast, in her dreams she was responsible for having, accidentally, caused car crashes or she had had needles stuck in her legs with blood pouring out. And yet, she looked at her own blood and felt no pain.

It took a year until Laura could tell me her "true" story. It was difficult for her to talk about it. She was very embarrassed. However, one of her dreams helped us, as dreams often do. It bore witness to what had really taken place in an apparently ordinary family. The dream told us about her split complex, and opened up a path to integration. Paraphrasing Jung's words,[15] we can say that this strong feeling-toned dream created this path. This dream became significantly more important as the analysis progressed and served as a reference point for me and eventually for both of us. Over the years, we both repeatedly referred to it as "The Hänsel and Gretel Dream".

It's night and I am walking in a forest and arrive at a cottage. I go closer to the windows so I can look inside. There are two children, I know that they are brother and sister. They are playing very quietly with a crab, a cockroach, a spider and an octopus, all real animals and incredibly over-sized. I think they are all genetically modified. The sister is feeding the animals. I am afraid for the children. They are in danger. But soon I real-ize that the children are not afraid because all the animals are amputees. Each of them is missing a limb, a leg, a claw, a tentacle. That's why they are not dangerous.

Dreams tell our stories, and this dream helped us to get to know Laura's story. Over the years, we became more grateful for this dream: it opened a window onto her horrific experiences as a child and gave her a way to finally begin to get in touch with her inner world. We "have been graced by the presence of … [this] dream" (Kalsched, 2013: 186). It gave witness to her experience. As in our first encounter, a shiver ran through me, as she told me the dream. It was as if I was standing there, close to Laura, at the window, looking inside her home. Now, I could see the giant animals, the terrifying monsters inside. I, too, was afraid of them. They could devour us. Now, I started seeing where this shiver, like the one that I experienced at the very beginning, came from. It was signalling to me that there was a house filled with terror inside Laura's story. That house was filled with the anger and destructiveness that had marked her childhood and which she had tried to hide from herself. I asked her what she thought the dream was about. After a few minutes of silence, Laura whispered that she was ashamed of what she was about to say. Then, for the first time in her life, she was able to tell some-one her true story.

Handling Unbearable Contradictions

Despite her mother being caring and providing wonderful home-cooked meals for her children, she would violently and cruelly beat Laura and her younger brother, without any reason, daily, throughout their childhood. She would beat them because they were playing and laughing, or because they had moved an object or simply because they were there. This meant that they could never predict when the beating would happen. During these furi-ous onslaughts, Laura used to shield her brother with her body, because "In those moments, I KNEW our mother could kill us". In fact, even when they had fallen on the floor, she would continue to beat them, blind with rage. If Laura's father sensed that his wife was moody, he would go out, leaving his children to the mercy of their mother. On several occasions, Laura would say, referring to her father, "I pitied him". After having beaten her children, her mother ordered them not to cry. And they learnt not to cry. They had to cut themselves off, or become amputees, from their grief and despair. Also, they couldn't allow themselves to experience their potentially destructive rage. It was then that I could grasp the meaning of my early embodied countertransference. I was frightened by the rage and destructiveness that had been buried within Laura.

The Mother Complex brings with it memories and affects linked to the image of the mother, as well as behavioural responses to this image. The core of the Mother Complex reflects a child's experience of the mother's ability and inability to care and protect him. Laura's experience of her mother meant that she had been dramatically wounded by her and had to block out her own mother's inconceivable rage. Even more challenging for her, was that she had to push down her own rage towards her mother. This was why the giant animals had all been amputees. They had been deprived of their damaging power. To survive, and to keep on functioning in her daily life, Laura had tried to eliminate the hurt by splitting off the dread, unbearable rage and grief in relation to such a cruel and heartless mother. How could she imagine her mother as a potential killer? She had had to find a way to manage the powerful contradictions that her mother presented. As it almost inevitably happens in these kinds of cases, Laura had to split the image of the aggressive, destructive mother from the caring mother, who was able to take care of her children and cook good meals for them as did the old witch in Hänsel and Gretel.

Murray Stein (2003) underlines that, while the defences in the defence system are usually very effective in protecting psychic life, they often come at a high price for the individuation process since "like autoimmune diseases that attack the body, they also have the unfortunate effect of undermining and often destroying the social and psychological viability of the people they are meant to protect" (Stein, 2003: 214).

The person goes on living, but must withdraw some of his libido from the world since, in order to survive, energy is needed for the constant work of maintaining the split. Kalsched suggests (1996) that the archetypal defence system is meant to protect the core of the Self from the unbearable. "In order to avoid further devastation" (Kalsched, 1996: 143), archetypal defences function as Yahweh did in a story from the Old Testament. "When Yahweh became so outraged at the excesses of man that he was impelled to destroy the world, he made sure that one part of the creation was saved – this part was Noah, and to him were entrusted all the animal species, two by two" (Kalsched, 1996: 143) to ensure that life goes on. We can argue that this solution has an evident cost since the ark made by Noah is an extremely limited world, even if it keeps the individual safe. It is an ark, a boat, a sort of prison in some ways.

While the split helps functioning, over time this mechanism impercepti-bly reduces the quality and enjoyment of life. The self-care system had helped Laura to go on, to work and to successfully play music for many years, but now it was no longer allowing her to play her flute in her band. In the end, the cost of maintaining the split from the dramatic contradic-tions that had accompanied her childhood had become unbearable for her psyche. Finally, it was time for her to try to recall the memories of those powerful affects in her narrative and try to integrate them into a fuller life. It was time for her to enter the cottage in the forest as inside there may also be hidden treasure – the individuation process, which had been blocked for a long time.

Meeting the Shadow (Helped by a Dream)

> But then, you see, I do not want to know the complexes of my patients. That is uninteresting to me. I want to know what the dreams have to say about complexes, not what the complexes are. I want to know what a man's unconscious is doing with his complexes, I want to know what he is preparing himself for.
>
> (Jung, 1935, para. 171)

The Hänsel and Gretel dream told us that Laura was now ready to find the cottage in the forest – apparently reassuring us, as in the fairy tale. How was it that the children there were not afraid of the monsters? This question remained unanswered for a while, until Laura was able to realize that the children had no escape from the cottage and that they couldn't allow them-selves to experience fear when living there. Moreover, their father had regu-larly left Laura and her brother unprotected and alone at home with their mother. As we know, Hänsel and Gretel had also been abandoned by their father. He had accepted the will of his wife, without any endeavour to pro-tect his children. Once alone, Hänsel and Gretel needed to overcome the old witch by themselves. This is what had happened to Laura, since she had had to split-off the dread from her consciousness and keep it far away from the image of her caring mother.

Approximately halfway through our work together, Laura brought another powerful dream, which had really struck her. She was surprised by the image it offered her. The *Dream of Sana* marked a turning point in her analysis. Following Jung's words on dreams as instruments, or occasions, for the unconscious to tell us "what he is preparing himself for" (Jung,

1935), the *Dream of Sana* was telling us that now it was time for her to meet her Shadow (the black woman).

> It's night and I come back home from work. Inexplicably, I sense that someone lives in my house during the day, when I am at my office. Immediately, I notice some small details that help me realize that another woman is living in my house. I understand that she is a young black woman, a stranger whose name is Sana. She hides herself during the night, when I am home, and comes out during the day, when I am at work, living there as if it is her own house. Now I want to meet her.

What surprised us most about this dream was that Laura wasn't afraid of meeting this stranger. What is more, she wasn't upset about a stranger living in her house without her permission! I asked her why she wasn't afraid about this. Laura explained that she wasn't afraid because she KNEW this woman didn't represent a threat to her. For some inexplicable reason, she knew that this unknown woman was a friend to her. I suggested to Laura that perhaps this stranger represented a part of herself that she had been forced to hide from her mother's destructiveness, from herself as well, to keep it safe. Moreover, the woman's name was Sana – this word is an adjective in Italian, which means *healthy*. Maybe Laura was finally able to meet the *healthy part* of herself and eventually welcome it into her life? As Jungian analysts, we may think of the stranger inside her house as a shadow, which was also *healthy*, as shadows are if we are able to integrate them into our consciousness. The Shadow is an extremely interesting concept in analytical psychology since it refers to the "hidden, repressed, for the most part inferior and guilt-laden personality" (Jung, 1951, para.422), in other words it "personifies everything that the subject refuses to acknowledge about himself" (Jung, 1939, para. 513), such as aggression and destructiveness. What is more, the aggression and the destructiveness that are hidden in the Shadow are "also vital for survival" (Perry and Tower, 2023: 4), and bring with them a potential for creativity. Often, the Shadow consists of the aspects of our personalities that have been "relegated by our parental upbringing and environment into the realms of the unconscious" (Perry and Tower, 2023: 6) but can also include parts of ourselves that we have not allowed to come to light. For Laura, her shadow consisted of her aggression towards her mother, which was accompanied by destructive fantasies in relation to her and a strong feeling of guilt about this. Helped by the encounter with the stranger, this moment in analysis opened the way for Laura to recuperate energy through the integration of her shadow, as well as some resolution of the splitting of the complexes constellated around her Mother Complex.

The energy that had been dedicated to keeping the "other woman" hidden in the darkness of the Shadow was now available to strengthen her actual life. As Jung observed, the integration of the shadow brings with it "an enduring effect on the relations of the ego to the inside and outside world" (Jung, 1954b, footnote nr.18).

Compassion

During the 12 years of analysis, Laura and I worked together on reassembling her split parts. In the encounter with trauma victims, the ability of the analyst to acknowledge the patient's compassion allows them to experience their own compassion. The most important realization for Laura was finally to be able to see her mother as a victim herself of the cruelty of her own mother. This meant that she could begin to experience *compassion* towards her mother, as well as towards herself. As Krieger suggests, working on the autonomous complexes in analysis can help the patient differentiate "what is self and what is the internalized 'other'" (Krieger, 2019: 756), thus allowing "for *compassion for both*" (Krieger, 2019: 756, italics added). I think compassion is an experience of grace, a gift in life as well as in analysis. Perry and Tower describe the gift that the process of integration (of the Shadow as well as of split-off complexes) brings with it: "integration can transform the meaningless into the meaningful" (Perry and Tower, 2023: 7).

For Laura, the meaningless and obsessive thoughts that had forced her to ask for psychological help had opened a way for her to tell her story, to narrate it to herself and to hear it while recounting it to me. At last, the meaningless thoughts found their meaning: the unknown children she was afraid of harming now had names, Laura and her brother.

In our last session, Laura brought another moving dream.

> It's daylight, I am walking in a park and need to pee. There are toilets, but they are very dirty. I go in, anyway, and realize my feet are covered with poo. I leave and feel very embarrassed. I meet a man and a woman. They look at me and show me the way to a fountain, gently saying that I need to wash my feet. They are very kind. Then I find the fountain and wash myself. I feel their deep compassion for me. And this is the feeling that this dream left me with.

The reassembling of the complex releases the energy that had been used to maintain the split. In this way a new energy is made available for the ego. As

David Sedgwick claims, "As the web of emotions and thoughts connected with a complex becomes conscious ... the complex loses its strength and autonomy. Indeed, as a complex becomes integrated, in a certain way it ceases to be a 'complex'" (Sedgwick, 2001: 31).

Just before leaving my studio, Laura told me, clearly excited, that she had started playing her flute again with her band and that they were about to leave for a series of concerts around the USA.

Notes

1 The first experiments started in 1902, as reported by the Editorial note in vol. 2. In 1904 the first article on this subject was published (see Jung and Riklin, 1904).

2 In 1901 Theodor Flournoy, reflecting on the case of the medium Helene Smith, was the first to write about cryptomnesia – a latent memory that reappears and is mistakenly experienced as new information.

3 Helped by Peterson and Ricksher, amongst others who had travelled to the Burghölzli from abroad to work on the Association Experiments.

4 As Krieger (2019) observes, the term "feeling toned complex" had already been introduced by Theodor Ziehen (1898), but it was Jung who linked it to the WAT and gave it a psychodynamic interpretation (Jung, 1973, quoted in Krieger, 2019).

5 The ego-complex in a normal person is the highest psychic authority. By this we mean the whole mass of ideas pertaining to the ego, which we think of as being accompanied by the powerful and ever-present feeling-tone of our own body (Jung, 1907, para. 82).

6 "These patients have, in fact, autonomous complexes, which at times completely destroy the self-control" (Jung, 1911a, para. 1352).

7 In her book *Archetype, Attachment, Analysis*, Jean Knox (2003) suggests that the concept of *Emotion Schemas* (Bucci, 1997) is identical to Bowlby's *Internal Working Model*. However, the most recent re-conceptualizations of the *Emotion Schemas* (Bucci, 2009; Bucci, Maskit and Murphy, 2015) highlight similarities with the Jungian concept of the complex, which I think could be seen as only an element of the *Internal Working Models*.

8 Smiling behaviour has been observed in blind newborns as well (Freedman, 1964), thus confirming the hypothesis of a smile reflex. Furthermore, four-dimensional ultrasound studies have shown that babies (when still a foetus) also smile in the womb (Kurjak et al., 2005).

9 According to Parker and Taylor, the deficits in ego development include "a failure to develop adequate higher-level defenses and other cognitive capacities to regulate affects" (Parker and Taylor, in Taylor, Bagby, Parker, 1997: 91).

10 Adverse Childhood Experiences.

11 Amongst the many researchers, we can mention the works on alexithymia and psychosomatics disorders by Graeme Taylor (1987; Taylor, Bagby and Parker, 2003), and the remarkable work on Emotional Schemas in the Multiple Code Theory by Wilma Bucci (1997, 2021). Besides these, we must also refer to the important contributions by Bessel van der Kolk (2014) and Vincent J. Felitti (Felitti et al., 1998; Felitti, 2002).

12 "We have to thank the French psychopathologists, Pierre Janet in particular, for our knowledge today of the extreme dissociability of consciousness" (Jung, 1934, para. 202).

13 See Paul MacLean's triune brain model (1949, 1970).

14 This case was presented, in a different form, at the IAAP 19th Congress (Copenhagen 2013).

15 "The strong feeling-tone, then, creates a path" (Jung, 1907, para. 183).

References

Astor, J. (2001) "Is transference the 'total situation'?", *Journal of Analytical Psychology*, 46(3): 415–430.

Beck, J.G., Grant, D.M., Read, J.P., Clapp, J.D., Coffey, S.F., Miller, L.M. and Palyo, S.A. (2008) "The impact of event scale-revised: Psychometric properties in a sample of motor vehicle accident survivors", *Journal of Anxiety Disorders*, 22(2): 187–198.

Bleuler, E. (1906) *Affektivität, Suggestibilität, Paranoia*. Halle a.S: Marhold.

Bucci, W. (1997) *Psychoanalysis and Cognitive Science: A multiple code theory*. NY: Guilford Press.

Bucci, W. (2009) "Lo spettro dei processi dissociativi. Implicazioni per la relazione terapeutica", in L. Solano and G. Moccia (eds) *Psicoanalisi e Neuroscienze*. Milano: Franco Angeli.

Bucci, W., Zoppi, L. and Solano, L. (2001) "Teoria del codice multiplo e attività referenziale. Significato e impieghi nella ricerca sulla salute", in L. Solano, *Tra Mente e Corpo. Come Si Costruisce la Salute*. Milano: Raffaello Cortina.

Bucci, W., Maskit, B. and Murphy, S. (2015) "Connecting emotions and words: The referential process", *Phenomenology and Cognitive Sciences*, 15(3): 359–383.

Charet, F.X. (2000) "Understanding Jung: Recent biographies and scholarship", *Journal of Analytical Psychology*, 45(2): 195–216.

Colman, W. (2015) "A revolution of the mind: some implications of George Hogenson's 'The Baldwin Effect': A neglected influence on C.G. Jung's evolutionary thinking (2001)", *Journal of Analytical Psychology*, 60(4): 520–539.

Cyrulnik, B. (2009) *Resilience*. London: Penguin Books.

Dalzell, T.G. (2007) "Eugen Bleuler 150: Bleuler's reception of Freud", *History of Psychiatry*, 18(4): 471–482.

de Rienzo, A. (2021) "The day the clock stopped. Primitive states of unintegration, multidimensional working through and the birth of the analytical subject", *Journal of Analytical Psychology*, 66(2): 259–280.

Dieckmann, H. (1991 [1999]) *Komplexe: Diagnostik und Therapie in der Analytische Psychologie*. Berlin: Springer Verlag.

Escamilla, M, Sandoval, H., Calhoun, V. and Ramirez, M. (2018) "Brain activation patterns in response to complex triggers in the Word Association Test: Results from a new study in the United States", *Journal of Analytical Psychology*, 63(4): 484–509.

Evans, R. (1964 [1979]) *Jung on Elementary Psychology*. London: Routledge & Kegan Paul.

Felitti, V.J. (2002) "The relation between adverse childhood experiences and adult health: Turning gold into lead", *The Permanente Journal*, 6(1): 44–47.

Felitti, V.J., Anda, R.F., Nordenberg, D., Williamson, D.F., Spitz, A.M., Edwards, V., Koss, M.P. and Marks, J.S. (1998) "Relationship of childhood abuse and household dysfunction to many of the leading causes of death in adults", *American Journal of Preventive Medicine*, 14(4): 245–258.

Ferenczi, S. (1932 [1988]) *The Clinical Diary of Sandor Ferenczi*. J. Dupont (ed.), M. Balint and N.Z. Jackson (trans.) Cambridge, MA: Harvard University Press.

Freedman, D.G. (1964) "Smiling in blind infants and the issue of innate vs. acquired", *Journal of Child Psychology and Psychiatry*, 5(4): 171–184.

Freud, S. (1900) *Die Traumdeutung*. Leipzig and Wien: Franz Deuticke.

Freud, S. (1901) *Zur Psychopathologie des Alltagslebens*. Berlin: Krager.

Gottlieb, G. (2007) "Probabilistic epigenesis", *Developmental Science*, 10(1): 1–11.

Haule, J.R. (1983) "Archetype and integration", *Journal of Analytical Psychology*, 28(3): 253–267.

Hogenson, G.B. (1998) "Response to Pietikainen and Stevens", *Journal of Analytical Psychology*, 43(3): 357–372.

Hogenson, G.B. (2001) "The Baldwin effect: A neglected influence on C.G. Jung's evolutionary thinking", *Journal of Analytical Psychology*, 46(4): 591–611.

Hogenson, G.B. (2004) "Archetypes: Emergence and the psyche's deep structure", in J. Cambray and L. Carter (eds) *Analytical Psychology. Contemporary Perspectives in Jungian Analysis*. London: Brunner-Routledge.

Hogenson, G.B. (2009) "Archetypes as action patterns", *Journal of Analytical Psychology*, 54(3): 325–337.

Hogenson, G.B. (2019) "The controversy around the concept of archetypes", *Journal of Analytical Psychology*, 64(5): 682–700.

Horowitz, M., Wilner, N. and Alvarez, W. (1979) "Impact of event scale: A measure of subjective distress", *Psychosomatic Medicine*, 41(3): 209–218.

Jacobi, J. (1957 [1959]) *Komplex, Archetypus, Symbol in der Psychologie C.G. Jungs*. Zurich: Rascher Verlag.

Jung, C.G. (1902) *On the Psychology and Pathology of So-called Occult Phenomena*. CW1. Princeton, NJ: Princeton University Press.

Jung, C.G. (1905) *Experimental Observations on the Faculty of Memory*. CW2. Princeton, NJ: Princeton University Press.

Jung, C.G. (1907) *The Psychology of Dementia Praecox*. CW3. Princeton, NJ: Princeton University Press.

Jung, C.G. (1911a) *On the Doctrine of Complexes*. CW2. Princeton, NJ: Princeton University Press.

Jung, C.G. (1911b) *Morton Prince, "The Mechanism and Interpretation of Dreams": A Critical Review*. CW4. Princeton, NJ: Princeton University Press.

Jung, C.G. (1912) *The Theory of Psychoanalysis*. CW4. Princeton, NJ: Princeton University Press.

Jung, C.G. (1934) *A Review of the Complex Theory*. CW8. Princeton, NJ: Princeton University Press.

Jung, C.G. (1935) *The Tavistock Lectures*. CW18. Princeton, NJ: Princeton University Press.

Jung, C.G. (1936) *Psychological Factors Determining Human Behaviour*. CW8. Princeton, NJ: Princeton University Press.

Jung, C.G. (1939) *Conscious, Unconscious, and Individuation*. CW9/1. Princeton, NJ: Princeton University Press.

Jung, C.G. (1948) *Foreword to Harding: "Woman's Mysteries"*. CW18. Princeton, NJ: Princeton University Press.

Jung, C.G. (1951) *Aion. Researches Into the Phenomenology of the Self*. CW9/2. Princeton, NJ: Princeton University Press.

Jung, C.G. (1954a) *On the Nature of the Psyche*. CW8. Princeton, NJ: Princeton University Press.

Jung, C.G. (1954b) *On the Psychology of the Trickster Figure*. CW9/1. Princeton, NJ: Princeton University Press.

Jung, C.G. (1957) *Foreword to Jacobi: Complex, Archetype, Symbol*. CW18. Princeton, NJ: Princeton University Press.

Jung, C.G. (1963) *Memories, Dreams, Reflections*. A. Jaffé (ed.) London: William Collins.

Jung, C.G. (1973) *C.G. Jung Letters. Volume 1, 1906–1950*. G. Adler (ed.) London: Routledge.

Jung, C.G. and Riklin, F. (1904) *The Associations of Normal Subjects*. CW1. Princeton, NJ: Princeton University Press.

Kallivayalil, R.A. (2016) "The Burghölzli Hospital: Its history and legacy", *Indian Journal of Psychiatry*, 58(2): 226–228.

Kalsched, D. (1996) *The Inner World of Trauma. Archetypal Defenses of the Personal Spirit.* New York: Routledge.

Kalsched, D. (2013) *Trauma and the Self. A Psycho-Spiritual Approach to Human Development and its Interruption.* New York: Routledge.

Kandell, E., Koester, J.D., Mack, S.H. and Siegelbaum, S. (2023) *Principles of Neural Science.* 6th edition, New York: McGraw-Hill.

Kehyayan, A., Best, K., Schmeing, J.B., Axmacher, N. and Kessler, H. (2013) "Neural activity during free association to conflict-related sentences", *Frontiers in Human Neuroscience,* 7: 1–9.

Knox, J. (2003) *Archetype, Attachment, Analysis. Jungian Psychology and the Emergent Mind.* London: Brunner-Routledge.

Kohs, S.C. (1914) "The association method in its relation to the complex and complex indicators", *The American Journal of Psychology,* 25(4): 544–594.

Krieger, N.M. (2019) "A dynamic system approach to the feeling toned complex", *Journal of Analytical Psychology,* 64(5): 738–760.

Kurjak, A., Stanojevic, M., Andonotopo, W., Scazzocchio-Duenas, E., Azumendi, G. and Carrera, J.M. (2005) "Fetal behaviour assessed in all three trimesters of normal pregnancy by four-dimensional ultrasonography", *Croatian Medical Journal,* 46(5): 772–780.

Lanius, R.A., Vermetten, E. and Pain, C. (2010) *The Impact of Early Life Trauma on Health and Disease: The Hidden Epidemic.* Cambridge: Cambridge University Press.

MacLean, P.D. (1949) "Psychosomatic disease and the visceral brain: Recent developments bearing on the Papez theory of emotion", *Psychosomatic Medicine,* 11(6): 338–353.

MacLean, P.D. (1970) "The triune brain. Emotion and scientific bias", in F.O. Schmitted (ed.) *The Neurosciences.* New York: Rockefeller University Press, pp. 336–349.

Martin-Vallas, F. (2013) "Are archetypes transmitted or emergent? A response to Christian Roesler", *Journal of Analytical Psychology,* 58(2): 278–285.

Morton, J. and Johnson, M.H. (1991) "CONSPEC and CONLERN: A two-process theory of infant face recognition", *Psychological Review,* 98(2): 164–181.

Perry, C. and Tower, R. (2023) *Jung's Shadow Concept: The Hidden Light and Darkness Inside Ourselves.* New York: Routledge.

Petchkovsky, L. (2017) "Advances in functional brain imaging technology and developmental neuro-psychology: Their applications to the Jungian analytic domain", *Journal of Analytical Psychology,* 62(3): 415–433.

Petchkovsky, L., Petchkovsky, M., Morris, P., Dickson, P., Montgomery, D.T., Dwyer, J. and Burnett, P. (2013) "fMRI responses to Jung's Word Association Test: implications for theory, treatment and research", *Journal of Analytical Psychology,* 58(3): 409–431.

Peterson, F. and Jung, C.G. (1907) *Psychophysical Investigations with the Galvanometer and Pneumograph in Normal and Insane Individuals.* CW2. Princeton, NJ: Princeton University Press.

Roesler, C. (2019) "Theoretical foundations of analytical psychology: Recent developments and controversies", *Journal of Analytical Psychology,* 64(5): 658–681.

Roesler, C. and van Uffelen, T. (2018) "Complexes and the unconscious: From the association experiment to recent fMRI studies", in C. Roesler (ed.) *Research in Analytical Psychology: Empirical Research.* London: Routledge.

Roesler, C. (2022) *C.G. Jung's Archetype Concept. Theory, Research and Application.* London: Routledge.

Saban, M. (2016) "Jung, Winnicott and the divided psyche", *Journal of Analytical Psychology,* 61(3): 329–349.

Schmidt, M. (2012) "Psychic skin: Psychotic defences, borderline process and delusions", *Journal of Analytical Psychology,* 57(1): 21–39.

Sedgwick, D. (2001) *Introduction to Jungian Psychotherapy: The Therapeutic Relationship*. New York: Routledge.

Solano, L. (2001) *Tra Mente e Corpo. Come si Costruisce la Salute*. Milano: Raffaello Cortina.

Solano, L., Zoppi, L., Barnaba, L., Fabbrizi, S., Zani, R., Murgia, F., Nicotra, M., Pennebaker, J.W. and Seagal, J. (2001) "Health consequences of differences in emotional processing and reactivity following the 1997 earthquake in Central Italy", *Psychology, Health & Medicine*, 6(3): 267–275.

Sommer, R. (1894) *Diagnostik der Geisteskrankheiten*. Wien: Urban und Schwarzenberg.

Sommer, R. (1904) *Kriminalpsychologie und Strafrechtliche Psychopathologie*. Leipzig: Barth.

Stein, M. (2003) "Spiritual and religious aspects of modern analysis", in J. Cambray and L. Carter (eds) *Analytical Psychology: Contemporary Perspectives in Jungian Analysis*. Routledge: Hove.

Stevens, A. (2002) *Archetype Revisited*. London: Brunner-Routledge.

Taylor, G.J. (1987) *Psychosomatic Medicine and Contemporary Psychoanalysis*. Madison, CT: International Universities Press.

Taylor, G.J., Bagby, R.M. and Parker, J.D.A. (1997) *Disorders of Affect Regulation: Alexithymia in Medical and Psychiatric Illness*. Cambridge: Cambridge University Press.

Taylor, G.J., Bagby, R.M. and Parker, J.D.A. (2003) "The 20-item Toronto alexithymia scale. IV. Reliability and factorial validity in different languages and cultures", *Journal of Psychosomatic Research*, 55(3): 277–283.

Weiss, D.S. and Marmar, C.R. (1997) "The impact of event scale – revised", in J.P. Wilson and T.M. Keane (eds) *Assessing Psychological Trauma and PTSD*. New York: Guilford Press, pp. 399–411.

Wilkinson, M. (2006) *Changing Minds in Therapy: Emotion, Attachment, Trauma and Neurobiology*. New York: Routledge.

Ziehen, T. (1898a) *Psychophysiologische Erkenntnistheorie*. Jena: G. Fischer.

Ziehen, T. (1898b) *Die Ideenassoziation des Kindes*. Berlin: Reuter & Reichard.

Zoppi, L. (2017) "Chilled to the bone: Embodied countertransference and unspoken traumatic memories", *Journal of Analytical Psychology*, 62(5): 701–709.

Zoppi, L. (2023) "'Blade Runner' und die Welt des echten Lebens. Analytisches Setting und Übertragungsdynamik", *Analytische Psychologie*, 54(1): 120–129.

Chapter 2

Trauma and the Inner World

The Self-Care System as a Resistance to Healing

Donald Kalsched

Introduction to the Model: The Self-Care System

In this chapter, I want to share with the reader some of my discoveries in psychotherapeutic work with the adult survivors of early childhood trauma. In keeping with Jung's ideas, my focus will be on the inner world of my patients, by which I mean primarily dreams and other products of the imagination, but also, and most especially, on the feelings and emotions that are such an important constituent of the inner world. Based on many years of work (see Kalsched, 1996, 2013), I believe that dreams give us a picture of how the psyche tries to defend itself against the potentially soul-crushing impact of trauma and the unbearable emotions that flood the personality following it.

The defences that I am describing are imagined in dreams and other imaginal contents of the psyche, accessible through the psychotherapy process with early trauma survivors. They present an archaic and typical (archetypal) "system" of interlocking self and object images together with their associated affects. These powerful affect-images operate unconsciously but greatly influence the patient's self-esteem and relational life in the world.

The idea that the unconscious routinely symbolizes the powerful violent agents of defensive processes and shows how they operate to attack or anesthetize vulnerable feelings in the inner world, is not something that Jung described in the dream-life of his patients. This is because most of Jung's patients were within the "neurotic" spectrum of a "conflict psychology" and their inner dynamics could be understood under the principle of *compensation*. Such patients had "personal complexes" that could be integrated, leading to a greater sense of wholeness. The patients I am describing were the victims of very severe early trauma and therefore had to dissociate to survive. The remnant pieces of their early fragmentation had never been present in the ego before and hence their integration was the worst imaginable thing. Jung once described them as victims of "collective complexes" where

DOI: 10.4324/9781003298076-3

archetypal powers held sway and where, "something so devastating [appears to have happened] to the individual that his whole previous attitude to life breaks down" (Jung, 1920/48, para. 594). We now understand this "devastating something" as unthinkable trauma in early life.

I call this assemblage of inner defensive "powers" the *Self-care System*, hereinafter abbreviated as "SCS". The system is a dissociative system. It comes into being in situations of extreme early trauma in a person's life. It is devoted to self-regulation of the child's psyche and it accomplishes this equilibration through a process of severe dissociation. The system tries to control how much affect is allowed to be experienced by the conscious ego, in order that the host personality is not undermined by anxiety, and can pursue its normal life in the world without the distraction of trauma-linked memories and painfully disturbing emotions. When therapy begins with a patient in whom this system exists, traumatic memories and affects begin to return, early traumatic remnants of experience begin to formulate, and the defensive "system" emerges to fight this integration process. Hence it becomes a significant resistance to healing.

My effort to describe an inner "system" in the psyche is a form of model-building that is basic to any scientific endeavour. Over years of clinical work, one looks at the data (in this case the dreams of people who have suffered severe early trauma) as they emerge in the work. Here one can observe certain themes and patterns which suggest a potential "system" or structural model which are linked to definable stimulating "moments" in the transference field. Finally, one can apply the model to future cases to see if it fits the data and if it's helpful in the psychotherapy of trauma survivors.

The model I'll be suggesting appears to define the inner world of patients who have experienced severe, early trauma in infancy and/or earliest childhood. This is a time when the ego is still an "archipelago" of islands in a sea of unconsciousness and before the various components of experience have integrated or been "formulated". That's Donnel Stern's (1997) word for the fact that the infant's earliest experience is a fragmented collage of pieces (i.e., affects, images, sensations, scraps of memory) that will eventually coalesce into a whole experience and come under the aegis of a central ego and a coherent identity. If trauma strikes at this earliest stage, then dissociative defences appear to be extreme and systematic – conspiring to keep everything "dis-aggregated", atomized and therefore unconscious.

Because there is no coherent ego yet formed at this early stage, defences cannot be seen as those normal defences described by Freud as ego-defences or by Jung as "complexes". They tend to be more severe and "primitive".

Michael Fordham (1974) recognized this fact and called such defences "defences of the Self".

Fordham's notion is a useful one because it calls attention to an apparent "intelligence" in the whole psyche, operating to defend a core of selfhood against impingement, even before the ego is consolidated. Fordham (1976) speculated that defences of the Self were operative in cases of early infantile autism, where the child seals itself off from a hateful mother and becomes completely un-responsive. He wondered why the normally synthetic function of the Self did not lead to symbolic capacities in the autistic children he was observing. He had the idea that under normal circumstances there was an "original self" in infancy that contained all the psycho-physiological potentials of the whole personality, existing even before birth as a unique individual, separate from the mother. This primary self, he thought, carries "archetypal expectations" and "predispositions". It "de-integrates", moving into the environment, seeking a "fit" for its archetypal expectations and then "re-integrates", forming the basis for true internal objects which are both "in here" and "out there" and paradoxically both.

But if the "fit" between the baby's archetypal expectations and the mother's provision is bad – in other words, if trauma impinges at this early time, then defences of the Self enter the picture, interrupting the de-integration/re-integration cycle and preventing an internal world from forming. In this case, says Fordham (1976), a "persistent over-reaction of the defence-system may start to take place, *leading to an accumulation of violence and hostility which is split off from any libidinal and loving communication with the object that may take place*" (Fordham, 1976: 90–91, italics for emphasis). This split between violence and vulnerability is a major feature of what I call the Self-care System, as we will see in the case below.

Fordham didn't focus on defences of the Self as part of a dissociative *system*, but the Self-care System can be thought of as an extension of his idea into the adult life of trauma-survivors where it appears in dreams as well as various forms of what are known as *enactments*.

We should note that the idea of the self-care system is broader than Jung's idea of discrete *complexes*, although it is built on some of the same assumptions. The model shares with Jung the idea that the psyche is *dissociable* by its very nature and exists *in parts*, each of which embodies a particular self-state or affect-constellation. It shares Jung's conviction that the psyche dissociates because of painful, frightening or disagreeable *emotions*, many of which are derived from childhood trauma. It confirms Jung's discovery that dissociation sometimes uncovers and exposes patterns in the deeper strata of the psyche that are both archaic and typical, that is, *archetypal*.

And finally, it affirms that anything that overcomes dissociation and helps the psyche to integrate these parts makes the patient better, while anything that increases division and splitting makes him worse.

It is important to keep in mind that *dissociation is a defence against painful or overwhelming emotion,* and also that emotion (affect) is the vital dynamic energy of the human psyche. "The essential basis of our personality is affectivity", Jung claimed (1907, para. 78). So, we're following in his footsteps with that understanding. However, Jung did not give the reality of *defences against affect* the same centrality that I'll be giving them in this paper. Nor did Jung emphasize the central role of aggression in the defence of dissociation that I will be giving it – especially aggression against the vulnerable child parts of the inner world. I have become convinced that in many, if not most, cases of severe dissociation, the central agency of dissociation is aggression and that, at least in the traumatized personality, much of the psyche's instinctive aggression is bound up in, or "dedicated" to, defence instead of to ongoing life in the world or relationships.

The system of defences which I'll be describing is archetypal and mythological, that is, pre-personal. It is largely invisible to the "naked eye" because its archetypal "parts" are unconscious and one of the main reasons they stay unconscious is that, because the archetypes are so powerful, *we identify with them.* They give the fragmentation-prone ego a "boost". In certain triggering situations, they "take over" the ego and alter it according to the strong feelings they embody. Even in normal complexes, Jung acknowledged that the complex alters the central ego and leaves an "affect ego" in its place (Jung, 1934). Because of its strong emotional content, we identify with the affect and think that it is "us" while failing to recognize that we are identified with an aggressive "system" that is ultimately a defence against our weaker, more vulnerable feelings. Fortunately, the invisible patterns presented by the SCS become visible in dreams. We can also observe them in the patterns of relationship that often emerge around certain trauma-triggering events including what we call "enactments" in the psychoanalytic situation.

To summarize, the SCS, as I understand it, came into being to help us manage the *painful emotions and un-remembered trauma* of early childhood that threaten to de-stabilize the personality, and thus *to defend a vulnerable core of the traumatized childhood psyche from further violation.* This means preventing certain painful emotions from becoming conscious in the ego, dissociating them, "killing" awareness of them or blocking them from associating with the ego. This can be a violent affair constituting an attack by the child's instinctive (archetypal) aggression against its own vulnerable emotional life. Because feelings are the window to life, defences can become formidable anti-life and anti-individuation forces in the inner world. As far as I know, Jung did not discuss this destructiveness as related to our defences against vulnerable emotions.[1]

One could think of the SCS as a "compartmentalization system" that includes normal complex-formation within its structure but goes beyond it with regard to the "severity" of trauma that it defends against. In addition to what Jung described as normal ego-complexes, the SCS oversees more "primitive" emotions that are a part of early infancy and early traumatic neglect or impingement. These "vehement emotions" (van der Hart, Nijenhuis and Steele, 2006: 5) or "affect precursors" (Krystal, 1988: 89) are "volcanic", undifferentiated, extreme emotions that are typical of early infancy and regressed states in the adult. They remain un-transformed by relationship in the early infant/mother dyad like 880 volts of un-transformed energy direct from the "power company" of the brain stem. Hence, they are not yet conscious "feelings" that can be spoken about or utilized in normal ego-functioning.[2] They tend to be totalistic and extreme, reflecting their derivation in psychosomatic states of contentment (love) vs pain and discomfort (hate).

Because of the power of these archaic affects, the defences necessary to control them are also extreme, hence the preponderance of aggression and violence in the defences of the SCS. These dissociative defences allow trauma survivors to go on with normal life, but at a cost. Because of defensive compartmentalization these patients function better in the outer world, but they often suffer from feelings of "fraudulence." They struggle with low self-esteem, intense feelings of shame and various self-destructive behaviours where their unconscious anger cuts them off from a painful reality that they must avoid at all costs.

An Example of the SCS in Operation: Mike and the Child-killing Bomber

A 40-year-old high school football coach named "Mike" came to see me, for what his wife described as "anger issues". Apparently, Mike was repeatedly involved in various road rage incidents and he often got into fights in bars. He was seemingly addicted to his rages. He had been arrested several times and his career was threatened. But then there was another symptom that worried his wife. A new baby had been born, Mike's second son. The boy was born with a condition of severe jaundice, which had mostly been managed at the hospital, but now that the infant was home, and out of medical danger, Mike still couldn't stop worrying. He spent many sleepless nights

standing over the baby's crib, frantically checking his breathing, his temper-
ature, crying over the imagined loss of him.

When I first saw him, Mike was highly agitated, could not sit down in his
sessions, and spoke to me in dramatic, hyperbolic language while pacing
back and forth like a wild stallion. Gradually, over several weeks, he sat down
and we began to explore his history which included regular beatings and
other humiliations by his militaristic father for Mike's uncontrollable, impulsive behaviour. Mike had apparently been "inconsolable" as a toddler, especially when his younger brother was born when he was 18 months. His rages,
incessant crying and acting-out made his parents desperate. In one of Mike's
memories, his father had literally put a dog-collar on him and attached him
with a chain to a dog-run in the front yard to keep him from running away or
destroying things when the parents were away. In his teen years, Mike became
a juvenile delinquent and a criminal: acting out his rage and spending several
months in jail for various offences (mostly breaking and entering). His father
wouldn't speak to him for years and withdrew into his alcoholism.

When Mike entered Junior High School, his athletic ability and physical
attractiveness saved him. He became a football star and slowly learned how
to channel his violence into scoring touchdowns, racing cars and going out
with "hot" girls. His coach became like a father to him and treated Mike as
his "favourite son", hence Mike's successful career in coaching.

As his therapy began and Mike settled into the empathic field of my attention in his weekly hours, he began to feel some of the raw pain and tearful
sadness underneath his macho-defences. This process was not easy for him
and his SCS routinely threw up many forms of resistance to feeling. Usually,
he would present some horrific detail about his childhood with a dismissive
cynical attitude, like the dog-chain incident. Then, out of the corner of his
eye, he would see the painful look on my face as I was affected by the humiliation that he must have experienced as a little boy. This gave him permission to feel some of his own pain and the result was, increasingly, that he
could let himself drop into his own vulnerable emotional experience: a lot
of it was grief and sadness he had not let himself feel before. His new access
to feeling excited him but also began to worry him. He confided later in the
therapy that he'd had the fantasy that I was perhaps trying to "feminize"
him and turn him into a homosexual!

During that early period in our work, where he was opening up his pain,
he brought the following dream:

We're in a huge hotel. I am a bodyguard for this child who seemed sacred
or special in some way, luminous, almost like the Christ Child. He's in an

adjoining room. Somehow, the child doesn't know who he is. I can feel the presence of an evil person, someone who has come for the boy and is very close by. I become vigilant … alert! Then there's an explosion set off by the 'evil one'. I run into the child's room. He's about five years old. The explosion occurred next door to him. The child is in shock. I recognize him and know who he is … the images of his life flash by me. I sit down next to this boy: "Who are you?", I shout. "Do you know who you are?" His eyes remain fixed, then roll up in the back of his head. I see a little smile on his face. Perhaps, I have made contact with him? But he won't look at me. I feel so frustrated. I leave the room crying out of helplessness. Then, in a final part, I'm trying to tell this dream to a man upstairs. A woman present has instructed me to tell him the whole story. I'm relieved at the prospect of this but am blocked (like I've had electro-shock or amnesia). I can't remember the boy's life story. I think perhaps I should go back for his history but I'll never escape the "evil one" if I do. I feel compelled to wake myself up.

A couple of Mike's associations were important. To the child in shock, he associated his own hardened inner child. This was the part of him that had stopped attaching to anyone … at least until his therapy started. But this child, the dream now made it clear, was somehow "sacred". It held something of his own vital potential. He also felt huge compassion for this child and, in his associations, remembered once seeing a picture of himself having his hair washed by his mother. On my suggestion, he brought the picture into therapy and showed it to me. "I look so innocent", he said with tears in his eyes. "You were innocent", I said.

In other words, Mike was beginning to feel compassion for the traumatized "boy" in himself. When he could see this boy as a vulnerable *part* of himself (and not as the whole of him), his pain was more tolerable and he could feel more of it (I would call this a slow dis-identification from the powerful archetypal affect/images in his SCS). It corresponded to a growing ability to suffer the real injuries of his childhood.

This would probably not have been possible, were it not for the fact that Mike and I had a kind of "macho" rapport as the work developed. This masculine connection, which contained a good deal of mutual affection, came partly from the fact that we shared a kind of "irreverent" sense of humour, but also because, as luck would have it, we both happened to be building our own houses in the woods of Connecticut and New York State respectively. We lived 50 miles apart but kept running into each other at lumber companies and tractor stores. These meetings were at first uncomfortable for both of us, but then became enjoyable. At the beginning of many ses- sions, before descending into more vulnerable material, we would share "war stories" about our respective building struggles, bodily injuries and successes. We each owned a tractor for landscaping work and Mike loved to kid me about how his tractor was much bigger than mine. It was this kind of kid- ding and shared "tough-guy" energy that made his sharing of childhood vulnerability possible.

Returning to his dream, Mike recognized the explosion set off by the evil one as the rage that spilled out of him whenever he felt hurt or shamed which included his many road-rage incidents. This anger, which was part of the dissociative "mechanism", helped him to cover up and defend against the pain and torture of his early life. And to the "man upstairs" he associ- ated me, his analyst (my office was upstairs in the village where I practiced). A female presence in his dream instructed him to "tell the whole story" to this man, and that's what he was doing.

Mike could relate to the dream ego's ambivalence in telling his story as part of him was blocked by dissociation (the electro-shock and amnesia) and afraid that if he allowed himself to know his history and feel his early pain, it would arouse his violent defences, that is, the "evil one". This pro- cess of recovering his feeling-memories against the oppression of his defences was precisely what was happening in his therapy. He was dropping his violent defences and letting the young and innocent part of himself feel the heart-breaking pain and helpless dependency of his early life.

Comment

This dream and my work with Mike back in the 80s (which is described at length in my book *Trauma and the Soul* (2013: 127–158), was my first glimpse into how the violent energies in the psyche are employed by the SCS for defensive purposes. The "evil one" in his dream is a personification of his own primitive aggression – now directed at the vulnerable "boy" in himself. This was not literally to kill it, but to kill his consciousness of it and render it the "not-me" child in himself. This violence is best understood as the instinctive upwelling of rage in Mike's childhood self as he was being neglected or abused.

Ronald Fairbairn (1981) gave eloquent theoretical expression to this dynamic. Fairbairn asked himself the question "What does the abused or neglected child do with its desperate neediness on the one hand and its rage and anger on the other?" The answer, in his words, was as follows: the child seeks to circumvent the dangers of expressing both [needy] and aggressive affect towards his object "by *using a maximum of his aggression to subdue a maximum of his libidinal need*" (Fairbairn, 1981: 115).

This results, says Fairbairn, in an unconscious attack by an "internal saboteur" upon the "libidinal ego" that is, the immature needs and vulnerability resident in the inner world. In other words, *aggression becomes the "engine" that drives the dissociative system*. It's where the *splitting* energy comes from – funnelled back into the inner world to attack and oppress the vulnerable libidinal parts of the personality.

Wilfred Bion (1959) seems to agree with Fairbairn. He called the splitting energy in the psyche "attacks against linking" and spoke of how dissociation dismembers whole experience, rendering it into "beta bits" which are not allowed to come together in symbolic images – what he called "alpha function". James Grotstein (1981: 92) corroborates Bion's insights and further adds that "aggression and destructiveness are the primary instrumentalities of the defense organization".

In Mike's case, we can see how the different "parts" of the SCS are arranged and how they enter his outer life and the therapy relationship. His

Figure 2.1 "The Good and Evil Angels Struggling for Possession of a Child", William Blake

newborn jaundiced baby boy, who Mike was crying over in nightly rituals of anticipated grief, is a perfect *stand-in* for the wounded *inner* child in himself who he has already lost to dissociation. In other words, his early *unremembered loss* of this part of himself (to his dissociative defences), is now accessible as a feared *future* loss of his "actual" child … his second son.

Angels as Archetypal Powers

The accompanying illustration shows the "parts" of the Self-care System as I have come to understand them, and as they appeared in Mike's dream. It is one of William Blake's illustrations from the Tate Gallery in London called the *Good and Evil Angels Struggling for Possession of a Child*. I think of it as a self-portrait of the psyche's dissociative defensive operations perpetrated by the two Angels representing *archetypal affects and dynamic structures* from another dimension of the unconscious that Jung called the "collective unconscious". To say these powers are "Angels" is another way of saying they are archetypal, which is another way of saying they are extremely powerful, "primitive", pre-personal, daimonic entities – mostly un-transformed by experience.

The Dark Angel, representing aggression, rage, violence and negation, is by far the most powerful force in the defensive system and does most of the dissociating. (We met him as the "mad bomber" in Mike's dream.) The Dark Angel would represent the "fight" part of the autonomic nervous system's triad of *fight, flight, freeze*. Clearly, some version of Lucifer in Blake's image, the Dark Angel, is shackled to the flames of Hell, which became his abode after he "fell" from Heaven in early mythology. In terms of object-relations, the Dark Angel would be the persecutor, that which Kleinian analysts call the "bad object": the great accuser in the psyche, the nihilist, the critic who fills the host personality with shame and despair. Eckhart Tolle (1999: 29ff) calls this figure the "pain body".

As outlined by Fairbairn, the Dark Angel gets its energy from the hatred and aggression which the traumatized child feels in its moments of abuse, but can rarely express toward its abusers. Such trauma survivors live with the enduring threat of annihilation, hating themselves when they could not risk hating those who harmed them. This angel persecutes the child within the system, muttering accusations that try to blame the "child" for the pain suffered by the host personality. Mike constantly listened to its voice in his head: "You're Stupid! What's the Matter with You! You're Bad, Bad, Bad! You're Disgusting!" These tirades amounted to aggressive attacks against the vulnerable "child" in Mike's inner world.

On the right of Blake's illustration stands another angel with a frightened child in its arms. I call this the Bright Angel and see it as a kind of opposing twin of the Dark Angel on the left. It is not shackled to the flames of Hell, but instead has normal seeing eyes and some compassion for the child in the system. I like to think of this angel as Lucifer's other half: Lucifer in his pre-fallen state as the bearer of light. If the Dark Angel is persecutory, the Bright Angel is protective. But both are devoted to dissociation.

In terms of object-relations, the Bright Angel would represent what Winnicott (1960: 142) called the "caretaker self" and Ferenczi (1932) the "progressed self", both of which exist mostly in the mind. As a spirit-being, this angel is associated with the celestial or upper regions, including those aspects of the mind which allow us to transcend our physical limitations, including the impossible realities of our mortality and death, especially our vulnerable feelings in the body. If the Dark Angel personifies the "fight" response, this one personifies "flight" and possibly also "freeze". The motto of both angels is like that of the Jewish Defense League: "Never Again!" Never again will this child experience such unbearable pain. Never again will this child attach to someone who can hurt him or her like this.

As guardian and protector of the child, the Bright Angel tries to hold the child away from its impossible pain, providing hopeful illusions, when hope seems to have vanished. Often appearing as feminine, her goal is also disso-ciation. But the Bright Angel uses "softer methods". She can cast spells, put the ego in a trance or throw an invisibility cloak over a traumatic memory. Sometimes she seduces the patient's ego with substances like alcohol or drugs, or invites it into an imaginative fantasy realm, creating an alternative reality for it to live in.[3]

So, to summarize, the Dark Angel represents *violence and the negative affects of hatred, malice, domination, shame, and attack.* By contrast, the Bright Angel represents *illusion* and all the soothing images and fantasies associated with *hope, comfort and safety, including primitive "love" and com-passion.* Both are necessary forces of dissociation, when trauma is extreme in the child's early life, each trying, in his own way, to keep the child away from the painful feelings in reality that have been impossible to entertain consciously. Each trying, through dissociation, to keep the child uncon-scious of its vulnerable feelings.

The Child

Finally, in Blake's image there's a "child" and this child turns out to be what the two angels in the SCS are defending. That doesn't mean they "like" this child. In fact, the Dark Angel often hates this child and tries to "kill" the ego's connection to it. We might think of the child as *a personification of the impossible human suffering of the patient*, a suffering that's rendered unconscious by these defences. Because the child is also dissociated, it can't remember explicitly what happened to it, but it carries the *implicit* memory of trauma in its little body, full of fear and powerlessness, vulnerable helpless feelings on the one hand, hateful anger that it can't express outwardly on the other. It is being kept prisoner in the system "for its own good" so to speak. At least that's what the system tells it. A major goal of psychotherapy will be to get this child "out" of the imprisoning fortress it's in. This means helping the host personality of the patient to experience the pain of this wounded inner child within a window of tolerance and thus making the child's unconscious suffering *conscious*. Doing this liberates both the child and the overworked defences which imprison him.

How the SCS Enters the Relational Field: Enactments

Because the "powers" in the SCS are "primitive" and laced with vehement emotional energy, they are extremely seductive to patients. Moreover, when such patients enter the analytic dyad, the angels and demons, innocent children and wounded children in the "system" inevitably find themselves in the relational field. This sets the stage for what are commonly known as "enactments" (Maroda, 1998).

Enactments were formerly known as "acting out" and were looked down upon in psychoanalytic discussions. Now, however, they are seen differently as a jointly created behavioural interaction, fuelled by strong unconscious emotion in both patient and analyst, where both parties describe themselves as slightly or completely "out of control".

According to Maroda (1998: 520), "Enactment is an affectively driven repetition of converging emotional scenarios from the patient's and the analyst's lives. It is not merely an affectively driven set of behaviours, it is necessarily a repetition of past events that have been buried in the unconscious due to associated unmanageable or unwanted emotion."

Maroda feels we must not be afraid of our strong feelings in our connections with patients. She says:

> What I began to realize after many years of clinical experience is that quite often patients would effectively stimulate in me the exact emotions they had experienced with someone else in the past. (And I would do the same with them). What turned out to be therapeutic was the constructive

expression of these deeply felt emotions, as well as the mutual working through of the subsequent emotional and behavioural events.

(Maroda, 1998: 531)

Enactment with Mike

In retrospect, it seems inevitable that Mike and I would share enactments of various kinds. But one was very memorable and almost "blew up" the therapy. Recall that Mike came into therapy primarily for help with his "anger" issue, expressed in various "road rage" incidents. It turned out that Mike had a long-standing history of acting out his anger. It started in adolescence and almost always involved incidents with teachers or authorities whom he felt humiliated by. For example, he had terrible learning disabilities and was always behind in school, feeling stupid, copying other kids' homework and cheating in exams. If he was caught and shamed by the teacher in front of the class, he would always retaliate. He would sneak into the school and defecate on the teacher's desk. Often he was arrested for these and other burglaries, but he rarely spent time in jail. His mother would post bail and the priests from the local church would intervene on his behalf. But his father would have nothing to do with him after these incidents and gave him the "silent treatment". Mike was desperate for help from his Dad, but he never got it.

Bernard Brandchaft (2007), who wrote about the "pathological accommodation" of traumatized children, reminds us that our trauma surviving patients, caught in their own compliance and rebellion patterns, will inevitably annoy us and get under our skin and that, inevitably, some of the dark powers inherent in the defensive system will get tangled up in the transference. When this happens, Brandchaft says: "no amount of interpretation, or of mirroring, or of gentle provision can reach the soul of a person so destroyed by the powers of shame and darkness. Only the determined grappling, *mano a mano*, with the powers of evil can connect and affirm their right to their resistance" (Brandchaft, 2007, cited in Orange, 2011: 215).

The following account of an incident with Mike contains exactly such a *mano a mano* moment.

For the first several years of work, I was spared any confrontation with Mike's volcanic anger. I knew how "touchy" he was whenever I intervened in his "victim/perpetrator" narrative and tried to engage his "younger" feelings underneath. His whole SCS was designed to protect the innocence at the core of his system, so if I suggested he was partly responsible for something that had gone wrong, such as a fight with his wife or a disagreement with his boss, he would flare inwardly but never express it to me outwardly.

I think, in all honesty, that I was sufficiently afraid of his anger, and knew not to push him in these moments.

We might say that Mike's aggression tended to be split off from the positive transference and acted out in his incidents of road rage outside the hour. However, as he would continually report such incidents to me, and as these dangerous and compulsive explosions continued to erupt despite our work on them together, I began to feel my own version of fatherly irritation.

As with many men who have suffered traumatic humiliation in early life, almost any frustration in our modern world could trigger Mike's humiliation, shame and helplessness. Immediately his tyrannical rage would come up as a defence to cover up these unbearable vulnerabilities. This could happen if his kids didn't do what he told them to; if his wife wasn't responsive to him; if someone cut into the line in front of him in the grocery store. And it happened repeatedly on the road. Someone would speed by him and cut in front of him, creating that old familiar "dissed" feeling inside. Up would come his rage! Down would go his foot on the accelerator, up would come his middle finger and out would come the "F" words until he and the other driver were often pulled off on the side of the road and Mike was bellowing like a wild bull. Archetypal energies would pour through him and sometimes he was temporarily out of his mind. Because Mike was 6 feet 2 inches and over 200 pounds, he sometimes hurt his adversary in these fights. Then he would feel terrible remorse about what he had done and sometimes drive his now bloodied antagonist to the hospital. His self-recriminations after these events were intense, made worse by the lectures he got from his wife and the obvious disapproval he felt from me.

Knowing that his eruptive anger was a defence against the shame and humiliation he had experienced in childhood (on his dog-chain and in the beatings from his father), and with the dream images of his evil bomber and traumatized child in my mind, I repeatedly tried to help these two dissociated self-states get together. We did active imagination with these inner figures. We reviewed each road-rage incident slowly, step by step, to see where he was triggered, paying attention to his states of activation, returning to his breathing and connecting the dots with early experiences. For a while, these body-sensitive techniques seemed to work. The road-rage incidents decreased. But if a stressful period ensued in Mike's life at work or in his marriage or with his kids, he would often regress and revert to these old patterns and the road rage incidents would occur again.

I began to feel ineffective, helpless and inadequate as his therapist. He told me that his wife wondered why his therapy wasn't working and I began to feel defensive although I had the same questions she did. I also started to think that he wasn't trying, that despite the appearances of regret, he really didn't mean it. I began to wonder about anger management groups I could get him into. I began to think of medication.

Then came the session of our "enactment". Mike came in and confessed superciliously (and with a cynical grin on his face) to yet another incident of road rage in which he had terrorized another man half his size. He was completely activated again, and I could find no regret, no guilt or remorse in him, only the pumped-up hyperarousal of this addictive violence. Sensing my discomfort, he changed the subject to some "urgent" issue about his wife. I sat seething, trying to listen with that old familiar feeling of helplessness and irritation with my own anger activated. Recovering my senses, I suggested that he was avoiding the most important thing we needed to talk about and asked him what he was feeling. "About what?" he said with cynical irritation. At that point, something snapped in me, and I lost my mind (at least, my analytic mind). Somewhere from a far-off place inside, I heard myself say to him: (with apologies to those of you who may be offended by the language), "Look", I said …

"Look … you are threatening everything you've created in your life – your profession, your family, your relationship with your wife, the boys, your relationship with me, and that new friendship with that little boy inside you – all for the temporary high of your little shit-fit rages. You think you're getting even or administering some kind of sick justice but the fact is you're simply indulging yourself like a two-year-old. You're just emotionally incontinent! That's your problem. You can't hold it! When are you f**ing gonna learn to hold it?

A deafening silence filled the room. "F** you!" he said, turning his head away fuming … "I'm outa here!". And he lurched out of his chair, slammed the door behind him and locked himself in the bathroom on the other side of the waiting room. (Fortunately, there were no other patients waiting.) I sat in stunned silence for a moment, slowly came back into my body, then followed him and stood outside the locked bathroom door.

"Mike", I said, "I am really, really sorry. You didn't deserve that outburst from me. It wasn't any better than yours on the highway! Let's not let this wreck our connection. Let me in so we can process this together. We've got too much going for us. There's a lot at stake".

An agonizingly long few minutes later, I heard the door unlatch from inside. I went in. He was seated on the toilet lid, head in his hands. I sat on the bathtub and put my hand on his shoulder. Several minutes went by with both of us finally coming back into our bodies. Then I noticed Mike's eyes begin to tear up. I waited for him to say something, but nothing came. "What're you feeling?" I asked. He looked up at me and saw the tears rimming my eyes also. "I don't know", he said … "Sad … grief about my father I guess". Then Mike really began to sob.

"Nobody ever cared!" he said. "I had to take care of it all by myself … I was always crying out for help in my acting out, but nobody got it … 6 arrests before I was 18 and my father never spoke to me about it! All they could do was make me bad. You're not making me bad".

"You're not making me bad". Suddenly, I felt a huge upwelling of relief and gratitude inside my chest, relief because I really *had* "made him bad", at least in my mind, and I felt terrible about it. I had really hated him, for a moment, and it hadn't destroyed him. And it hadn't destroyed us. Both love and hate, the good and the bad, were held together in this moment for each of us but love was stronger, and hence the relationship was both preserved and deepened. Mike took my hand and we just sat looking at each other in this wet, beautiful moment. It was like the Balm of Gilead, healing and reconciliation poured down on us both. Trauma repeated, acted out, but repaired, right there in the session. The little boy and the murderous protector (in both of us) were present and getting to know each other.

Reflections on our Enactment

In retrospect, I think Mike and I lived through what the late Paul Russell (1998: 24) called "the crunch", by which he meant repetitions of injuries in important earlier relationships (in this case Mike and his father) that could not contain strong affect. These injuries were now "delivered into the treatment situation as a crisis and a threat to the treatment relationship itself". Russell points out that when relationships cannot contain and process the inevitable mixture of positive and negative feelings that are a part of life, then trauma is the result. "It is traumatizing because the individual must attempt to do the containing himself", says Russell. "The essence of trauma is that without [relational] containment, feelings cost the individual the relationship" (Russell, 1998: 25). This is what had happened to Mike and his father.

One of the ways to think about Mike's situation is that the trauma of unshared emotionality (both positive and negative) with his father was too painful to remember, so it had to be dissociated. And, unconsciously, he sought out a relationship in which it could be repeated. Repetition, says Russell, has to do with what we cannot feel, so it's a kind of affective incompetence. The repetition compulsion is an "organized system of affective incompetence" (Russell, 1998: 7). In other words, a dysfunctional feeling system.

In the typical repetition, the patient gets attached to the analyst in what looks like a working alliance, but then things start to get complicated. The patient begins to focus on some aspect of us that recaptures the past. With Mike and me, this was the father whose disapproval now found an echo in my own disapproval, and whose abandonment of his son's need and acting-out had left him full of hate and shame.

As advice to those of us caught in these impasses and repetitions with patients, Russell (1998) offers an important reminder:

> [the things the patient complains about] he says, "are real parts of ourselves that do, to some degree, prove their point. *However odious, this aspect needs to be located in us, and for us to try to disown or disavow it, to ascribe it to 'transference' is to sever the patient's emotional connection with us.* The only thing that works is negotiation, namely a negotiation around whether things have to happen the same way this time".
>
> (Russell, 1998: 9; italics added)

The thing that was odious for me in this example was my own hatred of and contempt for Mike's defensively-inspired behaviour, and my own feelings of helplessness and failure as his therapist. The thing that was odious to Mike was the old, familiar feeling of shame at failing one more time to please the man he loved and whose pride in him he so desperately needed.

Fortunately, I did not dissociate my hatred for long. Once enacted, I could own it, and this made my apology possible. That was the beginning of a negotiation towards a different outcome. Allan Schore makes the therapist's affective integration of love and hate, internally, an essential ingredient of such moments:

> when a therapist's wounds are hit, can she regulate her own bodily based emotions and shame dynamics well enough to be able to stay connected to her patient? Can the therapist tolerate what is happening in her own body when it mirrors her patient's terror, rage and physiological hyperarousal? Herein lies the art of psychotherapy. For a therapist to stay with a dissociating patient who is projecting his trauma onto her takes many years of experience. More importantly the therapist needs to have worked deeply with her own trauma *and has to keep working with it* (italics added). A successful therapeutic relationship precipitates emotional growth not only in the patient but also in the therapist.
>
> (cited in Sieff, 2015: 132)

A Post-Enactment Dream

Some time after our "enactment" session, Mike had a dream. The dream presents an image of healing and reconciliation between a "father" and his lost, orphaned "son". It profoundly moved us both and became an important image for our later reflection. Here's the dream:

> I'm a part of a police force and we're chasing this young man who's about the age of my oldest son ... 10 or so. He looks like an Afghani child, neglected and lost. He carries an old newspaper in his hand. This boy has eluded us for years, yet now that we've captured him, I'm confused. He looks at me imploringly and says "is it time?" ... tentatively handing me a newspaper. The front-page article is about this lost boy, and how much his father wants him back ... he's been lost or abandoned or abducted! In that moment, I recognize him as my son! (As if he'd been the child of an old girlfriend I'd gotten pregnant). I'm overcome with grief and longing. All I can say is "I love you". I reach out for him in an embrace and wake up deeply moved.

This beautiful dream heralded a major shift in our work together and a major integration in Mike's psyche between a younger "un-fathered" part of himself that was clearly "his", yet had become "bad", a fugitive, shame-ridden, hence lost to his ongoing life owing to the defensive system that had "abducted" him. Mike was in tears as he told this dream, tears of recognition that this lost boy was himself and that there was a part of him that had been deeply wounded (in his relationship with his actual father) but was now starving and impoverished in his own war-torn inner Afghani landscape – in other words, his own orphaned "son". It was seemingly this father-wound – both inner and outer, and shared by both of us – that Mike and I "enacted".

Mike's acting-out had provoked me into my own shame complex, defended in myself by making him "bad" (my hatred), just like his father had done, no doubt after similar provocation. Here is the early injury "delivered into the treatment situation as a crisis" referenced by Russell above (1998: 24). Yet defensive hatred wasn't all I felt toward Mike, and my apology had introduced the deeper affection that united us and that his real father could never express. Hence the love and hate that had become frozen in a defensive spiral with his actual father, could get un-frozen in our transference enactment, and his feelings (and mine) could flow once again. When Mike looked at me in the bathroom with tears in his eyes, felt my affection for him and was able to say "you're not making me bad", he saw through the projection, and the abandoned "boy" in himself could return. The father-wound was re-lived in the moment (repeated), but with a new outcome.

It would be important to acknowledge that this was also a healing moment for me. Out-of-control anger and hatred is not a comfortable part of my analytic "identity" and the eruption that occurred in my enactment with Mike left me feeling shame-ridden and "bad" about myself. His ability to see through this to my deeper affection and "good" intentions ("you're not making me bad") felt like forgiveness, hence my own upwelling of tears and gratitude. Dissociated parts of myself could come together in this moment also and I felt inwardly reconciled.

One of the striking features of Mike's "Prodigal Son" dream is that the "News"-paper reveals that the boy's father wants him back – that it is indeed "time" for him to return. And then there occurs the epiphany that Mike *is* this boy's father, that is, the story is happening NOW, and Mike is no longer outside the narrative but an intimate part of it. The distance between the dream ego and the dissociated child-self collapses. They fall into each other's arms.

In this example, we're given a glimpse of the way the psyche seems to celebrate (symbolically) the recovery of its own lost wholeness and the healing of its dissociated parts such as a father's embrace of his lost son. In this case, and in many others that I presented in *Trauma and the Soul* (Kalsched, 2013), the recovery of this lost wholeness seems to be represented in dreams by the return of an unacceptable "child" from some state of unconscious alienation. Moreover, this "child" is often numinous, soul-like in its pristine innocence and truthful aliveness.

We can't help asking ourselves: "Who is this child, who seems to be the central concern of the defensive system?"

I have described this child as primarily the wounded empirical child of the patient's early life. A great deal of early-trauma therapy is involved in trying to recover this wounded inner child and, with him, some of the un-remembered pain consigned to unconsciousness by dissociative defences. Much of my time with Mike was spent doing this.

But sometimes, in the course of the work, not often, but often enough, there's a glimpse into another aspect of the inner child and this has to do with the pure joy, pre-traumatic innocence and aliveness of the child that sometimes comes to presence. Jung (1949) thought he saw in this "child" a half-spiritual premonition of the psyche's potential wholeness, its divine spark and potential for creative renewal and healing. There was something "more", something ineffable about this child and Jung spoke of this additional dimension as *entelechy*, a vital principle of aliveness that in its unfolding guides the development and functioning of all life-forms, including the human personality (Jung, 1949, para. 278).

This dimension of the child, Jung identified as the archetypal child. He saw it as the vital formative principle central to renewal and regeneration in all the great world religions. Frequently, this more-than-human "child" who, according to the universal stories, will eventually turn out to be the hero or heroine of a whole culture, or an inspired leader, or a healer, does not know who he is at first and lives in exile in a foreign land like Moses or Oedipus. The uncovering of this child's destiny moves through his personal suffering to his trans-personal destiny and vocation. It's as though, beside the memory of childhood pain and suffering (in the empirical child), there's another "memory" of a very particular creativity – that is, his or her unique and unrepeatable personal gift.

Dancer and choreographer Martha Graham puts it this way:

> there is a vitality, a life force, an energy, a quickening, that is translated through you into action, and because there is only one of you in all time, this expression is [sacred and] unique. And if you block it, it will never exist through any other medium and will be lost.
>
> (cited in de Mille, 1991: 45)

Winnicott (1960) called this core the "true self" and affirmed that it was a sacred centre of aliveness in all of us. For Jung, it was the "divine child" deeply buried in the unconscious of us all like a seed, patiently awaiting his realization. In my first book, I referred to this mysterious core as the "imperishable personal spirit" (Kalsched, 1996) and in my second book, simply as the embodied "soul" (Kalsched, 2013).

So, we have to think of the child in the Self-care System as a dual child. A child of dual parentage, on the one hand the empirical suffering, wounded child, carrying the implicit memory of trauma; on the other hand, the innocent, pre-traumatic vital, alive child, the child created in the image of God so to speak. As we all know, this dual child image is at the centre of the Christian myth and also at the centre of Jung's authorship.

For Jung, the analytic adventure of individuation and the pursuit of our wholeness was therefore a *spiritual journey*, as well as a secular, material one. Margaret Arden, a British Psychoanalyst, was also aware of this fact and connects the spiritual dimension of our work with the "child" we have been observing in the material I've presented. Arden (1998) says:

> For me, the transformation produced by insight in the consulting room is symbolically equivalent to the spiritual journey towards enlightenment.

Psychoanalysis is a new version of the ancient theme shared by all the great religions. The loss of illusion, the giving up of attachment to a false reality, the inevitability of suffering and expiation are all present in psychoanalysis … Every person who seeks analysis is on a personal pilgrimage.

The Christian maxim "unless you become like little children, you shall not enter the kingdom of heaven" is my marker of the true self. False self-behaviour is usually manipulative and destructive of psychic truth. All our theories can be seen as ways of unravelling the destructive processes or defences which the patient uses. The miracle of psychoanalysis, and it is a miracle, is that when a person comes to understand the core of his or her childhood experience, all the anger, all the rejection of life, turns out to have been for one purpose: to preserve, at whatever cost, the child who is capable of love.

(Arden, 1998: 4–5)

Notes

1 Gustav Bovensiepen (2022) has argued recently that Jung never had an adequate concept of aggression or destructiveness – leaving it all to the "dark side of God" or the archetypal "shadow". He suggests that Jung had a too romantic notion of the "child" and never describes the "evil" child "who can become an evil or destructive hero". I think he's right in his assessment of Jung. But for me, Jung's lack of an adequate concept of aggression and destructiveness comes from his failure to understand early trauma and the violent archetypal defences that attack and injure the vulnerable feeling-self of the traumatized child. Possession by these defences is what turns the original vulnerable and innocent child, "evil".

2 Jung's use of the word "feeling" to characterize one of the four function-types of consciousness has led to confusion in the use of the word. In the child's early development, "feelings" do not yet exist. Vehement emotions and archetypal affects predominate. Slowly, as these affects differentiate (with the aid of language) and can be talked about, they become conscious feelings. So, a great deal of early trauma work in psychotherapy is an effort to transform unconscious suffering, in the form of unconscious emotion and unformulated experience, into conscious feelings and hence, into conscious suffering.

3 I am not the first to discover a kind of protective, angelic spirit in the unconscious material of trauma survivors. Sandor Ferenczi (Clinical Diary, 1932) spoke about a miraculous personified Being in the inner world of one of his most severely traumatized patients – a being that had a special relationship with the patient's inner child. Ferenczi and his creative patient called this being "Orpha" and referred to it as an "Astral Fragment" who – just like Isis in the ancient Osiris myth – at a moment of traumatic dissociation, would exit through a hole in the head and roam the whole universe in search of solace for the patient, putting her fragmented parts back together again, soothing her with "spiritual" love in the absence of human love and often witnessing the child's trauma from a position "above".

References

Arden, M. (1998) *Midwifery of the Soul: A Holistic Perspective on Psychoanalysis: Collected Papers of Margaret Arden*. London, Free Association Books.

Bion, W.R. (1959) "Attacks on linking", in *Second Thoughts: Selected Papers on Psychoanalysis*. New York: Jason Aronson.

Bovensiepen, G. (2022) "Destructiveness: a 'Neglected Child' in the theory of analytical psychology", *Journal of Analytical Psychology*, 67(4): 999–1019.

Brandchaft, B. (2007) "Systems of pathological accommodation and change in analysis", *Psychoanalytic Psychology*, 24(4): 667–687.

de Mille, A. (1991) *Martha: The Life and Work of Martha Graham*. New York: Random House.

Fairbairn, W.R.D. (1981) *Psychoanalytic Studies of the Personality*. London: Routledge.

Ferenczi, S. (1932 [1988]) *The Clinical Diary of Sandor Ferenczi*. J. Dupont (ed.) Cambridge, MA: Harvard University Press.

Fordham, M. (1974) "Defences of the Self", *Journal of Analytical Psychology*, 19(2): 192–199.

Fordham, M. (1976) *The Self and Autism – Library of Analytical Psychology, vol. 3*. London: Heinemann.

Grotstein, J. (1981) *Splitting and Projective Identification*. New York: Jason Aronson.

Jung, C.G. (1907) *The Psychology of Dementia Praecox*. CW3. Princeton, NJ: Princeton University Press.

Jung, C.G. (1920/48) *The Psychological Foundations of Belief in Spirits*. CW8. Princeton, NJ: Princeton University Press.

Jung, C.G. (1934) *A Review of the Complex Theory*. CW8. Princeton, NJ: Princeton University Press.

Jung, C.G. (1949) *The Psychology of the Child Archetype*. CW9/1. Princeton, NJ: Princeton University Press.

Kalsched, D. (1996) *The Inner World of Trauma: Archetypal Defences of the Personal Spirit*. New York: Routledge.

Kalsched, D. (2013). *Trauma and the Soul: A Psycho-Spiritual Approach to Human Development and its Interruption*. New York: Routledge.

Krystal, H. (1988) *Integration and Self-Healing*. New Jersey: Analytic Press.

Maroda, K. (1998) "Enactment: When the patient's and analyst's pasts converge", *Psychoanalytic Psychology*, 15(4): 517–535.

Orange, D.M. (2011) *The Suffering Stranger*. New York: Routledge.

Russell, P. (1998) *Trauma, Repetition & Affect Regulation: The Work of Paul Russell*. J.G. Teicholz and D. Kriegman (eds) New York: Other Press.

Sieff, D.F. (2015) *Understanding and Healing Emotional Trauma: Conversations with Pioneering Clinicians and Researchers*. London: Routledge.

Stern, D.N. (1997) *Unformulated Experience: From Dissociation to Imagination in Psychoanalysis*. New Jersey: Analytic Press.

Tolle, E. (1999) *The Power of Now: A Guide to Spiritual Enlightenment*. Novato, California: New World Library.

van der Hart, O., Nijenhuis, E. and Steele, K. (2006) *The Haunted Self: Structural Dissociation and the Treatment of Chronic Traumatization*. New York: W.W. Norton & Co.

Winnicott, D.W. (1960) "Ego distortion in terms of true and false Self" in *The Maturational Processes and the Facilitating Environment*. London: Hogarth Press, pp. 140–152.

Part I

Early Relational Trauma

Chapter 3

Countertransference in Working with Early Relational Trauma

In Dialogue with the Body

Daniela Eulert-Fuchs

Introduction

Trauma is a violent intrusion into psychic experience, an event that overwhelms the psyche's coping strategies and leads to a fundamental shattering of trust. Mental regulatory capacities collapse. Massive defence mechanisms and a break in the continuity of life occurs (Winnicott, 1971).

The role of the analyst in working with trauma patients has been subject to debate for a long time. After Freud abandoned his seduction theory, at the end of the 19th century, trauma as the cause of mental illness moved into the background. In psychoanalytic treatment, the focus moved to unconscious fantasy and, with regards to method, on insight and interpretation. A deviation from this attitude could lead to exclusion from the psychoanalytic association, as the controversy with Bowlby showed (Bohleber, 2014).

There is now no doubt that trauma has massive effects on psychic development and that the analyst is inevitably drawn into the early life and relational world of the analysand. Early relational trauma ruptures a person's horizon of expectations and violates archetypal hope (Eulert-Fuchs, 2020). Traumatic experiences are not connected to the thinking and feeling "I" but lead an unconnected life of their own in the depths of the psyche and are excluded from representation and symbolization.

If conventional treatments involve thinking and feeling again that which has already been thought and felt, in the case of trauma, the analysis concerns feeling and thinking what could have never been felt and thought until now. The traumatic experience that cannot be managed, and is therefore split off, causes mental alienation, stagnation and psychic death (Winnicott, 1967). Although not stored in cognitive memory, and yet always present, traumatic experiences are major players in psychic life, like foreign bodies that bind psychic energy and prevent one from living. The inaccessible, and often strongly secured, realm of traumatic inscription can only be read by means of its traces. Traces that not only the patient, but also we analysts,

DOI: 10.4324/9781003298076-5

would often rather not follow. Nevertheless, these traces must be taken seriously if we want to gain access to the hidden, buried lives of our patients.

Paraphrasing Christa Wolf, from her *Kindheitsmuster* (1976), the past never dies, it becomes the present and comes alive in the relationship with the analyst. He too will experience the trauma, albeit in a lesser form, as well as turbulences in the setting and in his body and mind. In the encounter with the patient, deficits in representation and symbolization, that become evident intersubjectively, need the other to be transformed. This is particularly evident in the work with traumatized patients. And this makes special demands on the analytic attitude. Kinston and Cohen (1986) point out that this work carries a high risk of re-traumatization and places an extraordinary burden on the analyst, as Schmidt and West also emphasize (Schmidt, 2012; West, 2016, 2017). In recent years, much emphasis has been placed on the requirement for therapeutic regression of the analytic couple. This has a long tradition in French psychoanalysis and was propounded with the concepts of the double and the chimera (Green, 1975; de M'Uzan, 1993). As early as 1993, de M'Uzan addressed the defensive movements that regressions trigger in the analyst. Another much-cited work is that of the Botellas, who asked themselves how one can gain access to an area of the unconscious which they call "mémoir sans souvenir" (Botella and Botella, 2005). Levine, Reed and Scarfone (2013) also address the regression of the analytic couple, especially in the context of non-represented states.

All these authors vividly describe how the analyst generates – or experiences them as phenomena emerging from the intersubjective field – images via his own reverie and arrives at an initial understanding that eventually informs an interpretation that drives the process. In my first vignette, with seven-year-old Jan, I will attempt to show that images, as Civitarese advocates, are "not a *sine qua non*" (Civitarese, 2013: 222) since, in some circumstances, they may be absent. However, it is by no means my intention to disparage the importance of interpretation in analytical work. Interpretation, given at the right moment, remains an invaluably powerful instrument for the analyst. It can clear the chaos and reduce anxiety, establish order and orientation, especially in neurotic conflicts, but, in my experience, it is not always available to us. Here I am mainly thinking of treatments where thinking symbolically remains impossible over a long period of time. From these experiences, my reflections have developed over the years to culminate in this chapter.

I aim to show that the analytic, transference-focused work, especially in the case of early relational trauma, often first needs preliminary work in the implicit relationship as a basis. Using clinical material, I will try to demonstrate that the willingness to absorb and work through early projections, and to include early bodily experience in the analytic process, is fundamental for this (Eulert-Fuchs, 2022). The fact that the body is so essential in this process is related to the internalization processes in early childhood. The formation of representations consists of the combination of internalized experiences of interaction and phantasmagorically formed ideas of being with the other. These experiences, conceptions, fantasies and expectations are stored in implicit memory and are accessible primarily through bodily sensations and affects embedded in the body (Samuels, 1994; Martini, 2016; Godsil, 2018; Kalsched, 2020).

I am convinced that these must be brought to life in the analytic field before they can be transformed. This phenomenon, which I call "reverie of the shared body", requires, first and foremost, the participation of the analyst in primary process experience. Understanding will ultimately follow, as if by itself. I call it "reverie of the shared body" because in this experience there is no clear separation, neither between body and mind nor between you and me. Rather, there is a dynamic, unconsciously shared experience from which a new "I and You" and "I with Myself" can eventually develop. It is therefore my hypothesis that this reverie has both essential communicative and therapeutic elements which contribute to a transformed understanding of self and world.

In this chapter, which is focused mainly on clinical work, I would like to offer three vignettes which attempt to give an (unvarnished) idea of my work with early relational traumata as it occurred in the consulting room. My goal is to describe an analytical attitude that doesn't primarily aim for insight but tries to enter into dialogue with the body and that which presents itself as unknown in body and mind.

Schwartz-Salant warns:

> Transference and countertransference dynamics cannot be apprehended without a clear understanding of how the subtle body may be experienced in the interactive field. The therapist must be able to recognize subtle states of mind. These states cannot be differentiated into mental or physical states of being, but quite palpably combine both. ... treatment situations oblige the therapist to deal with irrational elements that exist not only in the patient but also in himself or herself.
>
> (Schwartz-Salant, 1989: 8–9)

When we allow for these irrational elements, as Schwartz-Salant recommends, and turn to that which we do not know, we may discover something new and connect the body with the mind. This, according to my experience, allows analysands to frame their own images and words and set a process in motion that enables an integrated, new understanding and a life beyond traumatic repetition.

Clinical Examples

In this regard, my treatment of a young boy stands out. Even though this was conducted over 20 years ago, my reflections on this child analysis continue to this day. You could say that I was at a loss for words, but my patient, a seven-year-old autistic child, found his way out of his speechlessness and learned to use words and images for himself. As a result, Jan became one of my first and most important teachers.

Jan had experienced neglect, rejection and persistent alienation from his primary caregivers. I cannot go into more detailed anamnesis here, nor is it essential for my considerations. In fact, this experience was not an isolated one, albeit particularly pronounced and thus also formative. I found myself in a situation that felt alien and incomprehensible: physical/psychological malaise, embarrassing states of excitement and inexplicable physiological reactions: hot, cold, leaden tiredness and emptiness. These feelings were very distressing and often bordered on the unbearable. Language, including my inner dialogue, was lost to me for a long time.

Jan came to me through a colleague. He had withdrawn himself. Jan was aggressive, hurting himself and others, untenable at school and in danger of losing his place there. He no longer came out of his room, did not speak, but sometimes had screaming fits which could not be calmed down for hours. Most of the time he was silent and beyond the reach of anyone. When I met Jan, I was still very naive in terms of child analysis with many concepts, but little experience, some might say. I myself would have wished a more experienced colleague for him, but no one was willing to work with him.

And so, our journey began:

Small, delicate, with water-blue eyes and translucent skin, he prances about the consulting room. His feet do not seem to touch the ground, his eyes wander, his gaze does not settle. My greeting echoes around the room, fading into nothingness. Eventually, he sits down and expends much energy drawing unrecognizable objects, compulsively executing the smallest details. This seems to tire him, and yet he is unable to stop. He calls it "landscape of machines". While he is drawing, I feel far away, exposed, isolated. What Jan wanted to tell me remained unheard, even though he showed me so clearly his distress and his attempts to keep it at bay. What was so obviously in front of me remained hidden. I didn't understand, didn't have access to him or myself, as though I was part of this bleak and dead meaningless landscape.

The sessions frightened us both.

For months, he uttered only barely identifiable, crude guttural sounds while he turned his back to me and enacted his, initially stuporous, then stereotypically compulsive, violent and sadistic play scenes. These were games of extreme cruelty in which small, defenceless beings were tortured and tormented by overpowering tyrants, in an endless loop with no escape. In ever new and more brutal variations, body parts were severed and people buried alive.

At first, I am terrified, then I feel nothing. An emptiness takes hold. The body becomes cold and stiff. Thoughts surface without context or meaning, there is a tension that is difficult to describe which makes being inside me almost unbearable. Thin, sharp silence. Then it is as if my breath had stopped. It was impossible to give words to my understanding, however incomplete. For a long time, I felt on guard, as though I was inhabiting a strange and hostile country, a jungle beset by unknown dangers. At the same time, I remained as though trapped in myself and my isolation. I felt useless and redundant. The sessions were endless. Every time, he left the room as wordlessly as he had entered it. Not a sound in between. This was repeated session after session, week after week.

A void dominated the room. This was not about understanding. It was about mental survival. I had fantasies of cancelling sessions, but something inside me made me persevere, something about Jan had touched me. It was as though he had asked me an unformulated and unthought question: can you keep hope alive? A hope which is hard to believe in (it sometimes feels like working against gravity), and which Winnicott describes as "an unconscious assumption [in the patient] (which can become a conscious hope) that opportunity will occur at a later date for a renewed experience in which the failure situation will be able to be unfrozen and re-experienced" (Winnicott, 1955: 18).

Jan had developed reliable autistic mechanisms to keep his inner distress at bay, which he did not want to give up lightly. He shared his isolation and dissociation with me. I, too, felt alien and not at home in my body. I struggled with bewilderment and wanting to fall asleep. Again and again, I had small lapses which I felt terribly ashamed of. In hindsight, I think that I often experienced what Green (1975) calls the representation of a missing representation. I was confronted with psychic holes (Kinston and Cohen, 1986), unsymbolized areas of mental experience, which were followed, unavoidably, by my own inability to dream, referred to by Cassorla (2013) as "non-dream".

Within my body, I had sensations that were hard to identify and hard to bear. This was something akin to anxiety, panic, loneliness. Cold and isolation. Sexual arousal pervaded my body, I was confused, ashamed and suffered on with the treatment which, so I thought, hardly deserved that name.

After Jan had not spoken for more than half a year, I suddenly and unexpectedly heard his clear voice:

"What does it need to gain trust?" he enquired.

"Time, I believe", I heard myself answer.

Jan sighs.

Something comes alive in me, a small, bright movement, a glimmer of hope?

A short time later, Jan brings me his Tamagotchi – an electronic pet; he explains how it needs to be fed to survive. Before the mid-term vacations, he forgets it. I learn how to feed the "animal". When he returns, he checks to see if it's been taken care of and remarks with satisfaction: "It's fine".

Jan comes alive, he wakes up, begins to paint and build in the sand. For many months he works hard.

Images emerge. Scenes of disaster. Black holes on paper and sand.

More and more sand images appear in which Jan designs different variations of a landscape of death where nothing survives. Meteors hit, hurricanes destroy the world, an army of aliens takes over the earth and poisons everything. Nothing survives.

Jan had begun to pour his experience into images. In one picture all scenarios of destruction merge, he calls it the catastrophe of Janithillia.

"One can't really survive there, isn't there anything one could do?" I ask.

"No, impossible", he says, but builds a bunker and a lightning conductor then moves a step closer to me.

In "The Lord of the Rings", Ithillia is a land between Gondor and Mordor, between good and evil, which the hero has to cross during his path of individuation. It is both inner psychic space where dissociated parts meet and an intermediary space, the place of encounter and hope. Will we succeed in writing a new story?

At school, Jan is supposed to write essays, but he tells me that he can't think of anything to write. His mother has only mockery for him. She informs me:

"That's why we hired you, to fix him".

We are both affected by this statement. I tell Jan:

"We could try to make something like a word salad ... you say whatever comes to mind, I write it down and, in the end, we see whether it makes a story?"

"I don't know. I can't think of anything", Jan replies.

"It doesn't matter, no hurry, who knows ..."

At first, it's slow, halting, laborious but, over time, words and ideas tumble out of him like from an overstuffed sack that's been closed for too long. For many months, writing stories becomes his favourite activity. Jan smiles and says:

"The monsters party, they are not evil, but maybe sometimes they scare people".

He draws the monster party and tells me, excitedly:

"You know, they are nice monsters, one of them will soon tell us about his experiences, how he flew over the world, what he has seen, and that he has reunited with his best friend, an explorer".

He paints pictures of himself and the friend exploring the world together. They travel to faraway countries and explore alien planets. There are parties to celebrate and an unlimited supply of the most wonderful sweets. Instead of a life-and-death struggle, now there are royal riding tournaments and knightly campaigns.

Jan finds a friend in school and throws himself into fencing. He writes stories about villages that could withstand curses and invaders, and towards the end of the fourth year of therapy, he makes a laughing face in the sand and tells me that he was very busy now and probably wouldn't be back after the summer break. When he left, he gave me a long handshake.

What had happened?

For years, Jan had tried in vain to connect with his mother and finally he had forbidden himself to hope. It was as if he had wiped her out internally, depriving her of meaning to render her harmless. This also made it difficult for us to connect and it took him a long time to find out if his analyst would be able to bear his story, to listen to him body and soul. The only way to figure this out was to involve her through me, to expose her to the same indigestible inner distress he had experienced and to test her extensively. In Jan's case, experience came before understanding. It had no label. No name. It hit me first hand, directly and almost overwhelmingly.

Jung said that, first and foremost, analysis is a process of experience. I agree, and see this as the shared experience of both analyst and patient. In 1935 Jung wrote that "A person is a psychic system which, when it affects another person, enters into reciprocal reaction with another psychic system" (Jung, 1935, para. 1) and this inevitable interaction is "the only thing with which I as an individual can legitimately confront my patient" (Jung, 1935, para. 2). Lesmeister (2009: 272) speaks of the "imprint of the self in the other". With regard to the Jungian idea of a mutual influence between patient and analyst, Schwartz-Salant suggests that the psychic energies that are activated in the analytic encounter can be so unsettling that "many therapists sometimes choose to retreat into a conceptual framework that promises the safety of their being able to gain control over their affects … rather than voluntarily suffer them" (Schwartz-Salant, 1989: 7).

Bion (1962) calls "facts that cannot be thought" beta elements. Beta elements are raw bodily states that are not yet mentalized. They belong to proto-mental experience, which does not yet differentiate between mental and physical. These indigestible elements of psychic life, which the child cannot process by himself, must therefore be eliminated: into the analytic session and through the body and mind of the analyst. This is what had happened to me with Jan.

In imposed silence, Jan had made me experience his isolation and distress. He confronted me with sensory-physical states that made me doubt the relevance of my work. We had both lost not only language but hope, too. In my view, this is not only unavoidable, but an important stage in the work. It is my contention that the willingness to accept and incorporate projections is crucial to the success of treatment and that the body, especially in early relational trauma, plays a crucial role in the countertransference, as Zoppi (2017) also touchingly illustrated. Why is this so?

Representation, Body, Defence

Early communication is a communication of bodies. A poetry of bodies.

Mothers and fathers answer the baby's first expressions with their eyes, words and gestures. The most important unit for the evolving and developing life is the dyad. "Being together" or being a "self with other", therefore, best describes the unit that guarantees survival. These experiences of interaction are internalized and represented. The first representations to be formed are thought of as representations of relationship (Brown, 2011). They carry, at their core, the fundamental affect of the dyad and the primary defence which cast their shadow over any further representation. Whether representations are formed or the imago fades depends upon the quality of care (Winnicott, 1967) and whether a libidinous cathexis of the body is possible (Anzieu-Premmereur, 2013). Development and consolidation of representation therefore depend on the continuous and dependable support of the caregiver. In fact, while a tolerable degree of frustration and absence stimulates the mental mechanisms of coping, fantasy and symbolic processing, these fail in the case of trauma.

When the affective activation of the experience exceeds a manageable degree, defence mechanisms emerge in babies as young as three months, which are also visible to the outside observer. I remember a four-month-old baby who was filmed at our department while being swaddled in the context of an interaction diagnostic. She did not react to her mother talking to her but constantly averted her gaze. When a colleague stepped up, the baby smiled at her and interacted vocally.

Avoiding gaze as a sign of the dysfunctionality of the relationship was specific to the interaction with the mother. At that age, the defence still is directed specifically at one person, as Anzieu-Premmereur (2013), suggests. Later it is generalized (Stern, 2003). So even the first processes of defence concern a specific form of interaction, of being with another. This dyadic inscription "self with other", which is deeply rooted in implicit body memory, has an affective core, a basic emotional tonality – something like "I feel looked after, held, full and happy with the other person" or, on the contrary, "I feel unwell, hungry, alone, persecuted, overwhelmed by anxiety, I am falling, breaking apart". The representation comes with a corresponding unconscious expectation of future experiences with relationships: of what I will experience with a different person and how I will feel.

Wilma Bucci (2001) has helped us to understand that the representation of the dyad is stored sub-symbolically and precedes self-representation. Beaten or abandoned children are convinced that they deserve it; they think of themselves as being worthy of punishment (Fonagy, 2002). The critical view of oneself experienced as a child is internalized and turned against the self as well as externalized in the form of expected criticism. The distortions of self-representation and the underlying affect colour and shape reality. This is also relevant for the analytical situation. The distortion of reality, and this is my basic hypothesis, must be communicated, experienced (also physically) and processed in the analytical field before new forms of experience can be represented. The transformation of self-representation can only happen through relationship.

I would now like to use two short vignettes to illustrate that the "reverie of the shared body" not only serves to communicate primary experiences of relationship with implicit expectations, but also to transform these and eventually represent new experiences.

Kleo

Kleo, a professionally successful young woman, came to me because she felt uncomfortable in the presence of others. She spent a lot of time and effort on being neat and "stylish". But still she always felt inadequate and out of place. For a long time, she had no words. During the sessions, she cried frequently and for long periods of time. She did not know why. There had been no dramas in her upbringing, everything, according to her, had been normal. Only at the very beginning she remarked, laughingly, that her mother had told her: "You were such a terribly ugly baby". Kleo hated herself and nearly starved herself to death. This disgust, directed not only at her body but at everything related to it, spread in the room like an invisible, amorphous mass that stuck to me and made me wish to be disembodied myself. I felt scrutinized from head to toe. I found myself unattractive, scruffy and poorly dressed. Before our sessions I checked the toilet and myself (whether everything was perfect), and afterwards I felt an almost irresistible craving for chocolate.

Objectively, Kleo was a very attractive woman but the longer we worked together, the less pretty I found her. I thought her nose was too big, her skin too large-pored and pale, and her eyes colourless. I was unable to find any compassion for her. I became cold and indifferent. My mouth was dry, my thoughts dead. It was as though her mother's gaze had petrified us both and drained our emotional life. I was afraid of the sessions and afraid of her gaze. Nothing escaped her. Sharply and curtly, she said:

"You misspelled my name. Kleo with a K, not a C".

Then she reverted to a frosty silence. I feel my body, too, running dry and freezing. I shiver, my breath is short and shallow. I stay with my breath. It deepens. I lean back.

As if through a kaleidoscope, I can see Kleo as a little girl – she puts on a dress, turns in front of the mirror, wants to show herself. I feel sadness.

"You probably think that I don't just misspell you, but that I also fail to see you properly, that I can't properly decipher and piece together the letters of your life. You must feel I don't understand you".

Kleo gives me a long look and replies:

"I have never been seen. The only thing that was ever noticed was my outstanding performance".

She falls silent. Her eyes are wet. This short dialogue was a "turning point" in our work. Kleo had experienced the painful internalization of a critical, even contemptuous, gaze. She had not been libidinously cathected by her mother to a sufficient degree and this impacted the cathexis of her own body. In our work, she had not only told me how she felt, but transferred this gaze onto me. She had made me experience how she looked at herself and felt looked at. This perception made me suffer, but it covered me like a veil that could not be pushed away. While I remained in this distorted perception, I shared Kleo's despair and distress. Remaining in this shared experience enabled me, and this is my hypothesis, to base my words on a shared experience and to phrase them emotionally in such a way that Kleo was able to feel that they resonated with sincere empathy. Through this physical-sensual experience, the countertransference fantasy had added a visceral understanding to the analytical process and given it life. Kleo began to take an interest in her inner life and to no longer avoid the pain. Increasingly, we witnessed her begin to take an open and, toward the end of therapy, empathic look at herself.

In early childhood development, the gaze of the primary caregiver is of great importance. Dialogues between primary caregiver and baby show how the child feels held in the eyes of the other. Still face studies bear witness to the holding function of the gaze and how great is the despair when it is interrupted. The baby struggles to resume eye contact with the mother and, if this does not happen, it finally collapses into sadness and resignation (Tronick, 2003). The gaze is existential, literally forming a second skin. Not to be seen means not to exist.

Hans

In the case of Hans, this unremembered experience shaped his reality, but only his body really knew about it. Hans, in his early forties, had come to see me because he was unable to bear closeness. He could not be touched. Hans was a banker, was good with numbers and comfortable with them. He was attractive, wealthy, successful and very lonely. He longed for a relationship, for a family, but could not commit and did not know why. He only had affairs that meant little to him. In recent years, he had sleep disturbance, nightmares and headaches that affected his productivity.

Hans was motivated to change. He came regularly, three times a week. Every time he lay down on the couch, he held me tightly with his gaze. I liked Hans, but his gaze made me uncomfortable. When he lay down, he would turn to me. He looked at me, didn't blink, didn't modulate, but just stared at me. I felt fixed, controlled, trapped in a kennel. At the same time, the floor caved in beneath me, I swayed as I sat, I felt dizzy and sick. I even experienced a gap, a small amnesia. Where was I? What had happened to me? At that moment, I remembered Hans' dream images, or rather dream fragments, which woke him at night He said that they were like scenes of a horror movie, but remained meaningless to him. I "understood" these images, fragmented body parts and cut-off limbs, "physically", as it were, as an expression of an agonising severance that had torn his identity to pieces. Hans had experienced this painful separation before he had internalized a secure image of himself and others. This occurred before he consistently experienced himself as a subject. His mother had left the family shortly after his birth. I had known of this before, but this knowledge had to root itself in my body to be effective. I returned his gaze. It was as though our eyes were touching, as though we met and shared a knowledge that didn't have words yet. Hans' body sank into the cushions. I leaned back. The floor was steady once more. A warm silence carried the rays of a late summer sun into the room.

Hans had let me know how much he feared falling into a bottomless void and breaking apart. This experience didn't represent itself in me as a thought or fantasy, but as a physical-sensory reverie, a sensation rooted in the body, which first triggered a defensive movement, and finally helped me to link my knowledge and thoughts about Hans as well as symbolic images. The physical-sensory reverie resulted in a new perspective, a gaze that carried a different tonality. Schwartz-Salant explains that "a capacity to see the patient through an imaginal lens … proves to be a containing vessel" (Schwartz-Salant, 1989: 4). This, I am convinced, was communicated to Hans.

The Therapeutic Absorption of the Unconscious, In Memoriam to Fordham's: Representation, Symbolization and the Double

That which ultimately carries the process forward remains a secret and may or shall remain so. I suspect, however, that through the implicit experience shared with an other, an emotional connection is created which is unconsciously perceived by both (Civitarese, 2013).

Jung draws on alchemy to amplify complex and difficult to understand transference and countertransference mechanisms. He writes of the meeting of two chemical bodies (Jung, 1946), of the *participation mystique* (Jung, 1921), of the psychoid (Jung, 1954) and of the subtle body (Jung, 1989). Schwartz-Salant (1986) also deals extensively with the subtle body and finds correspondence with Winnicott's transitional space. The borders of I and you, body and soul, blur. Here, I draw comparison to the earliest communication between parent and baby in which body and mind are experienced as an inseparable interwoven whole. Similarly, my hypothesis is that the repeated experience of a shared emotional-bodily state in the analytic space also gives rise to a shared subtle body that interacts and communicates. In this state, pre-verbal experiences are replicated and a form of primary relatedness emerges, in which the other is not yet "an other", instead he is a transformational process. This is something that Bollas (1987) described in terms of the transformational object, while Treurniet (1995) talks of the object as a process and Winnicott (1965) of the environmental mother. This process predominantly concerns communication of bodies: gesture, gaze, voice, intensity, sound, shape and, above all, affect-tuning and temporal alignment.

Reflecting on Fordham's developmental psychology of the primary self, the process could be thought of as follows. First, *de*integration, that is, the opening towards the world and objects, which is the relational aspect. Then *re*integration, the inner process of assimilation. Together, both constitute the dynamics of development. If, however, the external world, and above all the objects, are not receptive, offer little resonance space and respond as little as occurred with my patients, then it is no surprise that this unfolding process is stunted, a rigid defence becomes erected, and the implicit expectation of relationships will develop accordingly. After all, we also have to deal with this rigid defence initially in the analytical process. However, in the shared unconscious of the analytical relationship what occurs is an exchange of the "two selves" which starts an unconscious process of mutual opening.

The analyst therefore, in a sense, opens his self, exposes it to distress and allows it to be touched and used. Inside him, depending on his individual constitution, subjective complexes and defences, an initially unconscious process of digestion begins. This can be seen as an assimilation of "deintegrates", a confrontation which always involves one's own early traumatic experiences. One can assume that, in this process, the flexible activity of the self, which absorbs and integrates, communicates with the world and with oneself. Growth can be restricted at times and even paralysed. The anaesthetizing and paralysing activity of the "self-care system" (Kalsched, 1996, 2013), of the "demon", can also seize the analyst. As a result, the analyst, too, will inevitably lose hope from time to time. This oscillating process of infection and coping that the analyst consciously and unconsciously undergoes, makes him a "transformational object" that can be internalized. Schore (2003) speaks of a necessary conversation between limbic systems of both analyst and patient. To me, not rejecting this unconscious process, but to embrace it and suffer it, rather than just endure it, encompasses the mystery of the inner alchemical becoming and the opportunity for transformation.

I think that it is this experience in particular that produces a mostly imperceptible, slow transformation in the representation of relationships that occurs below the threshold of perception. Old convictions regarding the way it feels to be with an other, which are rooted in physical memory, are undermined. New possibilities are initially regarded with a critical eye, then tested in depth, and later slowly taken into consideration. This doesn't happen through insight, but through repeated experience, it takes time and repetition (Leuzinger-Bohleber, 2014).

The key affective note changes nearly imperceptibly. In most cases, we realize this only in retrospect. In the countertransference too, this becomes perceptible with feelings of relief and a first budding of hope because rigidity, impasse and defence no longer dominate the scene. In my opinion, these are signs that a new representation for "being with" have developed, which then are the precondition for new representations of "being with oneself". The significant change is visible in the transformation of the fundamental affect of the primary dyad. I understand this as an expression of archetypal hope being reactivated and anchored individually, physically, as well as intersubjectively as a new relational experience. The new experience of relationship allows for a different perception of the self, a transformed "I with myself" and thus a more positive cathexis of the body.

In the symbolic material, this development of a new perception of self, a new experience of being with oneself, of "I with myself" often appeared in dreams and, in the work with children, with above-average frequency, as a doppelgänger. This doppelgänger, or imaginary companion, shows itself primarily in pictures. This double, alter ego or doppelgänger, has friendlier features than the frightful monsters from the first phases of work. It has features of an affirmative presence that explores the world and the other with openness and interest. It unlocks new living spaces of expansion and exploration.

This development is rather consistent with Françoise Dolto's developmental concepts, which state that the doppelgänger develops in a dialectic relationship with the other (mostly the mother) in whose gaze the child mirrors itself (Dolto, 1985). The "I–you", she argues, for the child is the doppelgänger. She argues that the doppelgänger is the reflection of inner security, the substrate of identity through which we have the certainty of being the same over time and space. This, to her, is the essential element of mental health. The affirmation in mother's gaze becomes an affirmation of the self. Its absence condemns the individual to search for this mirror in the outside world or avoid it. Recent research on mirror processes shows their enormous significance in the development of the self. Gergely and Watson (1996) describe a complex mechanism (which I cannot go into here), which leads to the formation of representations through marked reflections and different stages of introjection.

I suspect that in the analytical space, the mainly unconscious, distorted self-perception must first be taken on and worked through in order to allow for a new perception of the self. Again, this endeavour is not about the analyst generating images, but about creating and holding a space in which new experiences of relatedness can be made and internalized through the experience of affect mirroring, affect regulation and modulation. Anne Alvarez (2010) argues that today, more than before, this is about a work beyond words, not only about working through, but about "taking in", where the focus is on questions of introjection, internalization and identification. Colman, too, argues that what is at stake here is more what comes from the self of the analyst, which the patient feels on the unconscious level (Colman, 2003).

In Kleo's case, it was a matter of an affirmative and appreciative view of the self. The underlying tone of contempt had to be addressed and eventually overcome intersubjectively. In the last quarter of our work, the "double" showed up in her dreams; a female figure helped her furnish her new house. The atmosphere in the room changed. I felt relief, started to relax, and looked forward to the sessions with her. Nearly imperceptibly, Kleo changed the way she looked at herself – as she remarked years later. The cathexis of her body, too, became positive. Towards the end of the analysis, she returned from her summer holidays in a light linen dress and colourful sandals. On entering the door, she said:

"I wasn't able to imagine that it would be like this someday, but when I looked at myself in the mirror, I noticed that I don't think I am that bad ..."

With Jan, it was about changing an affective landscape marked by coldness, exclusion, isolation, despair and rejection. These affects had to be experienced and processed intersubjectively. The analyst was challenged not only to cultivate an attitude of not knowing, but also to lose hope. To lose hope means to consider annihilation, the annihilation of the hoped-for, the known, the familiar and to encounter nothingness. (Jan's black holes had this effect on both of us for months.) Nothingness is not the absence of something. Nothingness is the existential otherness of everything that can be thought or imagined. It is radical, and I knew in my body that Jan had encountered this nothingness in the intermediary space before anything new could emerge. In this radically open space, the countertransference imperceptibly transformed. Hope emerged. An "I-You" could establish itself, then a "We", and finally a new "I-with-Myself". Jan travelled through space with his doppelgänger friend in a space-shuttle, together they explored the world, space and mastered many adventures. At first, Jan needed a companion who mirrored him completely and was not in any way different. Only later did a two-dimensional mirroring become a three-dimensional triangulated space that tolerates difference and allows for subjectivity and thus autonomy.

Hans' basic emotional note was his early abandonment, its impact on the self and his fundamental conviction that it would remain like this forever.

With Hans, it was about overcoming fragmentation, the formation of a skin and the development of an identity. This, too, became a bodily intersubjective experience before understanding and speaking about it could have a transformative effect. He had to experience and express his distrust and fear in many ways, and that this was viscerally understood and contained. This development needed time. After years, his dreams changed as benevolent and helpful figures appeared. He began to draw and to write. He wrote letters to an imaginary female friend and found words that captured his yearning and gave it shape. It is not important whether we can talk and interpret, says Winnicott, but whether we can wait for the patient to find words himself and to understand. At best, we can enable language (Winnicott, 1971). Sensual-poetic language knows the intimation of the unspeakable, the touch and the persistence of the enigma. Hans said: "Hope and death are close relatives. If I don't have to erase you during your absence, then I no longer need to erase the part of myself that misses you. By the way, have you noticed I don't need to look at you anymore?".

Conclusion

Analytic work with early relational traumata requires a participation in early primary process experiences in order to enable traumatic residues to come to light and be transformed. The willingness not to know and yet to explore something new is one precondition. The other, is to allow implicit relational experiences to come alive in body and mind. In this "reverie of the shared body", pre-verbal experiences are recreated. The unremembered can reveal itself, the new can emerge. An emotional connection develops and with it, trust. The rupture in primary hope can thus be worked through. The process has active as well as passive aspects: active in the effort to maintain openness and receptivity; passive in that understanding implies a dimension of allowing rather than of constructing. Slowly, the implicit is able to become explicit as dissociated mental content takes shape and can be named. This is connected to the emergence of a thinking/feeling "I" and a sense of the meaningful. It not only allows for processing and transformation, but also for historicizing the trauma. As Civitarese (2013) observes, temporality, continuity, and meaning are re-established.

The task of the analyst is to maintain the willingness to go where one cannot go alone; to stay with what has no name; to lose her bearings, to accept confusion and to keep the flame of hope burning.

The alchemical opus that Jung consulted to amplify the mysterious processes of transference is well suited to this paradox. Understanding transforms, an understanding that connects body and mind. From the holistic understanding that comes from bodily-sensory experience, parts that were initially disconnected can be joined together, creating a new language, a language rooted and re-anchored in the body. This is a language that touches. It carries the silence, the rhythm and the physicality of early processes of exchange: the gaze between mother and child while nursing, which carries in itself the sensual experience of being breastfed, but is so much more than that. It brings with it the roots of hope and trust, and the mystery of what can come to life, if we are able to dream and trust.

> To make a prairie
> It takes a clover and a bee
> one clover, and a bee,
> And revery
> The revery alone will do
> If bees are few
>
> (Emily Dickinson, 1896)

In the trans-modal sensory communication that we have underlined as being at the core of the analytic encounter, language and body are connected in a holistic dance which ambiguously and multidimensionally spans time and space. Now, the archetypal hope that was ruptured in the primary relationship can once more become anchored in the intersubjective experience and in the body. In this way, the analytic couple, defying the goddesses of fate, spins a new thread and exhorts influence on a seemingly sealed fate, which creates paths out of dead repetition into a living becoming. This allows for a symbolic attitude, in its true sense, and gives imagination the status that Jung intended in human life. We cannot rewrite history, but the tension between need and desire, and not their confusion, opens spaces for that which "cultural experience" (Winnicott, 1967) represents.

References

Alvarez, A. (2010) "Levels of analytic work and levels of pathology: The work of calibration", *The International Journal of Psychoanalysis*, 91(4): 859–878.

Anzieu-Premmereur, C. (2013) "The process of representation in early childhood", in H.B. Levine, G.S. Reed and D. Scarfone (eds) *Unrepresented States and the Construction of Meaning*. London: Routledge, pp. 240–254.

Bion, W.R. (1962) *Learning from Experience*. London: Heinemann.

Bohleber, W. (2014) "Auf der suche nach repräsentanz – analytisches arbeiten an der cchnittstelle von ungedachtem und symbolisch repräsentiertem", *Psyche*, 68(09): 776–786.

Bollas, C. (1987) *The Shadow of the Object: Psychoanalysis of the Unthought Known*. New York: Columbia University Press.

Botella, C. and Botella, S. (2005) *The Work of Psychic Figurability: Mental States without Representation*. New York: Brunner Routledge.

Brown, L.J. (2011) *Intersubjective Processes and the Unconscious. An Integration of Freudian, Kleinian and Bionian Perspectives. The New Library of Psychoanalysis*. New York: Routledge.

Bucci, W. (2001) "Pathways of emotional communication", *Psychoanalytic Inquiry*, 21(1): 40–70.

Cassorla, R.M.S. (2013) "In search of symbolization: The analyst's task of dreaming", in H.B. Levine, G.S. Reed and D. Scarfone (eds) *Unrepresented States and the Construction of Meaning*. London: Routledge, pp. 202–219.

Civitarese, G. (2013) "The inaccessible unconscious and reverie as a path of figurability", in H.B. Levine, G.S. Reed and D. Scarfone (eds) *Unrepresented States and the Construction of Meaning*. London: Routledge, pp. 220–239.

Colman, W. (2003) "Interpretation and relationship: ends or means?" in R. Withers (ed.) *Controversies in Analytical Psychology*. New York: Brunner Routledge, pp. 352–362.

de M'Uzan, M. (1993) "Während der sitzung: überlegungen zum psychischen geschehen im analytiker", *Jahrbuch Psychoanalyse*, 31: 77–100.

Dickinson, E. (1896 [2004]) *Poems: Three Series, Complete*. Urbana, IL: Project Gutenberg.

Dolto, F. (1985) *Praxis der Kinderanalyse. Ein Seminar*. Stuttgart: Klett-Cotta.

Eulert-Fuchs, D. (2020) "The other between fear and desire – countertransference fantasy as a bridge between me and the other", *Journal of Analytical Psychology*, 65(1): 153–170.

Eulert-Fuchs, D. (2022) "What does the virus do to the analytic container? Thoughts on the frame in times of pandemic", in S. Carpani and M. Luci (eds) *Lockdown Therapy: Jungian Perspectives on How the Pandemic Changed Psychoanalysis*. London: Routledge.

Fonagy, P. (2002) *Affect Regulation, Mentalization, and the Development of the Self*. New York: Other Press.

Gergely, G. and Watson, J.S. (1996) "The social biofeedback theory of parental affect-mirroring: The development of emotional self-awareness and self-control in infancy", *International Journal of Psychoanalysis*, 77(6): 1181–1212.

Godsil, G. (2018) "Residues in the analyst of the patient's symbiotic connection at a somatic level: unrepresented states in the patient and analyst", *Journal of Analytical Psychology*, 63(1): 6–25.

Green A. (1975) "The analyst, symbolization and absence in the analytic setting (on changes in analytic practice and analytic experience). In memory of D. W. Winnicott", *International Journal of Psychoanalysis*, 56(1): 1–22.

Jung, C.G. (1921) *The Problem of Types in History of Classical and Medieval Thought*. CW6. Princeton, NJ: Princeton University Press.

Jung, C.G. (1935) *Principles of Practical Psychotherapy*. CW16. Princeton, NJ: Princeton University Press.

Jung C.G. (1946) *The Psychology of the Transference*. CW16. Princeton, NJ: Princeton University Press.

Jung C.G. (1954) *On the Nature of the Psyche*. CW8. Princeton, NJ: Princeton University Press.

Jung, C.G. (1989) *Nietzsche's Zarathustra: Notes of the Seminar Given in 1934–1939*. Jarret, J. (ed.) London: Routledge.

Kalsched, D. (1996) *The Inner World of Trauma: Archetypal Defences of the Personal Spirit*. London: Routledge.

Kalsched, D. (2013) *Trauma and the Soul. A Psycho-spiritual Approach to Human Development and its Interruption*. Hove: Routledge.

Kalsched, D. (2020) "Opening the closed heart: affect-focused clinical work with the victims of early trauma", *Journal of Analytical Psychology*, 65(1): 136–152.

Kinston, W. and Cohen, J. (1986) "Primal repression: Clinical and theoretical aspects", *International Journal of Psychoanalysis*, 67(3): 337–355.

Lesmeister, R. (2009) *Selbst und Individuation: Facetten von Subjektivität und Intersubjektivität in der Psychoanalyse*. Frankfurt am Main: Brandes & Apsel.

Leuzinger-Bohleber, M. (2014) „Den körper in der seele entdecken: embodiment und die annäherung an das nicht-repräsentierte", *Psyche*, 68(9–10): 922–950.

Levine, H.B., Reed, G.S. and Scarfone, D. (2013) *Unrepresented States and the Construction of Meaning*. London: Routledge.

Martini, S. (2016) "Embodying analysis: The body and the therapeutic process", *Journal of Analytical Psychology*, 61(1): 5–23.

Samuels, A. (1994) *Vielgestaltigkeit der Seele: von der Notwendigkeit innerer Demokratisierung*. Zürich: Schweizer Spiegel-Verl.

Schmidt, M. (2012) "Psychic skin: Psychotic defences, borderline process and delusions", *Journal of Analytical Psychology*, 57(1): 21–39.

Schore, A.N. (2003) *Affect Regulation and the Repair of the Self*. New York: Norton.

Schwartz-Salant N. (1986) "On the subtle-body concept in clinical practice", in N. Schwartz-Salant and M. Stein (eds), *The Body in Analysis*. Wilmette, IL: Chiron Publications.

Schwartz-Salant, N. (1989) *The Borderline Personality. Vision and Healing*. Wilmette, IL: Chiron Publications.

Stern, D.N. (2003) *Die Lebenserfahrung des Säuglings*. 8th edition. Stuttgart: Klett-Cotta.

Treurniet, N. (1995) "Was ist psychoanalyse heute?", *Psyche*, 49(02): 111–140.

Tronick, E.Z. (2003) "Things still to be done on the still-face effect", *Infancy*, 4(4): 475–482.

West, M. (2016) *Into the Darkest Places. Early Relational Trauma and Borderline States of Mind*. London: Karnac.

West, M. (2017) "Trauma, self-disclosure and the pressures on the analyst", *Journal of Analytical Psychology*, 62(4): 585–601.

Winnicott, D.W. (1955) "Metapsychological and clinical aspects of regression within the psycho-analytical set-up", *International Journal of Psychoanalysis*, 36(1): 16–26.

Winnicott, D.W. (1965 [2018]) *The Maturational Processes and the Facilitating Environment*. London: Routledge.

Winnicott, D.W. (1967) "The location of cultural experience". In *Playing and Reality*, London: Tavistock Publications, pp. 95–103.

Winnicott, D.W. (1971) *Playing and Reality*. London: Routledge.

Wolf, C. (1976) *Kindheitsmuster*. Berlin: Suhrkamp.

Zoppi, L. (2017) "Chilled to the bone: Embodied countertransference and unspoken Traumatic memories", *Journal of Analytical Psychology*, 62(5): 701–709.

Chapter 4

The Body Roots of Traumatic Experiences

From Unsymbolized Body Memory to Bodily Reverie

Mariella Battipaglia and Giovanna Curatola

Introduction

This work was inspired by a clinical vignette approached from different theoretical frameworks, with a specific focus on Jungian and neuroscientific perspectives. Our aim is to bridge these different viewpoints and highlight how cognitive-affective neurosciences, analytical psychology and post-Bionian thinking can be of help in exploring bodily phenomena that arise during trauma treatment. These phenomena include enactments, body symptoms and other somatic experiences that manifest in the transference and require a specific therapeutic attitude.

To foster a more fruitful dialogue across different theoretical frameworks, we need to avoid confusing neuroscientific theories with analytical perspectives. This approach aims to prevent excessive saturation or reductionism on either side. Such a dialogue can be productive when it values "not knowing beforehand" (Fordham, 1993), as it allows for the emergence of new organisations according to the Theory of Complex Dynamic Systems (Lansing, 2003). "Generative emptiness" is an experience of *staying without knowing* (Jung, 1935), and is valued as an important instrument in analytical work. However, it is very challenging for the analyst to work with the unspeakable, namely experiences that belong to pre-representational and pre-symbolic levels of psychic functioning. The clinical vignette is taken from the analytical treatment of Carolina, a patient suffering from a severe eating disorder. It will show the challenges the analyst can be confronted with when the patient has suffered early relational trauma. From infancy, disturbances of the body schema and body image are characteristic of patients suffering from eating disorders. The concept of body schema pertains to an individual's perception and understanding of his own body, influenced by sensory and kinaesthetic experiences of it moving in the room. The body image is the mental representation of the body shaped by the individual's emotional experience and by the symbolic meanings attributed to the body through

DOI: 10.4324/9781003298076-6

interaction with the primary carer (Schilder, 1950) as well as from the individual's life experiences.

Disorders pertaining to the schema and to the image of the body are intricately linked to the developmental stages from birth, as shown by Infant Research (Stern, 2004), supported by neuroscience (Damasio, 1994), in accordance with Winnicott's view of *psyche-soma* (1949) and Bion's *proto-mental* (1962). Moreover, a lack of successful integration between the body and the mind within the intersubjective matrix has been shown in the genesis of psychopathology and appears as symptoms in the analytical field.

From a Jungian perspective, keeping in mind the bodily roots of the archetype (as suggested by Knox, 2003), we must consider the influence that the negative aspects of the Great Mother Archetype (Neumann, 1983) can have on the development of the child. In some cases, it can take the appearance of a voracious being who feeds on the vitality of the child, preventing the emotional growth and differentiation needed to initiate the individuation process. In connection with the negative aspects of the Great Mother Archetype, there is often the Orphan Archetype, which evokes powerful issues of abandonment, deprivation, loss of hope and isolation often observed in individuals who have experienced trauma.

The clinical case presented shows how psychic pain can take shape in the body when the subject has to deal with overwhelming experiences. As we know, these states are experienced by the subject, but not consciously processed, instead they persist in the unconscious mind without being integrated (Mancia, 2006). They exist as unrepresented or unsymbolized aspects of our psychological life. Processing unsymbolized experiences requires "engagement at the level of the psychoid unconscious" (Lagutina, 2021: 20) which is unreachable by consciousness and therefore unknowable. The psychoid is the place where the psychological and physiological realms meet and of whose existence we have only indirect knowledge (Jung, 1946). During regressive experiences in analysis, it is not uncommon for unexpected contents to surface through sensory perceptions and reverie. These experiences may be accompanied by a temporary decrease in the level of consciousness and a lowering of defences.

The theory of affect regulation (Hill, 2015) proposes that optimal affect regulation, both in intensity and attentional flow, is essential for self-development and mental health since affects and emotions organise mental states and psychic manifestations. Affect regulation in the mother-child dyad involves intercorporeal interactions, attunement and mother-mentalizing feedback from her child in attachment behaviour. The concept of affect regulation is also linked to Bion's notion of reverie (1962), which pertains to the mother's capacity to be receptive and to assimilate sensory input (*beta elements*) from the child's primitive and rudimentary unconscious. The mother in turn re-projects the transformed sensory data (*alpha elements*) into the infant after she has made them tolerable, thus allowing them to be integrated into an experience. Deficits in affect regulation and the reverie process, due to early traumatic experiences, have been shown to be determining factors in the emergence of psychopathological conditions.

The Clinical Experience with Carolina

Since childhood, Carolina had suffered from being terribly overweight. Ten years before we met (she was 40 at the moment of our encounter), she had had a sleeve gastrectomy, removing part of the stomach, which resulted in her losing about 80 kilos. However, the process of losing weight did not continue and Carolina remained obese. It was tiring for her internal organs to carry this excessive weight. She came to therapy in order to understand something about what was happening to her.

Carolina had difficulties in acknowledging and experiencing the physiological needs and sensations of her body. She had been living with it as an enemy. It was a body which hosted something strange and hostile to her. She had never thought her body might have something to tell her.

During our initial sessions, Carolina shared some traumatic family experiences. The first she could remember was her father's death when she was four years of age. Her mother and brother hid this fact from her for about six months (in order to protect her) and instead misinformed her that her father had gone away on a business trip. Later, her mother let her know that it was at this time that she had started overeating and that the paediatrician had recommended letting Carolina "eat as much as she wanted because she was mourning her father's loss in this way". Moreover, there were other family events, such as the onset of her brother's mental illness in adolescence (he is bipolar), her mother's compulsive gambling, financial problems and debts, which meant that the family environment was based on emotional instability. Carolina was bright and, despite all of this, graduated as a medical doctor which finally gave her economic independence. This attitude towards food continued from childhood and remained unchanged, together with chronic emotional fragility and difficulty in regulating and mentalizing her emotions and behaviour. Overfeeding was still the only psychophysical experience in which she felt autonomous. She used it to sedate her emotional arousal and pain, denying the harm she was doing to herself. Immediately afterwards however, she was overwhelmed by a sense of helplessness and shame. Only when her mother died, was Carolina able to see and feel the real weight of her body: "It was the only moment in which I was afraid of my body. I became conscious of the fact that I could die if I continued like this. In that moment, I decided to pay for a partial gastrectomy, and I lost 80 kilos, but now something is blocked again".

Carolina's body had always been a difficult place in which to live. Sometimes it seemed that emptiness (the absence of an internalised good mother object) assailed her like an enemy, taking possession of her; at other times, she treated her stomach like a dustbin, into which she could throw "the disorganized affects" that she couldn't manage. In the meantime, her physical form also served as a point of connection with the terrestrial realm. Her weight gave a perception of stability. Her corporeal bulk was seemingly aimed at counterbalancing certain attributes of her inconsistent and ambivalent maternal representation. Based on Carolina's accounts, it could be understood that her mother may have also experienced bipolar disorder with its concomitant emotional instability, compulsivity and ambivalence.

During our first year of therapy, Carolina never brought a dream to analysis. When I asked her if she dreamt, she replied "No!" often commenting that dreams were not important, revealing her concrete outlook on her daily experience. In one session, she told me that she was voiceless, "Perhaps I have the flu", and for an instant she seemed to me to be a young cold girl looking for some heat in the armchair.

She then started talking about a terrible experience she had just had: as a radiologist, she had done a CT scan on her friend's body to check her post-covid lungs and discovered serious liver cancer. Carolina then quickly added, with a disapproving frown on her face, that one of her other friends, a psychologist, had told her that she had lost her voice because she didn't want to inform her friend of this diagnosis. In that frown, I could see the sense of contempt that Carolina felt towards her own body, which was constantly letting her down and always denying her emotions. I could also see her contempt for life, which continued to disappoint her. I imagined that she also wanted to warn me not to give her simple interpretations, as her psychologist friend had done, but that she expected something more. So, I didn't comment at all. While she was telling me about her experience, I had a powerful countertransferential experience of desperation and pain, which I imagine was very syntonic to hers. I felt the danger of her possible psychic breakdown. I was concerned that Carolina would not be able to endure the potential loss of her close friend, a "survivor" like her, with whom she often identified owing to a common past of traumatic neglect. With a feeble voice,

Carolina declared: "Once again another person I love is going to die very soon". She was afraid she wouldn't be able to cope with all this. I wondered if she was also afraid of my inability to support her at that very moment?

I was thinking about how important it must be for a friend to have a caring person nearby when one receives a cancer diagnosis, a kind person who promises that she will be by your side during the ordeal of cancer treatments, who may even be able to reduce one's suffering with her medical expertise. Was my thought inspired by a need to establish a connection with Carolina during this terrible moment? I didn't interpret, but I told Carolina that it must have been helpful for her friend to have Carolina by her side in this moment of extreme difficulty. Could Carolina feel me by her side? Could I provide her with the reassurance that she would be able to get through this experience of pain and of facing death? I tried to be present with Carolina. Her deep pain and desperation took me back to a time when I heard that one of my family members had cancer. At that time, I felt terrified, and I remember that I even experienced derealization as an extreme attempt to put a distance between myself and that unbearable reality. I found myself wondering: "Why am I remembering such a traumatic mechanism of dissociation? Perhaps something has been dissociated in Carolina, too?". And again, I told myself, "Don't leave; let things happen". Asking these questions and talking to myself helped me feel a sense of deep tenderness towards myself. I could also recall another feeling I had not recognised then: I had felt ashamed about my experience of derealization, and probably a part of me had been looking at myself with the same frown of disapproval as Carolina had done. This event brought me closer to Carolina, and my compassion for myself helped me to disidentify from her and understand why she felt persecuted by her painful and shameful feelings. The experience of now being mute might have again engendered feelings of being persecuted by her own body.

In that moment, I imagined myself very small (similar to the transformation we can see in Alice in Wonderland) and I felt as if I was able to shrink enough to travel inside Carolina's body, the place that was so hated, the place of her worst nightmares. With my imagination working so actively, I felt alive and real as Carolina's body had now become a concrete and secure place to explore where I could meet many wonders. Now, I was in her throat, and I could see her vocal cords, which were alive and energetic, vibrating, trying to let all the desperate pain out. Thanks to my countertransferential experience of this embodied disperceptive phenomena, I was able to observe her vocal apparatus, which was intact and ready to cry out, while Carolina was trying to manage the unbearable anguish, in order to survive.

We were now in a dimension where the soma supports the psyche (Winnicott, 1949). In this dimension, the analyst's sensory reverie is linked to bodily perceptual experiences. After such a challenging countertransference transformation ("transformation in hallucinosis", Bion, 1970; Civitarese, 2015), I came back to myself, to my body, to my vocal cords and I tried to say something, but I had to cough persistently to clear my throat before speaking. I was pondering the meaning of that cough. What was my body signalling to me? I realised I felt the need to modulate my voice as much as possible in order not to burden Carolina with my pain-filled words. I had to be careful with regard to the challenging affects that were emerging, by paying attention to the musicality of my voice and the sweetness of the words, even if they were words of pain. Unfortunately, I didn't do it in time. Carolina watched my coughing episode with a sense of apprehension and promptly recalled when, as a medical student, she accompanied her mother for a brain scan. She had clear memories of the warm emotional atmosphere and the caring voice that the doctor used when he told them about her mother's brain tumour. It was a reassuring tone of voice, even though he was giving them terrible news. She remembered the ray of hope that his voice gave them. At the same time, a memory emerged in me: I remembered the singing lessons I attended when I was a child, which included breath control and diaphragmatic movements. It was as if, in that very moment with Carolina, I had to connect mind and body to regulate the affective flow in the challenging process of identification and differentiation. This was necessary to hold together the threads of the fabric of the affective experience that Carolina and I were sharing. Then I relaxed and recalled the famous painting *The Scream* by Munch.[1] I told Carolina that perhaps it was as if she herself had been involved in the CT scan with her entire body and with her vocal cords functioning; she too had wanted to scream but hadn't been able to; she too would have liked to use the same compassionate tone of her mother's doctor, but she hadn't been able to find it inside herself. It was the same voice I had been looking for when I had coughed earlier in the session.

Carolina smiled at me with a tender face and said: "Yes, inside myself I really screamed, silently, and no sound or words came out". We smiled at each other, both emotionally moved, and quietly shared an authentic new experience of mutual emotional acknowledgement and tenderness.

Bovensiepen (2002) emphasises the process of creating a symbolic space through associating the analyst's reverie with a symbolic attitude. Like the early mother-child relationship, this can help transform emotional experience in the transferential relationship, thus favouring the development of a symbolic space.

In that moment with Carolina, I hadn't made an interpretation but instead used her recall and her reverie as a therapeutic tool to contain the affect and foster awareness, helped by the image of Munch's painting. When working with a patient who has difficulties symbolising, it is important that the analyst uses his symbolic attitude, to give value to the countertransference, not interpreting the transference so that the patient's defences are not challenged. We both shared a genuine experience of *mutual tenderness* (Macrillò, 2015), triggered by her memories of the doctor's voice, my memories and reverie, and the powerful feelings we were sharing. This can be understood as a first attempt to represent an emotional experience that bridges its bodily roots with the symbolic level. It had been fundamental in order to avoid a psychic breakdown for both of us. And now it was something that gave new affective value, a new situation, a new level of being (Jung, 1958) that allowed Carolina and I to face her emotions when dealing with death. We had to give up our defences without feeling humiliated about this. It is precisely this sense of humiliation, which accompanies any traumatic experience, that steals our vital energy and reduces us to a state similar to death. The experience of humiliation and loneliness was accepted and embraced within an intersubjective intercorporeal framework.

Clinical Discussion

Reflecting on traumatic experiences in childhood, Ferenczi (1932) linked together dynamics of fragmentation, dissociation, identification with the aggressor and an inversion of the parent-child relationship, defining these as a confusion of languages between adults and children.

Confusion can also occur between the internal and external worlds, especially between the body and mind. Bodily reaction to trauma puts the subject in a condition lacking appropriate defensive strategies. In these situations, raw sensations and sensory-motor traces are not subjected to regulation of the intensity of their affective values. Consequently, they cannot be processed through imagination nor mentalized. This means that they cannot reach a proper psychological representation. In the absence of reflexive function, the experience of me-ness (the implicit sense of being the owner of an experience or action in the first person) and the preservation of boundaries between the self and non-self are profoundly affected.

As Carolina showed, children who have suffered traumatic experiences in relationship with their parents manifest a specific difficulty in thinking about their own and other's mental states (Carolina also had particular difficulties in thinking about her bodily states). These children tend to have problems regulating, thinking about and expressing emotions and are therefore more vulnerable to re-traumatization in later life.

Considering the clinical situation from a neuroscientific perspective, the interoceptive and exteroceptive aspects of the body's sensory experience form a reciprocal and interconnected relationship. This connection allows the analyst and patient to collaborate in the process of transforming raw bodily sensations into meaningful representations, verbal communication, and ultimately, shared experiences. The patient-analyst interaction can be conceptualized as a complex and multifaceted domain in which, especially at challenging moments in analysis, various elements from different levels of communication (such as bodily, imaginal, affective, verbal and non-verbal) may not yet be fully integrated. Processing and integrating all this information into a meaningful and coherent narrative is an important task for analysis. Supported by the analyst's multidimensional listening attitude, all these levels can give rise to an integrated affective shared experience, a "living, third thing", as Jung suggested (1958, para. 189).

Drawing upon the perspective of dynamic systems operating in a state far from equilibrium, neuroscience examines the concept of mind as arising from an ongoing stream of conscious and/or unconscious mental states that are intricately linked to complementary organisational mechanisms of integration and segregation (Kelso and Tognoli, 2007). The cognitive processes that establish connections between perceptions, memories, thoughts and feelings in a cohesive framework that leads to awareness of internal stimuli, is in line with the Jungian idea of the dissociability of the psyche. Due to the ability of the psyche to dissociate, the analyst can engage in regression while also maintaining a distinct position as an emotional container, through the process of segregation. This allows for the integration of different affective and representational levels present within the relational context. Mind-brain integrative mechanisms have therapeutic importance when holding dissociative and regressive processes in an effort to reach a representation. Interestingly, using Jung's Word Association Test to clarify the physiological processes subtended to psychological dynamics, Jungian scholars (Escamilla et al., 2018; Petchkovsky et al., 2018) have shown that, as a response to word stimuli, different brain areas are sequentially involved. These areas are related to bodily responses, affectivity, emotions, memory and semiotic meaning. Following activation, they are linked in an integrated gestalt, suggesting the organisation and then emergence into consciousness of a feeling-toned complex. The complex can be seen as a psychic structure that links affective values, memories, thoughts and feelings (Jung, 1907).

The Brain-Body and the Mind

The phenomena we are discussing fit within the framework of a body-mind dialogue as defined by embodied cognition (Damasio, 1994). Body-mind dialogues and their connected processes start in intrauterine life and continue through relational and social interactions (Johnson, 2017). From the beginning, embodiment is weaved together with self-development as an uninterrupted mind-body integration process. This process is embedded in, and enacted through, the primary relationship as part of a wide range of biological, psychological, linguistic and cultural environments (Colombetti and Thompson, 2008). Studies concerning implicit memories during the first two years of life indicate a common ground between different psycho-analytic theories (Mancia, 2006) and neuroscience. Unconscious implicit infantile memories, which are attributed to the immaturity of neurophysiological structures, are not actively engaged in the processes of removal; although they are elements of the unconscious, they will never become completely conscious. These are responsible for emotional habits and patterns of unconscious and automatic behaviours. Clinical practice has shown that these implicit memories follow a process of automatic recall and association that makes the patient susceptible to further re-traumatization. Implicit memories often occur as sensory-motor traces that interfere with the transference-countertransference dynamics, affect dreams, the analyst's reverie, as well as preverbal and perceptive factors. This substratum of implicit memory is directly related to complexes. As they are far from ego consciousness (Bovensiepen, 2006) and therefore closer to the unconscious part of the ego complex (Caetano and Machado, 2018), a very particular feature of implicit memories is the possibility for them to be re-lived in varying forms of reverie. Somatic reverie and somatic countertransference derive from the unconscious experiences of the patient and analyst together (Battipaglia and Curatola, 2023), as well as from those that the analytical pair co-construct during the sessions, thanks to the function that Jungian analysts call the *transcendent function* (Jung, 1958).

The sensorial experience in the analytic field can be understood as a self-regulated action, where the affects activated in the shared field between patient and analyst can help new connections to form between the body and the mind of both participants. When body and mind are dissociated, they become two opposite poles, which cannot be joined together. This results in a loss of flow of communication between conscious and unconscious for the analytical couple.

Carolina's body, with its physiological and painful vitality, found itself struggling with the actual experience that was brought into the session (her friend's illness). Traumatic memories occasionally interfere with the experience of the temporal context and this makes it more challenging for the subject to link specific memories to what they are experiencing "here and now". Carolina's traumatic experience with her friend seems to have reactivated past traumatic traces, beginning with the silence that surrounded her father's death, then the experience of the loss of her mother, as well as when Carolina acted out the decision to undergo a gastrectomy. These were instances where bodily affects and vitality, even in their painful manifestations, have not had a chance to emerge. These *symbolization gaps*, in the organisation of the sensory-affective fabric of the self, resulted in an endless recurrence of the trauma.

The activation of traumatic affects also has an impact for the analyst, often leading to experiences similar to those of the patient, even if they have already been processed by the analyst. This can be seen as an attempt to form a representation of the phenomena that is taking place within the analytic field guided by the emotional shared encounter. These encounters are effectively described by the concepts of *contagion* and *alchemical processes* (Jung, 1946). The *gaps in symbolization* elicit bewilderment and vague physical sensations in the analyst, along with somatic disperception and mental states such as reverie (de Rienzo, 2021).

Several functions can facilitate an opening to this unconscious dimension for the analyst. These include the reverie function, the analyst's sensitivity to subliminal sensory-motorial levels, states of *participation mystique* and the use of physiological resonance in countertransference. They can potentially facilitate an opening to the psychoid dimension of the unconscious (Lagutina, 2021). The analyst's unconscious identification with the patient, and subsequent dis-identification, can be regarded as an essential tool which allows for the necessary interplay between conscious-unconscious thus helping to give meaning to experiences.

The connections between body, brain and mind, and their possible representations in consciousness, without any hierarchical pre-eminence, are well synthesized by Jung:

> I use the word 'image' simply in the sense of a representation. A psychic entity can be a conscious content, that is, it can be represented, only if it has the quality of an image and is thus representable. I therefore call all conscious contents images, since they are reflections of processes in the brain ... In this way we can form an idea of the nature of the psyche. It consists of reflected images of simple processes in the brain, and of reproductions of these images in an almost infinite series.
>
> (Jung, 1926, paras 608–610)

The *almost infinite series* can be seen as a process of complex non-linear dynamic systems in which mental states emerge from the relationship between different levels of conscious and unconscious functioning. These dynamics can involve both intra-level and inter-level elements, and their interaction gives rise to the "emergence" of higher-order functions which can influence lower ones, as indicated by several Jungian authors (Knox, 2003; Cambray and Carter, 2004).

The Brain-Body, the Mind and the Other: The Synchronization of Integrative-Dissociative Dynamics

Empirical data from Infant Research suggests a new model of interpersonal unconscious communication referring to bio-behavioural synchronization at different levels and subsystems of the mother-infant dyad. The development of interpersonal synchronization and the importance this has in allowing the attunement of emotional states between members of a dyad (as well as in coordinating the dynamics of social groups) are well documented (Nowak et al., 2017).

According to Zadbood et al. (2017), the construction of shared neural representations, via synchronization of brain activities, facilitates the retrieval of episodic memories through the reactivation of sensory-motor memories. Interestingly, when individuals share a collective emotional experience, they both undergo the recollection of their own memories that differ in subject matter but hold equivalent emotional significance. This can also be observed in clinical scenarios, such as when the analyst recalls subjective memories with traumatic emotional intensity, while listening to the patient's narrative. The same areas that are active during recall are also active during prospective thinking (the act of mentally simulating the future), as well as during the construction of imaginary events, which helps to transmit and share one's thoughts and experiences with others. In embodied simulation and intentional attunement theory (Gallese, 2022), internal representation of body states associated with actions, emotions and sensations is evoked in the observer as if he himself were facing a similar action, experience or emotion. According to affective neuroscience (Damasio, 1994), the attribution of an affective meaning (valence) to an attention-attracting external or internal stimulus (salience) can be the element that drives and sustains integration in the flow of shared mental states between analyst and patient. Only afterwards, can memories of previous events and cognitive evaluations of them be linked together into a narrative. These processes, which support mentalization, are strongly influenced by the subject's attachment style and affect regulation ability in the intersubjective space. In the clinical vignette presented, we have an example of this dynamic when the analyst has to regulate a painful affective experience by connecting body and mind, helped by the childhood memories of her singing lessons which emerged out of the blue.

The analyst's reflexive function, and the use of reverie as an emergent process, can allow for a symbolic understanding, which sometimes takes its cue from a "bodily understanding" – if we are able to see the poietic function of the bodily phenomena. This bodily-poietic function enables us to be more receptive to sensory information to facilitate mental representativeness. Therefore, it is a tool for the analyst which favours the integration of dissociated feelings and memories.

In the clinical vignette, it is possible to delineate the flow of transference-countertransference between patient and analyst and the coordination of the dynamics that generates a *living third thing* (Jung, 1958). We can consider bodily experience as something that comes alive, perhaps with the help of an imaginary scream, as in the memory of Munch's picture. Bodily experience was registered at some level in Carolina when she was faced with pain and death. The result was an emergent new quality of the experience, namely a shared tenderness, activated in the interplay of the body-to-body encounter, but also between body and mind, conscious and unconscious of patient and analyst. Sometimes it is precisely this emergence of the living, vital body that opens up the recovery of experiences of the self, in critical moments of analysis.

Conclusions

The Multi-Layered Nature of the Jungian Unconscious

> The unconscious is … everything of which I know, but of which I am not at the moment thinking; everything of which I was once conscious but have now forgotten; everything perceived by my senses, but not noted by my conscious mind; everything which, involuntarily and without paying attention to it, I feel, think, remember, want, and do; all the future things that are taking shape in me and will sometime come to consciousness: all this is the content of the unconscious.
>
> (Jung, 1954, para. 382)

Jung's statement about the unconscious and its contents is the reference point for clinical and theoretical research concerning the role of body-mind dialogues in the analyst-patient dyad. The psychopathology of trauma focuses on how sensory and emotional memories can avoid symbolization. This is clear when we witness the emergence of the body in transference and countertransference dynamics, as well as in enactment phenomena. These are understood as related to dissociative defences or to a non-cohesive self-organisation, resulting from a failure of integrative processes. Integrative processes constitute the scaffolding of mental functioning in intersubjective and socio-cultural dimensions. Clinical evidence has led us to consider the presence in the unconscious mind of a more primitive, unrepressed unconscious (Mancia, 2006) which is related to the concept of the body as a perceptive and organisational component of body-brain-psyche dynamics. Many authors have offered diverse perspectives about the structure of this pre-symbolic and preverbal domain. In the meantime, cognitive neuroscience has formulated its own theory of the unconscious, which is linked to the embodied mind and memory processes (Johnson, 2017).

In line with Jung's notion of an unconscious continually committed to associating and dissociating its contents (Jung, 1954), the flow from one mental state to another implies experiencing momentary disorganisation and then, hopefully, a following re-organisation. This is in line with the idea of the continuous activity of deintegration and reintegration processes of the psyche as conceived by Fordham (1985). This dynamic is also well represented by body-brain/mind dialogues in their interaction between the external and internal world, isomorphic with subjective phenomenological experience (Kelso and Tognoli, 2007).

We can see the analytical field as something in which the matrix of transferential processes is *co-constructed* by patient and analyst (Wiener, 2009: 96), or, in other words, as a network of co-transference relationships where the analyst's body is part of the setting and is one of the tools available in the analyst's toolbox (Manica, 2020). The analyst's toolbox helps us to accommodate complex dynamics to establish a continuous inner dialogue between the various states of the self, including states of body and mind, which sometimes express themselves and can also be left unrepresented. The functional roots of a biological nature that link the mind to the processes concerned with instincts, affects and emotions are in the psychoid psyche. Jung's psychoid concept "links body and mind, instinct and spirit, with the imaginal and the symbolic, emphasising the teleological aspect of its organising function in the service of individuation" (Addison, 2019: 67). Jung's theory seems to suggest a further articulation of body and mind dimensions in the psychoid. It offers a link to the collective unconscious, where instincts and archetypes are correlated since they express themselves in action and perceptions.

Moreover, the psychoid is involved in developmental processes from the very beginning of life, as Knox has suggested, embodying the archetypes in the sensorial and affective matrix of mother-child relationships (Knox, 2003).

The transference matrix, which is first rooted in the mother-child relational matrix, is hopefully characterised by reciprocity since the analyst is invited to move in a common field of unconsciousness. At the same time, this matrix is also asymmetrical, as the analyst's role is to think about what is fluctuating between words and images, even somatic ones.

In this chapter, we advocate for the inclusion in analytic thinking of specific occurrences in the analytical process, where several levels can be linked together. These levels encompass the conscious and unconscious realms, the mind-body connection, the patient-analyst dynamic and the temporal dimensions of the past and future. In this light, the clinical case presented underlines moments in which the dialogues between clinical experience and theoretical constructs, both analytical and neuroscientific, can lead the way to new interpretative potential.

Note

1 Damasio (1994) hypothesises that the explicit mental images we evoke emerge from a synchronous and temporary activation of neural patterns occurring in memory.

References

Addison, A. (2019) *Jung's Psychoid Concept Contextualised*. London: Routledge.

Battipaglia, M. and Curatola, G. (2023) "Corpi che sognano: le rêverie sensoriali alla luce del dialogo tra psicologia analitica e le neuroscienze", *Studi Junghiani*, 57.

Bion, W.R. (1962) *Learning from Experience*. London: Heinemann.

Bion, W.R. (1970) *Attention and Interpretation*. London: Tavistock Publications.

Bovensiepen, G. (2002) "Symbolic attitude and reverie: Problems of symbolization in children and adolescents", *Journal of Analytical Psychology*, 47(2): 241–257.

Bovensiepen, G. (2006) "Attachment-dissociation network: Some thoughts about a modern complex theory", *Journal of Analytical Psychology*, 51(3): 451–466.

Caetano, A.A. and Machado T.C. (2018) "Complex in memory, mind in matter: Walking hand in hand", *Journal of Analytical Psychology*, 63(4): 510–528.

Cambray, J. and Carter, L. (2004) "Analytic methods revisited", in J. Cambray and L. Carter (eds) *Analytical Psychology: Contemporary Perspectives in Jungian Analysis*. London: Routledge.

Civitarese, G. (2015) "Transformations in hallucinosis and the receptivity of the analyst", *The International Journal of Psychoanalysis*, 96(4): 1091–1116.

Colombetti, G. and Thompson, E. (2008) "The feeling body: Towards an enactive approach to emotion", in W.F. Overton, U. Mueller and J.L. Newman (eds) *Developmental Perspectives on Embodiment and Consciousness*. London: Routledge, pp. 45–68.

Damasio, A. (1994) *Descartes' Error: Emotion, Reason and the Human Brain*. New York: Putnam.

de Rienzo, A. (2021) "The day the clock stopped. Primitive states of unintegration, multi-dimensional working through and the birth of the analytical subject", *Journal of Analytical Psychology*, 66(2): 259–280.

Escamilla, M, Sandoval, H., Calhoun, V. and Ramirez M. (2018) "Brain activation patterns in response to complex triggers in the Word Association Test: Results from a new study in the United States", *Journal of Analytical* Psychology, 63(4): 484–509.

Ferenczi, S. (1932) "Confusion of tongues between adult and the child", *Contemporary Psychoanalysis*, 24: 196–206.

Fordham, M. (1985) *Explorations into the Self*. London: Academic Press.

Fordham, M. (1993) "On not knowing beforehand", *Journal of Analytical Psychology*, 38(2): 127–136.

Gallese, V. (2022) "Inconscio e neuroscienze", in A.M. Nicolò, G. Giustino and M. Vigna-Taglianti (eds) *La Mente Sensoriale e lo Spettro Allucinatorio*. Milano: FrancoAngeli.

Grotstein, J. (2007) *A Beam of Intense Darkness: Wilfred Bion's Legacy to Psychoanalysis*. London: Routledge.

Hill, D. (2015) *Affect Regulation Theory: A Clinical Model*. New York: W.W. Norton & Co.

Johnson, M. (2017) *Embodied Mind, Meaning, and Reason: How Our Bodies Give Rise to Understanding*. Chicago, IL: University of Chicago Press.

Jung, C.G. (1907) *The Psychology of Dementia Praecox*. CW3. Princeton, NJ: Princeton University Press.

Jung, C.G. (1926) *Spirit and life*. CW8. Princeton, NJ: Princeton University Press.

Jung, C.G. (1935) *The Tavistock Lectures. On the Theory and Practice of Analytical Psychology*. CW18. Princeton, NJ: Princeton University Press.

Jung, C.G. (1946) *The Psychology of the Transference*. CW16. Princeton, NJ: Princeton University Press.

Jung, C.G. (1954) *On the Nature of the Psyche*. CW8. Princeton, NJ: Princeton University Press.

Jung, C.G. (1958) *The Transcendent Function*. CW8. Princeton: Princeton University Press.

Kelso, J.A.S. and Tognoli, E. (2007) 'Toward a complementary neuroscience: metastable coordination dynamics of the brain', in L.I. Perlovsky and R. Kozma (eds) *Neurodynamics of Cognition and Consciousness*. Berlin: Springer.

Knox, J. (2003) *Archetype. Attachment, Analysis. Jungian Psychology and the Emergent Mind*. London: Routledge.

Lagutina, L. (2021) "Meeting the orphan: Early relational trauma, synchronicity and the psychoid", *Journal of Analytical Psychology*, 66(1): 5–27.

Lansing, J.S. (2003) "Complex adaptive systems", *Annual Review of Anthropology*, 32: 183–204.

Macrillò, A. (2015) "Sulla libertà di essere veri", *Psicoanalisi e Metodo*, XIV: 73–90.

Mancia, M. (2006) "Implicit memory and early unrepressed unconscious: Their role in the therapeutic process (how the neurosciences can contribute to psychoanalysis)", *International Journal of Psychoanalysis*, 87(Pt 1): 83–103.

Manica, M. (2020) *Psicoanalisi del Traumatico. Sogno, Dissociazione e Linguaggio dell'Effettività*. Roma: Alpes.

Neumann, E. (1983) *The Great Mother: An Analysis of the Archetype*. Princeton, NJ: Princeton University Press.

Nowak, A., Vallacher, R.R., Zochowski, M. and Rychwalska, A. (2017) "Functional synchronization: The emergence of coordinated activity in human systems", *Frontiers in Psychology*, 8: 945.

Petchkovsky, L., Petchkovsky, M., Morris, P., Dickson, P., Montgomery, D.T., Dwyer, J., Burnett, P. and Robertson-Gillam, K. (2018) "Functional brain imagery and Jungian analytical psychology: An interesting dance?", in S.J. Golubic (ed.) *Neuroimaging – Structure, Function and Mind*. London: IntechOpen.

Schilder, P. (1950) *The Image and Appearance of the Human Body*. London: Routledge.

Stern, D.N. (2004) *The Present Moment in Psychotherapy and Everyday Life*. New York: W.W. Norton & Co.

Wiener, J. (2009) *The Therapeutic Relationship: Transference, Countertransference, and the Making of Meaning*. College Station, TX: Texas A&M University Press.

Winnicott, D.W. (1949) "Mind and its relation to the psyche-soma", in *Collected Papers: Through Paediatrics to Psychoanalysis*. London: Routledge.

Zadbood, A., Chen, J., Leong, Y.C., Norman, K.A. and Hasson, U. (2017) "How we transmit memories to other brains: constructing shared neural representations via communication", *Cerebral Cortex*, 27(10): 4988–5000.

Chapter 5

Working with Early Relational Trauma and Borderline States

The Role of Unconscious Communication

Lara Lagutina

Introduction

In this chapter, I explore some disruptions in the earliest developmental processes that can leave a long-term imprint in the form of splitting of the ego, reliance on dissociation and persistence of borderline states of mind – part of the sequelae of early relational trauma. I will offer an extended clinical illustration of the analytic process with a patient who suffered birth trauma. The role of unconscious communication, based on symbiotic relatedness (or 'unconscious identity' [e.g. Jung, 1912/1952]), is explored in working with states of persistent self-hatred, terror, aloneness and suicidal despair. I will also try to convey a shared sense throughout the process that, underneath the pain we both had to bear, the analysis has been guided by something deeply meaningful and purposeful in my patient's unconscious.

The Caesura of Birth, Symbiotic Relatedness and Psychic Skin

A number of psychoanalytic authors have reflected on the function of symbiotic relatedness between mother and foetus (and later mother and baby), where communication is essentially unconscious in that it relies on the two people intuitively "getting" and knowing each other's experiences (e.g. Searles, 1962; Mahler, 1968). This way of communicating is essential to the baby's survival and its quality can be described as psychic. As the child grows and starts separating from the mother, he increasingly starts relying on more explicit ways of communicating through signs, words and gestures while the original mode of communicating is gradually left behind and forgotten.

Having said that, the reliance on unconscious communication is never entirely lost and sometimes manifests, for example, between people with strong emotional bonds, such as mother and child, lovers or patient and analyst. This way of relating is inherent in the Jungian notions of *Unus*

DOI: 10.4324/9781003298076-7

Mundus and *participation mystique*, which refer to our deep sense of inter-connectedness with the world around us and is at the root of our creative engagement with life. It is also the basis of synchronistic experiences (e.g. Lagutina, 2021).

It therefore appears that this earliest form of connectedness reaches beyond the personal link between the two people involved. Martin Buber (a contemporary of Jung) expressed this poetically, saying that the womb in which the baby dwells is not solely that of the human mother. He refers to a mythical Jewish saying which states that "in his mother's womb man knows the universe and forgets it at birth" (Buber, 1923: 76). Buber's intimations strike me as deeply Jungian.

Freud's famous dictum comes to mind here as well: "There is much more continuity between intra-uterine life and earliest infancy than the impressive caesura of birth allows us to believe" (Freud, 1926: 138). A caesura is both a break and a pause, which connects two parts (e.g. of a line of verse) without severing the continuity – not dissimilar to the experience of normal birth. In keeping with this, Winnicott (1949) suggests that the process of birth is not inherently traumatic and in the normal course of development is experienced more like a transition. The period of intrauterine gestation is followed by the extrauterine one (Montagu, 1971, quoted in Lutenberg, 2009). Here the child is still highly dependent on the mother and relies on her capacities for holding and containment in order to preserve his sense of continuity of being. If this process is successful, he will gradually come to feel safely contained ("at home") within the boundaries of his own skin. This was beautifully expressed by Winnicott (1947) as the psyche coming to indwell in the body.

Anzieu (2016), in exploring the baby's emerging capacity to feel safely contained, talks about the development of *skin-ego* (or psychic skin). He suggests that initially the membrane of psychic skin is experienced as a common boundary with the mother on one side and the child on the other – figurative of their symbiotic union. He considers this an essential illusion, which later in life can come alive in such states as being in love. This experience is later internalised in the gradual process of separating from the mother and acquires a wider symbolic quality as the skin-ego which not only holds the internal contents together but also mediates our connection to the world around us. Anzieu further observes that as the physical skin envelops the body, the ego envelops the psyche and is closely linked with our capacity for thought. A healthy psychic skin is permeable and is symbolically capable of filtering out toxins and taking in nourishment, serving as the boundary between external and internal, I and not-I, and directly linked to ego strength and ego functions, such as reality testing.

Bick observes that the original state of the baby is that of total helplessness, where "parts of the personality have no binding force amongst themselves and must therefore be held together ... by a skin functioning as a boundary" (Bick, 1968: 484). If the mother is unable to provide a consistent safe and attuned presence, the baby will not feel held (e.g. if the mother is absent for too long, or is depressed, emotionally overwhelmed or cut off). As a result, in a highly vulnerable state of unintegration, the baby experiences anxieties of the most terrifying nature, also referred to as unintegration anxieties (Bick, 1968; Symington, 1985; Mitrani, 1993), such as falling forever, spilling into space, dissolving or fragmenting and so on. These anxieties far exceed the baby's capacity to contain them and instead are "catalogued" by the body-ego. In this way, states of unintegration (Winnicott, 1945), which in the normal course of events serve as precursors for our later capacity for relaxation, may become associated with anxieties of the most catastrophic kind.

Bion (1977) proposed that in addition to the mother's holding capacity, adeptly described by Winnicott, it is also important that she is capable of containing. The containing function involves the capacity to receive the infant's primitive communications through reverie, to metabolise these primitive anxieties and return them to the infant in a form that is rendered meaningful and digestible. In other words, she needs to have a capacity to transform beta elements into alpha through her alpha function. The mother's failure to do this may result in the infant's projections being stripped of the little meaning they initially had and returned to him as nameless dreads.

In response to these unthinkable dreads, second skin defences are employed, involving muscle tension, sights, sounds, smells or inappropriate use of certain mental functions or innate talents. These defences are interwoven with primitive omnipotent proto-phantasies, through which dependence on the object is replaced by pseudo-independence (Bick, 1968), which persist in later life.

Ogden (1989) develops these ideas further, in his formulation of the concept of the autistic-contiguous position linked to the early pre-symbolic experiences of common boundaries and surfaces touching each other. He says that "this primitive psychological organisation under normal circumstances contributes to the barely perceptible background of sensory boundedness of all subsequent subjective states" (Ogden, 1989: 128). Ogden proposes that a rudimentary sense of "I-ness" arises from these relationships of sensory contiguity (the experiences of being touched, held and spoken to by the mother). This sense of boundedness and cohesiveness becomes the foundation of "a place where one lives" (cf. Winnicott, 1971) and of the beginnings of the experience of cohesion of the self.

Later in life, if the person's sense of cohesiveness of the self is tenuous, there may be an underlying fear of fragmentation and of going mad. Ogden describes how in the analytic hour patients may attempt to re-establish a sensory floor of experience (Grotstein, 1987, quoted in Ogden, 1989) by activities such as hair twirling, stroking of the lips or cheeks, focusing on familiar shapes of the pictures on the walls or the rug on the floor and so on.

Symbiotic Relatedness and the Structural Void

With all this in mind, what happens if the caesura of birth is experienced as a traumatic rupture, such as that in birth trauma? One clinical theory that seems very relevant here is that of Lutenberg's primary and secondary symbiosis and the structural void, which can form the background of borderline conditions.

Similar to other authors, Lutenberg (2009) suggests that in the normal course of events, the newborn baby is in a state of a linking perinatal (or 'original') symbiosis with the mother (e.g. Mahler, 1968). Later in life, this symbiosis fades into the background but continues to exist as our fusion with the infinite universe. It nourishes us, forming the basis for further development and differentiation. These ideas have resonance with the Jungian concept of the psychoid unconscious.

If, however, something goes wrong (as in birth trauma), the natural process of transition and differentiation is "aborted by the sudden eruption of unbearable experience (terror)" (Lutenberg, 2009: 92) and the structural void is created. Interestingly, Lutenberg likens this experience of the severance of the symbiotic link with that of being temporarily "orphaned" (cf. Lagutina, 2021). He considers this experience of bond-breaking highly traumatic – generating a psychic catastrophe. The resulting nameless terror remains in an unthinkable frozen form, as an accretion of beta elements (Bion, 1962) and forms the core of the void.

Lutenberg stresses that for the structural void to be generated, the psychic trauma has to occur in the period of *extrauterine gestation*. In Winnicott's (1969) thinking, this corresponds to the time of the transition from a "subjective object", that is from object relating to object usage, and the creation of transitional space. The area of the structural void gets split off and later co-exists with other parts of the personality, where development proceeds as normal.

The void is usually compensated by a secondary symbiosis (usually the symbiotic bonds with another person). Instead of mourning, the person can rely on object substitution, where the objects of attachment are interchangeable. Here, when a link with one person breaks, they are soon replaced by another. The void may remain unnoticed until such time when a threat of separation is experienced, triggering not only separation anxiety, but also a nameless terror linked with the void.

Lutenberg clarifies that the secondary symbiosis is reactive and defensive, and therefore pathological, making the individual intolerant of separation. When the secondary symbiosis proves an insufficient defence, new defensive structures can be generated, such as borderline conditions or a complete withdrawal from the outside world as in autism. The breakdown of the secondary symbiotic defence can precipitate uncontrolled acting-out, a psychotic episode or psychosomatic crisis. However, Lutenberg suggests that it can be a benign psychosis, capable of bringing about a psychic evolution, if a good holding container, such as that of analysis, is available during such crises.

It is interesting to compare Lutenberg's thinking with Bleger's (1967) ideas about the "dumb" symbiosis, which gets deposited in the analytic frame and remains inaccessible for analysis until such time when either the frame is broken or the threat of it breaking is experienced. It seems to me that in his paper Bleger explores the dynamics of what Lutenberg described as secondary symbiosis.

Analysis, Regression to Dependency and the Role of Unconscious Communication

Addressing these early issues, such as the structural void and the appearance of holes or lacerations in psychic skin (e.g. Schmidt, 2012), requires regression to dependency in order to re-establish the original symbiosis (e.g. Searles, 1962; Winnicott, 1974). Reflecting on the stage of "the necessary return" in the transference (for both neurotic and psychotic patients) to the phase of symbiotic mother-infant relatedness, Searles (1962) suggests that the hallmark feature of this phase is characterised by feelings of fond contentment with each other in the analytic couple. He observes that this phase is often preceded by feelings of ambivalence as both members of the dyad defend against these deeper vulnerable feelings. He notes that although the feelings of mutual relatedness are crucially important for the treatment, his supervisees often needed help

> in seeing that … at a deep level, [the analyst] has become one with the so ambivalent patient; that for the latter's recovery it is not only permissible, but essential that he be able to enter increasingly into a fond, mutually dependent, playful and contented oneness with the patient, now functioning in the transference as a healthy infant or young child.
>
> (Searles, 1962: 592)

Jung recognized the importance of supporting regression in the patient until "the prenatal stage is reached" in order to "make contact with a core of the self", "the lost heart of the self" hidden in the unconscious and often having an aura of numinosity around it. He saw this as the ultimate (although unconscious) goal of regression (Jung, 1912/1952, paras. 508–10).

For the analyst, establishing this original symbiosis also means taking the patient in and being open to the creation of unconscious identity. This inevitably challenges the integrity of the analyst's own psychic skin by activating pre-existing fault lines in it, which can be both painful and frightening. However, from the perspective of the wounded healer archetype, we can also say that our own wounds are essential for the work to succeed. Interestingly, Merchant (2012) takes this idea even further, suggesting that the presence of early relational trauma should be one of the selection criteria for accepting future analysts into training.

It is curious, however, that although the role and significance of symbiotic relatedness and unconscious communication is widely acknowledged in psychoanalytic literature (Freud, 1933; Bion, 1962; Ogden, 2004; Birksted-Breen, 2019), Jung's pioneering thinking on the subject is hardly ever referred to. Yet, his concepts such as synchronicity, *Unus Mundus* and the psychoid unconscious seem to me very important for understanding the basis of reverie (Bion, 1962), the analytic third (Ogden, 1994) and "thought transference" (Freud, 1933) – the processes linked to unconscious communication.

In the clinical example that follows, I have attempted to trace the process of regression to dependency, which entailed engaging with the structural void linked to birth trauma. Part of this process involved a gradual re-generation of badly lacerated psychic skin. As Winnicott (1974) astutely observed, regression to dependency is often connected to a need to experience "the breakdown that has already happened". Unconscious communication has been a significant feature of this analysis, helping my patient feel that, despite his mistrust that I (or anyone else) truly cared, we were deeply connected and he wasn't alone in his process. The emergence of unconscious communication often happened at times when he felt particularly desperate and disconnected, manifesting as reveries, "thought transference", dreams and sometimes unconscious enactments.

I hope that this illustration conveys a sense of the work in which "the whole being of the doctor as well as that of the patient plays its part" (Jung, 1929, para. 163). I have been deeply affected (as well as "infected") by the experience and have definitely felt that "the doctor is as much 'in the analysis' as the patient" and "is equally a part of the psychic process of treatment and therefore equally exposed to the transforming influences" (Jung, 1929, para. 166).

Clinical Illustration

The Beginning

Nicholas is a middle-aged man who wanted therapy on account of his deeply ingrained pervasive fear, shame, self-hate and sense of disconnectedness from his body. He related a history of multiple suicide attempts and told me that he felt unable to sustain relationships or to love. He described his relational history as that of serial dating with an underlying fear of being abandoned and a feeling that he always had to have a "backup" – someone else waiting in the wings in case his existing relationship broke down.

I later learned that he was a breach birth, born two weeks premature and spent the first 24 hours of his life in an incubator. He knew that he had some kind of breathing difficulties at birth but didn't know whether there were any other complications which had necessitated him being incubated. Based on some clues which later appeared in his dreams and in the transference, both of us wondered whether he might have been born with the umbilical cord around his neck and needed to be resuscitated. Later on, as the work deepened, the incubator metaphor emerged powerfully in different shapes and forms.

The work began at a frequency of once weekly. After our first short break, Nicholas started missing sessions and then sent me an email informing me that he was breaking off from therapy. I responded by inviting him back and suggesting that he may need a higher frequency of sessions. This seemed to help him feel held and to settle back into the work as well as to acknowledge his underlying need for a stronger container. This pattern was to be repeated as Nicholas found the analytic breaks difficult and would become withdrawn and angry with me both before and after.

Nicholas' initial dream proved highly symbolically significant as the process unfolded:

> I am in an observation cage with a friend going underwater to see sharks. Once underwater, I cut my finger and sees the sharks gathering around attracted by my blood. I then look up and notice that the top of the cage is missing and that I am vulnerable to attack.

During the first year of our work, Nicholas shared with me his sense of deepening trust. He said that it felt both important and frightening, because he had never trusted anyone in his life. This trust felt unsettling as he also noticed a voice in him telling me: "Don't mess with me!". As the trust grew, his fear of psychotic breakdown and suicidal feelings increased along with his need to know whether he really mattered to me. The fear of being rejected and shut out by the other came alive in the transference. Thus, he noticed that I had a door installed on the entrance to a room which he would pass on his way to my consulting room and felt that I did that to protect myself from him.

About a year into our work together, he had another significant dream.

"I am in a field with a friend, and we are building a house. We have laid the foundation, and now I need to figure out how to lay bricks to build the walls."

Nicholas found the dream a hopeful indication of where he was in his process – we have laid the foundation, which was an important start. He was very aware that he had never had a sense of home. It seemed to me that, now that the foundation was there, he needed to build a safe container (of his own psychic skin represented in his initial dream as a cage with the missing top, with terror, hate and other powerful unconscious forces threatening to destroy him). The theme of psychic skin also emerged in other forms over the subsequent years. In one session, an image of his psychic skin with holes in it came up for me in my reverie and I decided to share it. In response, Nicholas exclaimed: "Oh, I've remembered … As a child, I was really scared that a door would fall out of an aeroplane, and I would fall out!".

I also noticed that as the work increasingly started to involve early states of mind (and after Nicholas had moved to work on the couch), he developed a particular way of starting his sessions. He would bring the tips of his fingers together in a shape reminiscent of hands held in prayer and would stay in silence for a minute or two. The gesture seemed to help him re-establish a sensory floor as well as a deeper connection with himself and a sense of being present in the room with me.

Following that dream and over the next few years, the first glimpses of Nicholas being able to feel himself inside his skin and in his body started emerging. In his external life, he was able to form a committed relationship and later build a home with his partner. However, despite feeling real care and a strong connection with her, Nicholas remained deeply ambivalent about the relationship, questioning whether she was the right woman for him. Also, the inevitable breaks in our analytic container still invoked powerful responses in his unconscious (e.g. dreaming on a summer break of falling out of an aeroplane and into the sea with sharks).

Through exploring the vicissitudes of his relationship with his partner, the realization gradually formed that, to a degree, his relationship served to cover up something in him that felt much more disturbing – a terrifying void at the core threatening to flood him with terror. He had a fear that if he broke up with her, he would have to face something so unbearable inside that he might fall apart, have a psychotic breakdown or commit suicide. The terrifying pull of the void was captured vividly in a memory he once shared with me – of a bridge over a dirty river with toxic water. The bridge had holes in it and was taped off, but he climbed on it anyway, and almost fell through a hole. "Should I try to keep away from these feelings?" he asked. It seemed to me that we both sensed that we were dealing with the dynamics of secondary symbiosis (without calling it that).

Gradually, Nicholas came to recognise that if he didn't face that terror, he would not be able to have a close, committed relationship with anyone. Things came to a head in the seventh year of the now three-times-a-week analysis, when the couple decided to separate and Nicholas moved out to live on his own. Just prior to that, he had a dream, which for him carried a prophetic significance:

> I am on an island with my partner. There is a funeral there. My partner is staying for the funeral, but I need to go back home by boat. I am on the boat with my father. I know that there are pirates in those waters and that the journey is dangerous. We reach a place with a narrow passage through a cave. This place is particularly dangerous, and yet we need to get through.

The Descent

The best way I can describe the subsequent year is as a descent into the underworld – with Nicholas feeling filled with terror, loneliness, a profound sense of isolation, suicidal despair and self-persecution. He battled with his alternating feelings of rage, self-hatred and envy of other people, who he felt were much better off (myself included). He would wake up at 4 am feeling that he was on the verge of a breakdown. I felt that we were going underwater together in that observation cage, not knowing when or how the descent would end. I was very aware that it was crucially important for me to stay close to him in that process, to be able to face the risks and bear my own anxiety. Sometimes, his suicidal feelings were so intense that he felt that they would never change and that there was no point for him to continue his struggle. At other times, he would ask me to give him hope, tell him that his feelings would change and that he would get through to the other (brighter) side. Much as I wanted to offer him hope and reassurance, I was also aware that it was very important for me to truly accept his suicidal feelings (to accept and meet him where he was and not reach for the wished for "better" self in him) and that even saying that I hoped that his feelings would change in the future would have been a subtle way of rejecting his feelings in the here and now, emotionally abandoning him and not surviving as an analyst for him (Winnicott, 1969).

At times my anxiety was very intense, especially when I felt that his state was particularly fragile and he felt flooded by fear of madness and suicidal feelings. One such experience occurred in a session just before a long weekend due to a rupture, which happened when I openly challenged some of his self-destructive choices. Even though what I said felt valid and important, I was aware that he was left feeling angry and unsupported by me, which added to his already fragile state. And yet, I had to bear these feelings. Then, over the weekend, I had a dream. In the dream, Nicholas and I had our next session. We talked and reconnected and I woke up with a sense of relief … and thought that perhaps this was a good sign …

When I saw Nicholas next, he started by telling me that he had noticed beautiful flowers in my front garden. There indeed was a sense that something had shifted and there was a greater sense of connectedness. He also told me how difficult he found our previous session and I acknowledged that it was difficult for both of us. We then proceeded to discuss the experience of the rupture.

On another occasion, when I was similarly left holding intense anxiety over a weekend, I got caught up in an unconscious enactment. On the Saturday morning, I accidentally sent him a text message intended for a colleague. The message itself was quite neutral in content, but what struck me when I discovered it later on, was that somehow I managed to change the name of the colleague to "Nicholas"! It truly felt like the unconscious in action. The next Monday, Nicholas told me that he had woken up feeling very low and depressed and then he saw my message! He felt touched, even after he realised that it had been sent in error, because something in him could feel that it was about my letting him know that he was on my mind.

On a more positive note, that year also allowed us to engage closely with his ambivalence about dependence, his hate of his vulnerable self and infantile needs. Little by little, he was able to allow himself to need me and to go deeper into regression.

There were a few sessions when he shared with me a fantasy of putting a cord around his neck and strangling himself in front of me. We wondered whether this was an expression of his hatred of me as well as his need for me to feel his pain. In the transference, sometimes I became an emotionally absent mother impermeable to his pain. One of the stories he had heard from his mother, which seemed significant to me, was that of her forgetting him, leaving him in a pram by a shop window and only remembering once she was back home. As a teenager, he felt a burden to his parents who were unable to recognise his suicide attempts as a cry for help. He remembered once overhearing them discuss giving him up for adoption.

I was also experienced as the archetypal Great Mother, overflowing with milk and abundant resources, which he so desperately needed, but who withheld them. One particularly painful issue between us concerned the intensity of his need for my touch. This need seemed multifaceted, a mixture of erotic feelings, Oedipal longings and early infantile needs. We discussed the various ins and outs of that need in terms of the transference dynamics, but although my interpretations (e.g. acknowledging that I was unable to reparent him and that, painful as it was, there was a need to mourn what he didn't get as a child) seemed to help contain the need somewhat and relieve the pain temporarily, the need itself didn't lessen in intensity. Sometimes he asked me: "What is the point of continuing our work if my deepest needs can't be met by you?" At one point, he found a female practitioner who offered body and energy work. "She offers me what you cannot", he said, followed by: "Why do I feel so annoyed with you after my sessions with her?". I found myself holding intense conflicting feelings in response to his need. There were times when I felt a strong urge to respond to his longing concretely. It felt particularly valid when we worked with his earliest experiences in regression, such as his sense of profound aloneness and isolation, which seemed linked to "the incubator". At the same time, I was very aware that if I were to touch him or hold his hand, I would become the seductive mother he dreaded. And yet, by not touching him I was experienced as the depriving mother. I felt that it was important to find a way of meeting his need symbolically – of touching him without actually physically touching him …

And there was yet another theme, which gradually emerged, concerning his fantasy of tying a cord around his neck in front of me – related to his birth trauma. The relevance of that theme slowly surfaced in the field between us as his regression deepened. Below, I will share part transcripts from three sessions which illustrate the emergence of, and our engagement with, this theme. The sessions are not consecutive.

The Incubator Session

Nicholas tells me that he has been struggling with intense painful feelings …
At one point over the weekend, he felt as if he was in a glass incubator and

couldn't reach anyone. Later, he found a photo of himself as a baby in an incubator. He couldn't look at the photo because it was too painful. He then continues to talk about his self-hate and disgust.

I choose to share my countertransference response: "I feel deeply moved by that image of you in the incubator ... I feel that you are really connected with baby Nicholas now ... and I am struck by how that experience – feeling profoundly alone and isolated – seems to have also produced deep shame ..." In my resonance with him, I also feel the pain related to the absence of touch in that experience and choose to name it, saying that I can feel how much baby Nicholas needs to feel held.

N: Yes! And he needs it from you!
L: I think he needs it from both of us...
   (I feel that we are both holding the pain of the absence of touch and the longing).
   Later in the session, he asks me whether I know what it's like – whether I have ever been to that place of really not wanting to go on, to live ... I feel that the question is coming from somewhere deep inside him and that he has taken a risk to ask it. We are now seven years into the work and, on this occasion, I choose to respond directly: "Yes, I know what it is like not wanting to be alive and finding life unbearable."
N: And is there a way out?
L: Well ... I am still here.
N: Thank God!

By the end of the session, Nicholas tells me that he feels grounded and comfortable in his body, which for him is a rare experience. In the next session, he tells me that after the previous session he felt deeply moved, close to me and to other people. He proceeds to tell me about a friend who sent him a genuinely caring message and becomes tearful: "I cry easily these days ..." I respond: "Something is thawing ..."

The Mouse Session

N: I was at work earlier today and found it very hard to participate in a meeting, to speak ... I feel so invisible and vulnerable ... There is something just SO vulnerable in me ... I hate it ...
   (I feel that we are in the familiar territory of his intolerance of his vulnerable self and his hate of it and choose to keep silent.)
N: ... The other day I found a tiny little mouse in the garden. He was shaking, terrified ... And I couldn't just leave him there, I took him into the

house … Imagine what it must be like to be an animal and to have to live with the threat of attack all the time.

L: I feel in touch with something very young in you, something that feels very frightened and vulnerable …

N: (seems moved and reflective) … Yes …

L: It brings to mind that image of you in the incubator … And I am aware that we have given some thought and space to that experience, but where this takes me now is to what must have happened before that … there was a reason you needed to be in the incubator in the first place … I can't imagine what it must have been like for you … I am thinking about that tiny terrified mouse.

N: (becomes tearful) … This reminds me of a DJ I liked as a teenager, his name was Terror Danger … imagine that … but yes, my birth … Somehow, I have a sense that I didn't want to be born and was resisting it all I could …

(Nicholas then mentions a friend who had been a source of support for him but who did not respond to his last message. He tells me that he feels let down by her.)

L: What do you imagine might have happened?

N: I think she found me too much … It is not easy to be around someone who is suicidal, in such a difficult state …

L: … I wonder where that experience is between us … the part of you that fears that you are too much for me?

N: (eyes fill with tears) Yes, I know … but there is something even more painful … I felt it at the start of our session today and I feel it now … It is hard for me to talk about it …

L: … and there is something very painful about these feelings …

N: Yes, strange as it may be … It is so painful to feel that I want to be close to you and I can't have that…

L: … There are different dimensions of closeness … What is it that you feel you can't have: physical closeness, emotional closeness, sexual?

N: All of these, I think … You have such warmth and no matter what I bring this doesn't change …

(For a while, we stay in silence with the feelings in the room.)

L: … I am in touch with that very vulnerable part of you – baby Nicholas – and I wonder where he is in relation to this and how he is feeling now.

N: (feeling and reflecting) … He is there and also feels the pain …

L: I wonder whether he is allowed to be part of our relationship … It feels as if he really needs to feel safe and held, but perhaps his needs frighten you – the intensity of your need for closeness – and not just with me (I refer to his fear of closeness with his partner) … because you fear that it may take over and will be too much for me … And then it's as if hunger turns to greed and it frightens you.

N: … Yes, it's true … but what do I do about this, about the greed?

L: The greed I think comes from the fear that you will not get enough, that your need will never be met …

(In the silence, I feel a sense of closeness between us …)

N: Yet when I start feeling close, this terror comes up – that I may lose it … (We talk about a possible meaning of his fear – of his need being too great, not getting enough, possible implicit memories in that area …)

L: … But actually, in a healthy nursing couple the experience of feeding is mutually enjoyable. It is when the baby can't feed – this is what is much more painful for both …

N: I have never thought about it this way … I see … Yes, I get it … I feel that we are in a very important area…

The Cave Session

Nicholas talks about his terror, which is always there deep down and which sometimes he feels flooded by. He recalls the dream about a boat journey through the cave. I am aware that he is in a very fragile state, going in and out of dissociation. I invite him to stay in touch with the here and now where he can hear my voice and feel the fear. After about a minute, he reports feeling more present and in touch with his body.

N: Yes, I know, this is what I need, it would not be right trying to avoid that terror …

L: Tell me more about your feelings in that cave …

N: In my dream?

L: In your dream and in your mind …

N: It is dark … there are eyes looking at me from all sides – animals. We are in the boat … there is a light at the front of the boat and I am terrified that if the light goes out, that will be it – death – the animals will attack us.

L: … I wonder what you consciously know about your birth process …

N: I know! As I was telling you this dream, I also had a sense – this is about my birth! I don't know much information. I was a breach birth and then I was put in the incubator, but I don't know why … Maybe because of that, but it's unlikely …

(At this point I found myself wondering again whether perhaps he was born with the umbilical cord around his neck and experienced asphyxiation … Was that the reason he ended up in the incubator? I do not say this out loud though.)

L: It is unlikely … And you are really scared that the light will go out – the light of consciousness perhaps …

N: That I will die? I also have a sense that I really didn't want to be born, and ever since then as if part of me is not here … as if it was left behind.

L: I wonder whether actually the light did go out at some point and then you woke up on the other side? And there is this gap you are struggling to bridge and the terror …

N: Yes, this resonates with my own sense of it …

L: And this is what is coming up now … that very early experience and unprocessed terror.

(I feel that a lot is happening in the space between us.)

At the end of the session, Nicholas says: "I feel that you really met me today where I needed to be met … I feel feelings in all my body now, not just in one tight place …"

Reflecting on these experiences and looking back at our work together over the years, I have come to recognise that there has been a series of dreams related to his birth trauma. Below are some of them:

"I am holding a baby in my hand, breathing warmth on her. She starts dis-integrating, then comes back together. I bring her back to her mother, who puts her in an incubator. She survives …"

"My friends and I are resuscitating a baby whale in a pool."

"A young boy is floating in water, nearly drowning, I rescue him."

The Way Up and Integration

About nine months from the start of the descent, Nicholas and I started noticing the first signs of what felt like a dawn – a sense of the darkness gradually lifting. He started reporting more frequent experiences of feeling embodied and feeling safe and comfortable in his skin.

Then he had a dream, which he described as very big, which made his hair stand on end:

There is a woman dressed in military uniform, she is the commander. She lifts up her gun and shoots in the air. This is the signal to the troops that the war is over. Then there are troops marching in the streets holding up their guns – signalling that it is over, and they are going home. In the blue sky there is a big full moon. One side of it is bright, the other is dark – it is like a Yin-Yang symbol.

In my experience, it is often the case with big dreams like this that they keep unfolding in one's life over months or even years to come. At present, I have an overall sense that significant changes are slowly taking place deep inside Nicholas, although more time is needed for these changes to fully manifest. We can see new shoots coming through in his external life too. For example, he is increasingly able to hold opposing feelings and states of mind in his awareness without collapsing into just one extreme position, such as self-hate and suicidal despair. His ability to contain his feelings, to stay present and inhabit his body has definitely grown as the work continues.

Discussion

I was struck by the rich symbolic significance of two images that came up repeatedly in Nicholas' process: the underwater observation cage in his initial dream and the walls of the incubator. Both images represent containers but with quite different qualities. Whereas the cage with the missing top surrounded by sharks can be seen as a reflection of his psychic skin with holes in it (wide open to the powerful and dangerous forces of the unconscious), the incubator seems to have the opposite qualities – the walls that isolate rather than contain – an impenetrable defence of a second skin. It seemed that our challenge was to help him re-grow his primary psychic skin – a living and breathing membrane that would transcend these two opposites and help him feel both contained and connected to the world around him. As the analytic process unfolded, I also wondered whether the symbolism of his initial dream referred back to his intrauterine and birth experiences. This dream offered us guidance concerning the qualities of the psychic dimensions we would have to revisit – this time together.

Winnicott (1949) observed that to wish for a new birth is not unusual. However, it seems that in birth trauma this unconscious wish acquires a particular significance. Nicholas said that he felt himself impregnated in me and, at times, I felt as though I was carrying him inside of me. That work in deep regression needed to happen before he could start separating from me. In order to achieve that, we needed to establish a symbiotic union where, in Anzieu's (2016) words, the skin is experienced as a common boundary between mother and baby, as well as between the baby and the world around, where exchanges are largely based on unconscious communication. Part of that work had to do with facing the structural void saturated with terror.

It is hardly surprising that in working with this very early level of experience the need to be touched (re)emerges powerfully. In that process, however, the analyst faces a challenge as to how to meet this need in an adult patient where it is often mixed with other feelings, such as sexual ones. It seems to me that a thoughtful and considered use of self-disclosure can offer a symbolic way of offering "touch". Such self-disclosure can also be experienced as a "moment of meeting" (Stern et al., 1998). Interestingly, Feldman (2014) sees moments of meeting as forming the foundations of the primary skin function, which can be developed within a secure frame and a containing analytic skin.

In thinking about working analytically with birth trauma, I found Winnicott's reflections on the subject helpful and insightful. Winnicott (1949) believed that not every birth is inherently traumatic and, in fact, that the majority of people have normal births that do not create a traumatic break in the continuity of being. However, when the birth is traumatic, the experience can determine the pattern for all subsequent persecutions and paranoid ideation. He suggests that one factor that can be traumatic is related to a very long birth, when the baby is stuck in the birth canal and is in the grip of something external, feeling helpless and not knowing when it will end. Another factor has to do with the delay in breathing (and not the initiation of breathing per se). He suggested that, later in life, such persons may be drawn to experiences linked to asphyxiation (e.g. through sexual practices). He also observed that when a break in the continuity of being happens during the process of birth, it can create a pattern whereby intellect begins to work as distinct from the psyche and the person starts "cataloguing" their experiences to be addressed at a later date. Such persons may then bring to analysis carefully collected memories of all persecutions they can remember. All these observations seem very relevant to my work with Nicholas.

Furthermore, Winnicott believed that birth trauma can only become a meaningful experience in analysis in the context of regression to dependency and that there is no such thing as working with birth trauma on its own. This resonates with my experience in that Nicholas' birth did not become represented in the space between us as a meaningful experience (even though he had intellectually known some difficult facts about his birth) until the analytic relationship had been well established, including the level of unconscious identity, when he was able to go deeper into regression. It was only then that the traumatic experiences related to his birth started to emerge in our joint dreaming process. For me, this often happened through reverie and felt particularly significant when our thought and feeling processes synchronistically coincided in sessions. My sense was that it was not something we thought about intellectually, but rather something that spontaneously emerged in the process when the time was right.

And last but not least, I felt struck by the rich symbolism of Nicholas' Ying-Yang Moon dream. I believe that this dream speaks about his individuation process – perhaps the birth of the new, more balanced (Ying-Yang) relationship with the Self. Jung thought that the Self may appear in dreams "in the form of a totality symbol, such as the circle, square or cross (or mandala) … When it represents a *complexio oppositorum*, a union of opposites, it can also appear as a united duality, in the form, for instance, of tao as the interplay of yang and yin …" (Jung, 1921, para. 790). Exploring the symbolism of the Moon (or *Luna*) and drawing upon ancient alchemical sources, Jung sees the Moon "with her antithetical nature" as "a prototype of individuation, a prefiguration of the self" and "the psychologem of the pregnant anima, whose child is the self". Quoting from William Mennes, Jung says that Luna "is really the mother of the sun, which means, psychologically, that the unconscious is pregnant with consciousness and gives birth to it" (Jung, 1955-56, para. 219). The references to a new birth and the embodiment of a new sense of self seem quite remarkable.[1] I think that this is indeed a big dream, which heralds the start of a new phase in Nicholas' process which is likely to keep unfolding in the time to come. The treatise of Wei Po-yang, also quoted by Jung, captures this beautifully: "The way is long and obscurely mystical, at the end of which the Ch'ien (yang) and the K'un (yin) come together" (Jung, 1955-56, para. 403n).

Note

1 When I showed Nicholas this manuscript for his permission to publish, he was struck by the synchronicity as, unbeknown to me, he intended to call his future daughter "Luna".

References

Anzieu, D. (2016) *The Skin-Ego*. London: Karnac Books.
Bick, E. (1968) "The experience of the skin in early object-relations", *International Journal of Psychoanalysis*, 49(2-3): 484–486.
Bion, W.R. (1962) *Learning From Experience*. New York: Basic Books.

Bion, W.R. (1977) *Seven Servants*. New York: Jason Aronson.
Birksted-Breen, D. (2019) "Pathways of the unconscious: When the body is the receiver/instrument", *International Journal of Psychoanalysis*, 100(6): 1117–1133.
Bleger, J. (1967) "Psycho-analysis of the psycho-analytic frame", *International Journal of Psychoanalysis*, 48(4): 511–519.
Buber, M. (1923[1970]) *I and Thou* (trans. W. Kaufmann), New York: Charles Scribner's Sons.
Feldman, B. (2014) "Creating a skin for imagination, reflection and desire", in A. Cavalli, L. Hawkins and M. Stevns (eds) *Transformation: Jung's Legacy and Clinical Work Today*. London: Karnac.
Freud, S. (1926) "Inhibitions, symptoms, and anxiety", in *SE XX*. London: Hogarth Press, pp. 77–175.
Freud, S. (1933) "New introductory lectures on psycho-analysis", in *SE XXII*. London: Hogarth Press, pp. 1–182.
Jung, C.G. (1912/1952) *Symbols of Transformation*. CW5. Princeton, NJ: Princeton University Press.
Jung, C.G. (1921) *Psychological Types*. CW6. Princeton, NJ: Princeton University Press.
Jung, C.G. (1929) *Problems of Modern Psychotherapy*. CW16. Princeton, NJ: Princeton University Press.
Jung, C.G. (1955–56). *Mysterium Coniunctionis*. CW14. Princeton, NJ: Princeton University Press.
Lagutina, L. (2021) "Meeting the orphan: early relational trauma, synchronicity and the psychoid", *Journal of Analytical Psychology*, 66(1): 5–27.
Lutenberg, J.M. (2009) "Mental void and the borderline patient", in A. Green (ed.) *Resonance of Suffering: Countertransference in Non-Neurotic Structures*. London: Karnac Books, pp. 89–120.
Mahler, M.S. (1968) *On Human Symbiosis and the Vicissitudes of Individuation*. New York: International Universities Press.
Merchant, J. (2012) *Shamans and Analysts: New Insights on the Wounded Healer*. New York: Routledge.
Mitrani, J.L. (1993) "'Unmentalized' experience in the etiology and treatment of psychosomatic asthma", *Contemporary Psychoanalysis*, 29(2): 314–342.
Montagu, A. (1971) *Touching: The Human Significance of the Skin*. New York: Harper & Row.
Ogden, T.H. (1989) "On the concept of an autistic-contiguous position", *International Journal of Psychoanalysis*, 70(1): 127–140.
Ogden, T.H. (1994) "The analytic third: working with intersubjective clinical facts", *International Journal of Psychoanalysis*, 75(1): 3–19.
Ogden, T.H. (2004) "This art of psychoanalysis: Dreaming undreamt dreams and interrupted cries", *International Journal of Psychoanalysis*, 85(4): 857–877.
Schmidt, M. (2012) "Psychic skin: psychotic defences, borderline process and delusions", *Journal of Analytical Psychology*, 57(1): 21–39.
Searles, H.F. (1962) "Problems of psycho-analytic supervision", in *Collected Papers on Schizophrenia and Related Subjects*. London: Maresfield Library.
Stern, D.N., Sander, L.W., Nahum, J.P., Harrison, A.M., Lyons-Ruth, K., Morgan, A.C., Bruschweiler-Stern, N. and Tronick, E.Z. (1998) "Non-interpretive mechanisms in psychoanalytic therapy: the 'something more' than interpretation", *International Journal of Psychoanalysis*, 79: 903–921.
Symington, J. (1985) "The survival function of primitive omnipotence", *International Journal of Psychoanalysis*, 66(4): 481–487.
Winnicott, D.W. (1945) "Primitive emotional development", *International Journal of Psychoanalysis*, 26: 137–143.

Winnicott, D.W. (1947) "Mind and its relation to the psyche-soma", in *Through Paediatrics to Psycho-Analysis*. London: The Hogarth Press.

Winnicott, D.W. (1949) "Birth memories, birth trauma and anxiety", in *Collected Papers: Through Paediatrics to Psycho-Analysis*. London: Tavistock publications.

Winnicott, D.W. (1969) "The use of an object", *International Journal of Psychoanalysis*, 50(4): 711–716.

Winnicott, D.W. (1971) "The place where we live", in *Playing and Reality*. New York: Basic Books.

Winnicott, D.W. (1974) "Fear of breakdown", *International Review of Psychoanalysis*, 1: 103–107.

Part II

Dissociative Processes in Trauma

Chapter 6

PTSD

Feeling-Toned Complexes and the Twilight of Self-Awareness

Gianluigi Di Cesare and Patrizia Brogna

The Traumatic Experience Between the Objective and Subjective Paradigm

Generally, trauma is seen as the result of subjective reactions to an event experienced and perceived as traumatic, but also as the consequence of the response of the subject to objectively traumatic events (earthquakes, natural disasters, accidents, etc.). Trauma is an event in which the Self is attacked and both its biological and psychic survival is endangered. Despite these different perspectives, from a first-person perspective (i.e., aimed at understanding human experience through one's own subjective experience) and from a third-person perspective (aimed at understanding the human experience through its manifestation), trauma and traumatic experiences represent a challenge in searching for the "truth" of what happened in the psychic experience.

The first perspective, known as "first-person understanding", underlines the subjective character of the response to an event that does not necessarily have an objectively traumatic value. This perspective not only highlights the evolutionary-relational aspect of the response to trauma, but also introduces the anthropological conception of "vulnerability-to" psychic splitting when facing trauma which resonates with Jung's notion of "an inner predisposition" to trauma (Jung, 1912, para. 217). This is the perspective of psychoanalytical, philosophical and psychodynamic theories.

The second perspective, or "third-person understanding" – characteristic of the so-called "exact sciences" – refers to the objective determinant of the traumatic event in the individual reaction and response. In this case, the emphasis is on the typology of the event rather than on the individual predisposition to trauma. In the Diagnostic and Statistical Manual of Mental Disorders 5 (DSM-5) (APA, 2013) there is an attempt to bypass this difference in the definition of a traumatic event, which is indicated both as

DOI: 10.4324/9781003298076-9

objective (perceived as objectively serious) and as subjective (perceived as subjectively serious).

From an exegetical analysis, the "interpretation" factor is crucial for a clinician attempting to understand the psychological situation of a patient and, if needed, make a diagnosis for him. In fact, Post-Traumatic Stress Disorder (PTSD), more than other psychiatric disorders, exposes the clinician to a doubt – first and foremost – of an interpretative nature.

Challenges to Psychiatric Diagnosis (by Means of the DSM-5)

Dissociative or psychotic symptoms seem to share a common framework in the fragmentation of self-consciousness, where they can be roughly defined and ascribable to other serious psychopathological disorders (schizophrenia, psychosis, mood disorders, personality disorders, etc.).

The first version of the Diagnostic and Statistical Manual of Mental Disorders (American Psychiatric Association [APA], 1952) was published during the Korean War (1950–1953) and included the diagnostic category of "Gross Stress Reaction", indicating extreme behavioural reactions of a normal individual to a stressful event. The disorder was not investigated further, or clearly defined, and was seen as showing spontaneous remission.

The DSM-II (APA, 1968) introduced post-traumatic disorders into the category of "Transient Situational Disorders", including acute reactions to exposure to stressors - such as a brief psychotic episode. Still in this version of DSM-II, the post-traumatic stress disorders were usually seen as showing a rapid spontaneous remission.

Finally, it was in DSM-III (APA, 1980) that the diagnostic category of PTSD was introduced, following the aftermath of the Vietnam War, with its huge sequela of severe psychic disorders affecting soldiers and war veterans.

In short, the diagnostic criteria included the occurrence of a stressful event "outside the range of common experiences". In DSM-III, there were only two clusters of symptoms, which were intrusive memories and avoidance behaviours towards trauma-related stimuli, whereas in DSM-III-R (APA, 1987), a third cluster was added, which was related to increased arousal. However, the criterion indicating the presence of clinically significant distress was not yet reported.

In the fourth edition, DSM IV-TR (APA, 2000), temporality was introduced as a discriminating factor for the intensity of the traumatic impact and then for the diagnostic process discriminating immediate responses from those that occurred later than the traumatic event itself.

It was with DSM-5 (APA, 2013) that the discriminating factor of dissociative phenomena was introduced, in addition to the more precise systematization of behavioural and externalizing criteria of traumatic outcomes, already present in DSM IV-TR. In particular, DSM-5 focuses on the different diagnosis of:

1 Depersonalization: recurrent and persistent experience of feeling detached from, and as if one were an outside observer of, one's mental processes or body (e.g., feeling as though one were in a dream; feeling a sense of unreality of self or body or of time moving slowly).
2 Derealization: persistent or recurrent experience of the unreality of surroundings (e.g., the world around the individual is experienced as unreal, dreamlike, distant, or distorted). Note: To use this subtype, the dissociative symptoms must not be attributable to the physiological effects of a substance (e.g., blackouts) or other medical conditions (e.g., complex partial seizures).

(APA, 2013: 274)

Another change introduced in the fifth edition of the DSM is the significant attention paid to adverse childhood experiences (ACE, which are understood as non-specific risk factors for mental health in general.) In fact, negative life events, trauma and bereavements, understood as adverse childhood experiences, are considered non-specific risk factors that can increase the probability of the onset of various physical or psychological illnesses; but they can also influence their course and worsen the prognosis. Other serious psychiatric disorders, such as schizophrenia and bipolar disorder, are seen as resulting from a marked biological vulnerability as well (Etain et al., 2013).

ACEs, the umbrella term for traumatic experiences during childhood, have a significant effect on the biological, psychological and social functioning of those who experience them. These experiences are usually caused by the child's main caregivers and can be produced both directly (as with sexual abuse, psychological abuse, physical abuse and neglect) or indirectly (a psychiatric illness of the caregiver, death, alcoholism or drug addiction) (Dube et al., 2001; Caretti, Craparo and Schimmenti, 2013).

A significant contribution came from the first wide scale, longitudinal epidemiological study of ACE aimed at simultaneously assessing several categories of child abuse and adverse experiences together with the cumulative effect of these experiences on the adult (Anda et al., 2007).

The results from this study pointed to significant interconnections between physical and mental health and traumatic experiences during childhood and adulthood. The role of relational trauma and, in particular, of a trauma in the attachment bond (Liotti and Farina, 2011) is evident in the different diagnostic categories of DSM-5. Adverse childhood experiences are associated with 44% of psychopathologies emerging during the development of the child and they can also explain later psychological disorders. The same DSM-5 includes post-traumatic stress disorders in childhood in its classification, giving greater importance to the relationships between children and parents within the framework of relational disorders, recognizing that trauma can have an effect for an entire lifetime (Dube et al., 2001).

Traumatic events often lead to a diagnosis of PTSD with symptoms such as flashbacks, dulling and/or numbing of emotions, loss of interest, disruption to circadian rhythms or insomnia, behavioural problems and social isolation. PTSD frequently occurs in comorbidity with other psychiatric disorders. Researchers agree that traumatic events are one of the central factors involved in the genesis and continuation of most psychopathologies (Gross, 2015). The presence of PTSD, alongside other mental disorders, significantly exacerbates symptoms in terms of higher numbers of suicide attempts and substance abuse. It also worsens the progression of those diseases (Quarantini et al., 2010).

The close correlation between childhood traumatic experiences and severe psychiatric disorders, besides Post-Traumatic Stress Disorder, is highlighted in recent scientific literature with particular reference to disorders related to the affective sphere of emotional tonality (Etain et al., 2013). It has also been observed that the comorbidity of traumatic events and other psychiatric disorders can have a negative impact on the response to both therapeutic and pharmacological treatment, since trauma-related avoidance strategies, such as social isolation and behavioural disorders, worsen affective regulation (Fonagy et al., 2017a, 2017b). Mental illness resulting from violence and traumatic events is one of the largest public health problems we currently face.

Trauma means that it is impossible for the subject to find meaning due to an inability to mentalize the experience, as the psychic integrity of the self is challenged to its limits. The subject is unable to find words for the immediate, disruptive and shocking experience of his own impotence. Without a coherent narrative that would give meaning to his personal history, the subject is unable to overcome what happened. Studies on the interconnection between traumatic experiences, attachment style, personality disorders and lack of mentalization, support this transience of meaning (Liotti, 2005; van der Kolk, 2014).

Unanimously, all the studies on traumatic experiences seem to highlight how, following exposure to a traumatic event, the capacity for mentalization and symbolization becomes more difficult. Traumatic experiences are understood as causing a deficit both in the continuity and coherence of the processes that attribute meaning to experience, as well as in the sense of unity to the perception of the Self (Kalsched, 1996, 2013). Personal meanings cannot be framed within one's own personal history. They remain incommunicable, unrepresentable, unspeakable: trauma steals their voice.

In the processing of traumatic memories, we believe that the reconfiguration of the traumatic experience is at the core of the healing process. This is particularly true when trauma occurs during early childhood and then arises in the form of bodily memories (Caretti, Craparo and Schimmenti, 2013). The experience of being unable to give meaning to what happened drags the traumatized person into anguish.

A Survival Story: The Naked and Abandoned Self

M was about 21 years old when she reached our public health service Complex Operative Unit "Prevention and Early Interventions".[1] Her case was referred by the Psychiatric Diagnosis and Treatment Service (SPDC) where she was hospitalized following a major suicide attempt, which happened in somewhat confused circumstances. From what we initially understood M, while on vacation with her mother abroad, experienced a psychotic crisis with perceptual phenomena and delusional ideation. This crisis, triggered by a large intake of cannabis, was experienced by her as "the end of the world" and resulted in an actual "leap into the void" that left her lifeless on the ground, after a fall of ten metres from a building. Immediately hospitalized, she did not suffer life-threatening injuries, but still had several major fractures. After a few days, she was transferred to Italy and, because of the persistence of psychiatric symptoms, hospitalized in the SPDC. During the hospitalization, M appeared frightened and confused. She described, in a chaotic way, the events prior to the suicide attempt and continued to insist that she was Jesus. A diagnosis of schizophrenic disorder was made, and a psychopharmacological therapy based on long-acting injectable antipsychotics (LAI) was established. Ten days later, she was transferred to a subacute clinic where she remained for about a month. M later recalled her anguish related to that hospitalization, characterized by the presence of shadowy figures in white coats who said incomprehensible things that frightened her even more. During the first period of hospitalization, she met a clinical team from our Operative Unit who had the task of continuing her treatment. The team immediately adhered to the diagnostic hypothesis formulated and acted accordingly, confirming the drug therapy started in the SPDC. After her discharge from the clinic, M came to the Unit several times, but always with a wary and suspicious attitude. After a few meetings, she refused to continue the pharmacological therapy, citing important side effects: in particular, she spoke about the "death" of a part of her brain which she identified as on the right side, as well as more typical side effects like fatigue, drowsiness and weight gain.

These statements confirmed her delusional state and led to a strong response from the team who, given the seriousness of the clinical situation, suggested further hospitalization. M refused hospitalization and abandoned the therapeutic program, stating that she wanted to continue with a private specialist. After a few months, the Operative Unit was contacted again by her mother who reported a worsening of the situation as M had also abandoned her private therapy. After several emails, we managed to get her back to the service and a new treatment with our team started.

She was both scared and disappointed, afraid to speak because she was worried about the possible consequences and angry because she continued to feel bad: "My brain no longer works. The drugs burned it. I have read that this can happen and that, despite having stopped using the medicines, it won't come back as before".

These words, her tone of voice and the overall way in which she expressed her complaints elicited the image of a frightened and sad girl which moved the whole team to feel more tenderness towards her. This was in contrast to the experience of the previous team who perceived in her an arrogant psychotic pretentiousness. It was our emotional experience which led to a new approach and helped create a container – a vas hermeticum – for M and her history.

After a couple of meetings, M told us that she couldn't fully reveal what had happened to her and was still happening to her because, if she did, she feared being hospitalized. We promised that, no matter what she told us, the content of her words would never be the reason for hospitalization.[2] M was then able to gradually trust us and to start sharing her story. It revealed a very traumatic family history, characterized by emotional neglect, abandonment, episodes of violence and poverty.

M's History of Neglect

M had survived, demonstrating a remarkable strength and resilience, but trauma inevitably had left its mark on her psyche. From the early, highly conflictual separation of her parents, M initially lived with her mother, then with her father and eventually with her maternal grandmother who became an important figure. M's relationship with her was strongly affective and very problematic. Grandmother was a serious hoarder who compulsively filled the house with countless useless objects. Moreover, since the choice to live with the grandmother had been opposed by father and mother, both parents refused to contribute financially. For this reason, M and her grandmother lived on the breadline, without electricity, cooking on a small stove and washing with cold water. M's mother linked financial support to M returning to live with her. Her father, on the other hand, with whom M had lived in previous years, had passively accepted the wishes of his second wife, who refused to have M and her brother in their house. Despite this situation, M continued to get good grades at school, met a young man and fell in love. Soon, this romance turned into a nightmare: her boyfriend would hit her for no reason, told her how to dress and controlled her. When M tried to leave him, he began to threaten her. He followed her, suddenly appearing in front of her house, tried several times to attack her and threatened to kill her.

As a result, M finally accepted her mother's invitation and joined her abroad. She experienced a short period of relative calm but then, after a few months, perhaps also due to increased consumption of cannabis, she began to perceive a progressive change in reality that was anguished and persecutory. The surrounding reality began to change, was less familiar, and led her to the experiential contingency that Blankenburg (1971) defines as *loss of natural evidence*, a situation in which the world around us ceases to be immediately understandable. The loss of common sense predicates the experience of objects and people as strangers full of ambiguity, forcing one into a continuous interpretative process. People's faces lose their usual physiognomy and become progressively distorted. Danger lurks in every corner, but is masked by apparent normality. It was at this point, when looking in the mirror, unable to find meaning in all her suffering, that M was able to discover a similarity between her face and that of Jesus. Confusion and malaise seemed to reside within an image that contained and gave meaning to her experience. M, however, failed to completely identify with the numinous power of this image, as her ego was still capable of criticism. She started to doubt what seemed to her an almost absolute truth. She moved away from the mirror and went to her mother, searching for someone who could give her back her sense of human experience.

The mother immediately answered M's question (Who am I? Am I Jesus?), with steely certainty saying: "Finally you have noticed!". And then she dealt a decisive blow to M's last traces of sanity by telling her, candidly, that she was not her father's daughter, having instead been conceived by her mother's amorous encounter with an extra-terrestrial being. M emerged from this brief dialogue even more bewildered and lost. The world became increasingly foreign and terrifying. People, especially men, seemed to look at her with a threatening gaze. She ran through the city chased by her ghosts, unable to call for help in a world full of enemies. Her race ended on the roof of a building from which, now in the grip of a nameless terror, she threw herself thinking that she could finally end her suffering. This story, briefly summarized here, came out gradually, in numerous weekly sessions (M was in psychotherapy at our outpatient mental health service). In these sessions, M had coherent discursive passages full of sadness, but these also alternated with moments in which her thoughts suddenly became concrete. In these moments, she had delirious ruminations on, amongst other things, relationships with UFOs and experiencing her body as foreign and paralyzed. In this situation, in which psychotic and non-psychotic functioning of the psyche alternated in an apparently random pattern, we decided to take our time and not immediately use pharmacological therapies. This decision was based on the fact that M seemed able to build a transference relationship where she could feel sufficiently safe to continue exploring her story. She was frightened about the idea of being psychotic or, as she often said, of falling back into psychosis. As the sessions continued, M, who had a rich vocabulary, was able to describe more clearly what she had gone through.

It was as if, at times, her world suddenly lost its familiar sense and was transformed into an unknown and dangerous one. In those moments, certain situations and people became confusing. The world could suddenly become difficult to understand, marked by an atmosphere of alarm and danger. Instead of epistemic trust (Fonagy and Allison, 2014; Fonagy et al., 2017a, 2017b), M seemed to have developed an epistemic hypervigilance that put her in a constant state of alert. "When I hear a door slamming, when I hear footsteps, even though somewhere in my brain I know it's my father who has come home, I'm terrified that it might not be him, that it might be someone who has broken into the house to hurt me."

On these occasions, the clinical picture seemed to shift towards a more clearly psychotic pathology, configuring a real paranoia. One might think that it is the outward projection of aggression and hatred – emotions strongly linked to trauma – that colour the world in a persecutory way. Even in this case, however, it is important to be aware of a possible differential diagnosis. In our opinion, it is more probable that in situations experienced by M as characterized by alarm and epistemic hypervigilance, a process occurred in which the abandoned and traumatized child takes over her adult part. In these moments, M is really a child and lives as if the anxious situations experienced in the past were present. Trauma, in fact, determines an overlap between past and present where memories are transformed into something that is actually taking place. Her adult mind recedes into the background and this causes a loss, albeit transitory, of her relationship with reality. Not taking these dynamics into account would lead to identifying her symptoms as psychotic and to intervening with pharmacological therapy.

In addition to this, she reported other disorientating experiences such as seeing a blue light that sometimes surrounded people, which she felt indicated possible extra-terrestrial encounters. At other times, however, everything seemed to return to normal and M could exist in a human world. During the sessions, it became clear that it was the affective element that determined the transition from one state to another. M's world was unfamiliar and full of an overwhelming enigmatic quality that forced her continuously to be vigilant. Even the most neutral situations, such as a person speaking to her in a waiting room or a mother holding a child, would trigger a disturbing question: "What's behind it? What are they hiding from me?". According to the theory of evolutionary systems (Panksepp and Biven, 2012; Schore, 2015), and the mechanistic hierarchical model (Holmes, 2020) where perception is the result of an interplay between internal generative models of reality and sensory data, we could say that this interplay mechanism was not working for her. By contrast, her generative models were rigid and repetitive. They described a hostile, unreliable and chaotic world. There was also something missing in the process whereby the generative model is progressively and continuously updated. In other words, the functional plasticity that normally supports general functioning and is aimed at responding to adaptive requests was lacking. The internal generative models failed to become more complex and flexible, in so doing they returned her to the same vision of reality. Moreover, we could observe that, in M's life, there were quite different alternating states. There was a dimension of apparent normality, that seemed to correspond to safe relational and affective situations with low emotional intensity. However, there was also another dimension – perhaps the more frequent one – of a more subjective experience with increased impressionability, distractibility and attention to details, cognitive interference, depersonalization, derealization, hypersensitivity to stimuli and fluctuating experiences of primary self-reference. This subjective experience, with its constant state of alarm and fear of having another psychotic episode, seemed strongly linked to the description of her basic symptoms (Gross, 2015).

The Mosaic of the Self: From Scattered Tesserae to a First Composition

In Jungian theory, the psyche is thought of as structurally dissociable, composed of a set of functional units aggregated according to specific affective tones (feeling-toned complexes) and coordinated by a main complex, the Ego.

The feeling-toned complexes, according to Gullotta and Alfani (2010) can be seen as a set of psychic contents (images, thoughts, memories, fantasies) which are related to each other by a common affective state. The more intense the affect, the more powerful the effect of the complex on the personality and the related representations that appear (or impose themselves) on the consciousness of the subject.

The ego-complex, linked both to the body and to self-representation, should orient consciousness and maintain direction in different situations: "The ego-complex in a normal person is the highest psychic authority. By this we mean the whole mass of ideas pertaining to the ego, which we think of as being accompanied by the powerful and ever-present feeling-tone of our own body" (Jung, 1907, para. 82).

Depending on their charge and how much energy they subtract from the psychic economy, we can speak of "healthy" or "pathological complexes". The latter subtract energy from the ego-complex that is then not able to remain stable and becomes overwhelmed by an autonomous complex. From the relational history of M and the intensity of her perceived symptomatology, it would seem that she was still immersed in an uroboric totality in which positive and negative elements were fused together (Neumann, 1956). She found herself overwhelmed by the power of this undifferentiated archetype. In fact, M seemed to have lost herself in her unconscious, abandoned in the company of horrors too great to be understood and managed on her own.

Caregivers should metabolize, soften and differentiate excessively strong affects in their infants, thus facilitating the symbolizing and humanizing of archetypes. If, on the other hand, this does not happen, as in the case of M, there is a psychic collapse. The emotional Ego (Jung, 1934) is dragged between two polarities: inflation or depression. In the absence of these emotions being *humanized* by dynamic and loving interactions with caregivers, the child's Ego is forced to identify with the archetypal bipolar energies that possess it.

According to Kalsched (1996, 2013), the mind tries to protect itself by activating primitive defences that turn off the Ego's ability to register overwhelming feelings of pain and depressive anguish. According to Fairbairn

(1952), the psyche uses its archaic aggressiveness as an agent of self-splitting. In so doing, the Ego protects itself while the affects and feelings are fragmented and encapsulated, preventing an integration of emotional experience. "The resulting architecture of the inner world is then bifurcated between a grandiose omnipotent (archetypal) defensive structure on the one hand which aggressively persecutes (while protecting) a mortified, humiliated, wounded 'innocent' child-self on the other, in order to keep it in" (Kalsched, 2013: 132).

Repeated and continuous experiences of relational failure, connected to the lack of affective attunement of both the caregiver and the context of care, with neglect and/or abuse, even in muted forms, can affect the development of the child's affective regulation skills and her physical and emotional response to external/internal stimuli.

As described by van der Kolk (2014), isolated traumatic episodes can produce single biological and behavioural responses without necessarily involving the whole personality. Instead, chronic abuse and neglect seem to have a more global effect on all the regulatory processes, both biological and psychological, thus producing the most devastating effects.

Investigating traumatic experiences while considering their extent can help the clinician to better identify the possible origin of the reported symptoms. As shown in this clinical case, the lack of information about the patient's traumatic childhood led the clinicians, initially, to categorize the symptom of "loss of control and loss of reality" as purely psychotic, despite their post-traumatic nature.

As Jung suggested, "the explosion of affect is a complete invasion of the individual, it pounces upon him like an enemy or a wild animal" (Jung, 1928, para. 267). In this fragmentation of the soul (Ferenczi, 1932), body/mind integration is wounded and the core of the Self cannot be incarnated (Kalsched, 2013).

In these fragmented, meaningless experiences, the child tries to find meaning and an explanation for his "not being loved". For the subject, the experience of not being loved or not being seen are introjected and understood as the subject not being able to live up to other's expectations or feeling unworthy of love. They shape beliefs and ideas of personal inadequacy and guilt. As a compensation for not being loved, they can also lead to grandiose ideas e.g., being divine (Schmidt, 2012) or "extra-terrestrial".

From studies on attachment and neuroscience we can make further considerations. The consequences of unresolved trauma for mothers or caregivers can lead to alterations in mood and stress management that damage affective regulation in the relationship with their child. This intersubjective psychopathogenic mechanism could underlie the intergenerational transmission of both relational trauma and dissociative defences when experiencing overwhelming and disturbing affective states. The mother's or caregiver's trauma can be transferred to the child even without active maltreatment (Mucci, 2014).

A Room for Trust: Challenges to Analytic Work

With traumatized patients, the work in the analytic room is often difficult because there is an inability to trust others and so the patients remain in a state of vigilance and fear. As Robert Stolorow (2007) explains, emotional trauma is "a catastrophic loss of innocence that permanently alters one's sense of being-in-the-world" (Stolorow, 2007: 16) and of being *safe in the world*.

In her encounter with the second team of therapists M perceived, probably for the first time in her life, that she could begin to trust someone. During the sessions, the positive transference that the patient had been progressively building allowed for a new form of attachment. M reported that the drugs prescribed by the previous team had "burned" her right brain, which we know allows for the emotional processing of experience and is the centre of creativity and imaginative capacity. What is more, during her first access to psychiatric services, M did not find a therapeutic space that could help her recover her capacity for non-verbal processing and social interactions. Instead, emotional communication had been brooked within a non-therapeutic alliance, where the first team of therapists was under pressure to admit her to hospital and give her drug therapy. In their urgency, there had been no time to form an alliance between M and the therapist. Thus, M found herself unable to process the unconscious affective contents, the *beta* elements described by Bion (1962), which remained in the mind as psychic fragments that couldn't be assimilated or narrated.

This case raises numerous theoretical and clinical issues. First, the trajectory of the changes in the disorder were linked to the change in both diagnostic and therapeutic methods. The first approach, responding to the most striking aspect of the symptoms (delusion, hallucinations) had quickly settled on a diagnosis of schizophrenia which was followed by an almost exclusively pharmacological treatment. The second focused instead on the possible traumatic origin of the same symptoms, thus giving space for a listening and therapeutic relationship with the patient. It seems as if, paradoxically, the old argument between Bleuler and Jung on the organic or psychological nature of schizophrenia had been revived. According to

Bleuler (1911), the symptoms of schizophrenia could have a psychological origin, but the cause of schizophrenia is to be found in an unidentified process of organic nature that results in the alteration of associative processes. "Dissociation", according to the Bleulerian etymon, is understood as the basic disorder of the disease. This dissociation could remain subclinical until psychological conditions trigger full-blown symptomatology. For Jung, on the other hand, the process is more nuanced, precisely because of the great importance attributed to affectivity, considered the true engine of psychic life (Gullotta and Alfani, 2010).[3] Moreover, Jung, wrote (1907) of an unspecified constitution or disposition where both an original psychic weakness and an abnormal increase in the traumatic intensity of affects could produce the same result, namely the emergence of the disease.

In Jung's "non-specific factor" hypothesis, we find a close affinity with the concept of "anthropological vulnerability" provided by phenomenological psychopathology (Stanghellini, 2007). Here trauma is seen as the consequence of the encounter between the nature of the event and the individual response to it. Conceived in this way, it can be seen as the origin of different disorders, where the phenotypic expression could represent the result of multiple factors. These could include the cumulativeness and precocity of traumatic experiences, the degree of maturation of the Nervous System and any additional protective or risk factors that the person has encountered.

The Transdiagnostic Nature of Dissociative Phenomena

Starting from early adverse and chronic experiences, characterizing a traumatic development, it is possible to outline distinct psychopathological trajectories that lead to clinical pictures in adolescents/young adults with large areas of overlapping symptomatology.

For this reason, it becomes interesting to investigate these transdiagnostic organizers, which can represent real endophenotypes, that are a link between a "before" (the trauma), relating to early genetic and environmental factors, and an "after", characterized by a multiplicity of symptoms. Among these factors, a particular role is played by the wide range of phenomena included in the concept of dissociation. The transdiagnostic nature of dissociative phenomena is linked to their heterogeneity, which phenomenologically can be distinguished between symptoms of detachment and symptoms of compartmentalization. The first category includes both experiences of detachment from oneself, from one's body, from one's emotions and from reality, such as depersonalization and derealization and symptoms of emotional anaesthesia, déjà-vu and autoscopic experiences outside the body. The second category includes experiences such as dissociative amnesia, intrusive traumatic memories, somatoform phenomena and dissociative identity disorder (DID) (compartmentalization of normally integrated functions such as memory, body, motor skills and identity).

In the presence of a previous trauma, not known to the consciousness of the subject, we can observe that even the pre-delirious atmosphere (Jaspers, 1959), as well as the basic symptoms, could in some cases be interpreted as the gradual re-emergence of frightening psychic elements, linked to the traumatic experience. From this perspective, delusions could have the protective function of preventing the full re-emergence at the conscious level of an overwhelming affect connected to the traumatic experience.

If psychosis is an attempt by the subject to protect himself from affects progressively emerging in consciousness, and potentially overwhelming it, this suggests, according to Moskowitz, Dorahy and Schäfer (2018), the existence of a dynamic relationship between psychosis and dissociation; the more the subject can dissociate the less he needs to create delusions, as the contents that could trigger delusions are outside the subject's consciousness thanks to the protective function (Poletti, 2021).

The development of the Self can be understood as the progressive capacity of the mind to represent itself (Parnas and Henriksen, 2014). Here, we need to look at the distinction between the reflexive Self and the minimal Self (Dennett, 1991; Parnas and Handest, 2003), where the former can be understood as the narrative centre around which memories, representations, stories, and decisions revolve (Dennett, 1991). The minimal Self, on the other hand, does not have the experience of time and does not express itself verbally or through any other kind of conscious representation. It concerns the primary experience of the Self, allowing the experience itself to be lived and felt as subjective. The basic constant of the functioning of the minimal Self is self-referral, that is, the perceived and lived experience that belongs to the subject, as can be seen from the use of the pronoun "I" (Poletti, 2021).

The minimal Self thus corresponds to a direct, tacit and implicit access to our conscious experience of the world, unmediated by reflexive functions of a superior cognitive order. It is a multidimensional construct whose primary functions are a sense of ownership and a sense of agency.

The emergence of the reflexive Self does not eliminate or replace the minimal Self, which continues to operate on an implicit level: these two levels of Self operate in parallel. The minimal Self provides the backbone for the functioning of the reflexive Self. Only abnormal, pathological or experimentally induced conditions might bring out of the shadows the implicit and tacit structure of the subjective experience of internal and external reality, in other words the minimal Self.

Neurobiological vulnerability and parents' inadequate responsiveness may diachronically affect the child's ability to integrate – that is, to sustain the bidirectional exchange of information between inner and outer worlds (sensorimotor and intersubjective) – thus producing, over time, a fragile sense of agency. In this framework, genetic and environmental risks could combine and empower each other, because they could damage the functioning of the mind: the minimal pre-reflective and preverbal Self.

The presence of a subjective vulnerability at the level of the minimal Self can help to explain the conceptual affinity between psychosis and dissociation. On the one hand, this conceptual affinity refers to the idea of a unity of psychic disorders, so that different syndromes would simply be expressions that differ in size but not in nature. On the other hand, it emphasizes the pathogenetic value of traumatic experiences, gives value to the patient's history and engages the therapist in an attentive and participatory relationship, that is capable of providing the patient with the maximum amount of psychological experience he can tolerate (Jung, 1939). It also encourages the therapist to maintain enthusiasm and confidence in his own therapeutic intuition (Jung, 1939) and to work while keeping his imagination active, because we cannot understand something that we cannot imagine (Calland, 2022).

Finding Meaning: From Chaos to the Analytical Encounter

In M's case, it was this possibility to see her imaginatively as a "neglected" child (Bovensiepen, 2022) that activated a different approach, together with the ability to accept the risk of entering an apparently delirious world with her, without being frightened and without having to resort to immediate diagnostic objectification. It also seems that this clinical situation could symbolize the difficulties of developing one's individuality which can result from traumatic experiences. The way M experiences the world and the speed with which an internal representation, imbued with distrust and danger, is activated in the face of apparently neutral life situations, suggests a deep original disorder that involves primitive layers of the psyche, layers in which the psychic and the somatic are still one and the same (Jung, 1948). The activation of M does not occur only at the level of thoughts or sensory perceptions but involves the whole body. Her sense of alarm is expressed through perceptual distortion (trees suddenly become people who have malicious intent) and somatic activation (the heart beats faster, the stomach tightens) that radically changes her relationship with the world. The biggest problem is that this activation not only seems real for her but it extends to all life situations. It is as if a mechanism which is deeper than that which can be inferred is operating underneath. The depth and extension of the representations which are assimilated in an automatic and rigid way, suggest the existence of an archetypal level. This term lends itself, as in many Jungian writings, to multiple readings. We understand the archetype precisely as a form without content, not an inherited representation, but an inherited possibility of representation.

"The archetype in itself is empty and purely formal, nothing more than a *facultas praeformandi*, a possibility of representation which is given *a priori*" (Jung, 1938, para. 155). From this perspective, Jung states that for children, before meeting the real parents, the encounter is with the parental archetype. It is then up to the real parents to allow the archetype to humanize itself by transforming itself into more diversified elements where the emerging ego-complex can activate a path of integration and differentiation. In the case of M, as well as in all those cases in which there is a very early traumatic experience, it is this process of humanization of the archetype that is missing (Schwartz-Salant, 1989). The archetype of the mother, then, instead of transforming and articulating itself in the relationship with the real mother, remains (if the mother is absent or unavailable) at an archetypal stage, that of the Great Mother simultaneously bringing nourishment and destruction. In this situation, the subject cannot relate to others in a healthy way because the relational aspect guided by the maternal archetype is lacking. Relationships will be framed by ambivalent affects, alternating between desire and fear thus paralyzing the patient who will not be able to experience his real life. Looking again at M's story, we can understand why she, when faced with any relational situation, was prone to immediately perceive its dark side and was therefore unable to decipher what was happening in the world around her. That is why, for most of the time, she found herself immersed in an affective state of alarm. This led M, via the defensive mechanism of avoidance, to abandon the situation itself, seeking refuge in her room and solitude. The enigmatic quality of the world around her, however, does not disappear and activates a mechanism of continuous rumination in a desperate attempt to come to terms with it. M's relationship with her grandmother, although characterized by problematic elements, seems to have represented the only protective factor capable of preventing her from falling into a psychotic world, thanks to a partial humanization of the maternal archetype.

What is more, the paternal archetype, unable to express itself with a real father – as opposed to an extra-terrestrial paternity – can only remain in the dimension of a divine or, more precisely, non-terrestrial being, thus framing, through a non-human birth, the motif of the divine child who will then find his own form in the image of Jesus. The divine father, however, is also characterized by maximum goodness, but also by the persecutory nature of his judgement. Thus, M related – in her only attempt at a romantic relationship – with a violent and possessive male figure who punishes her for the slightest mistake. In this situation, development is blocked at an archetypal level and therefore is rigid but active and can lead to a fascination with the divine world. M tried to find an explanation – on an intellectual level – for her suffering through esoteric studies, becoming passionate about UFOs and participating in meetings and conferences on the subject, until she became convinced of her double birth. As she was the daughter of two parents who separated immediately after her birth and who had never had a relationship with her, she was fascinated by theories about the relationship between humans and extra-terrestrials. These theories assert that extra-terrestrials select, among humans, people from whom they can subtract their soul in order to strengthen their own lives by becoming immortal which leaves humans de-animated and soulless (Stanghellini, 2004).

As Ferenczi (1932) noted, trauma is a real death or loss of the soul and therefore M felt empty, devoid of strength, and continuously invaded by contents foreign to the Self. Moreover, as Kalsched (2013) opined, if patients, during their developmental years, have lost the normal channels of self-esteem, the attempt to collect self-esteem through heroic identification with divine energies represents "the ways the self-care system provides for the survival of the soul in trauma – albeit at the cost of ego-flexibility and stable self-esteem regulation. In this way, trauma turns us into 'children of God' and leaves us with a life-long struggle to become human again" (Kalsched, 2013: 133). The evolutionary process that the latest therapy has started should lead to differentiation and humanization of these primordial images. For the first time in her life, thanks to the new therapeutic relationship, M felt accepted and heard. The analytical space became a centre of meaning and order, where previously there was only chaos and despair. The therapeutic couple, consisting of a psychiatrist and a psychologist,[4] could metaphorically have represented the role that Jung attributes to the "godfather" and the "godmother" (Jung, 1936/37), namely the possibility of moving from the archetype of parents to a more human and less frightening relationship.

Perhaps, by clearly stating the safety of the therapeutic space we provided – "whatever you say, you will not be hospitalized" – together with waiting for the patient to be ready to collect the fragments of her traumatic story and then integrating them into a possible narrative, allowed for her experience to be framed between past, present and future, in this way, activating her individuation path.

A special thanks to Isabella Panaccione, Psychiatrist, Psychoanalyst in training, colleague and friend "in the district".

Notes

1 The Complex Operative Unit "Prevention and Early Interventions" (PIPSM) is a public mental health service of the Local Health Authority (ASL ROMA 1) for patients between 14 and 25 years.
2 In Italy, hospitalization constitutes one of the many possible ways of psychiatric intervention. If the patient has openly communicated suicidal intent or if there are signs of his dangerousness, he must immediately be included in a full-time care program, even without hospitalization.
3 Bleuler (1906, 1911) gave great importance to affects, considering them as the real engine of psychic activity. However, with regard to schizophrenia, he hypothesized an organic origin, while conceiving a psychic origin for the symptoms.
4 The Complex Operative Unit "Prevention and Early Interventions" (PIPSM), is a public health service. Our procedures require that the first therapeutic sessions are carried out by a therapeutic couple, consisting of a psychiatrist and a psychologist. Once the therapeutic treatment has been chosen, the sessions are carried out only by the psychologist, for the psychotherapeutic work.

References

American Psychiatric Association (1952) *Diagnostic and Statistical Manual of Mental Disorder*, 1st edition. Arlington (VA): American Psychiatric Association Publishing.

American Psychiatric Association (1968) *Diagnostic and Statistical Manual of Mental Disorder*, 2nd edition. Arlington (VA): American Psychiatric Association Publishing.

American Psychiatric Association (1980) *Diagnostic and Statistical Manual of Mental Disorder*, 3rd edition. Arlington (VA): American Psychiatric Association Publishing.

American Psychiatric Association (1987) *Diagnostic and Statistical Manual of Mental Disorder*, 3rd edition. (text rev.) Arlington (VA): American Psychiatric Association Publishing.

American Psychiatric Association (2000) *Diagnostic and Statistical Manual of Mental Disorder*, 4th edition. (text rev.) Arlington (VA): American Psychiatric Association Publishing.

American Psychiatric Association (2013) *Diagnostic and Statistical Manual of Mental Disorder*, 5th edition. Arlington (VA): American Psychiatric Association Publishing.

Anda, R.F., Brown, D.W., Felitti, V.J., Bremner, J.D., Dube, S.R. and Giles, W.H. (2007) "Adverse childhood experiences and prescribed psychotropic medications in adults", *American Journal of Preventive Medicine*, 32(5): 389–394.

Bernstein, D.P. and Fink, L. (1994) "Initial reliability and validity of a new retrospective measure of child abuse and neglect", *American Journal of Psychiatry*, 151(8): 1132–1136.

Bion, W.R. (1962 [1984]) *Learning from Experience*. London: Routledge.

Blankenburg, W. (1971) *Der Verlust der Natürlichen Selbstverständlichkeit: Ein Beitrag zur Psychopathologie Symptomarmer Schizophrenien*. Berlin: Parodos.

Bleuler, E. (1906) *Affektivitat, Suggestibilitat, Paranoia*. Verlag Classic Edition.

Bleuler E. (1911) *Dementia Praecox oder Gruppe der Schizophrenien*. Leipzig und Wien: Franz Deuticke.

Bovensiepen, G. (2022) "Destructiveness: A 'neglected child' in the theory of analytical psychology", *Journal of Analytical Psychology*, 67(4): 999–1019.

Calland, R. (2022) "Facilitating the emergence of hidden dissociative identity disorder: Finding the lost maiden medusa", *Journal of Analytical Psychology*, 67(1): 73–87.

Caretti, V., Craparo, G. and Schimmenti, A. (2013) *Memorie Traumatiche e Mentalizzazione: Teoria, Ricerca e Clinica*. Roma: Astrolabio.

Dennett, D.C. (1991) *Consciousness Explained*. London: Penguin Books.

Dube, S.R., Anda, R.F., Felitti, V.J., Chapman, D.P., Williamson, D.F. and Giles, W.H. (2001) "Childhood abuse, household dysfunction, and the risk of attempted suicide throughout the life span: Findings from the adverse childhood experiences study", *JAMA*, 286(24): 3089–3096.

Etain, B., Aas, M., Andreassen, O.A., Lorentzen, S., Dieset, I., Gard, S., Kahn, J.P., Bellivier, F., Leboyer, M., Melle, I. and Henry, C. (2013) "Childhood trauma is associated with severe clinical characteristics of bipolar disorders", *The Journal of Clinical Psychiatry*, 74(10): 991–998.

Fairbairn, W.R.D. (1952) *Psychoanalytic Studies of the Personality*. London: Routledge.

Ferenczi, S. (1932 [1995]) *The Clinical Diary of Sandor Ferenczi*. J. Dupont (ed.) Cambridge, MA: Harvard University Press.

Fonagy, P. and Allison, E. (2014) "The role of mentalizing and epistemic trust in the therapeutic relationship", *Psychotherapy (Chicago, Ill.)*, 51(3): 372–380.

Fonagy, P., Luyten, P., Allison, E. and Campbell, C. (2017a) "What we have changed our minds about: Part 1. Borderline personality disorder, epistemic trust and the developmental significance of social communication", *Borderline Personality Disorder and Emotion Dysregulation*, 4(11).

Fonagy, P., Luyten, P., Allison, E. and Campbell, C. (2017b) "What we have changed our minds about: Part 2. Borderline personality disorder, epistemic trust and the developmental significance of social communication", *Borderline Personality Disorder and Emotion Dysregulation*, 4(9).

Fuchs, T. (2021) *In Defence of the Human Being: Foundational Questions of an Embodied Anthropology*. London: Oxford University Press.

Gross, J.J. (2015) *Handbook of Emotion Regulation*. New York: Guilford Press.

Gullotta, C. and Alfani, F. (2010) "I complessi e le cause della dementia praecox", *Rivista di psicologia analitica*, 30(82): 93–104.

Holmes, J. (2020) *The Brain has a Mind of its Own. Attachment, Neurobiology, and the New Science of Psychotherapy*. Confer Books.

Jaspers, K. (1959 [1997]) *General Psychopathology*, (trans. J. Hoening and M.W. Hamilton). Baltimore and London: Johns Hopkins University Press.

Jung, C.G. (1907) *The Psychology of Dementia Praecox*. CW3. Princeton, NJ: Princeton University Press.

Jung, C.G. (1912) *The Theory of Psychoanalysis*. CW4. Princeton, NJ: Princeton University Press.

Jung, C.G. (1928) *The Therapeutic Value of Abreaction*. CW16. Princeton, NJ: Princeton University Press.

Jung, C.G. (1934) *A Review of the Complex Theory*. CW8. Princeton, NJ: Princeton University Press.

Jung, C.G. (1936/37) *The Concept of the Collective Unconscious*. CW9/1. Princeton, NJ: Princeton University Press.

Jung, C.G. (1938) *Psychological Aspects of the Mother Archetype*. CW9/1. Princeton, NJ: Princeton University Press.

Jung, C.G. (1939) *On the Psychogenesis of Schizophrenia*. CW3. Princeton, NJ: Princeton University Press.

Jung, C.G. (1948) *On Psychic Energy*. CW8. Princeton, NJ: Princeton University Press.

Kalsched D. (1996) *The Inner World of Trauma: Archetypal Defences of the Personal Spirit*. New York: Routledge.

Kalsched, D. (2013) *Trauma and the Soul*. New York: Routledge.

Liotti, G. (2005) "Trauma e dissociazione alla luce della teoria dell'attaccamento", *Infanzia e adolescenza*, 4(3): 107–126.

Liotti, G. and Farina, B. (2011) *Sviluppi Traumatici: Eziopatogenesi, Clinica e Terapia della Dimensione Dissociativa*. Milano: Raffaello Cortina Editore.

Moskowitz, A., Dorahy, M.J. and Schäfer, I. (2018) *Psychosis, Trauma and Dissociation: Evolving Perspectives on Severe Psychopathology*. New York: John Wiley & Sons.

Mucci, C. (2014) *Trauma e Perdono. Una Prospettiva Psicoanalitica Intergenerazionale*. Milano: Raffaello Cortina Editore.

Neumann, E. (1956) *The Great Mother: An Analysis of the Archetype*. Princeton, NJ: Princeton University Press.

Panksepp, J. and Biven, L. (2012) *The Archaeology of Mind: Neuroevolutionary Origins of Human Emotions*. New York: W.W. Norton & Co.

Parnas, J. and Handest, P. (2003) "Phenomenology of anomalous self-experience in early schizophrenia", *Comprehensive Psychiatry*, 44(2): 121–134.

Parnas J. and Henriksen M.G. (2014) "Disordered Self in the schizophrenia spectrum: a clinical and research perspective", *Harvard Review of Psychiatry*, 22(5): 251–265.

Poletti, M. (2021) *Prima della Schizophrenia*. Roma: Giovanni Fioriti Editore.

Quarantini, L.C., Miranda-Scippa, A., Nery-Fernandes, F., Andrade-Nascimento, M., Galvão-de-Almeida, A., Guimarães, J.L., Teles, C.A., Netto, L.R., Lira, S.B., de Oliveira, I.R., Post, R.M., Kapczinski, F. and Koenen, K.C. (2010) "The impact of comorbid posttraumatic stress disorder on bipolar disorder patients", *Journal of Affective Disorders*, 123(1–3): 71–76.

Schmidt, M. (2012) "Psychic skin: Psychotic defences, borderline process and delusions", *Journal of Analytical Psychology*, 57(1): 21–39.

Schore, A.N. (2015) *Affect Regulation and the Origin of the Self: The Neurobiology of Emotional Development*. London: Routledge.

Schwartz-Salant, N. (1989) *The Borderline Personality: Vision and Healing*. Wilmette, IL: Chiron Publications.

Stanghellini, G. (2004) *Disembodied Spirits and Deanimated Bodies: The Psychopathology of Common Sense*. Oxford, UK: Oxford University Press.

Stanghellini, G. (2007) *Antropologia della vulnerabilità*, Milano: Feltrinelli Editore.

Stolorow, R. (2007) *Trauma and Human Existence: Autobiographical, Psychoanalytic, and Philosophical Reflections*. London: Routledge.

van der Kolk, B. (2014) *The Body Keeps the Score. Brain, Mind, and Body in the Healing of Trauma*. New York: Viking.

Chapter 7

Trauma and Dissociation

A Psychodynamic Perspective

Emanuela Mundo

Introduction

In her book *Coming into Mind* (Wilkinson, 2006), Margaret Wilkinson examines the interactions between mind, brain and traumatic experiences from a Jungian standpoint. From this perspective, this chapter will explore what constitutes a traumatic event for a particular patient (with reference to Jungian Complex Theory) and the consequences of this on his subjective experience. The clinical implications of the impact of an event which was traumatic for a patient will also be discussed. These correlates, which are observed in the clinical setting, vary from the more common (from conversion to dissociative phenomena) to the less common (i.e., Dissociative Identity Disorder – DID – and its variations). Trauma-related clinical phenomena are often not discrete in the clinical setting; in fact, they may be observed as on a continuum or as a frequent shifting from one phenomenon to another with different intensity. The clinical effects which we can observe in traumatized patients are related to changes that trauma induces on mind-brain interactions which have been described in the literature and are evolving with current research. Among these trauma-induced changes, particular attention will be given to the *kindling* phenomenon, which I feel is critical for the patient and for the patient-clinician interaction.

What happens to the clinician's mind-brain system in its encounter with a traumatized patient? This meeting may become, for the therapist, a traumatic experience in itself, which needs to be recognized and processed both in and out of the session. Managing dissociation in the clinical setting with traumatized patients is of paramount importance for the outcome of the treatment. Some recommendations on how to deal with correlates of traumatization which may arise in psychodynamically-oriented therapy will also be discussed.

DOI: 10.4324/9781003298076-10

The possibility that a traumatic experience may become an opportunity for healing and transformation of both the patient's and therapist's mind-brain system will be addressed. The reference diagnostic guidelines used in this chapter are taken mainly from the Second Edition of the Psychodynamic Diagnostic Manual (PDM-2) (Lingiardi and McWilliams, 2017) rather than from the Fifth Edition of the Diagnostic and Statistical Manual (DSM-5) (American Psychiatric Association [APA], 2013), since PDM-2 has been designed to be psychodynamically-oriented.

What is Trauma?

Following the first theorization of trauma by Sigmund Freud as the trigger for neuroses (1894), Carl Gustav Jung highlighted a critical aspect that is at the core of the present work, namely the subjective nature of the traumatic experience. Jung was the first psychoanalyst, although not the only one, to suggest that there is an individual predisposition to be traumatized by in fact any event, even by fantasies (Jung, 1912). In *On the Psychology of the Unconscious* Jung states:

> the intensity of a trauma has very little pathogenic significance in itself, but it must have a special significance for the patient. This is to say that it is not the shock as such that has a pathogenic effect under all circumstances, but in order to have an effect, it must impinge on a special psychic disposition, which may, in certain circumstances, consist in the patient's unconsciously attributing a specific significance to the shock. Here we have a possible key to the "predisposition".
>
> (Jung, 1917, para. 9)

Actually, Jung, early in his work, minimized the impact of exogenous trauma on complex formation,[1] instead emphasizing that complexes are caused by endogenous trauma caused by conflictual fantasies.

In more recent times, supporting this hypothesis, Donald Kalsched (1996) has claimed that the pathological effect of trauma requires an external event and a psychological internal factor. Thus, outer trauma alone doesn't induce dissociation/splitting. A wide field of research in both clinical psychology and psychoanalysis has been dedicated to the study of inner psychic characteristics of trauma victims. This field is called victimology (van Dijk, 1999; Yilmaz, 2021) and is not the focus of this chapter. Trauma is described, by diagnostic manuals for mental disorders (e.g., DSM-5-TR, APA, 2022), as a specific event outside the range of normal events. This is a very broad description which is not helpful when applied to psychodynamically-oriented clinical observation. In fact, this is more inclined not to focus on the severity of the external life event, instead it looks at the unique predisposition of the individual to be traumatized.

A more subject-oriented definition of trauma is found in the PDM-2, which identifies five different types of trauma according to a more relational context, including consideration of different ways they affect the individual, his/her subjective predisposition and age at the occurrence of trauma:

Type I, impersonal/accidental/disaster/shock trauma, which are not intentionally caused by anyone. This category has recently been expanded by some diagnostic manuals (e.g., DSM-5-TR, APA, 2022) to include illness and medical conditions;

Type II, interpersonal trauma, perpetrated by a human being on another. This type of traumatic experience can be either a one-off or repeated over months/years. The interpersonal dimension of the trauma is particularly important with regard to symptom severity, which is worse when the perpetrator is someone known or related to the victim (or who has a role or relationship that involves nurturance or protection that is used to dupe the victim). This pattern is called "betrayal trauma". Type II betrayal trauma typically involves a child's parents or caregivers, with one abusing the child, while the other is negligent. Another typical situation is a sentimental relationship between two individuals, one of whom may be traumatized by stalking, aggressive or even violent behaviour. A common feature of Type II trauma is when the victim turns to others for help, but they are not able to help, or when the victim is shamed or blamed for the traumatic event, which could be regarded as a *second* injury in itself. When it happens that the person who blames the victim is a parent or a caregiver, this becomes a core component of betrayal trauma;

Type III, identity trauma, based on largely immutable individual characteristics (ethno-racial group and features, gender, gender identity, and sexual orientation) that become a focus for victimization;

Type IV, community trauma, based on identity, derived from belonging to certain cultures, traditions, cultural and/or community minorities, which may be attacked, isolated or discriminated;

Type V, ongoing, layered, based on re-victimization and re-traumatization. Type V trauma includes "cumulative trauma". The definition of "cumulative trauma" (Khan, 1974) originally refers to recurrent unmet needs and neglect that have an accumulative devastating effect on child development. This partially overlaps with Winnicott's description of "primitive agonies", the experience of which is unthinkable (Winnicott, 1974).

This type of trauma is critical for professionals who treat traumatized individuals because of transference (the therapist is experienced as the negligent or abusing parent) and countertransference (experience of mistrust, attempts to reparent the patient) issues related to re-traumatization in therapy.

The Many Faces of Dissociative Phenomenon

Defining dissociation in the clinical field of trauma is difficult since dissociation may appear in different phenomena (i.e., conversion, depersonalization/derealization and dissociation). Also, it is not uncommon to observe overlapping or shifts from one dissociation phenomenon to another within a session or in different sessions with the same patient.

The term *conversion* was coined by Freud (and linked to the diagnosis of hysteria, Breuer and Freud, 1895) to designate mostly neurological (but also somatic) symptoms not related to any organic condition. Rather, these symptoms arise from a partial repression of either unbearable events, intolerable/forbidden wishes and/or impulses which produce an excess of excitation. Freud originally attributed the "sum of excitation" to external trauma. With the well-known concept of "primary gain" he suggested that for a subject it is better to suffer the symptom than to be conscious of the forbidden wish or impulse. *La belle indifférence* of the patient to their symptoms is the expression of primary gain. Although the symptoms disturb the patient, they are preferable to the unbearable alternative (Mundo and O'Neil, 2017).

The generic understanding of conversion refers to any "psychogenic" symptom that mimics an organic, mostly neurological, condition, frequently related to traumatic experiences either experienced or fantasized. The medical diagnosis of conversion requires a psychogenic aetiology. The final diagnosis is often made by a neurologist, who excludes the presence of organic disease, and then may refer the patient to a psychiatrist or therapist.

It is quite common to witness a clear example of conversion in clinical practice with traumatized patients. As an example, a female patient of mine wakes up with a strong headache and hand/fingers dysesthesia (from Mundo and O'Neil, 2017). During a session, she describes an apparent innocuous argument with her sister where she reports: "I wanted to strangle her!". This verbalization may cause the pain and the "pseudo neurological symptoms" to vanish, a clear signal of the somatic conversion of unbearable feelings towards her sister. The primary gain is that it is better for the patient to have pain and dysesthesia than to recognize her conflicting and unbearable feelings towards her sister. Further treatment may also reveal something more.

In this clinical example, I found that identical pain and neurological symptoms emerged as a result of having been beaten in the head 30 years ago. The onset occurred following a nightmare the night before, which was triggered by the appearance of a man on the street who reminded her of her original assailant (her father).

In *depersonalization/derealization*, the central symptom is the feeling of being detached from the self, one's own body (depersonalization), the environment or the social context (derealization) while reality testing is intact (this is a differential diagnosis for psychotic conditions). Depersonalization may feel like a general sense of one's body not being one's own; of being "me" in a body which is somehow "not me". The experience commonly includes the whole body, and more rarely parts of it: "Parts of my body feel as if they are artificial". Other somatic states commonly co-occur (e.g., dizziness, blurred or altered vision). Most patients can also experience anxiety symptoms, either psychic or somatic. Depersonalization varies from mild to severe and when it is severe may be extremely unpleasant. In some cases, depersonalization may even induce quietness, when its defensive function is most effective. In derealization, the world seems unreal, or as if it is seen from under a glass. The patient may say "I feel strange, as if I were cut off from the world and the world is strange and detached to me" as in the self-report questionnaire by Sierra and Berrios (2000: 161–162). Depersonalization and derealization can exhibit a wide range of symptomatic distress and social impairment. The extreme emotional pain of subjects often appears incongruent with their apparent ability to function. Symptom intensity may be constant or may wax and wane, sometimes triggered by specific situations (e.g., artificial light, crowded places). Common precipitants of depersonalization and derealization are panic attacks, cannabis intoxication and psychosocial stressors.

The therapist may find that a patient with depersonalization or derealization presents as silent, monotonous, or emotionally "flat". What is more, the therapist may experience a variety of emotional states himself including emptiness, unreality, sleepiness, distraction or boredom. These feelings may be seen as a defence against a clinical situation that lacks feelings, fantasies, memories and dreams, in which the therapist may find himself at a loss as to how to interact or interpret symptoms and silences. The possibility of a transference-countertransference enactment should be always considered (e.g., the patient or the therapist may abruptly interrupt the session, the therapist may fall asleep).

Dissociation. Over the past century and a half, the meaning of the term "dissociation" has evolved considerably. Dissociation was originally seen as a type of hysteria, related to conversion, but distinct from depersonalization. It included amnesia, fugues, certain altered states of consciousness and multiple personalities.

It is not the aim of this chapter to describe the evolution of the concept of dissociation with its polymorphic clinical equivalents. Instead, I think it would be more useful to describe the different "faces" of dissociation to aid clinicians and therapists in dealing with these phenomena and help the patients "undo" dissociation, as Wilkinson states (2006). Dissociation needs to be undone because it implies a sort of self-maintaining state that seriously affects the mind-brain system in both the patient and, possibly, the therapist.

Dissociation is described in the DSM-5 as "the disruption of and/or discontinuity in the normal integration of consciousness, memory, identity, emotion, perception, body representation, motor control, and behaviour" (APA, 2013: 291). To better recognize dissociation, it should be remembered that dissociative symptoms may appear as "negative" or "positive". "Negative" dissociative symptoms involve the absence or the withdrawal of something, such as dissociation of memory (amnesia), sensation (conversion anaesthesia) or affect (emotional blunting). Examples of "positive" dissociative symptoms are the intrusion of something, such as the sensory re-experiencing of a trauma (flashbacks, hyperarousal), or any other intrusion of affect, knowledge, sensation or behaviour (action, unintended vocalization, etc.). Looking beyond the definitions, describing dissociation as a subjective experience appears to be more useful for the clinical management of dissociation itself and its consequences during psychodynamic therapy. It should be remembered that dissociation can be seen as a continuum from conversion symptoms to the disruption of a sense of self, as well as in the physiological integration of consciousness, memory, identity, emotion, perceptions, body representation, motor control and behaviour.

Another quite rare form of dissociation is called *"dissociative multiplicity", as described in PDM-2*. This is a plurality of consciousness, most obvious in DID, in which two types of dissociation (dissociation as described in diagnostic manuals and depersonalization/derealization) commonly co-occur. The most recent estimate of the prevalence of DID is 1.5% in the general population (APA, 2013). This figure is worthy of some critical consideration as it appears to be high and may be an epiphenomenon/secondary effect of other disorders (e.g., auditory hallucinations, delusional perceptions in schizophrenia; rapid changes of mood and behaviour in mood disorders).

In DID it appears that there is more than one self occupying the centre of consciousness, that there is more than one centre of subjective experience, alternatively dissociated or depersonalized/de-realized. In DID every experience may be experienced as alien, as "not-me". The range of symptomatic expressions varies widely, however, from person to person, and may also vary over time within the same individual. Some DID patients seem to have led relatively "normal" lives until a trauma in adulthood precipitates a general deterioration in their adaptive functioning.

The "default" subject, the one who most often interacts with "the real world", often referred to as the "host", may remarkably be without subjective symptoms, apart from experiencing that he or she has recurrent intervals of "lost time". Such individuals may discover something about their manifest behaviour from outside evidence or from other people who witnessed them during the amnestic interval. The "host" role is just that, and over time this role may be taken on by different alter-egos, known in DID as "alters".

If the alternate subject, or alter, appears in a therapy session, he may likewise be remarkably/surprisingly without subjective symptoms and may give a coherent account of experience during the interval in question. While the host may be ignorant of other selves, most of the alters are usually cognizant of the host and often of each other or, at least, of some subset of the others. More often, especially in the consulting room, the host does have symptoms which may include amnesia, depersonalization, derealization and any variety of "intrusion" symptoms from other self-states. Intrusions (and withdrawals) include others' voices, flashbacks, intrusion and withdrawal of emotions, thoughts, impulses, fears, sensations and so on.

Psychodynamic authors have approached dissociative psychopathology from many different perspectives. Hypnoid hysteria can be traced back to Breuer and Freud's *Studies on Hysteria* (1895), which placed altered states of consciousness under psychodynamic examination. Brenner (2001) explained dissociative multiplicity using Freud's (1938) "Splitting of the Ego in the Process of Defence". Tarnopolsky (2003) viewed dissociative multiplicity through the lens of Kleinian splitting. Several authors draw on the work of Fairbairn (1944) or Kohut (1984) to reinstate dissociation within the psychoanalytic frame. Bowlby's attachment theory (1982) has attracted wide attention for highlighting the role of attachment deficits in the aetiology of dissociative phenomena as severe as DID. Watkins and Watkins (1997), borrowing the concept of ego state from Paul Federn (1952), developed the ego state theory. The idea of ego states has led to a general interest for different states of self, beginning from infancy. This has led to a reconceptualization of psychodynamic thinking in order to frame a multiple self-state model of mind. The normal mind is now seen as constituted by a multiplicity of states, and DID emerges as a particular constellation from that multiplicity.

The multiple self-state model of mind arose from attachment theories and relational psychoanalysis, and has undergone robust research testing in infant attachment research and behaviour studies. In clinical cases of chronic trauma, the patient finds himself having to cope with different ways of being and experiencing himself. This leads to an inability for the subject to understand what has happened or what is happening in the moment. The resulting segregation of emotion, behaviour, and experience obstructs the creation of a coherent autobiographical narrative and altered subjectivity (Mundo and O'Neil, 2017).

The experience of severely dissociated and DID patients is quite complex and varies widely within the same individual at different times and across different individuals. These patients commonly experience "three realities" (Mundo and O'Neil, 2017). The first is "objective" reality – the reality that most people share. The second is "subjective" reality, or what is real for a given single consciousness – the locus of subjective experience. The third reality is generally experienced by alters, not always by the host: an internal virtual or phantom landscape, sometimes called the "inscape", wherein the various alters experience each other as cohabiting this space, much as different real people experience each other in the first reality.

A critical issue for clinical management is understanding the relationship patterns of dissociative patients, which can vary widely. DID patients may show a wide range of capabilities to function, for example, certain self-states look after the home, spouse and children, while others look after work. Good functioning may be more apparent than real and may appear more adaptive in certain contexts than others (e.g., workplace). The traumatic pattern may be compulsively repeated with other partners with patterns of re-victimization. Furthermore, the traumatic relationship may be re-experienced with the therapist from whom severe mistreatment is unconsciously feared. Patients with a history of trauma may seek help but rarely trust clinicians, and clinicians without special training can be scared or discouraged to treat dissociative patients and they can even suffer for vicarious traumatization or dissociation (see paragraph below). In addition, therapists working with severely traumatized patients may have to face hate and attacks during sessions and also, out of the sessions (e.g., outbursts, dramatic interruptions of the sessions, repeated acting out, self-injuries). Fordham states that in trauma, "the predominance of defence systems leads to the accumulation of violence and hostility" (Fordham, 1976: 91).

Donald Kalsched has developed further Fordham's seminal notions, suggesting that "early trauma liberates powerful volumes of volcanic hate in the infant psyche" (Kalsched, 2015: 481). Developments in attachment theory and affective neuroscience have already opened analysts to the understanding that the severe wounding of early unremembered trauma is not transformable through interpretation (Mundo, 2006; Fonagy, 2010). Instead, it will inevitably be repeated in the transference, leading to mutual "enactments" between the analytic partners and, hopefully, to a new outcome (Kalsched, 2015).

These are serious challenges for the therapists that may require specific training for managing difficult situations, and primitive defence mechanisms (e.g., projection, projective identification).

Trauma and Dissociation

It should be remembered that psychoanalysis arose from Freudian studies on trauma. Even though the history of trauma across the different psychoanalytic orientations is not the focus of this chapter, some aspects, which could be relevant for understanding secondary traumatization, neurobiology of kindling and its clinical management need to be considered.

The Freudian concept of *Nachträglichkeit*, as an example, is a sort of second injury, a generic repetitive additional effect which crosses the spectrum of trauma and severe neglect. This word has been translated into English as *deferred action* (Eickhoff, 2006), and more precisely translated into French as *après coup*, or "after shock". Jacques Lacan made it a central concept in French psychoanalysis, across different writings and at different times in the construction of his theoretical frame. *Après coup* occurs whenever new knowledge, life or the analytic experience induces a revision of past traumas. According to Lacan, the subject is born originally experiencing a trauma (Lacan, 1955) and any event may be traumatic for a subject, at a certain point, according to his phantom construction (Lacan, 2013). For most psychoanalytic theoretical frames, we manage traumatic events in the clinical setting as a re-traumatization that refers to some original trauma, either fantasized or experienced.

Freud and Breuer, who co-authored *Studies on Hysteria* (1895), originally identified the root of hysteria in women as child sexual abuse and specifically incest. Freud eventually reversed that emphasis to focus on the child's fantasies of sex instead of the reality of sexual abuse. However, other Freud contemporaries, notably Pierre Janet and Sandor Ferenczi, retained a focus on the trauma of childhood abuse, considering dissociation as the primary way used by a child (and later an adult) to cope with an unbearable event. As stated before, Jung formulated the concept of the traumatic complex which binds the concepts of trauma and dissociation in a clear way: "a traumatic complex brings about the dissociation of the psyche. The complex is not under control of the will and for this reason it possesses the quality of psychic autonomy" (Jung, 1928, para. 266). Jung also describes these complexes as "splinter psyches", dissociated fragments, which have become split off *because of* traumatic experience.

Contemporary literature is full of examples of cause-effect dynamics between trauma and dissociation, complex post-traumatic conditions and a wide variety of dissociative phenomena. Post-Traumatic Stress Disorder (see Chapter 6) involves an alteration of the self and these familiar indicators: many traumatized individuals describe having a pre-trauma and a post-trauma self and see the traumatic experience as a life-changing discontinuity. Misunderstanding or minimization of this subjective impact can lead to unhelpful comments and questions by the therapist that may retraumatize the patient as occurs in betrayal trauma.

Neurobiological Effects of Trauma: The Mind-Brain Relationship and Kindling

As stated in the Introduction of this chapter, the impact of a traumatic event depends on the psychological and biological predisposition of an individual to effectively process the actual event. According to some researchers (Schore, 2002; Mundo, 2009), traumatic experiences occurring during infancy, when the individual has not yet achieved the neurobiological development of some brain areas (i.e., hippocampus) and a complete representational ability, may have a different impact on the psychological development than more potentially traumatic experiences that occur later in life. Early traumatic experiences can be understood as embodied encounters with primary nurturing figures, which remain incorporated in memory as well as in synapses. One of the major consequences of early relational trauma is the difficulty – and sometimes impossibility – of integrating these early somatic-affective experiences into an individual's own narrative memory.

These clinical observations are consistent with the fact that, in the earlier stages of life, neurobiological structures are completing their neurodevelopment (e.g., neurogenesis, myelinization, differentiation, synaptogenesis, synaptic plasticity). Some authors have defined trauma as "the illness of brain/neuronal plasticity" (Ansermet and Magistretti, 2004: 129) implying that traumatic events induce damage in synaptic connections and in the possibility of creating new connections (useful for memory and learning processes) across neurons in different brain areas.

Structural and functional neuroimaging studies have pointed out that the main brain structures involved in encountering trauma are: the Hypothalamic-Pituitary-Adrenal (HPA) axis, the limbic system (with particular respect to amygdala and hippocampus) and the corpus callosum (for a more specific dissertation on neurobiology of trauma see Chapter 14).

One aspect that I would like to focus on in this chapter is what is known as the "kindling phenomenon". Kindling refers to a sort of sensitization of the neurobiological system (i.e., mainly limbic structures and their connections to the fear circuits and to the prefrontal cortex). The exposure to a stressor or a traumatic event sensitizes these brain structures adding "indelible ... engrams [that are] ... formed in the brain" (Rosen and Schulkin, 1998: 336). This sensitization implies that any event that may resemble the original traumatic event may elicit a "fear response", including hyperarousal, freezing and recurrent dissociation even in the absence of the traumatic event.

Neurobiological research has identified some changes occurring in individuals with post-traumatic dissociation that may also explain symptoms of a post-traumatic clinical presentation. Trauma affects the fear circuit that is regulated by the amygdala hippocampus system. Threats activate the fear system which releases stress hormones (glucocorticoids), inducing a change in the function of the cardiovascular system (increased blood pressure and heart rate, respiration rate and increased muscular response from the body). In addition to these adaptive responses, glucocorticoids are toxic for the part of the brain (hippocampus) which is responsible for historic autobiographic memory in such a way that when the amygdala overreacts the hippocampus downgrades its function. An interesting phenomenon occurring after acute traumatization is the so-called "kindling response". In kindling, a sensitized system may react *as if* the original trauma (single or multiple) is occurring when an almost neutral stimulus is present. In other words, psychological kindling is the changed pattern of neuronal responses to internal stimuli, clinically giving rise to flashbacks, nightmares and dissociation as a defence response.

Another interesting piece of neurobiological research explains one of the most frequent clinical phenomena: repetition compulsion. This had been observed by several psychoanalysts, including Freud, first in *Remembering, Repeating and Working Through* (1914) and later in *Beyond the Pleasure Principle* (1920) where he explains the repetition compulsion as an epiphenomenon of the death drive. Repetition compulsion consists in the tendency of the subject to expose himself to situations that resemble the original traumatic one(s) either symbolically or in reality and in re-living the trauma in dreams and re-enaction.

Some researchers have found that the repetition is associated with the release, in the brain, of endogenous opioids which reduce pain and have other effects inducing relief in traumatized patients. This biological mechanism may explain a kind of addiction of the victim to re-traumatization (Orlandini, 2004; van der Kolk, 2014). This addiction should be considered one of the primaries focuses of psychodynamic psychotherapy with traumatized patients.

Another issue which is related to the clinical understanding of trauma and dissociation is the neurobiological effect of dissociation itself. When kindling (and dissociation) occurs, stress hormones (e.g., glucocorticoids) are released into the blood stream and affect the brain structures that are already compromised in volume and function by the trauma(s). This particularly affects the hippocampus, which is a brain region expressing the largest number of receptors for glucocorticoids. This means that subsequent dissociations of a traumatized individual affect a brain region which is already damaged by the original trauma and dissociation. As a result, the functioning of the hippocampus is increasingly stressed with a subsequent further unbalanced relationship to the amygdala, which is, in turn, activated even more. These effects need to be recognized and corrected: excess of sensory memories, a hypersensitivity to external and internal stimuli and a blurred sense of self and identity. These brain effects have, of course, an impact on how the mind produces different degrees of dissociation and disruptive behaviours: this is a kindled response (Scaer, 2001).

Managing Dissociation in the Clinical Setting

The multiplicity of dissociative phenomena means that it is complex to manage dissociation in the clinical setting. This is a serious challenge for the therapist who is called to "undo" it when it occurs (Wilkinson, 2006: 94). There are many reasons why dissociation needs to be un-done in the mind-brain of patients. The first and self-evident one is that dissociation splits the psyche and, thus, it is the opposite of integration. The dissociative phenomena keep the traumatic experiences alive and active which prevents healing and transformation in treatment. Sensorial memories replace semantic memories, flash backs interrupt the continuity of the subjective experience and make the patient re-experience the traumatic event in both his mind and his brain. The time of trauma becomes suspended in a kind of eternal time, which repeats itself and interferes with a secure and cohesive sense of self. In addition, there are neurobiological consequences of re-experiencing trauma. The re-activation of the HPA stress system induces an excessive release of stress hormones (i.e., glucocorticoids) that are toxic for some brain regions (mainly the hippocampus) inducing cell death and seriously impairing hippocampus functioning with its connections to brain regions that are critical for integration (Mundo, 2009).

Dissociative phenomena may reappear (and quite often do) during treatment because of the treatment itself, when traumatic memories arise from the inner world of the patient. This experience of dissociation during the session is often traumatic for both the patients and the therapist, and needs serious consideration and management. First, the therapist should be prepared for this phenomenon which is at the core of the experience of treatment with traumatized patients. Depersonalization, derealization, physical symptoms, sudden interruption of speech, increased arousal, lack of emotional and motor control and other intrusion of affects, knowledge, sensation or behaviour are, as stated earlier, signs and symptoms of dissociation and need to be recognized by the therapist, even when they appear to be less severe or subliminal.

What does the therapist need to do, in order to "un-do" dissociation and prevent re-traumatization during the session? Following what we have learned from neuroscience research, during trauma and dissociation there is an imbalance in amygdala hippocampus functioning and an increased arousal. The amygdala (and its connections with cortical regions and the HPA) overreacts while the hippocampus does not function properly. Thus, we need to balance the function of these two brain structures (and their complex connections with other cerebral regions) and we can do this with the help of our main therapeutic instruments: holding and talking. The holding must be symbolic rather than actual (physical) since physical contact with patients may have a high traumatic potential. Rather, symbolic holding consists of different strategies also depending on the setting. In a vis-à-vis setting it may be maintaining eye contact and a sympathetic facial expression, while in a classical "on the couch setting", holding may imply different strategies, like talking to the patient with specific tones and words. Margaret Wilkinson (2006) explains these tools in a quite impressive way when she states that the therapist should not use primary colours but rather pastel colours: the voice should be low and quiet, words should be simple and reassuring, aimed to remind the dissociated patients that nothing bad is happening at that moment of the session and that in the *hic et nunc* of the session he is safe.

In a vis-à-vis setting the therapist's facial expression can be a very good tool for holding during the session, but we must be very careful with exposing the patient to excessive sympathy or disgust, fear or anxiety (Beauregard, 2007). Expressing excessive sympathy or fear or preoccupation for the patient's state of mind may increase the dissociative post-traumatic reactions, which can in turn increase the activity of the "kindled" (i.e., sensitised) amygdala, worsening the patient's mind-brain distress. A good holding strategy is also, if the setting does not imply eye contact (i.e., the patient is on the couch) to verbalize with quiet and simple words (the hippocampus is overstimulated) that the room of the session is a safe place, that what is happening in the patient's mind is not happening at the present moment but happened in the past and that the unbearable feelings can actually be recollected slowly and elaborated. Interpretation should be avoided when the patient is dissociated.

Vicarious Traumatization and Dissociation: The Experience of the Therapist with Trauma Victims

Patients often fear that their own therapy can affect the therapist in various ways. These concerns are quite appropriate, particularly when the patients have been traumatized. In fact, the therapist may suffer from secondary traumatization/dissociation. The therapist may be terrified by some aspects of the trauma and may feel tempted not to explore them any further; there may be some aspect of the patient's behaviour during the trauma that leads to "blaming the victim" (as in secondary betrayal trauma); or attention may be diverted towards the external perpetrators and into questions of justice and punishment, disregarding or putting aside the patient's inner suffering. In working with traumatized patients, therapist self-care is highly important.

Immersing oneself in the patient's trauma may lead to vicarious traumatization, resulting in emotional exhaustion, stress, irritation, frustration, stressful dreams or preoccupation. Vicarious traumatization especially occurs if the therapist is not adequately prepared or trained to face the gravity of the patient's trauma. Symptoms of vicarious traumatization include preoccupation with the patient's issues between sessions, insomnia and dreams about the patient, exaggerated enthusiasm or reluctance for the next session, dissociation (with its various expressions) during the sessions and while listening to the narratives regarding the traumatic event(s).

Moreover, when the personal histories of therapist and patient intersect, the specific neglect and trauma reported by the patient may trigger the therapist's own unresolved trauma, eliciting a re-experiencing, blunting, avoidance or arousal, which can further compound vicarious traumatization. On the other hand, traumatized therapists who have successfully worked through their past traumatic experiences may be particularly effective in the treatment of patients with similar histories (Mundo and O'Neil, 2017). However, even well-trained therapists need to face and carefully manage the anger and hatred of being traumatized. These feelings, as stated before in this chapter, are usually projected into the analyst and may induce enactments.

Patients with a history of secure attachment and a variety of personal and interpersonal resources, who suffer trauma-related conditions from a single-incident, may be able to approach the trauma early in the treatment and without a great deal of resourcing or pre-treatment focus. Patients with more complex trauma histories are more difficult to manage, especially when trauma events belong to childhood, are cumulative and there has been a "betrayal trauma" type. Patience is needed to tolerate the patient's deep mistrust. Perceived sensitivity to closeness may lead to distancing, which may re-enact the negligent non-abusing parent whose neglect allowed the abuse to happen in the first place.

In addition, the quality and severity of symptoms of traumatized patients may affect the subjective experience of the therapist as well as his mind-brain system. We should remember that in the clinical setting there are two mind-brain systems interacting and influencing each other: hyperarousal and release of toxic hormones for the hippocampus may affect both the patient and the therapist with various degrees of severity.

An encounter with DID may leave the therapist feeling completely de-skilled – at a loss. The patient often presents a vague, disjointed, or contra-dictory narrative, so anamnesis may produce confusion and a sense of futility. The dissociative structure (its self-states, their attributes and dynamics) may be so challenging that the clinician may become either immersed in it or completely detached as a defensive attitude. Also, the trauma history may provoke rescue fantasies in the therapist. Limits and boundaries may be tested by the patients who present themselves as "The exception" (Freud, 1916) in many ways. A child "alter" may excite the desire to reparent the patient. Claims of childhood traumatization may come with insistent requests to be believed. However, we need to remember that what could have been fantasized is possibly not what could have happened in reality. As Jung states: "There can of course be no doubt that many neuroses begin in childhood with traumatic experiences … but it remains equally true that hysteria, for instance, is only too ready to manufacture traumatic experiences where these are lacking, so that the patient deceives both himself and the doctor" (Jung, 1926/46, para. 201).

The patient may be rocked by seemingly interminable flashbacks, or else frozen into protracted affective numbing and amnesia. Therapists may suffer vicarious traumatization to the extent that they are unprepared to confront pervasive emotional and physical neglect in early childhood, together with early, severe, repeated emotional, physical and sexual traumatization that accompany this, with reactions ranging from outrage to denial. Specific training in dealing with traumatized patients or supervision with a trusted colleague is often critical.

Trauma as an Opportunity

Is it possible to consider the traumatic experience as an opportunity for the individual? *Kintsugi*, also known as *kintsukuroi* ("golden repair"), is the Japanese art of repairing broken pottery by mending the areas of damage with precious materials (e.g., gold, silver, or platinum). Symbolically, it requires not disguising the crack but rather treating the breakage and maintaining it as something even more valuable than the original object. Trauma becomes part of the history of the damaged object. The art of Kintsugi can be seen as representative of the main challenge for the dynamic psychotherapy of trauma: is it possible that what was unthinkable and unbearable, which led to a split in the psyche, may turn into a possibility for transformation of the individual? The treatment of traumatized patients should consider that repairing the damage that trauma has caused is not the primary goal. The premise of this chapter is that trauma is not something that can be described objectively but rather something that is specific for the individual. In other words, we cannot reduce trauma to what the diagnostic manuals define as an experience that exceeds the "normal experience" (DSM-5). We should consider the person first, his history, his unconscious, his inner predisposition to be traumatized by any event that triggers that specific and unique predisposition. Trauma remains something that hurts and disrupts the sense of self but not in the same way for every individual, just as the same event does not cause trauma in all individuals. As Jung (1917) reminds us, not all trauma causes illness, but it is only a "peculiar or exaggerated" reaction to trauma which does. The same experience can be traumatic for one person and not for another (Jung, 1926/46).

The natural consequence of this premise is that we should always consider the patient as a unique subject, as unique as the traumatic experience he has suffered. In addition, it should not be the primary aim of a psychodynamically-oriented treatment to repair trauma. Recollection of memory fragments of a whole picture or history is possible, and it is useful to reach a more cohesive sense of self and of one's own personal history. The whole picture of the story helps to undo "toxic" dissociation, and to relieve the patient's suffering. However, psychodynamic psychotherapy needs to go beyond, when possible: it needs to aim for *transformation*. The traumatic material, the wounds and what has been damaged, should be transformed into something precious for that individual: a chance for change. Something that was hidden may now be disclosed, working through the traumatic material and the transformative drive of the psychodynamic therapy may bring this to light as something special. This could be a patient's attitude that never had the chance to express itself, and so working through the traumatic event(s) may allow him have access to transformation and to new possibilities. A new and better life may arise from an apparently broken life. The new object, as in the Japanese art of "repairing" broken pottery, is then even more precious than the original one, because it has its own history, and it is transformed into something unique. Damage becomes, from this perspective, a chance for change, a way towards transformation.

The following clinical vignette may help focus better on some of the issues discussed in this chapter.

Alice started therapy at the age of 52, when her first daughter gave birth to a baby girl and Alice started helping her in the daily care of the child. The reason why she asked for treatment was the onset of intrusive images and thoughts of harming the little child, and particularly her genitals. In addition, the patient complained of "pseudo neurological" symptoms such as hand and finger dysesthesia, which had no organic cause but were related to physical contacts with her granddaughter (*conversion* symptoms). The symptoms (i.e., intrusive images and thoughts) were quite distressing and disturbing even though her usual functioning was intact. Alice was the first of two siblings, born into a wealthy family. Ever since childhood she had been attracted by art, colours, painting and sculpture. Her father died in a car accident when she was two years old and her mother, who she described as a cold and detached woman, remarried a few years later. Alice's mother forced her to study medicine, and she became a brilliant doctor. She had never been passionate about her work, but her overall functioning had always been impeccable. She met her husband at the age of 28 and got married two years later. She describes the relationship with her husband as affectionate and quite good, she gave birth to three children and gave up her work to take care of the family after the third pregnancy. During the treatment, while looking into the metaphoric meaning of the symptoms described in the first sessions, some traumatic memories started to emerge. The re-construction of the traumatic events was difficult and challenging, with Alice experiencing many *dissociative states* during the sessions (e.g., flashbacks, fugue, *derealization*) and out of the sessions (e.g., nightmares, a sort of somnambulism which took her to places in the house she never remembered reaching, *dissociative fugue*). I felt sometimes bored, found myself distracted from the patient and thinking about my own personal issues during the session, and experienced quite a disturbing depersonalization with a headache and back pain (*vicarious dissociation*). However, during subsequent sessions, some dreams led Alice to the recollection of significant memory fragments. In one of the most significant dreams, Alice stays in an empty house with many mirrors on the walls and she is watching her image in the mirrors but could not see anything but her face burning while other parts of her body are invisible. During the dream she had no feeling or pain, she just watched her face burning with a sort of detachment, as if in a movie. While working on the dream in the subsequent sessions, it came to light that Alice had been repeatedly sexually abused by her stepfather from the age of six to 13 years. The man used to force her to perform fellatio and Alice remembers being deeply disgusted and ashamed. Her burning face in the dream reminded her of the pain she had felt while being sexually abused. She tried to seek help from her mother, but she did not believe Alice, saying repeatedly that the narrations of the abuse were her fantasies and not reality (*second injury in betrayal trauma*). She therefore had stopped seeking help and had kept silent ever since. Although during the whole treatment the therapeutic alliance with her was good, sometimes Alice's transference made her too sensitive or susceptible to some words I had said or to the almost imperceptible movements I had made. These words or movements were perceived as signs of inattention or little consideration for her narrations, very likely reminding Alice of her mother's neglecting attitude. Occasionally, during the sessions, I could feel nauseated by Alice's mother's behaviour, at times even angry with her and so helpless that I could only say a few words. The countertransference was quite often driven to repairing the parental betrayal, thus shaping a re-parenting attitude. Besides this, during other sessions I had the bewildering experience of being in a bad dream and detached from the reality of the session (I was experiencing a *vicarious traumatization*). Then it happened that Alice discovered a shocking story regarding her stepfather. She had a talk with an old aunt, in order to collect information about her childhood, and so she could find out that her stepfather, who was a teacher at a high school, had been sentenced for paedophilia after a complaint by the father of one of his students. It was a very challenging time in analysis, where she was able to re-construct the terrible history of her childhood and puberty. During this painful work, Alice started to draw sketches after the sessions and then expressed the wish to start studying art. A dream depicted very clearly this important moment in the treatment:

> Alice is sitting on the floor of her room, in the house she lived in at the time of the abuse. A woman is giving her coloured pencils and a weird object to paint (like a small round table, broken in some way she cannot explain – "there were cuts or little fragments on the surface, but the table was nice and not completely broken"). She starts painting the little table while the older woman is observing her and saying only a few words: "It is good work playing with colours. You can even repair objects by only using colours, it is great, isn't it?".

The dream took several sessions to be interpreted properly but at the end we got to the conclusion that reparation was possible and that her original fascination for arts and painting was something precious that she could allow herself to follow in her life. After a few months, she began to attend an art academy and quite soon became a highly valued artist, fulfilling the ambition she had kindled since childhood. Alice has exhibited several of her art works in galleries and, moreover, won an international award for an art project aimed at supporting young children and women victims of sexual abuse.

Conclusions

As theorized by different psychoanalytical perspectives, trauma is a subjective experience that implies an individual psychic predisposition. Any encounter, any event may be traumatic for that specific subject (Mundo, 2022). Diagnostic manuals created for psychodynamically-oriented therapists (e.g., PDM-2) classify trauma according to the subjective experience of the traumatized individual and according to the dynamic of the "encounter" with the specific event also (e.g., "interpersonal/betrayal", "identity", or "community" trauma).

The concept of trauma is closely linked to the concept of dissociation. Dissociation is a multi-faceted phenomenon: it may appear as conversion symptoms, depersonalization/derealization, fugue, amnesia and DID. These dissociative phenomena may overlap or shift in the same patient outside and/or during therapy sessions. Clinicians treating traumatized patients must face and carefully manage the many faces of dissociation, in order for the dissociative phenomena to be "undone" (Wilkinson, 2006). Neurobiological studies have pointed out that trauma may severely affect the structure and the functioning of different brain areas, particularly the limbic system. This brain structure in traumatized patients is sensitized (the "kindling" phenomenon) so that any stimulus resembling the traumatic event(s) may trigger an exaggerated response and dissociation. The therapist should be trained to manage different critical situations when treating a traumatized patient. First, as mentioned above: dissociation may appear during the sessions and must be "undone". The therapist should use the instruments of the talking cure: symbolic holding (sympathetic and reassuring face expressions if the setting is vis-à-vis) as well as simple words and low voice (avoiding untimely interpretation), to balance the over-activation of the patient's mind-brain system. The second critical challenge for the therapist is to manage the anger and the hatred of traumatized subjects where these feelings may be projected into the therapist, inducing him to enactments. Third, the therapist should be aware that treating traumatized patients may lead to vicarious traumatization/dissociation: he can experience himself detached from reality, as in a bad dream, or even experiencing conversion symptoms, that need further training and supervision.

Finally, it should be remembered that trauma is not only a disruptive experience. It may be a chance for transformation. The unbearable wound may be transformed into something that could be precious for the subject: a new possibility not only to repair but to go beyond towards new opportunities to express attitudes which were never expressed before.

Note

1 Complexes are unconscious "feeling-tones", "splinter psyches", fragments, which may be activated because of traumatic experience.

References

American Psychiatric Association (2013) *Diagnostic and Statistical Manual of Mental Disorders, DSM*, 5th edition. Arlington (VA): American Psychiatric Association Publishing.

American Psychiatric Association (2022) *Diagnostic and Statistical Manual of Mental Disorders, DSM*, 5th edition. (text rev.) Arlington (VA): American Psychiatric Association Publishing.

Ansermet, F. and Magistretti P. (2004) *À Chacun Son Cerveau. Plasticité Neuronale et Inconscient*. Paris: Odile Jacob.

Beauregard, M. (2007) "Mind does really matter: Evidence from neuroimaging studies of emotional self-regulation, psychotherapy, and placebo effect", *Progress in Neurobiology*, 81(4): 218–236.

Bowlby, J. (1982) *Attachment and Loss (Vol. 1: Attachment)*, 2nd edition. New York: Basic Books.

Brenner, I. (2001) *Dissociation of Trauma: Theory, Phenomenology, and Technique*. Madison, CT: International Universities Press.

Breuer, J. and Freud, S. (1895) *Studies on Hysteria*. London: Hogarth Press.

Eickhoff, F.W. (2006) "On nachträglichkeit: The modernity of an old concept", *International Journal of Psychoanalysis*, 87(6): 1453–1469.

Fairbairn, W.R.D. (1944) "Endopsychic structure considered in terms of object-relationships", *International Journal of Psychoanalysis*, 25: 70–93.

Federn, P. (1952) *Ego Psychology and the Psychoses*. New York: Basic Books.

Fonagy, P. (2010) "Attachment, trauma and psychoanalysis: Where psychoanalysis meet neuroscience", in J. Canestri, M. Leuzinger-Bohleber and M. Target (eds) *Early Development and its Disturbances*. London: Routledge.

Fordham, M. (1976) *The Self and Autism: The Library of Analytical Psychology. Vol 3*. London: Heinemann.

Freud, S. (1894) "The neuro-psychoses of defence", in *SE III*. London: Hogarth Press, pp. 41–61.

Freud, S. (1914) "Remembering, repeating and working through", in *SE XII*. London: Hogarth Press, pp. 145–157.

Freud, S. (1916) "Some character-types met with in psychoanalytic work: I. The 'exceptions'", in *SE XIV*. London: Hogarth Press, pp. 311–315.

Freud, S. (1920) "Beyond the pleasure principle", in *SE XVIII*. London: Hogarth Press, pp. 7–64.

Freud, S. (1938) "Splitting of the ego in the process of defence", in *SE XXIII*. London: Hogarth Press, pp. 271–278.

Jung, C.G. (1912) *The Theory of Psychoanalysis*. CW4. Princeton, NJ: Princeton University Press.

Jung, C.G. (1917) *On the Psychology of the Unconscious*. CW7. Princeton, NJ: Princeton University Press.

Jung, C.G. (1926/46) *Analytical Psychology and Education*. CW17. Princeton, NJ: Princeton University Press.

Jung, C.G. (1928) *The Therapeutic Value of Abreaction*. CW16. Princeton, NJ: Princeton University Press.

Kalsched, D. (1996) *The Inner World of Trauma: Archetypal Defences and the Personal Spirit*. London: Routledge.

Kalsched, D. (2015) "Revisioning Fordham's 'Defences of the Self' in light of modern relational theory and contemporary neuroscience", *Journal of Analytical Psychology*, 60(4): 477–496.

Khan, M.M.R. (1974) "The concept of cumulative trauma", in *The Privacy of the Self*. New York: International Universities Press, pp. 42–58.

Kohut, H. (1984) *How Does Analysis Cure?* Chicago, IL: University of Chicago Press.

Lacan, J. (1955 [2006]) "The Freudian thing", in *Écrits* (trans. B. Fink, H. Fink and R. Grigg). New York: Norton & Co.

Lacan, J. (2013) "La logica del fantasma", in A. Di Caccia (ed.) *Altri Scritti. Testi Riuniti da Jacques-Alain Miller*. Torino: Einaudi, p.322.

Lingiardi, V. and McWilliams, N. (2017) *Psychodynamic Diagnostic Manual: PDM-2*, 2nd edn. New York: Guilford Press.

Mundo, E. (2006) "Neurobiology of dynamic psychotherapy: An integration possible?", *Journal of the American Academy of Psychoanalysis and Dynamic Psychiatry*, 34(4): 679–691.

Mundo, E. (2009) *Neuroscienze per la Psicologia Clinica. Le Basi del Dialogo Mente-Cervello*. Milano: Raffaello Cortina Editore.

Mundo, E. (2022) "Il trauma dell'incontro", in E. Mundo and F. Lolli (eds) *La Clinica Psicoanalitica del Trauma*. Litorale.

Mundo, E. and O'Neil J.A. (2017) "Symptom patterns: The subjective experience-S Axis", in V. Lingiardi and N. McWilliams (eds) *Psychodynamic Diagnostic Manual: PDM-2*. New York: Guilford Press, pp. 134–259.

Orlandini, A. (2004) "Repetition compulsion in a Trauma victim: Is the 'analgesia principle' beyond the pleasure principle? Clinical implications", *The Journal of the American Academy pf Psychoanalysis and Dynamic Psychiatry*, 32(3): 525–540.

Rosen, J.B. and Schulkin, J. (1998) "From normal fear to pathological anxiety", *Psychological Review*, 105(2): 325–350.

Scaer, R.C. (2001) "The neurophysiology of dissociation and chronic disease", *Applied Psychology and Biofeedback*, 26(1): 73–91.

Schore, A.N. (2002) "Dysregulation of the right brain: A fundamental mechanism of traumatic attachment and the psychopathogenesis of post-traumatic stress disorder", *Australian and New Zealand Journal of Psychiatry*, 36(1): 9–30.

Sierra, M. and Berrios, G.E. (2000) "The Cambridge depersonalization scale: A new instrument for the measurement of depersonalization", *Psychiatry Research*, 93(2): 153–164.

Tarnopolsky, A. (2003) "The concept of dissociation in early psychoanalytic writers", *Journal of Trauma and Dissociation*, 4(3): 7–25.

van der Kolk, B. (2014) *The Body Keeps the Score: Brain, Mind, and Body in the Healing of Trauma*. New York: Viking.

van Dijk, J.J.M. (1999) "Introducing victimology", in J.J.M. van Dijk, R.G.H. van Kaam and J. Wemmers (eds) *Caring for Crime Victims: Selected Proceedings of the Ninth International Symposium on Victimology - Amsterdam*, August 25–29, 1997. Monsey, NY: Criminal Justice Press, pp. 1–12.

Watkins, J.G. and Watkins, H.H. (1997) *Ego States: Theory and Therapy*. New York: Norton.

Wilkinson, M. (2006) *Coming into Mind. The Mind-Brain Relationship: A Jungian Clinical Perspective*. London: Routledge.

Winnicott, D.W. (1974) "Fear of breakdown", *International Review of Psycho-Analysis*, 1: 103–107.

Yilmaz, T. (2021) "Victimology from clinical psychology perspective: Psychological assessment of victims and professionals working with victims", *Current Psychology*, 40(4): 1592–1600.

Chapter 8

Eroticized Trauma and its Manifestations in the Transference

Martin Schmidt

Trauma-Related Complex

As we see repeatedly in this book, trauma is understood as an experience that overwhelms the mind, a devastating burst of excessive psychic excitation which disrupts the capacity for emotional containment, thinking and understanding. It can cause the psyche to fracture. In this way, trauma produces autonomous complexes: "Complexes are in fact 'splinter psyches'. The aetiology of their origin is frequently a so-called trauma, an emotional shock or some such thing, that splits off a bit of the psyche" (Jung, 1934, para. 204).

To compound matters, these complexes, which act as if they have a life of their own, are charged with fury and hatred. Building on Fordham's (1976) ideas, Kalsched (2015) became convinced that: "trauma liberates powerful volumes of volcanic hate in the infant psyche" (2015: 481). The child is often unable to channel this aggression towards those responsible for the trauma for fear of retribution. Instead, the complex directs the hatred against oneself driven by that which Bion (1967: 107) refers to as a sadistic or "ego-destructive superego", Fairbairn (1952: 136) an "inner saboteur" and Kalsched (2017: 478) the "dark angel". This accumulation of self-hatred makes one ill.

The trauma victim attempts to protect himself from this psychic tsunami by dissociation and repression but the effects of the unthinkable experience live on. Inevitably, in work at depth, the patient's psychodrama will come to life in the analysis in some way. This is even more the case in early relational trauma which happens before cognitive memory and language develop: "What we cannot forget ironically, is that which was never represented in memory in the first place" (Bollas, 2013: 71). West (2016) describes how early trauma-related patterns of interaction become installed in implicit memory (as opposed to explicit cognitive memory) and are relived in the therapeutic relationship as a trauma-related complex is constellated. Here,

DOI: 10.4324/9781003298076-11

the therapist becomes the re-traumatizing other and unwittingly triggers the trauma. This is particularly challenging when the trauma was sexual in nature.

Sexual Abuse as Trauma

Sex is, amongst other things, a form of aggression, whereas sexual abuse is a form of violence. Ego-syntonic aggression (aggression in service of the ego) is necessary to become independent, self-assertive and prevent others from exploiting one. Glasser (1979) defines violence in terms of the intended infliction of bodily harm on another person. However, I think this definition is too narrow for, in sexual abuse, the body is not always directly involved, for example, being forced to watch sexual acts can be a form of violation. Although sexual abuse can involve bodily pain, it is not usually the physical aspect of the encounter which is most traumatic as sexual violence predominantly impacts the mind rather than the body.

We can observe how a traumatic event (or sequence of events) such as sexual abuse produces a trauma-related complex with far-reaching ramifications which has a bearing on every aspect of the individual's life. The greatest devastation usually comes from a shattering of the child's emotional stability. His predictable, relatively safe and innocent world is corrupted forever. The experience of sexual violation is an episode of madness (one could say for both protagonists) because the victim is unable to make sense of, or process, the experience. Children who have been abused often report that something overwhelming has occurred which felt profoundly confusing, wrong, sinful, shameful, exciting and frightening. This turmoil is compounded if the perpetrator is a parent or a relative who then gaslights the child by labelling the transaction as "loving". In the aftermath, the child suddenly finds himself entering into a particular state of mind, indeed another world, where he is profoundly estranged from other children. This constitutes a brutal expulsion from the Garden of Eden, a shameful, bewildering loss of innocence where it is no longer possible to be a child, in the true sense of the word, again.

Bettelheim (1976) beautifully illustrates this in his interpretation of the Snow White fairy tale. He sees the seven dwarves as representing the seven asexual latency years between the Oedipal complex and puberty (from the ages of five to 12 years). Initially, the wicked stepmother tempts Snow White with a hair comb (which emphasizes the contrast between stereotypically long-haired girls and short-haired boys at puberty) and then a corset (which accentuates the hourglass figure of a pubescent girl). Snow White is enchanted by these lures for, in common with most little girls, she likes to experiment with "being sexy" by dressing up in mummy's clothes, shoes and make-up. Both gifts make her faint (the comb is poisoned and the corset too tight) as she is too young to sustain being sexually mature. Fortunately, the dwarves are at hand to revive her. After both attempts of seduction by the stepmother, they rescue Snow White from precocious sexuality and return her to the innocence of the latency period. However finally, like Eve, she is unable to resist sinking her teeth into the stepmother's apple (which represents sex itself). Now the Rubicon has been crossed. No more can the dwarves help her as the gates to latency and the garden of innocence are now irrevocably closed. Instead, she is lost in a world of her own and only a prince (a loving partner to accompany her into the world of adult sexuality) can save her. This fairy tale charmingly illustrates how sex, if it arrives prematurely, can cast the child out from the shelter of innocence into a precocious, perilous quasi-adulthood.

The trauma is reinforced if the young person feels unable to inform a parent about the abuse or if the parent does not believe the child (Ferenczi, 1932). This leaves him exposed to further mistreatment. In some cases, the experience of not being believed, or even being accused of being a liar and therefore left feeling crazy or betrayed, can be experienced as a greater trauma than the actual sexual abuse itself (see the case of Zara below). The child is left floundering, doubting his sanity, questioning who is responsible for what has happened and is rendered isolated, hermetically sealed in guilt, shame, fury and hatred.

Intromission

I would now like to look at the dynamics of what may be happening inter-psychically between the abuser and abused. Laplanche (1999: 133) uses a specific word to emphasize the particular nature of what is projected by the perpetrating adult and introjected by the hapless child in sexual abuse. He describes how, in this type of encounter, there is an "intromission" of a message from an enclaved part of the adult's unconscious which affects the child's psyche in a specific way. He deliberately uses the word "intromission" which means "the insertion of a penis into a vagina in sexual intercourse" to describe this projection of disturbed aspects of the adult psyche into the child's mind. The child passively receives these projections which he cannot translate. This violent introjection creates a rupture. As the sexual abuse is unable to be subjected to symbolic representation, gaps of un-representable experience are lodged as a foreign body in the child's mind.

One of my patients comes to mind here, a middle-aged woman, who was haunted by repetitive intrusive thoughts of sexual acts and a memory of interrupting her parents having sex (when she was seven years old). This image generated an intense sense of shame. She remembered her father's fury at her coming into the bedroom while her mother stared at her in silence. He screamed at her to get out and she ran away in terror. What struck me was that it was my patient, and not the parents, who experienced profound shame. It was as if the shame, that the parents were unable to feel, was fired into the little girl's psyche as an intromission ignited and fuelled by father's rage. This unprocessed attack from father with its injection of shame continued to be played out, as a repetition compulsion, in my patient's mind for years to come.

Eroticization as a Creative Form of Repetition Compulsion

Freud (1914) used the term repetition compulsion (*Wiederholungszwang*) to describe the unconscious tendency of a person to repeat a traumatic event or its circumstances. This can take the form of recurrent dreams, intrusive thoughts and symbolically, or literally, re-enacting the event. He noted how "the patient does not *remember* anything of what he has forgotten and repressed, he *acts* it out, without, of course, knowing that he is repeating it" (Freud, 1914: 150).

When an abused child becomes an adult, the distressing feelings associated with sexual trauma such as helplessness, shame, fear and pain can sometimes be reversed and converted into sexual feelings which are exciting, pleasurable and in the former victim's control. This eroticization of the trauma, I see as a creative form of repetition compulsion where the sexual abuse is re-visioned in adult sexuality. Bondage, discipline, domination, submission, sadism and masochism (BDSM) are sexual practices that can be seen as a form of eroticization of early childhood trauma. For example, those beaten and confined by their parents can find pleasure in being tied up and spanked consensually as adults. The premeditated beating of a child can be considered a form of sexual abuse as it involves a degree of sexual satisfaction for the perpetrator. Freud refers to this as sadism: "A portion of the destructive (death) instinct is placed directly in the service of the sexual function, where it has an important part to play. This is sadism proper" (Freud, 1924: 163).

Sometimes even very early trauma, such as birth trauma, may be eroticized. Winnicott (1949) directly connects difficult deliveries, where inhalation is restricted, with the development of later perversions that involve breathing obstruction: "The desire to be suffocated can be extremely strong and turns up as a masturbatory fantasy, in the acting out of which many who had no suicidal intention have died" (Winnicott, 1949: 188). The untimely demise of rock singer Michael Hutchence comes to mind here. Although his death was officially attributed to suicide, his lover, Paula Yates, is reported to have said (O'Rourke, 2011) that it was caused by auto-erotic asphyxiation (the practice of depriving the brain of oxygen to heighten orgasm) in a sex game that went wrong. However, I have been unable to discover whether Hutchence also suffered a birth trauma.

Some who have been traumatized by seeing mother have sex with father (or another person) or found themselves supplanted in mother's affections by a sibling may convert these feelings of humiliating rejection into the sexual exhilaration of cuckoldry. Here the patient now takes pleasure from watching his spouse have sex with another and is aroused by the humiliation of the spouse's new partner being more well-endowed or superior in performance. This cuckold fetishism is seen as a variant of masochism as the primary component is that of feeling humiliated but, importantly again, on one's own terms. The fetish does not work if the cuckold is humiliated against their will. DSM-5 (American Psychiatric Association [APA], 2013) is careful not to pathologize fetishism (as a fetishistic disorder) unless it causes significant psychosocial distress or impairment in the individual's life.

There is an element of repetition compulsion in these practices as the distressing event is repeated rather than remembered. However, I often see a creative dimension to the experience in my patients as it not only repeats the trauma but converts it into an enlivening experience – as opposed to Freud's attribution of repetition compulsion to the accentuation of the Death Instinct (Freud, 1920). Indeed, Freud later surmised that the repetition compulsion often included a potentially reparative dimension. He concluded that the repetition offers a kind of proto-containment that attempts, via action and discharge: "to control and lessen unpleasant or traumatic experiences" (Potamianou, 2015: 945). It could be argued that there is also hope for a different resolution, for a new life to come, for the subject who is trapped in repetition compulsion.

Perversions

Eroticization of trauma is sometimes labelled perverse. Freud (1905) understood perversion as the re-emergence, in adult sexuality, of bisexual, polymorphous, infantile aims and objects. For Klein (1927), perversion is a form of destructive narcissism while Stoller (1985) saw it simply as an erotic form of hatred because, in perverse enactments, the sexual partner is dehumanised and used as an object. The term perversion is itself controversial as it has been used in psychoanalysis, and elsewhere, to judge and pathologize unorthodox sexual practices. However, I think the term is still useful in that perverse relations accurately describe part-object, transactional interactions where the other is exploited and intimacy is avoided. In this sense of the term, many BDSM sexual practices are not perverse, for even though the sexual practices may involve fetishes or part-object relating, the very fact that the relations are consensual and carefully negotiated according to the particular desires of each partner means that the sex as a whole can be life-enhancing and intimate. Here, each partner offers themselves to be used as a part-object for the pleasure of the other and gains pleasure from meeting the other's wishes. In this way, the overall transaction can be seen as loving and not perverse. Indeed, in some patients, BDSM practices have become a lifeline which allows them not to be dominated by their childhood trauma but instead maintain a healthy functional role in society. A commonly reported experience in so-called perverse relations is not pain, but one of elation, release and freedom. As Royston (2001) suggests, this may be because it is the only way a true self, that has been confined by a traumatizing and invasive object, can find temporary expression. It is worth remembering, as Winnicott observed in relation to the perverse: "There is something of all this, as of everything else, in the healthy passionate sexual relationship" (Winnicott, 1949: 188).

However, it is also important to note that BDSM practices (and indeed any sexual behaviour) can be considered perverse if there is an obsessive, addictive, controlling and compulsive colouring which damages the relationship. This is particularly evident where sado-masochistic dynamics are not confined solely to the sexual domain but are also exercised in other aspects of the relationship. I recall a patient seen by one of my supervisees. She had sought psychotherapy in her late twenties following a string of disappointing relationships. Her childhood was marred by repetitive sexual abuse and beatings. However, as an adult, she relished being tied up, smacked and was attracted to sadistic men who could pleasure her in this way. These sado-masochistic acts not only coloured her sexual life but infiltrated all aspects of her relationships. Eventually, she was able to meet someone who was compatible with her, who shared her interest in BDSM but was also loving outside the bedroom. She declared that she could never imagine relinquishing her craving for BDSM, which she also understood as an eroticization of her early sexual abuse, because it made her feel truly alive.

It is not only patients who can be enslaved in an eroticized complex. Both male and female analysts are equally at risk of projecting their own feelings of infantile vulnerability and its associated perverse, shameful shadow aspects into their patients. This means we need to be mindful of our own prejudices in relation to sexual practices which we consider either alien or unacceptable to our own socio-cultural traditions. These include, for example, masturbation, use of pornography, practices of a sexual orientation different to one's own, prostitution and behaviour labelled "perverse" such as fetishism.

A Clinical Case

I would now like to look more deeply into how childhood sexual abuse can be both eroticized and transmuted using a case from my clinical practice. Following multiple hospitalisations for severe self-harm and depression, a 32-year-old woman (whom I will call Zara) was referred to me in the psychiatric rehabilitation centre where I worked as a psychologist and therapist. When we met, she was understandably anxious and quick to burst into nervous laughter to distract us both from her discomfort. I too was fearful; it was as if there was nowhere I could comfortably settle my gaze. If I caught her eyes, I felt as if I was culpable of a rude assault. If I looked away, I felt ashamed and embarrassed. After a while, she rattled off her life story in a somewhat perfunctory manner as if she had been asked for it many times before. While she was in this somewhat robotic state of mind, I felt that I had a chance to look at her. She had lank, greasy hair and clammy skin. By contrast, she was dressed to seduce with a short tight skirt and low-cut blouse. She nervously adjusted her hemline, squirmed in her chair and chewed her cuticles. Her exposed arms were covered in scars, some superficial scratches and others deep enough to have required stitching. I felt nauseous and wanted to escape, but was pinned to my chair. Zara described how her parents had divorced when she was five years of age and that she saw very little of her father from then on. Her mother, whom she portrayed as a weak character with a sullen disposition, became dependent on a string of unreliable men. Mother soon remarried, to a violent, coercively controlling brute who ruled the household with an iron fist.

Zara reported, without feeling, that her stepfather had repeatedly sexually abused her from the age of seven to 14. I felt strangely numb and asked whether she had told anyone about this or asked for help. She explained, with a hebephrenic smile, that when she tried to tell her mother, she was told not to make up such terrible lies. I felt suddenly enraged on her behalf and suggested that her mother's disbelief must have been devastating for her to hear. Her eyes then met mine as she remained silent. It felt as if I had made contact with her for the first time. I was mindful that my bodily reactions, my shame, nausea, numbness and rage were important indicators in our work. As Eulert-Fuchs (2022) highlights, it is inevitable when working with traumatised patients that we receive primitive projections, that are unformulated, which are often experienced somatically (Zoppi, 2017). These can inform us of the nature of early relational trauma. I was experiencing something of Zara's inner world which she had been unable to process.

Our sessions quickly became very intense and highly charged. She was very thin-skinned and would quickly fly into a rage, and even storm out of sessions, if she felt that I had got something wrong or didn't understand her. Like many trapped in borderline states of mind, she was consumed by shame which she found very difficult to articulate. This took a particular counter-intuitive shape in that it was easier (less shameful) for her to talk about sexual matters (because this made me uncomfortable and excited her) than everyday thoughts and feelings. I felt seduced, intimidated and controlled by her. If I managed to hold my attention on her feelings, she would turn the tables with intrusive, personal questions about myself, but despite her manic attempts to throw me off the scent, I could sense her deep sorrow which was thinly disguised by a flimsy, light-hearted air.

Traditionally, one of the most useful tools in the psychoanalytic method is interpretation: the putting of words to feelings to create meaning. This can liberate someone trapped in emotional turmoil: "Give sorrow words; the grief that does not speak knits up the o-er wrought heart and bids it break" (Shakespeare, 1861: 134). However, in the early stages of our work, I found that my interpretations were futile as it was almost impossible to help her find words to put to her trauma. Instead, I found this old adage from my analytic training to be true: that which is unable to be thought about and given words is either expressed through the body (somatised) or re-enacted. In the absence of any useful interpretation, as time went by, I endeavoured to read what she was feeling under her brittle façade. I tried to help her label her feelings, to make sense of what it was that I said, or did not say, that distressed her so much. Her violent projections were very difficult for me to hold and resist acting upon. Often, I wanted to retaliate or run away, to react rather than respond. I felt toyed with, flattered one moment, denigrated the next. Often, she reminded me: "You are a good person with a big heart … it's such a pity you are a useless therapist". Staying with this process was no easy task: "Containment is hard work. It involves a reworking of the traumatic experiences with all its emotional impact, and all the guilt, fear and hatred released by the original event" (Garland, 2002: 30).

Later, I discovered that, although very intelligent, she had struggled at school owing to difficulties in making friendships. She confessed that she couldn't really relate to, or trust, the other children. They felt alien as if they were living in a "Disneyland of happy families" unbeknownst to her. What is more, they were so "childish". This amused her and she giggled at the irony (children are meant to be childish). Her adolescence was recalled as a "wild time". In reality, it transpired that it had been blighted by dramatic mood swings, outbursts of rebellious anger and impulsive behaviours (such as petty theft and promiscuity). She developed a precocious fascination/ desire for sex accompanied by a premature onset of puberty (menarche) at 9 years of age which are common features of those who have suffered sexual abuse (Castillo Mezzich et al., 1997). Freud (1895) has emphasized the central role of the psyche in transforming surplus unwelcome excitation into forms of impulse, drive and affect. I understood this concupiscence in Zara as an expression and displacement of the unwelcome, excessive, psychic excitation she had received at the hands of her stepfather.

Zara proudly recounted that, at the age of 15, she was finally expelled from school and ran away from home. Her life then consisted of a string of abusive relationships with domineering older men who provided somewhere to live in return for sex. She found some solace in drink and drugs, but this proved ineffective in dulling her pain. I asked her to tell me more about her pain. She froze, her complexion became pale and then, after some minutes, she confessed that it was only when she began to slash her arms, thighs and vagina with a razor blade that she experienced relief from her psychic torment. I felt disgusted and perversely aroused at the same time as if half of my experience belonged to me and half to her. The link between sexual abuse and self-cutting is well documented (Zlotnick et al., 1996; Gladstone et al., 2004) however my colleagues and I noticed a much higher correlation between those patients who cut their inner thighs and vaginas with actual sexual abuse, than those who only cut their arms.

For years, Zara had dissociated from her pain and experienced states of depersonalization where she imagined looking down on herself from above. The slashing, with a cold, hard blade, brought her back to herself. I found myself wondering whether this self-harm was also a psychosomatic expression of the laceration of her psychic skin (Schmidt, 2012), the decimation of her own containing function, engendered by years of abuse and neglect. It was as if by symbolically revisiting, on her own terms, the earlier slashing of her psychic skin, she might rediscover and empower herself.

One day, she informed me that she had stopped cutting herself. I did not believe that this was a miraculous transformation produced by our sessions, but rather the latest development in a movement of her Self which, amongst other things, had brought her to therapy. When I asked why she had stopped, she told me that she had discovered a pornographic magazine called "Knicker Wetters" which catered for the needs of those who derive sexual pleasure from being urinated upon. She confided in me that she had long harboured a fantasy of urinating on men and having power over them, so she decided to contact the magazine. Within a matter of weeks, she had acquired four regular clients who paid good money for her services which involved little or no actual physical contact. She explained to me the different deals on offer, and I remember feeling very naïve, perhaps like one of the "childish children" she referred to at school. The gold service (named after "golden showers") involved directly urinating into the customer's face and mouth. The silver service (a pun on serving meals at formal occasions) involved urinating onto a glass coffee table while the client lay beneath the glass, free to observe but protected from getting wet. The bronze service (a pun on the colour of faecal traces deposited in underwear) involved the sale of used, soiled knickers. I was confused and asked why this had led to the cessation of cutting herself. She replied: "Can't you see? I have replaced one type of slashing for another!". For those unfamiliar with English vernacular, "to slash" means to urinate as well as to cut.

I was beginning to see how this eroticized acting out could be understood not only as revenge on her domineering stepfather, but also as a creative displacement and inversion of her wish to slash her own skin. Now, her hot urine is used to slash (on) another, rather than a cold blade used to slash herself. I also felt that it was perhaps a re-enactment of a degrading, abusive, transaction with her stepfather, but this time on her own terms. Her clients wanted to be dominated and humiliated by her. I found myself unsettled and somewhat embarrassingly excited by her telling of the story. Although I was not directly sexually aroused by imagining the encounters, I was not disgusted either. I think I felt enthused by the ingenious, creative and relatively safe way her unconscious had found to re-constellate her complex and displace her self-harm. It had made some meaning from the demeaning trauma.

She couldn't bear the idea that I might be looking down on her or judging her. The only way we could progress was if she felt that I was not pitying her or acting as if I knew what was best. For Zara, and many like her, understanding is more important than approval. She sought the attunement (understanding without the need to explain) which was sadly lacking in her infancy and felt exhausted and enraged by my need for her help in understanding her. It was as if I ought to know what she was feeling without the need to ask. It became increasingly clear to me that her experience of trauma began before the sexual abuse. Her mother had been inconsistent and neglectful from the outset. Zara relayed stories of being left out in the garden when her mother had lovers in the house, being sent to school in unwashed clothes and soiled underwear only to be mocked by the other children. Here, I thought of the possible eroticization of this deep humiliation in the "bronze service" she now offered her clients. Her aunt once told her that she discovered her crying alone in the house (when she was only two years old) because her mother had gone to visit a lover and "forgot" that she was home alone. This, in part, explained how an environment was created which fostered further trauma of a sexual nature.

I became increasingly important to her, but I was not allowed my own mind. In desperation, I fell back into the trap of justifying myself and making elaborate interpretations. Kalsched, in revisioning Fordham's (1974) "defences of the self", warns: "early unremembered trauma are not transformable through interpretation but will inevitably be repeated in the transference" (Kalsched, 2015: 477). One moment I would feel as if she was tyrannising me, the next as if I was the cruel sadist. She declared that she would feel less humiliated if we were equals. At first, she tried to do this by denigrating me (so that I too might feel powerless and humiliated) but then, when she felt she could trust me more, by seduction so that I might become one with her. At times, there was a strong pull to replay an incestuous relationship, a re-enactment of something which would, in reality, be sexually abusive but which, in fantasy, may heal and transcend the original abuse. Jung understood this tension from his own experience: "The feebler the rapport i.e., the less doctor and patient understand one another, the more intensely will the transference be fostered and the more sexual will be its form. Sexuality intervenes as a function of compensation for the lack of understanding" (Jung, 1928, para. 276). I came to see this as both a desire to control me and to fuse, to merge skin, both physical and psychic. It seemed to reflect both a regressive longing to return to a time of profound contact with mother and a repetition compulsion of the sexual abuse. I was surprised, and singularly impressed, by how forgiving and understanding Zara was of her mother. She did not give up hope of re-establishing a loving relationship with her.

In work with patients who have been sexually abused, it is common for the transference to be eroticized in some way. I have noticed three common constellations of the countertransference dynamics in such work. All of these were present at some stage in the therapy with Zara. The first is a fear that the analyst will, in some way, become the abuser and repeat the abuse by insensitive interventions and penetrating interpretations. This can lead to the analyst becoming defensive and over-cautious for fear of damaging the patient. The second, more common constellation, is the experience of being controlled and abused by the patient as the latter's vulnerable abused child self is projected or intromitted into the analyst and attacked. Last is the countertransference experience of becoming the parent who knows about the abuse but turns a blind eye to it. This can present a very difficult ethical problem particularly when the patient informs the analyst that the person who perpetrated the abuse is still a risk to others (e.g., a teacher or priest). The analyst is then confronted with the dilemma of whether to inform the appropriate authorities (potentially breaking the patient's confidentiality) or preserve the patient's wish for secrecy and, in so doing, collude with the abuse in silence and potentially endanger others.

Rather than labelling her new sexual professional activities as pathology, I felt admiration for the ingenuity of her unconscious. It had managed to help her find a way to rework her trauma on her own terms and replace the need for cutting herself. It also provided her with the financial means to become more independent and stable. I wondered about whether I was remiss by not taking a more moral/ethical position on her behaviour. By the time I had the opportunity to discuss her case in group supervision, she was earning more money than most of the staff in the rehabilitation centre. I mention this, because I divined that envy may have played a part in the dis-approval of some colleagues who encouraged me to challenge her or even try to stop her sex work as a condition of her being able to continue to attend the psychiatric rehabilitation programme. I mooted the idea to the team that you tell a tree by its fruit. After all, she was now happier, more stable and wealthier than she had ever been. Fortunately, the consultant psychiatrist Dr Brian Snowdon (also a Jungian analyst) who supervised our clinical team, was more aligned with my position. He stated that our work together and her solution may not have addressed the issues at the heart of her trauma complex, for example, the "nameless dread" (Bion, 1962: 183) and her primitive pernicious envy, but she had found a creative way of man-aging her trauma. I was reminded of one of the criticisms sometimes directed at Alcoholics and Narcotics Anonymous, namely that their members have displaced their dependence on addictive substances to dependence on group meetings. Even if there may be some truth in this, the AA/NA groups are a more benign and productive drug than alcohol or heroin. The same can be said of Zara's *modus operandi*.

As the therapy continued, she started a relationship with a man who did not seem to mind that she was a sex worker as long as she eschewed intercourse with her clients. Having physical contact with her clients had no interest for her, but being in control did. Throughout the therapy (which lasted for the three years that she was allowed to attend the programme), she never cut herself again and was noticeably less depressed. We tried, a number of times, to explore her trauma but with limited success (perhaps, in part, because we both knew we only had three years in which we could work together). It became clear that the greater unprocessed trauma was not the sexual abuse from her stepfather. She claimed that she found it easy to hate him and so he had become psychically insignificant. However, her mother's inconsistency, abandonment, failure to believe her, protect her and love her had cut Zara to the core. There was "a gaping hole of pain" inside her. She felt that she had been irretrievably damaged and emotionally disabled by her mother. Although nothing could assuage these feelings, she had found a way to live with the torment. At the end of the therapy, she shared with me what it was that she thought had helped. It was not so much that I believed her story and understood why she had joined Knicker Wetters, it was that I didn't stop the therapy or abandon her during the prolonged periods that she was very angry with me. This brought to mind Winnicott's (1969) seminal paper on "the use of an object" where he highlights the two most vital tasks of a parent (and analyst) in relation to a child's (and patient's) aggression, which are: first, to survive and second, not retaliate. We both worked very hard. It was a struggle for both of us to engage with each other and be emotionally present in the room. I did survive her attacks but, at times, did also retaliate (with mistimed judgemental interventions or justifications of my behaviour), though not to a degree that her faith in me and the therapy was broken.

Sexual Abuse as a Defence Against an Earlier Trauma

As can be seen with Zara, there may be deeper earlier trauma underlying sexual abuse which allows a toxic culture to develop. This can foster further trauma. It is also important to note, as Alessandra Cavalli (2014) controversially proposed, that sexual abuse can sometimes be sought by the child as a defence against "nameless dread" (Bion, 1962: 183). This is a term Bion used to describe the psychotic panic that can develop when a child's primitive anxieties are not contained. Cavalli argued that this uncontained affect could be perceived as more damaging and intrusive than sexual abuse itself: "Neglected children can be seduced by external abuse in the hope of being protected from affect that threatens to feel abusive from within. Paradoxically these children are drawn towards abusive situations in the hope of finding some ongoing shelter from unmanageable affect" (Cavalli, 2014: 31).

She describes her work with a patient (Mary) who, like Zara, was molested by her mother's partner (Mr X) at the age of eight, but who only disclosed this when he also started to abuse her younger sister. The patient "always felt that Mr. X was not ok, but she was seduced by the fact that she was feeling special, chosen by him. This is why she allowed him to do what he did" (Cavalli, 2014: 37). Cavalli continues: "By allowing Mr. X to abuse her, Mary was looking for an abusive way of looking after unmanageable feelings that her mother had not been able to contain" (Cavalli, 2014: 38). In the transference, Cavalli was experienced as the mother who was sadistically abusing Mary because she was unable to protect her from her terror. As Colman (2022) articulates in relation to this case, containment can sometimes feel abusive whereas sexual abuse can sometimes feel containing.

Eros: A Force Which Connects

As I have tried to show, trauma is often eroticized and comes alive in the transference. As the erotic derives from Eros, it may be helpful to revisit the mythological basis of Eros in the development of psychoanalytic thinking. Eros is not just about sex. It is a force which connects us with others: emotionally through love, mentally through imaginative conceptions as well as physically through intercourse. Eros brings creativity with it. In Greek mythology, Eros was thought to be one of the primordial Gods that created the cosmos. Night (Nyx) laid a germless egg from which love (Eros) sprang. Eros then mated with Chaos and hatched forth the human race. It is perhaps fitting to find that all humans are the product of love and chaos. In later accounts, Eros came to be known as the illegitimate son of the Goddess of love, Aphrodite (Venus) and her lover Aries (Mars) the God of war. Eros is attributed with very different qualities in youth and in maturity. As a child, he is referred to as Cupid the trickster who has the power to evoke desire or revulsion depending on whether one is struck, respectively, by one of his sharp gold-tipped or blunt lead-tipped arrows. Revulsion and disgust in the transference can be understood as embodiments of the negative erotic. In Renaissance art, Cupid is often portrayed as blindfolded to remind one that love is blind, can strike anyone at any time and alludes to the darkness associated with sin and trauma. Bettelheim (1984) reminds us not to confuse the mischievous irresponsible boy Cupid with the fully grown, powerful mature Eros who becomes wedded to Psyche. Psyche means both mind and soul. The Greek myth of Psyche and Eros, where mind and love become entwined, serves as an allegory for the nature of all human relationship.

Eros at the Heart of Jung and Freud's Thinking

Freud based his psyche-analysis directly on the affiliation between Eros (sexual love) and Psyche (mind). For Freud, Eros in the transference led back to actual childhood and a revisiting of incestuous desires of the Oedipal phase. Originally, he saw libido (the sexual drive) as the most important instinct but after the death of his daughter Sophie, his favourite grandson (Heinz Rudolf) and the onset of his own cancer (see Schmidt, 2013), he revised his thinking. Now he saw Eros as the life instinct (which encompassed sexuality) and Thanatos as the death instinct. This was an expansion of Spielrein's (1911) conception of life and death drives: "The aim of the first of these basic instincts is to establish ever greater unities and to preserve them … to bind them together; the aim of the second, on the contrary, is to undo connections and so to destroy things … for this reason we also call it the death instinct" (Freud, 1941: 70–71).

This marked a move towards a position which Jung had long championed, that is, that the libido is "psychic energy" and not just sexual energy. Jung had always viewed Eros from a broader perspective than just sexuality. For him, Eros represents a wish for renewal, a bridge between man's primordial, animal, bodily sexual needs and his spiritual divine calling: "the intermediary between mortals and immortals … a mighty daimon whose function is 'to interpret and convey messages'" (Jung, 1911–12, para. 242). He advocates a balance between man's animal and spiritual nature: "Too much of the animal distorts the civilized man, too much civilization makes sick animals" (Jung, 1917, para. 32). Interestingly, Jung attributes this powerful male God, Eros, to the relational, feeling function of feminine consciousness (Jung, 1955/56, para. 224). Its opposite is Logos, which he equates with masculine consciousness by which he means the capacity to think, discriminate and make judgements. However, although Jung agreed that Eros was a great binding and relational force, he did not hold with Freud's idea that Eros is equivalent to the life instinct. He saw this as a fundamental problem, because Freud seems to assume that the opposite of Eros (love) is death rather than hate. In Jung's formulation: "Logically the opposite of love is hate, and of Eros, Phobos (fear); but psychologically, it is the will to power. Where love reigns, there is no will to power; and where the will to power is paramount, love is lacking. The one is but the shadow of the other" (Jung, 1917, para. 78). This brilliant insight has illuminated our understanding of all human relationships in that it identifies the two core dynamics: love and power. In relationships predominantly guided by love, the need to demand, control or jealously check up on the other is absent. By contrast, in relationships governed by power, love is undermined. This is now at the heart of our

understanding of the difference between the eroticized and erotic transference and countertransference. Namely, that the former is concerned with
power and the latter with love.

Erotic and Eroticized Transference

Many psychoanalysts still see the erotic transference as primarily a defensive mechanism. Through clinical practice, we have become aware of many
ways in which a sexualised transference can be used defensively, for example, as a way of avoiding separation from the analyst (Jung, 1912, para.
439), as a means of psychic survival (McDougall, 1995), as a form of pseudo
intimacy when real intimacy is too traumatic (Kaplan, 1991); as revenge for
psychic injuries of the past (Meltzer, 1973), to eroticise aggression when
intimacy is liable to provoke it (Glasser, 1979) and as a method of hyper-
stimulation for a deadened self (Guntrip, 1968).

However, this classification gives no room for consideration of the erotic
transference as a positive, lively, creative and loving aspect of the analytic
relationship. Therefore, it was ground-breaking when Blum (1973) designated this defensive type of sexualised transference as erotized (eroticized)
transference. Eroticized transference and countertransference refer to a
dynamic between analyst and patient that has predominantly power, not
love, at its root. It is primarily defensive in nature with a wish to control the
other through seductive and sexually evocative words, imagery and behaviour. Some psychoanalysts (Blum, 1973; Kulish, 1986; Lester, 1990) consider this to be a form of delusional transference, a powerful resistance,
where the capacity to symbolise is absent. The manifestation of eroticized
transference is more common with patients who have experienced sexual trauma.

By contrast, the "erotic transference" proper can now be seen as the natural result of mutual empathy which develops when two people become close,
learn to trust and understand each other. It takes the shape of feelings of
curiosity, concern, affection, gratitude and love towards the other which
may or may not involve some sexual feelings. However, any sexual feelings
that may arise do not govern the relationship and do not need to be acted
upon. This is because the capacity to symbolise and reflect is very much
present which gives it a sense of freedom, creativity and play.

Perhaps it is for this reason that some Jungian analysts, for example
Lambert (1973) and Gordon (1993), distinguish between different types of
love in analysis, such as erotic, platonic, agapeic. Erotic love is usually
considered impulsive, compulsive, driven by desire and all-consuming. By

contrast, agape is considered neither envious, nor vengeful, nor inflated with pride or vanity, but kind, just and patient. Lambert recommends that the love of the analyst for the patient should be agapeic. However, I side with Rosemary Gordon who argues for a balance between the two. Without the erotic, analysis can be dull, lifeless, lacking colour, vitality and deep mutual engagement. There needs to be a mix of Eros and Thanatos, love and aggression.

Discriminating Between the Erotic and Eroticized Transference by Using One's Countertransference

How do we tell the difference between an erotic and eroticized transference and countertransference? Sometimes the erotic and eroticized transferences can become mixed up and hard to distinguish. Zinkin (1969) reports a case of feeling unmoved by his patient's declarations of love. This absence of a reciprocal countertransference, he felt, was a clear indication that the transference was eroticized. He argues that his lack of arousal in response to the patient's erotic feelings may indicate that what the patient is expressing is another impulse – possibly hate. If we feel seduced, tantalised, abused, bullied or controlled then clearly an eroticized transference is at play. This can be a feature of work with patients (like Zara) who have been sexually abused or traumatised. Our task is to contain and process this aggression, to understand its cause and function with the hope that this will bring about change hopefully to a more erotic transference.

The "true" erotic countertransference, which can have both agapeic and libidinal qualities, feels very different. It is usually born out of working through difficult issues with patients over a sustained period and involves getting to know and understand them deeply. We look forward to seeing these patients; we like them, are interested in them, curious about them and care for them. There is a sense of mutual appreciation and gratitude for the privilege of sharing this intimate journey with them. For patients who are schizoid, withdrawn, profoundly depressed and lacking in sexual energy, one of the aims of analysis may be to help them become an "erotic object". By this, I mean that they may be able to find themselves, and others, sexually attractive with the outward expression of Eros that this entails. Of course, there are dangers here. We can find patients attractive for a range of reasons, including ones that relate to the narcissistic wounds of the analyst. Sometimes an eroticized transference/countertransference can feel like an erotic one. The dangers of Cupid, the Trickster, playing games with both are also present. It is easy for compassion, empathy, care and concern to become confused with desire and erotic impulse. In this context, I think it is important to remember the relationship between Sabina Spielrein and Jung which highlights the dangers of working in this area.

Jung and Sabina Spielrein

Jung recognised, but was unprepared for, the power of the erotic in psychoanalysis. He realized that sexuality is a fundamental instinct and acknowledged its role in Freud's theory of repression. As we know, from his relationship with Sabina Spielrein, he was, himself, gripped at times by the daimonic power of Eros. Ironically, it could be argued that his work with Sabina was one of the most successful early cases of treatment by psychoanalysis.

When a child, she was beaten by both her parents and suffered sexual abuse at the hands of a relative. As a result, she developed multiple somatic symptoms (including tics and grimaces) and we can see the role of a trauma-related Oedipal complex in the series of infatuations she had with older men (e.g., her history teacher, an uncle and a doctor). She was admitted to the Burghölzli hospital at the age of 19 with a diagnosis of psychotic hysteria and obsessive sexuality. Her obsession with masturbatory fantasies of being beaten and her anal preoccupations can be understood as an eroticization of the beatings by her father (Graf-Nold, 2001).

In the course of the analysis, Jung and Sabina were held captive by an erotic complex activated between them. Apparently, there was no physical affair while she was in hospital and "they may never have consummated their deep attachment to each other" (Thomson, 2001: 76). However, something remarkable did happen. This bright adolescent girl, unable to think clearly because of her sexual obsessions, was able to leave the hospital and, within two years, excel at university. Jungian analyst Jean Thomson, saw this as an example of someone overwhelmed by Eros who, through a deeply intense analysis, was able to find her relationship with Logos. She argues that Sabina's: "cognitive capacity, which had been evident in diaries, was swamped by feelings" (Thomson, 2001: 79) and that "Jung's capacity to wrestle with her psychotic delusions gave her the serious attention and understanding she had never had before" and, what is more, he: "gradually helped her re-find the cognitive powers she had lost" (Thomson, 2001: 76–78). Bruno Bettelheim went so far as to claim: "It was what she experienced with Jung that cured her ... Jung's behaviour and attitude, as conveyed to her in their relation – call it treatment, seduction, transference, love, mutual daydreams, delusions, or whatever – was instrumental in achieving the cure" (Bettelheim, 1984: 77). The relationship with Jung gradually changed from patient to student to colleague. She was deeply troubled and heartbroken by the end of her relationship with Jung and sought counsel from Freud. However, it is reported that she regarded her experiences with Jung as overall more beneficial than otherwise (Carotenuto, 1986). Later, she married, had children and became a brilliant psychoanalyst in her own right publishing over 30 papers. Unfortunately, neither Jung nor Freud gave her the credit she was due.

I am not condoning Jung's behaviour, but I am trying to show that there is more to be gleaned from his and Spielrein's engagement with Eros than simply dismissing it as transgression. He clearly struggled with the erotic and eroticized transference and countertransference, as Thomson observed: "Jung was unable to deal with what he himself began to think of as a professional deviation" (Thomson, 2001: 78). Steinberg argues that "this may have led him to play down the significance of the personal component of the transference and try to find other means of treating his patients" (Steinberg, 1988: 36).

Conclusion

In this chapter, I explore how sexual abuse generates trauma-related complexes. The most traumatic element of sexual abuse is the psychological violence at its core (not the physical violence) as the perpetrator *intromits* uninvited, hostile affects into the victim. I also propose that the premeditated physical beating of a child can be understood as a form of sexual abuse as there is an element of sadism (sexual pleasure in inflicting pain) involved. Trauma produces extreme hate and fury, in reaction to this intromission, which then often becomes directed at the self as well as others.

The situation is complex. I suggest that some trauma associated with sexual abuse is more painful than the abuse itself. Sometimes betrayal by the parent who does not physically commit the molestation, but turns a blind eye to it or denies it or even blames the child, can produce a greater trauma than the physical abuse itself. As can be seen in the clinical case presented, there is often deeper earlier trauma underlying sexual abuse which allows a toxic culture to develop that fosters further trauma. What is more, sometimes sexual abuse is sought by the child in order to feel special, to compulsively repeat an earlier trauma or even to protect herself from a more terrifying trauma, for example, nameless dread.

I demonstrate, through the use of clinical examples (my own and Jung's relationship with Sabina Spielrein), how trauma-related complexes which arise in childhood as a consequence of sexual abuse, can be transformed, through eroticization, into behaviours which revision the trauma in a new way. Distressing feelings associated with sexual abuse such as helplessness, shame, fear and pain can sometimes be reversed and converted into adult sexual feelings which are exciting, pleasurable and in the former victim's control. This eroticization I see as a creative form of repetition compulsion.

Bondage, discipline, domination, submission, sadism and masochism (BDSM) are sexual practices that can be seen as a form of eroticization of early childhood trauma. I argue that these customs are often mislabelled as perverse (where perversion is understood as behaviour which is governed by power and not love, is exploitative, controlling, part-object, transactional and dehumanising). In this sense of the term, I contend that many BDSM practices are not perverse, for even though the sexual acts may involve fetishes or part-object relating, the very fact that the transactions are consensual and carefully negotiated according to the particular desires of each partner, means that the sex as a whole can be considered life-enhancing and intimate. Here, each partner offers themselves to be used as a part-object for the pleasure of the other and gains satisfaction from meeting the other's wishes. In this way, the overall transaction can be seen as loving and not perverse. Indeed, in some patients, BDSM practices have become a lifeline which allows them not to be dominated by their childhood trauma but instead maintain a healthy functional role in society. As Freud (1905) reminds us:

> No healthy person, it appears, can fail to make some addition that might be called perverse to the normal sexual aim; and the universality of this finding is in itself enough to show how inappropriate it is to use the word perversion as a term of reproach. In the sphere of sexual life, we are brought up against peculiar, and, indeed, insoluble difficulties as soon as we try to draw a sharp line to distinguish mere variations within the range of what is physiological from pathological symptoms.
>
> (Freud, 1905: 160–161)

However, I also qualify this perspective by stating that BDSM practices (and indeed any sexual behaviour) can be considered perverse if there is an obsessive, addictive, controlling and compulsive colouring which damages the relationship. This is particularly evident where sado-masochistic dynamics are not confined to the sexual domain but are also exercised in other aspects of the relationship.

These perverse dynamics can also be seen in the eroticization of the transference. It is important to distinguish, as Blum (1973) did, between erotic and erotized (eroticized) transference. Although the classical psychoanalytic view of erotic transference portrays it as defensive in nature, I support Blum's position in seeing erotic transference as a positive expression of the mutual empathy which develops when patient and analyst understand, learn to trust and care about each other. Eros is primarily concerned with connection and sex is only one dimension of the erotic. This is in stark contrast to eroticized transference which is perverse as it is based on a need to exercise power over the other through manipulation and seduction.

References

American Psychiatric Association (2013) *Diagnostic and Statistical Manual of Mental Disorders, DSM-5*, 5th edition. Arlington, VA: American Psychiatric Publishing.

Bettelheim, B. (1976) *The Uses of Enchantment: The Meaning and Importance of Fairy Tales*. Middlesex: Penguin Books.

Bettelheim, B. (1984) *Freud and Man's Soul*. London: Hogarth.

Bion, W.R. (1962) "A theory of thinking", in *Second Thoughts: Selected Papers on Psychoanalysis*. London: Maresfield Library, pp. 178–186.

Bion, W.R. (1967) "Attacks on linking", in *Second Thoughts: Selected Papers on Psychoanalysis*. London: Maresfield Library.

Bollas, C. (2013) *China on the Mind*. London: Routledge Taylor and Francis Group.

Blum, H.P. (1973) "The concept of erotized transference", *Journal of the American Psychoanalytic Association*, 21(1): 61–76.

Carotenuto, A. (1986) *A Secret Symmetry: Sabina Spielrein between Freud and Jung*. London: Routledge.

Castillo Mezzich, A., Tarter, R.E., Giancola, P.R., Lu, S., Kirisci L. and Parks, S. (1997) "Substance use and risky sexual behaviour in female adolescents", *Drug and Alcohol Dependence*, 44(2–3): 157–166.

Cavalli, A. (2014) "From affect to feelings and thoughts: From abuse to care and understanding", *Journal of Analytical Psychology*, 59(1): 31–46.

Colman, W. (2022) "Thinking the unthinkable: Trauma, defence, early states of mind in Alessandra Cavalli's work", *Journal of Analytical Psychology*, 67(4): 919–938.

Eulert-Fuchs, D. (2022) "What does the virus do to the analytic container? Thoughts on the frame in times of pandemic", in S. Carpani and M. Luci (eds) *Lockdown Therapy: Jungian Perspectives on How the Pandemic Changed Psychoanalysis*. London: Routledge.

Fairbairn, W.R.D. (1952) *Psychoanalytic Studies of the Personality*. London: Routledge.

Ferenczi, S. (1932 [1955]) "Confusion of tongues between adults and the child", in M. Balint (ed.) *Final Contributions to the Problems and Methods of Psycho-Analysis*. London: Hogarth Press, pp. 156–167.

Fordham, M. (1974) "Defences of the Self", *Journal of Analytical Psychology*, 19(2): 192–199.

Fordham, M. (1976) *The Self and Autism – Library of Analytical Psychology*, vol. 3. London: Heinemann.

Freud, S. (1895) "Project for a scientific psychology", in *SE I*. London: Hogarth Press, pp. 347–387.

Freud, S. (1905) "Three essays on the theory of sexuality", in *SE VII*. London: Hogarth Press, pp. 123–243.

Freud, S. (1914) "Remembering, repeating and working through", in *SE XII*. London: Hogarth Press, pp. 145–156.

Freud, S. (1920) "Beyond the pleasure principle", in *SE XVIII*. London: Hogarth Press, pp. 3–64.

Freud, S. (1924) "The economic problem of masochism", in *SE XIX*. London: Hogarth Press, pp. 155–170.

Freud, S. (1941) "An outline of psychoanalysis", in *SE XXIII*. London: Hogarth Press, pp. 70–71.

Garland, C. (2002) "Thinking about trauma", in C. Garland (ed.) *On Understanding Trauma – A Psychoanalytical Approach*. London: Karnac, pp. 9–31.

Gladstone, G.L., Parker, G.B., Mitchell, P.B., Malhi, G.S., Wilhelm, K. and Austin, M.P. (2004) "Implications of childhood trauma for depressed women: An analysis of pathways from childhood sexual abuse to deliberate self-harm and revictimization", *The American Journal of Psychiatry*, 161(8): 1417–1425.

Glasser, M. (1979) "Some aspects of the role of aggression in the perversions", in I. Rosen (ed.) *Sexual Deviation*, 2nd edition. Oxford: Oxford University Press, pp. 278–305.

Gordon, R. (1993) *Bridges Metaphor for Psychic Processes*. London: Karnac.

Graf-Nold, A. (2001) "The Zurich school of psychotherapy in theory and practice: Sabina Spielrein's treatment at the Burghölzli Clinic in Zurich", *Journal of Analytical Psychology*, 46(1): 73–104.

Guntrip, H. (1968) *Schizoid Phenomena, Object Relations and the Self*. London: Hogarth Press.

Jung, C.G. (1911–12) *The Transformation of Libido*. CW5. London: Routledge & Kegan Paul.

Jung, C.G. (1912) *The Theory of Psychoanalysis*. CW4. London: Routledge & Kegan Paul.

Jung, C.G. (1917) *On the Psychology of the Unconscious*. CW7. London: Routledge & Kegan Paul

Jung, C.G. (1928) *The Therapeutic Value of Abreaction*. CW16. London: Routledge & Kegan Paul

Jung, C.G. (1934) *A Review of the Complex Theory*. CW8. London: Routledge & Kegan Paul.

Jung, C.G. (1955/56) *The Personification of the Opposites*. CW14. London: Routledge & Kegan Paul.

Kalsched, D. (1996) *The Inner World of Trauma: Archetypal Defences of the Personal Spirit*. New York: Routledge.

Kalsched, D. (2015) "Revisioning Fordham's 'Defences of the Self' in light of modern relational theory and contemporary neuroscience", *Journal of Analytical Psychology*, 60(4): 477–496.

Kalsched, D. (2017) "Trauma, innocence and the core complex of dissociation", *Journal of Analytical Psychology*, 62(4): 474–500.

Kaplan, L.J. (1991) *Female Perversions*. London: Penguin.

Klein, M. (1927 [1975]) "Criminal tendencies in normal children", in *Love, Guilt and Reparation and Other Works 1921–1945*. 2nd edition. London: Hogarth Press and the Institute of Psychoanalysis.

Kulish, N.M. (1986) "Gender and transference: The screen of the phallic mother", *International Review of Psychoanalysis*, 13(4): 393–404.

Lambert, K. (1973) "The personality of the analyst in interpretation and therapy", in M. Fordham et al. (eds) *Technique in Jungian Analysis: The Library of Analytical Psychology*. London: Heinemann.

Laplanche, J. (1999) *Essays on Otherness*. London: Routledge.

Lester, E.P. (1990) "Gender and identity issues in the analytic process", *International Journal of Psychoanalysis*, 71(3): 435–444.

McDougall, J. (1995) *The Many Faces of Eros*. London: Free Association Books.

Meltzer, D. (1973) *Sexual States of Mind*. Perthshire: Clunie.

O'Rourke, J. (2011) "Deaths from auto erotic acts hidden", *The Sydney Morning Herald*, 28 August. Available at: www.smh.com.au/lifestyle/deaths-from-autoerotic-acts-hidden-20110827-1jfbq.html

Potamianou, A. (2015) "Amniotic traces: traumatic after-effects", *The International Journal of Psychoanalysis*, 96(4): 945–966.

Royston, R. (2001) "Sexuality and object relations", in C. Harding (ed.), *Sexuality Psychoanalytic Perspectives*, Sussex: Brunner-Routledge.

Schmidt, M. (2012) "Psychic skin: Psychotic defences, borderline process and delusions", *Journal of Analytical Psychology*, 57(1): 21–39.

Schmidt, M. (2013) "Freud's cancer", in J. Burke (ed.) *The Topic of Cancer: New Perspectives on the Emotional Experience of Cancer*. London: Karnac.

Shakespeare, W. (1861) *Macbeth*, in G. Brandes (ed.) *The Life and Work of William Shakespeare*. New York: Croscup and Sterling Co.

Spielrein, S. (1911 [1994]) "Destruction as a cause of coming into being", *Journal of Analytical Psychology*, 39(2): 155–186.

Steinberg, W. (1988) "The revolution of Jung's ideas on the transference", *Journal of Analytical Psychology*, 33(1): 21–39.

Stoller, R.J. (1985) *Observing the Erotic Imagination*. New Haven: Yale University Press.

Thomson, J. (2001) "The madness of love: A Jungian perspective on sexuality", in C. Harding (ed.) *Sexuality Psychoanalytic Perspectives*, Sussex: Brunner-Routledge.

West, M. (2016) *Into the Darkest Places: Early Relational Trauma and Borderline States of Mind*. London: Karnac Books.

Winnicott, D.W. (1949) "Birth memories, birth trauma and anxiety", in *Collected Papers: Through Paediatrics to Psychoanalysis*. New York: Basic Books, pp. 174–193.

Winnicott, D.W. (1969) "The use of an object", *International Journal of Psychoanalysis*, 50(4): 711–716.

Zinkin, L. (1969) "Flexibility in analytic technique", in M. Fordham et al. (eds) *Technique in Jungian Analysis Fordham: The Library of Analytical Psychology*, London: Karnac.

Zlotnick, C., Shea, M.T., Pearlstein, T., Simpson, E., Costello, E. and Begin, A. (1996) "The relationship between dissociative symptoms, alexithymia, impulsivity, sexual abuse, and self-mutilation", *Comprehensive Psychiatry*, 37(1): 12–16.

Zoppi, L. (2017) "Chilled to the bone: Embodied countertransference and unspoken traumatic memories", *Journal of Analytical Psychology*, 62(5): 701–709.

Chapter 9

The Black Sun of a Transgenerational Trauma

Dissociative Processes, Affects and the Symbolic Function

Fabrizio Alfani

Introduction

Contemporary psychoanalysis has accustomed us to consider the results of complex traumatic processes (not just events such as a car accident or an earthquake, but traumas caused by other human beings) as a variety of psychopathological forms and symptomatic manifestations, which can be very different from each other. For example, an adult who has suffered a severe trauma may show profound changes in consciousness that are symptomatically very different from the consequences of so-called early relational trauma.

However, it is possible to identify certain elements common to all these various clinical forms. We can observe how intense and dissociated affects related to trauma often penetrate the analytic relationship, influencing not only the patient's but also the analyst's ability to think and imagine. This reduction of the psyche's representational capacities (the partial paralysis of the symbolic function) hinders the processing of emotional experiences. This emotional infiltration, or "unconscious infection" (Jung, 1946), makes the analytical relationship very problematic, but at the same time it represents a therapeutic opportunity since it allows a live experience, in the "here and now" of the relationship, of the main affective constellations that inhabit the patient's psyche in a dissociated way.

As in the clinical case described in this chapter, it is not uncommon in the course of the analytic work for the therapist to enact affective content related to the autonomous complexes originating from the traumatic experiences lived by the patients. Sometimes these enactments allow the reactivation of the symbolic function through which previously dissociated emotions can be represented, imagined and experienced.

Dissociation and Autonomous Feeling-Toned Complexes

Jung very clearly stated that the psyche has a dissociative nature. In his view, dissociation is not only a pathological condition, but also a normal one, in

DOI: 10.4324/9781003298076-12

fact: "The psyche is far from being a homogeneous unit - on the contrary, it is a boiling cauldron of contradictory impulses, inhibitions and affects ... The unity of consciousness or of the so-called personality is not a reality at all but a desideratum" (Jung, 1938/54, para. 190). The contents of the psyche, "its original elements", are organized in *feeling-toned complexes*, which can become *autonomous* with respect to ego complex (Jung, 1934). At their core are affects, the strength of which influence the extent of the complex's autonomy.

As Jung wrote, complexes have different causes:

"The aetiology of their origin is frequently a so-called trauma, an emotional shock or some such thing, that splits off a bit of the psyche. Certainly, one of the commonest causes is a moral conflict, which ultimately derives from the apparent impossibility of affirming the whole of one's nature. This impossibility presupposes a direct split, no matter whether the conscious mind is aware of it or not.

(Jung, 1934, para. 204)

Therefore, the different aetiology of complexes can lead to two different interpretations of dissociation: a traumatic dissociation and a conflictual one, which has similarities with Freudian repression (Freud, 1915). The clinical and psychological consequences of the autonomy of the dissociated complexes essentially depend on two factors: the intensity of the affective charge of the complex and the psyche's ability to process and transform the affective experience.

A fundamental function of the psyche is to provide images and words for affective experiences. Affects are somatopsychic experiences, which are deeply rooted in the body (Damasio, 2010) and the psyche constantly attempts to make representable the affective states that accompany our existence (Bion, 1962), linking images and words with affects, in order to give meaning to the experience. This kind of psychic work is what Bion called "alpha function" (Bion, 1962) and is a fundamental aspect of the process generally thought of as "symbolic function". If the connection of images with affects and words does not succeed, a split between mind and body occurs that leads to a separation between body, emotions and thought. The processing and then transformation of affective states does not consist in making them into something other than what they are, but in making them available to be experienced by the subject in the most intimate and complete way for him. Alpha function does not turn hate into love or sadness into joy or anger into resignation or forgiveness. What it does is create the conditions for individual consciousness to be able to imagine, tolerate and experience hate, love, fear, sadness, joy and anger, without being overwhelmed by the intensity of these affects. In this way, alpha function enables consciousness to communicate and represent affects in the most articulate way. Thus, emotions and affects are transformed into feelings that nourish consciousness and its ability to dialogue with the unconscious (Jung, 1958; Kalsched, 2020).

The complexity of this process lies in the fact that the psyche is a battleground between conflicting tendencies. Acknowledging and experiencing the hatred and anger that dwell within us brings into conflict with our wish to be seen as good, loving and aligned with the prevailing positive values of collective ethics. Here we meet what Jung called the Shadow: "The shadow personifies everything that the subject refuses to acknowledge about himself and yet is always thrusting itself upon him directly or indirectly – for instance inferior traits of character and other incompatible tendencies" (Jung, 1939, para. 513). Every human being experiences dissociation between what he accepts and what he rejects of his own nature. Often this conflict leads to what is understood as normal dissociation, or as normal dissociative *processes* (Bromberg, 2006, 2011). As we know, dissociation can result not only from a conflict, in fact a traumatic experience can produce overwhelming affects that the psyche is not able to process and transform. Sometimes it is not possible for the individual to *suffer* this pain, and this paralyses the psyche's symbolic function and its development. This unbearable traumatic experience, untransformed and unelaborated, tends to reappear, although in dissociated forms, as the most frequent symptoms show us. These can be intrusive flashbacks that re-propose the traumatic scene, or somatic symptoms through which bodily memories of the trauma are expressed (which may fall under what Freud in 1917 called "repetition compulsion"); or they can be relational difficulties that tend to perpetuate in the patient "the breakdown of the relationship between the self and the nurturing other" (Laub and Auerhahn, 1993: 287).

As Mauro Manica states, the psyche is born and develops into an original intersubjective matrix, which begins as early as the placenta: "The mind like the body seems to have a placenta in which the intervillous space is not exclusively of the mother and is not exclusively of the fetus. It is a space in which mother and fetus co-create those proto-unconscious experiences from which the individual mind and all subjectivity will flourish" (Manica, 2022: 137). Every traumatic experience breaks this intersubjective matrix, and the gravity of trauma is greater the more: "it is realized as a *placental trauma*, the more it injures and breaks the continuity of this original intersubjective matrix" (Manica, 2021: 46). This basic, proto-unconscious, intersubjective matrix is a medium for the development of psychic functions. The strength and weakness of the psyche are rooted in this matrix.

One of the main relational experiences, which every human being has to manage, is both the presence and loss of the significant other. The relationship with the other is what enables the development of the psyche and, at the same time, it is also the main threat to its survival. An important task for the psyche is to process the loss of that *other* on whom its very survival is based. This ability depends upon the development of the symbolic function, which ensures that, even when the other is not physically present, his image continues to exist in the subject's internal world, with both cognitive and affective value. This makes it possible to maintain an affective bond with the other, even when he is not there. In this way, *loss* can turn into *absence*. As Maria Ilena Marozza observes, "The experience of absence contains within itself the germ of *psychic birth*, of that passage, that is which allows the physical-perceptual link with the object to be replaced by *intrapsychic representational play*" (Marozza, 2015: 100). Transforming loss into absence requires going through, feeling and suffering the grief caused by it. This is a painful experience that is necessary for psychic growth, in fact "We assume that the avoidance of loss, the failure of grief, will take a toll which is far more costly to the individual than loss which has been grieved… loss is necessary if one is to grow" (Russell, 2006: 86).

Dissociation as a Defense Mechanism or as a Deficit of Superior Psychic Functions

Traumatic experiences, and their related affects, produce both defensive dissociative mechanisms and *désagregation* (Janet, 1889) of the superior psychic functions.

The importance of affects and emotions in the genesis of dissociative processes was first recognized by Pierre Janet, who is considered the father of the concept of dissociation (Hellenberger, 1970; van der Hart and Dorahy, 2009). Janet understood dissociation as the consequence of a *deficit of the integrative functions of the mind*, a deficit caused by the disruptive effect (*désagregation*) of violent emotions on the higher levels of psychic functioning (Janet, 1889).

According to this idea, the mind *passively* dissociates as a consequence of the violent emotions that accompany traumatic experiences. Furthermore, if such experiences occur during the earliest stages of child development, they hinder the growth of superior psychic functions, such as consciousness and memory (Stern, 1985), mentalization (Allen, Fonagy and Bateman, 2008), the ability to regulate emotions (Schore, 2003) and the dialogue between consciousness and unconsciousness, which Jung called the "transcendent function" (Jung, 1958).

Another approach to dissociative processes is to consider them as a consequence of a defense mechanism of the psyche aimed at protecting itself from the repetition of intolerable experiences. According to this perspective, the psyche *actively* dissociates in order to avoid the repetition of disrupting experiences that can lead to further radical fragmentation and dissolution of a sense of self. As Kalsched writes: "Instead, dissociation appears to involve a good deal of aggression – apparently it involves an active attack by one part of the psyche on the other parts. It is as though the normally integrative tendencies in the psyche must be interrupted by force" (Kalsched, 1996: 13). According to Kalsched, the interruption of normal integrative tendencies in the psyche is not caused by the direct effect of vehement emotions, as Janet suggested, but by the psyche attacking itself to protect the sacred core of the self from the danger of annihilation. From this point of view, the dissociative process, understood as an active defense mechanism, entails the constitution of a hypercritical, sadistic and persecutory complex within the personality, full of fear, rage and hatred that are activated by the traumatic experience. This persecutory complex hinders the search for closeness and intimacy with others in every possible way. However, it also has a protective function: by preventing the subject from seeking closeness and intimacy in a relationship with the other, it tries to avoid the repetition of ancient traumatic experiences which provoked disorganizing and annihilating feelings. Dissociation is therefore achieved through these two mechanisms, one predominantly passive due to violent emotions disrupting superior psychic functions, and the second active, enacted by the psyche to protect itself from the danger inherent in any deep linking. However, these two models of dissociation can be usefully integrated, recognizing the role played both by *defense mechanisms* and the *deficit of superior psychic functions* in provoking dissociative phenomena (Alfani, 2020). As Laub and Auerhahn state: "It is the nature of trauma to elude our knowledge, because of both defense and deficit ... To protect ourselves from affect, we must, at times, avoid knowledge ... Trauma also overwhelms and defeats our capacity to organize it: ... our psychological abilities are rendered ineffective" (Laub and Auerhahn, 1993: 288).

Different Levels of Traumatic Experience

Clara Mucci (2018) concisely classified trauma according to three increasing levels of interpersonal traumatization. The first level is early relational trauma; the second maltreatment, neglect, physical and sexual abuse; and at the third level we find massive trauma (war, torture, genocide).

While the second and third levels reflect an increasing threat to physical and/or psychic survival, the first level is more directly related to a lack of affective attunement which takes the form of loss: the other, although physically present, is not psychologically there. Or, conversely, the subject perceives himself or parts of himself as not existing for the significant other. This can occur in the relationship between parent and child, when the parent is unable to mirror and empathize with the child's affective state. The parent can be either absent or too present, too far from the relationship or conversely too intrusive, that is, by using the relational field to evacuate his own disturbed psychic states or by invading and colonizing the child's mind (Schore, 2003).

In reference to autonomous complexes and their relationship with traumatic experiences, Jung states that the nuclear element of the complex is its affect, its emotional tonality. This nuclear element consists of two components: "first, a factor determined by experience and causally related to the environment; second, a factor innate in the individual's character and determined by his disposition" (Jung, 1948, para. 18). With respect to this "factor innate in the individual's character" we cannot help but wonder how these "innate" characteristics are

> profoundly shaped in early relationships with attachment figures, depending on whether they are recognized and confirmed or conversely rejected, misunderstood or simply not seen. More generally, the experience of the early relationship with the mother, and the influence exerted on it by the unconscious aspects of the maternal personality, contribute decisively to the development of the individual character, and this cannot be ignored in working with patients with severe personality disorders.
>
> (Alfani and Gullotta, 2008: 17)

The affective core of the complex is, to a great extent, the result of early relational experiences, which often have to do with the parent's failure in recognizing and confirming important aspects of the child's personality. The *trauma of nonrecognition*, as Bromberg underlines, "is an inevitable part of everyone's early life to one degree or another. In response to the trauma of nonrecognition, dissociative process becomes dissociative structure, at least in certain areas of mental functioning" (Bromberg, 2011: 69).

Indeed, patients may present the dissociative consequences of hidden, barely visible traumatic experiences that have been repeated over time, especially those from early development. Here, the breakdown of the relational context may not have the striking characteristics of survival-threatening physical violence, or of severe neglect or acted-out physical or sexual abuse, but rather consists of a persistent lack of affective attunement in the relationship with the other. It is what Masud Khan (1963) called "cumulative trauma" and, more recently, other authors have referred to as "the hidden trauma in infancy" (Bureau, Martin and Lyons-Ruth, 2010). Longitudinal studies show that the presence of dissociative symptomatology in childhood and adolescence correlates more with disorganized attachment and altered parent-child dialogue than with physical, sexual and psychological abuse or severe neglect (Lyons-Ruth, 2003). This is not to say that abuse and severe neglect do not lead to dissociative states, but that the tendency to dissociation is also triggered when the affective communication between parent and child is confused and disjointed, without this leading to abusive or neglectful behaviour. This is what Schore (2003) calls "early relational trauma".

Attachment studies have shown that these kinds of reactions are closely related to attachment disorganization (Main and Solomon, 1990). When a child feels fear or pain, he looks for protection and closeness to his parents, which activates the attachment system. However, the child's search for attachment figures can occasionally stir up painful memories in the parents, if there are unresolved memories of losses and traumas in their attachment relationships. The parent may react in an anxious, violent or humiliating way and may even dissociate himself (i.e., detaching from the relationship with his child and becoming psychologically absent). This can be extremely frightening for the child, often left alone and unable to understand. It alters the intersubjective matrix of the relationship, which becomes paradoxical and confusing, since the parent is, at the same time, "the source and the solution of the infant alarm" (Main and Hesse, 1990: 163). As Liotti writes: "Pathological dissociation is not necessarily always the outcome of violent, abusive, or humiliating interactions between an adult and a child. *Provided that activation of the attachment system is involved*, parental communications that are frightened or confused, but not obviously maltreatment of the infant, may set dissociative mental processes in motion" (Liotti, 2009: 56).

Attachment disorganization does not persist unchanged over time. In fact, it can be seen that around the age of three, many children whose relationship with the caregiver is characterized by disorganized attachment, begin to develop a more organized behaviour, which has been defined as *controlling behaviour* (Lyons-Ruth and Jakobvitz, 2008; Liotti and Farina,

2011). From the age of three onwards, instead of seeking attachment with the caregiver (which causes a disorganizing and annihilating experience) the child begins to take control of the relationship, developing either a caring or a punitive attitude towards the caregiver. These two attitudes are sometimes both present, alternating in the same individual.

The controlling strategies present many points of contact with the defense systems connected to dissociation, the main purpose of which is to protect a person from seeking closeness and intimacy in a relationship with the other, in order to avoid disorganizing and annihilating feelings. The inner demon of trauma described by Kalsched (1996) seems to be an inner personification of this need. At a conscious level, the relational style and behaviour may oscillate between the controlling caretaking system or the punitive one, but in both cases there is an inner demon whose role is to prevent, in a violent way, closeness, intimacy and the search for protection in the relationship with the other.

Nicholas and the Black Sun

For years, Nicholas's inner world had been characterized by anger and extreme sensitivity to feeling devalued and unrecognized by others. When I met him, he was 30 years old and had lived most of his life at home with both his parents and his paternal grandparents. In the last two years he had been living with his partner, the only reliable figure in his life and to whom he was deeply attached.

The atmosphere in the parental home had always been very quarrelsome: in particular, the grandmother was extremely critical and argumentative towards Nicholas's mother. From the age of 5, Nicholas had participated in family arguments by taking his mother's side, while his father sided with his own mother. He had asked for analysis because of persistent anxiety, insomnia and anger, mainly due to work-related situations. In addition, he also suffered from Crohn's disease and the intensity of his intestinal symptoms correlated with fluctuations in his mental states.

A few months after starting analysis, during one of the last sessions before the summer holidays, he arrived in a highly agitated state and asked if he could stand instead of sit in the chair. He explained that this was because the standing position allowed him to better manage his psychic state, which was a mixture of anxiety and anger. As he paced back and forth in the room, he told me that the past week had been a very difficult one and that he feared he would not be able to cope with all the tension he was feeling. At work, Nicholas felt ignored and exploited, but he could not fight back for fear of being fired. In addition, he had recently arranged some renovation work at home, but there were defects and the company that had carried out the work denied any responsibility. He felt mocked, which evoked a very strong anger and he feared he might explode at any moment. All this had had a devastating effect on his body, as his Crohn's disease flared up.

That session lasted an hour and a half, twice as long as usual. I told myself that I could not let him go in such an overwhelming angry state. Many of the things he had talked about (not being able to complain to his superiors at the office about the lack of proper consideration and the short-comings in the renovation of the house, for which no one wanted to take responsibility) sounded like unconscious references to our relationship, to his needs of being seen, which I imagined was related to the imminent break for the summer. I had the feeling that he was unconsciously testing me, to check if I was willing to accept his need to be seen or whether he would have to engage in a battle with me to claim his right to exist and be respected. I also felt that he was evoking something reminiscent of the quarrelsome atmosphere of his childhood. However, while *thinking* all this, I was unable to find the words to communicate it. I had the *feeling* that these were fundamental themes that had been present throughout his life, but my inability to make sense of what was happening between us made me feel as if I was paralysed. I felt that any attempt to put into words my feel-ings about what was happening between us would be too violent. In the same way, I could not bring our meeting to an end as it seemed to me that an interruption would be too violent at that moment too. It would be unbearable, for both him and me. I was certainly afraid of arousing a neg-ative transference reaction in him, afraid that he would become aggressive towards me. However, at the same time, I was strongly convinced that something very important for Nicholas's psychic life was happening in that session, and that the subsequent outcome of therapy would also depend on how we would be able to manage the affective dynamic that was being acti-vated between us. It was only later that I was able to understand how the inability to talk about the break in our relationship was likely related to an old experience of his, linked to grief and to the impossibility of talking about separation.

At a certain point, he said something that made me understand that he thought the next session would be our last. I reminded him that we had agreed to see each other until the end of the month, so we still had three sessions left. He nodded without making any explicit comment. Now, I felt I could end the session. Having mentioned the imminent separation for the summer holidays suddenly allowed me to cope with the conclusion of the session. I also noticed that my reminder that we still had three sessions left before the break considerably reduced his anxiety. The following sessions, which preceded the break, went much better.

Unfortunately, after a few months we had to stop because of the Covid pandemic, since he refused to do the sessions online. Altogether, we did not meet for almost six months. However, during those months Nicholas dedicated himself to studying for an examination that would allow him to change job and obtain a role more suited to his desires and training. He was successful and accepted a role that gave him the recognition, both financial and professional, that until then he had always been denied. However, he could not celebrate his success. When we met again in September, he told me that winning this competition had not calmed him down. The anxiety and insomnia, that had intensified during the preparation for the exam, had not resolved after the positive outcome of it. He continued to feel constantly threatened by something unknown and was afraid that his inability to rest at night would eventually drive him crazy.

At that moment, I was unable to see his anxiety as a possible consequence of our separation. It was only later that I could realize how separations made Nicholas feel terrified, angry and guilty. These emotions colonized my mind without me realizing it, hindering my ability to think and imagine. Faced with the persistence of his symptoms, I suggested he might try some medication. Until then, he had occasionally taken low doses of benzodiazepines prescribed by a previous doctor, but they no longer worked. I decided to prescribe him an antidepressant.

Nicholas accepted the prescription without hesitation. During the next session he said: "I cannot imagine where all this anxiety comes from, apparently there is no reason. This week I thought that *I am operating a kind of self-sabotage* to my detriment. I don't know why, but I feel like I am preventing myself from living peacefully." These words reminded me of the *inner saboteur* (Fairbairn, 1952), as well as the *inner demon of trauma* (Kalsched, 1996). I suggested that he try to dialogue with this inner saboteur, as if it were a character from his inner world. This proposal left him very perplexed and so I suggested he try drawing it instead.

The next session he came with a drawing of a black sun in a dark grey sky over a blue sea. The drawing was very simple, and he commented: "The saboteur takes me there. Perhaps the saboteur is the black sun. The black sun is not a black hole, it is a sun that sends its black light on all things." This drawing favoured the development of a greater capacity for self-reflection on Nicholas's behalf, who was then able to tell me, in the following session:

> I have noticed that lately I am trying to have a less negative view of the world. In the past, I used to believe that if my life was going badly, it was because others behaved badly towards me. I am realizing that I see things differently now: I don't look so much at the fact that others make me live badly, but I see that I am the one who is attributing this negative attitude to others. And then it is as if this negativity spills over onto me. *It's like the black sun turning the whole world around me black.*

Encountering the Inner Demon(s)

From that session on, his anxiety began to lessen, and dreams appeared in which he tried to escape unsuccessfully from devils, evil presences or tormentors. They were oneiric representations of that internal saboteur, the inner demon of trauma that had probably been inhabiting him since childhood. In a dream three months later, the devil appeared in a very different way:

> I am at my parents' house, in my room. On the bed is an iron pen. I try to pick it up, but it is so heavy that I can't lift it because there is a magnetic force attracting it downwards. I try to better understand what is happening and so I pick up a compass, which can't find North and seems to have gone mad. I realize that there is a strange force in the world, there are demons that open breaches in our dimension. Whenever the door to this other dimension is opened, 'paranormal' phenomena occur involving the earth's magnetism. I approach the door that allows passage into the other dimension, it is as if it were the door to hell. On the threshold stands a red demon with horns who says to me: "I am in your mind, but you will never find out where".

In this dream, the opening of a door between different dimensions in Nicholas's inner world brings with it a loss of orientation. This allows his oneiric ego to dialogue with the demonic representation of the inner saboteur, standing at the door of hell and claiming to be hidden in his mind. However, the demon is not just a threatening, silent presence, as in previous dreams; now there is a form of communication between the two. The opening of a door allows for this communication to happen, even if it causes profound disorientation. Through the demon, Nicholas's ego can speak to an otherness, a Shadow that had hitherto only manifested itself through evil and negative forms but which now has a more familiar aspect.

Some weeks later, dreams began to appear in which I was present as the analyst. Through one of these dreams, it was possible to recall a loss that had profoundly affected the history of Nicholas and his family, but which had never appeared in analysis.

> I'm with another guy, who looks like an old school friend of mine. We look almost like relatives, there is a very close bond. We commit bad deeds and are involved in drug trafficking. We exhume bodies from graves and then "pulverize" them. This activity generates great guilt and anxiety for me. I feel that what we are doing is totally wrong. My friend, unlike me, has no remorse, no scruples. In fact, he forces me not to talk about it with anyone. At one point we exhume a body, pulverize it and mix it with a drug, then sell it. This last act seems even more deplorable to me. I can't keep it all inside and I tell my parents everything, crying. Then I find myself in my childhood home, with you [the analyst]. The sense of anguish I feel is very deep, mixed with guilt. I tell you about the exhumation and pulverization of the bodies, and you give me an enlightening interpretation and the guilt immediately disappears.

In this dream, our relationship was ambivalent, positive and negative at the same time. I was the analyst offering an enlightening interpretation and freeing him from his fears, while we were a couple committing sacrilegious acts. We had been exhuming corpses and mixing them with a drug (which very likely was also a reference to the antidepressant I had prescribed).

However, in addition to this reading referring to our relationship, the setting of the dream prompted me to ask if there had been other deaths in the family. It was then that he told me that two years before his birth, his uncle, his father's brother, had died of cancer when he was only 14 years old. After his death, the grandmother had forbidden any expression of joy in the household and the grandparents visited their son's grave every day for the rest of their lives. If Nicholas's mother (at the time, in her early twenties) laughed or put on lipstick, his grandmother criticized her harshly, and this had been one of the main reasons for the quarrels that had marked his childhood.

Nicholas had never told me this before. Now, this helped to give new meaning to many of the things he had brought to analysis, as if the ghost of his uncle had continued to be present in the family. This unprocessed grief had not allowed the family to welcome the new life that was coming.

The ghost of the uncle and the associated immense grief had triggered a transgenerational trauma (Faimberg, 1988) which had unconsciously colonized Nicholas's psychic life from birth, and burdened him with a sense of guilt for something he was not responsible for: he was alive, while the uncle was dead. This also illuminated something Nicholas had repeated to me several times: "I have the impression that I have to be punished for something, even though I am convinced that I have done nothing wrong, that I am not at fault".

The intensity of the affects aroused by the experiences of separation and the peculiar importance they assumed in Nicholas's psychic world only emerged after the account of his uncle's death. Only then, were we able to better understand the meaning of the two clinical situations described above, namely the session before the summer holiday that lasted twice as long and Nicholas's intense anxiety that led me to prescribe medication.

At the time, I had been unable to feel and to think the fear and the anger that the long break in our sessions could have evoked in Nicholas. This reaction was linked to his transgenerational trauma, which brought with it an endless, unbearable grief. Moreover, I now realized why getting his new role at work evoked in him a deep guilt, related to his being alive while his uncle was dead. Only later, through dreams and through the drawing of the black sun, was it possible to give an image to these affective vicissitudes and to develop a capacity to symbolically represent what had been evoked in the therapeutic relationship.

In the first case, the unusual prolongation of the session can be understood as an attempt to deny the inevitable separation. In the second case, the prescription of the medication can take on multiple meanings. The drug can be seen as a form of nourishment that the analyst-mother offers to the patient-child in the absence of revêrie, that was paralysed at that moment. The medicine also has a shadow side: it can be seen as a poison, a drug that replaces and annihilates the symbolic capacities of the psyche by anaesthetizing them, mixing (as in the dream) the unprocessed remains of the uncle's death with the drug. Furthermore, the drug allows for the denial of separation, it can be perceived by the patient as an object that symbolically represents and replaces the analyst. The drug, unlike the analyst, is always available and the patient can take it with him wherever he goes, even when the therapy has stopped. In the relationship with the medication, the patient is not exposed to the vicissitudes of the relationship with the other, to its possible absences and to the threat of a definitive loss. However, there is a risk of replacing the dependence on the analyst with dependence on the drug.

Despite the short-circuiting of the capacity to imagine and think, these acts did not prevent the development of Nicholas's ability to symbolically represent the complex themes that conditioned his psychic world. On the contrary, they seem to have somehow facilitated it, perhaps because in both cases the analyst was unconsciously resonating with Nicholas's (equally unconscious) emotional demands. In fact, it was during the session following the pharmacological prescription that Nicholas spoke of a self-saboteur (internal persecutor) which prevented him from living more serenely. And then, when I asked him to draw the internal persecutor, he drew the black sun.

Black Sun, *Umbra Solis*, Shadow

Personal and Archetypal Resonances

The black sun is an image rich in meaning, also present in the works of many modern artists (Marlan, 2005). There are many references to the black sun in alchemical literature. The twelfth woodcut in the *Rosarium Philosophorum* (1550) depicts a sun plunging into a tomb and the commentary on the figure states: "Here Sol plainly dies again and is drowned with the Mercury of the Philosophers." The next image shows a winged hermaphrodite lying in the sepulchre, but the commentary refers again to the black sun: "Here Sol is made black unto pitch, with the Mercury of the Philosophers." The alchemical symbolism of the shining sun entering the tomb to go through a death experience alludes to a mercurial and transformative experience closely linked to the experience of pain and psychic death.

The nineteenth panel of the *Splendor Solis* (Trismosin, 1582/2021: 119), a 16th-century alchemical text, is also dedicated to the black sun, setting on the horizon of a barren landscape, with dry trees in the foreground, among which new vegetation grows. The next panel of the *Splendor Solis*, the twentieth (Trismosin, 1582/2021: 121), shows a room where a group of children are playing under the gaze of their mother sitting in the background. It is significant that the image of the black sun is followed by that of children playing, as if the contact with experiences of psychic death, linked to the black sun, enabled the activation of creative energies capable of renewing the experience of ourselves, playing with life and the inhabitants of our imagination (Sherwood, 2006).

Julia Kristeva's (1987) book on depression and melancholia is significantly titled *The Black Sun*, because this image is associated with the experience of psychic death linked to melancholia and depression. As Kristeva states, melancholic feelings resonate with "old traumas that I realize I have failed to mourn" (Kristeva, 1987: 14). But at the same time, melancholia is capable of profoundly transforming our view of the world and things as it allows for a nocturnal vision of our psychic world, enabling us to see what a consciousness dazzled by too much light is sometimes unable to recognize.

In "Mourning and Melancholia", Freud (1917) pointed out that depression is evoked by the predominance of a narcissistic attachment to the object.

In the normal grieving process, the object-directed libido remains attached to the lost object, even though the reality principle forces us to recognize its loss. The ego clings to the object, identifying with it for as long as necessary, until we are able to recognize that we can survive emotionally in the absence of the love object. At this point, the "grief work" allows us to accept the separation and loss, and we can see that the world without the love object is a world still worth living in.

In the case of melancholia, what is lost is a narcissistic object. The attachment to this object is not sustained by love for it, but predominantly by the ego's need to be constantly nourished by the relationship with this object. Then, when it is lost, "the shadow of the object fell upon the ego" (Freud, 1917: 249), that is, the loss of the object is transformed into a loss of the ego, which is experienced as dead. Thus, depression sometimes forces us to process old traumas, losses that we were not able to cope with. These are mainly early relational traumas that have prevented our vital narcissism from being adequately nourished (Green, 1983), leading us to unconsciously seek this narcissistic nourishment in our relationships with the outside world.

The journey into the dark night of depression, if mourning succeeds, can offer the possibility of emancipating ourselves from the excessive narcissistic demands that prevent a more satisfying object relationship (Ogden, 2012; West, 2020). We can also read Freud's statement from a Jungian perspective: the "shadow of the object" is not only what remains after its loss, but is also the dark side of the object, its Shadow (in a Jungian sense), that has fallen on the subject. This Shadow of the object – the Shadow of the parent – can make him psychologically absent or too present for the child, thus preventing a lack of recognition by the significant other. "Nothing exerts a stronger psychic effect upon the human environment, and especially upon children, than the life which the parents have not lived" (Jung, 1929, para. 4). We can think of the black sun (*umbra solis*) in Nicholas' drawing not only as his own shadow, but also as the dark side of the object, the shadow of the family that inhabited Nicholas's psyche. In a similar way, commenting on Joyce McDougall's case of Sorel, in which inability to process transgenerational grief is described (McDougall, 2000), Astor suggests that in the patient's psyche "we see the shadow not only of her experience but also of her parents' experience" (Astor, 2000: 71).

The image of the black sun, which we can understand as an archetypal image, spontaneously presented itself to Nicholas as he tried to depict the internal saboteur: an image that his hands drew beyond his awareness. Interestingly, with regard to the process just described, Grotstein – who is not a Jungian analyst – suggests that the transformation of emotional experience into images: "is facilitated by alpha function's access to inherent and acquired preconceptions, that is, archetypes, which are always pressing to surface but require a sensible experience for a vehicle" (Grotstein, 2000: 27).

After the creation of the image of the black sun, Nicholas was then able to make a radical change in his representation of himself and of the world. He began to feel less narcissistically victimized by a world filled with objects that had ignored his need for recognition. Now, suddenly, he had glimpsed the possibility of being the author of his own story. This was helped by acknowledging the existence of an internal saboteur, an Other inside himself who had exerted its influence on him since birth. This influence was like an astral constellation emanating the dark light of an irreparable loss, the power of which Nicholas had failed to realize. However, the presence of this internal Other helped him to survive the lack of adequate primary narcissistic nourishment he had suffered.

Paul Russell emphasized the importance that experiencing loss in one's life has for psychotherapy: "Psychotherapy, to the extent that it works, necessarily involves grief. The treatment process itself thus becomes a necessary loss, or, more accurately, it helps the person to *feel* a loss that has heretofore, for whatever reason, not been grieved. Psychotherapy consists of the facing down of one's necessary losses" (Russell, 2006: 86–87). In order to transform *loss* into *absence* we need to be able to *feel* the loss, to experience and suffer the pain it entails. However, as Bion (1970: 9) stated: "People exist who are so intolerant of pain or frustration (or in whom pain or frustration are so intolerable) that they feel the pain but will not suffer it."

It had been impossible for Nicholas's family to grieve the pain of their loss. The death of his uncle had caused an intolerable and unspeakable grief, a wound that had never healed and had created an emotional void in Nicholas's family; a void that had been filled with fear, anger and guilt. Despite the fact that he had lived in a house full of photographs of his uncle and had gone to the cemetery with his family every Sunday until he was 13 years old, they had never spoken at home about that death and the pain it brought with it. There had only been fragmentary news, such as what his mother had told Nicholas at the age of 10. Although the image of his uncle was in front of him every day, his death had no access to words, no access to a narrative. There were no words for such an endless grief. In a similar way, still referring to the case of Sorel (McDougall, 2000), Astor goes on with saying: "This is a family in which death features hugely, but without any of the shared experience of dying and without any mourning" (Astor, 2000: 73).

Even in analysis it had been very difficult to talk about the experiences of separation and loss, of feeling abandoned. The two clinical situations described are an example of this, and it is very likely that, in both cases, the difficulty of representing and verbally formulating the affects aroused by the separations had been relived in the transference-countertransference, colonizing my mind as well and enacted within the therapeutic relationship. It took a dream, which came after about two years of therapy, to be able to begin to narrate that trauma and what it had entailed in Nicholas's life.

Conclusions

One of the main goals of psychotherapy is the integration of dissociated complexes, which takes place mainly through the therapeutic relationship. As Jung says: "The transference is the patient's attempt to get into psychological rapport with the doctor. He needs this relationship if he is to overcome the dissociation" (Jung, 1928, para. 276).

However, the therapeutic relationship cannot be sufficient in itself, if it does not nurture the growth of a symbolic capacity to give form to previously unrepresentable psychic contents. Otherwise, there is the risk that the therapeutic relationship causes the development of an infinite dependency (or malign regression [Balint, 1959]), in which the analyst is the exclusive repository of the symbolic function necessary for the patient to live.

Sometimes, analyst and patient can meet in the analytic field, and become touched by the encounter with the other. This "touching" and "being touched" can allow the repair of the intersubjective matrix, that has been broken/injured by the traumatic experience. The symbolic function helps not only by making it possible to give images and then words to the patient's unspoken past, but also by highlighting the goal of individuation for the subject. The unconscious shapes a possible realization of this goal.

A year after the dream of the cemetery, a new dream appeared, set in a world of zombies. This world is transformed into a living world when the zombies see themselves reflected in a mirror, thus realizing they are dead. A sacred, revitalizing light then appears, breathing life back into that dead reality.

It is the apocalypse, the world is a grey place, populated by zombies. I see the scene as if it were a film. The protagonists of the story see their image reflected in a mirror and thus realize that they are zombies, as if the mirror showed them what they really are, the living dead. Suddenly they realize that the whole world is populated by zombies, but each of these zombies does not know they are zombies because they do not see themselves that way. Suddenly from the altar of a small, bare stone church comes a powerful beam of pure light, which shines down the side of a hill. From the hillside (which was previously barren and devoid of life forms) flowers and blades of grass begin to grow and the zombies become living people again. I remember a large tree that begins to produce green leaves.

This powerful dream refers to the possibility of self-reflection, offered by analysis (the zombies seeing themselves in the mirror). In a certain way, we can say that Nicholas had finally realized he had always been living like a zombie, in a world of zombies. In fact, it was exactly the *living dead* that his family was made of. Helped by the encounter with the Black Sun, Nicholas was then able to see his lifeless world, where now a light comes to give life to flowers and grass. Hope for new life is arising from the previous domain of death and pulverization.

As Jung wrote:

The treatment must do more than destroy the old morbid attitude; it must build up a new attitude that is sound and healthy. This requires a fundamental change of vision. Not only must the patient be able to see the cause and origin of his neurosis, he must also see the legitimate psychological goal towards which he is striving. We cannot simply extract his morbidity like a foreign body, lest something essential be removed along with it, something meant for life. Our task is not to weed it out, but to cultivate and transform this growing thing until it can play its part in the totality of the psyche.

(Jung, 1928, para. 293)

References

Alfani, F. (2020) "Continuità e discontinuità dei processi dissociativi", in M. Germani and M. Maulucci (eds) *Frammenti di Psiche*. Roma: FrancoAngeli.

Alfani, F. and Gullotta, C. (2008) "Trauma, complesso, dissociazione", *Studi Junghiani*, 14: 13–31.

Allen, J.G., Fonagy, P. and Bateman A.W. (2008) *Mentalizing in Clinical Practice*. Washington DC and London: American Psychiatric Association Publishing.

Astor, J. (2000) "Response to Joyce McDougall: The triumph of compassion over mourning", *Journal of Analytical Psychology*, 45(1): 69–73.

Balint, M. (1959) *Thrills and Regressions*. London: Routledge.

Bion, W.R. (1962) *Learning from Experience*. London: Heinemann Medical Books.

Bion, W.R. (1970) *Attention and Interpretation: A Scientific Approach to Insight in Psychoanalysis and Groups*. London: Tavistock Publications.

Bromberg, P.M. (2006) *Awakening the Dreamer. Clinical Journeys*. London: Analytic Press.

Bromberg, P.M. (2011) *The Shadow of the Tsunami and the Growth of the Relational Mind*. London: Routledge.

Bureau, J.F., Martin, J. and Lyons-Ruth, K. (2010) "Attachment dysregulation as hidden trauma in infancy: Early stress, maternal buffering and psychiatric morbidity in young adulthood", in R.A. Lanius, E. Vermetten and C. Pain (eds) *The Impact of Early Life Trauma on Health and Disease: The Hidden Epidemic*. Cambridge: Cambridge University Press, pp. 48–56.

Damasio, A. (2010) *Self Comes to Mind*. New York: Penguin Random House.

Faimberg, H. (1988) "The telescoping of generations: Genealogy of certain identifications", *Contemporary Psychoanalysis*, 24(1): 99–118.

Fairbairn, W.R.D. (1952) *Psychoanalytic Studies of the Personality*. London: Routledge.

Freud, S. (1915) "Repression", in *SE XIV*, London: Hogarth Press.

Freud, S. (1917) "Mourning and melancholia", in *SE XIV*, London: Hogarth Press.

Green, A. (1983) *Narcissisme de Vie, Narcissisme de Mort*. Paris: Editions de Minuit.

Grotstein, J. (2000) *Who is the Dreamer, Who Dreams the Dream? A Study of Psychic Presences*. Hillsdale, NJ: The Analytic Press.

Hellenberger, H.F. (1970) *The Discovery of the Unconscious. The History and Evolution of Dynamic Psychiatry*. New York: Basic Books.

Janet, P. (1889) *L'Automatisme Psychologique. Essais de Psychologie Expérimentale sur les Formes Inférieures de l'Activité Humaine*. Paris: Félix Alcan.

Jung, C.G. (1928) *The Therapeutic Value of Abreaction*. CW16. Princeton, NJ: Princeton University Press.

Jung, C.G. (1929) *Paracelsus*. CW13. Princeton, NJ: Princeton University Press.

Jung, C.G. (1934) *A Review of the Complex Theory*. CW8. Princeton, NJ: Princeton University Press.

Jung, C.G. (1938/54) *Psychological Aspects of the Mother Archetype*. CW9/1. Princeton, NJ: Princeton University Press.

Jung, C.G. (1939) *Conscious, Unconscious and Individuation*. CW9/1. Princeton, NJ: Princeton University Press.

Jung, C.G. (1946) *The Psychology of the Transference*. CW16. Princeton, NJ: Princeton University Press.

Jung, C.G. (1948) *On Psychic Energy*. CW8. Princeton, NJ: Princeton University Press.

Jung, C.G. (1958) *The Transcendent Function*. CW8. Princeton, NJ: Princeton University Press.

Kalsched, D. (1996) *The Inner World of Trauma. Archetypal Defences of the Personal Spirit*. New York: Routledge.

Kalsched, D. (2020) "Opening the closed heart: Affect-focused clinical work with the victims of early trauma", *Journal of Analytical Psychology*, 65(1): 136–152.

Khan, M.M.R. (1963) "The concept of cumulative trauma", *The Psychoanalytic Study of the Child*, 18: 286–306.

Kristeva, J. (1987) *Soleil Noir. Dépression et Mélancolie*. Paris: Gallimard.

Laub, D. and Auerhahn, N. (1993) "Knowing and not knowing massive psychic trauma: Forms of traumatic memories", *International Journal of Psychoanalysis*, 74(2): 287–302.

Liotti, G. (2009) "Attachment and dissociation", in P.F. Dell and J.A. O'Neil (eds) *Dissociation and the Dissociative Disorders – DSM-V and Beyond*. New York: Routledge, pp. 53–65.

Liotti, G. and Farina, B. (2011) *Sviluppi Traumatici*. Milano: Raffaello Cortina Editore.

Lyons-Ruth, K. (2003) "Dissociation and the parent-infant dialogue: A longitudinal perspective from attachment research", *Journal of American Psychoanalytic Association*, 51(3): 883–911.

Lyons-Ruth, K. and Jakobvitz, D. (2008) "Attachment disorganization: Genetic factors, parenting contexts, and developmental transformation from infancy to adulthood", in J. Cassidy and P. Shaver (eds) *Handbook of Attachment: Theory, Research, and Clinical Applications*. New York: Guilford Press, pp. 666–697.

Main, M. and Hesse, E. (1990) "Parents' unresolved traumatic experiences are related to infant disorganized attachment status: Is frightened/frightening parental behaviour the linking mechanism?", in M.T. Greenberg, D. Cicchetti and E.M. Cummings (eds) *Attachment in the Preschool Years*. Chicago: Chicago University Press, pp. 161–182.

Main, M. and Solomon, J. (1990) "Procedures for identifying infants as disorganized/disoriented during the Ainsworth Strange Situation", in M.T. Greenberg, D. Cicchetti and E.M. Cummings (eds) *Attachment in the Preschool Years*. Chicago: Chicago University Press, pp. 121–160.

Manica, M. (2021) *"E Quindi Uscimmo a Riveder le Stelle" – Il Dialogo di Bion con la Psicoanalisi*. Roma: Armando Editore.

Manica, M. (2022) "Il dialogo della psicoanalisi", in F. Feliziani (ed.) *A Tu, per Tu. Pensare l'Incontro Facendosi Incontro*. Roma: Piccola Barca.

Marlan, S. (2005) *The Black Sun: The Alchemy and Art of Darkness*. Texas: A&M University Press.

Marozza, M.I. (2015) *Ritorno alla Talking Cure*. Roma: Giovani Fioriti Editore.

McDougall, J. (2000) "Theatres of the psyche", *Journal of Analytical Psychology*, 45(1): 45–64.

Mucci, C. (2018) *Borderline Bodies: Affect Regulation Therapy for Personality Disorders*. New York: W.W. Norton & Co.

Ogden, T.H. (2012) *Creative Readings: Essays on Seminal Analytic Works*. London: Routledge.

Russell, P.L. (2006) "The role of loss in the repetition compulsion", *Smith College Studies in Social Work*, 76(1–2): 85–98.

Schore, A.N. (2003) *Affect Regulation and the Repair of the Self*. New York: W.W. Norton & Co.

Sherwood, D.N. (2006) "Alchemical images, implicit communication, and transitional states", *Spring*, 74: 233–262.

Stern, D.N. (1985) *The Interpersonal World of the Infant*. New York: Basic Books.

Trismosin, S. (1582/2021) *Splendor Solis*. S. Skinner, R.T. Prinke, G. Hedesan and J. Godwin (eds) Roma: Edizioni Mediterranee.

van der Hart, O. and Dorahy, M.J. (2009) "History of the concept of dissociation", in P.F. Dell and J.A. O'Neil (eds) *Dissociation and the Dissociative Disorders – DSM-V and Beyond*. New York: Routledge.

West, M. (2020) "Self, other and individuation: Resolving narcissism through the lunar and solar paths of the *Rosarium*", *Journal of Analytical Psychology*, 65(1): 171–197.

Part III

Sociological and Analytic Aspects of Trauma

Chapter 10

Social Trauma

Emilija Kiehl

They hang the man and flog the woman
That steal the goose from off the common,
But let the greater villain loose
That steals the common from the goose.
The law demands that we atone
When we take things we do not own,
But leaves the lords and ladies fine
Who take things that are yours and mine.[1]

This chapter is a continuation of the paper I presented at the III European Congress of Analytical Psychology in Trieste in 2015. There I explored the impact of the British socioeconomic class system on the individual sense of self. A version of the paper was later published in the Journal of Analytical Psychology (2016). The title, "You were not born here, so you are classless, you are free!", came from a statement made by a patient of mine in relation to my social status in British society as he perceived it.

After my presentation in Trieste, a British colleague congratulated me and said that it was good that someone finally approached this topic which is a taboo subject in Britain. Another British colleague commented that my paper viewed the British class system "from the outside". I wondered if the latter comment was in fact questioning the validity of my view, being "from the outside". I also wondered if, indeed, I would be writing about the potentially traumatic impact of the British social class system on the sense of personal identity, if I had been born in this system. Would I attempt to "see" a cultural class-complex from the inside?

The epidemiologists Wilkinson and Pickett, in their book *The Inner Level* (2018: 202), note that, "Many people tend to be evasive about class and status differences, and some deny not only their importance but occasionally even their existence. Personal interactions across class differences are often experienced as awkward and embarrassing." In this collection of research

DOI: 10.4324/9781003298076-14

material on the impact of socioeconomic inequality on mental health, they quote an excerpt from a book by professor of sociology, Andrew Sayer, *The Moral Significance of Class*, who found that:

> When people are asked in interviews what class they belong to, their replies are often awkward, defensive and evasive, treating the question as if it were … about whether they deserve their class position or whether they consider themselves inferior or superior to others … Class remains a highly charged issue because of the associations of injustice and moral evaluation. To ask someone what class they are is not simply to ask them to classify their socio-economic position, for it also carries the suggestion of a further unspoken and offensive question: what are you worth?
>
> (Sayer, 2005, in Wilkinson and Pickett, 2018: 203)

What is Trauma?

In his book *Involuntary Dislocation. Home, Trauma, Resilience, and Adversity-Activated Development*, Renos K. Papadopoulos (2021) warns that "Trauma – a word for all seasons", may have become one of those words "so popular and 'fashionable' … that their meaning becomes so elastic that it can stretch to refer to virtually any phenomenon loosely related to a vaguely understood theme" (Papadopoulos, 2021: 206–207). Papadopoulos explores the etymology of the word and a number of formulations, which have entered everyday discourse, to depict the ever-widening scope of life's situations where what we call trauma may develop. His thread takes us back to Homer, where we find that *trauma* (or wound), the noun of the Greek verb *titrosko* (to pierce or wound), extends its meaning beyond the physical, into the metaphorical dimension, which includes various forms of psychological injury (Papadopoulos, 2021).

Psychoanalyst Howard Levine (2021), agrees with Papadopoulos and explains his approach to the term:

> The concept of Trauma in psychoanalysis has suffered from overuse and inconsistent use. A review of Freud's writings beginning with the Project indicates that from the perspective of the impact upon psychic processes, Freud held a more consistent view of the concept that, if recognized, can help avoid the often fruitless etiological debates of internal vs. external cause, intrinsic (drive) vs. extrinsic (reality) factors, etc. What is more helpful from a clinical perspective, is to view the various challenges that a given set of potentially trauma-inducing circumstances might pose for an individual, consider each individual's highly subjective mode of

experiencing and responding to those challenges and take into account the supports offered in any instance by the specific familial, social or cultural surround.

(Levine, 2021: 794)

In other words, the events, situations or circumstances that may develop into a trauma for one person may not do so for another. As Levine goes on to say,

Each set of experiences that will be qualified as 'trauma' that any of us undergoes will to some extent be understood and integrated into our particular subjectivities according to our unique, subjective organizations of self, understandings of and position in the world.

(Levine, 2021: 794)

Papadopoulos (2021) writes about the plight of refugees and bears witness to the potentially traumatic experiences of people who have been displaced from the (in some cases at least relative) safety of their homes and familiar relationships. These are people who are forced to make the external and internal transitions of adjusting to unfamiliar living conditions, social perceptions and value systems in foreign, often hostile, lands.

Can the experiences of refugees seeking safety in places they do not belong to by culture, language or race, be compared to those born poor into socio-economic class systems of pronounced, ever-widening inequality, which, for the most part, favours the interests of the rich? Unlike the refugees, those of modest means do share some spheres of life such as language and certain aspects of culture with those in money and power, but how much do they feel "at home" in the system where their voice has little or no impact on the decisions which affect their lives? Does a person born in an affluent family feel more "at home" in such a society than a person who has to work hard just for food and shelter, let alone earn a "badge of dignity"[2] among their fellow citizens? Sennett and Cobb remind us that thinking about the impact of social inequality on sense of self-worth has been around for a while: "The humanists of the eighteenth century preached an idea of the worthiness of all men, of a natural dignity in man regardless of his position in society or his power" (Sennett and Cobb, 1972: 55). The humanists' idea, however, did not get much hold in the general perception of human value, even less so, it seems, in the societies which are driven by market forces and consumerism.

In a scene from the 1981 semi-documentary film "My Dinner with Andre" by Louis Malle, the New York playwright, Andre Gregory, shares with his fellow-playwright, Wallace Shawn, moments of spiritual awakening he had experienced on his travels around the world. Those glimpses into a different way of looking at the worlds, internal and external, brought into light Gregory's hitherto unconscious, or seen as given, social attitudes. He describes a moment when he entered his luxury apartment block and suddenly became aware that the old porter always calls him 'Mister Gregory' and he calls the old man simply 'George' - as if Gregory were an adult and George a child.

"If a man feels he obeys someone he ought to obey, what happens to his own self-image?" ask Sennett and Cobb (1972: 77).

Shawn (1985) published a play soon after this film, where his protagonist, Aunt Dan, makes the comment that she never, ever shouts at a waiter or a porter or a clerk in a bank or anybody else who is in a weaker social position then she is. Many people, if they are angry with a *powerful* person, will still speak to that person very politely and nicely, she adds, but if they are angry with someone *weaker*, they will shout and be nasty; they would try to humiliate that person. This is horrible and so *cowardly*, she exclaims.

In a somewhat humorous way, Aunt Dan then imagines how the festering resentment within the social perceptions of power, weakness, superiority and inferiority may one day overturn the class structure built on inequality. She observes people being ashamed of what they do as though working as a labourer, a clerk or a minor official, for example, makes them feel as if they had been unfairly singled out for some degrading punishment. It is as though everyone wants to be president, she remarks. But if everyone wants to be president, and no one wants to cook for the president, the president will have to cook for himself; if no one wants to bring food to the president's kitchen, he will have to buy it himself; if no one wants to work in shops, he will have to go into the countryside to grow his own food. This is a full-time job, and he will have to resign as president in order to grow that food.

Society as a Source of Trauma

Wilkinson and Pickett found that rich developed countries have, for some time, been suffering from high and rising rates of mental illness (2009: 7). *The Inner Level* is a sequel to *The Spirit Level*, their 2009 report on decades of research on the impact of socioeconomic inequality on both physical and mental health. Their findings show that social and health problems are more common in rich countries with big economic inequalities than in poorer but more equal societies. In countries where there are bigger differences in income, the social distances are also greater and social stratifications are experienced as more important. Their studies further show how the perception of one's status on the social scale profoundly affects physical and mental health, which may explain the substantial increase in rates of depression and social anxiety in the "developed countries". "Social status carries the strongest messages of superiority and inferiority" they wrote (Wilkinson and Pickett, 2009: 43). In *The Inner Level* they offer insights into recent research by psychologists and anthropologists on the origins of social inequality and its psychological impact, the "imprint of inequality", of what they call the Dominance Behaviour System on both the dominant and subordinate segments of societies. They found that social anxiety and selfish behaviour across generations are more prominent in more unequal societies, starting in early life with children bullying each other.

Since before the French Revolution, the idea that inequality is divisive and socially corrosive has been widespread. Now that we have sufficient data to compare inequality – as measured by income differences between rich and poor – in each country, it has become clear that this intuition is emphatically correct, perhaps more so than we ever imagined. Rather than a private hunch, it has – as hundreds of studies now show – become an objectively demonstrable truth (Wilkinson and Pickett, 2018: 16).

Social trauma was a part of the 2022 series of online talks by a group of American psychotherapists organized by the National Institute for the Clinical Application of Behavioural Medicine (NICABM). Amongst other areas and contexts of exploring trauma, clinicians from different schools of thought examined expressions of trauma, for example, in the body (van der Kolk); in interpersonal neurobiology (Siegel) and neuroscience (Lanius). They found that working with resentment as a response to social injustice, ongoing social oppression and historical marginalization, requires a different clinical approach to how we work with resentment about past events.

Over recent years, some explorations of the psychological impact of racism have tentatively entered the psychoanalytic and psychotherapeutic discourse but the effects of income inequality on sense of self-worth still remain largely unexplored.

The psychological impact of the socioeconomic hierarchy in Britain became a prominent theme in my work during my analytic training. Both my training patients were professional people from working-class backgrounds and they would bring up their feelings about class in the sessions. They described their families as "typical working-class people, uneducated and racist". Exploring their feelings about their class-roots, their desire to leave those roots behind and move up the social hierarchy, brought to light features of what I came to think of as a trans-generational trauma of being born in a society of pronounced economic and cultural inequality and privilege, based largely on money and property, which were often inherited, not earned. One of my patients described the typical working-class response to the British social system as a "paradoxical mixture" of resentment, self-loathing, guilt and pride. This multi-layered collective attitude may have arisen in the Victorian era when what became the working class emerged from the former peasantry who migrated to cities looking for work. On the one hand, they found themselves in harsh, sometimes appalling living and working conditions while, on the other, they were aware that they were part of the unprecedented rise of the British industrial and colonial power (Kiehl, 2016).

Dissociation is a common response to living with the sustained pain of trauma, sometimes with pride in place of humiliation. Thus, the class which was perceived as inferior intra-nationally had the opportunity to feel superior inter-nationally. Racism among the working classes may be thought of as coming from the unconscious hope for healing the pain and shame of feeling inferior at home by feeling superior towards "others" (in race, culture, ethnicity) both at home and abroad.

Historically, different forms of inequality have existed in different social arrangements, and the sense of self-worth within a social context, the "badge of dignity", has not always and everywhere been based on money as it has been in the market-driven neoliberal societies. In the social hierarchy of the now long-gone socialist Yugoslavia (my country of birth), the way of acquiring "a badge of dignity" was primarily through higher education (which was free, therefore, at least nominally affordable to all citizens) or by joining the political class. Material wealth alone (such as it was) did not earn you a "badge of dignity". On the contrary (albeit mixed with some envy), money alone was looked upon as an inferior means of earning respect in society. In comparison with good education, money did not induce a sense of social superiority nor did it guarantee a short-cut up the dignity-hierarchy as did the connections with the "right people" in the high ranks of politics, education and social institutions. Exploration of the impact of those, now almost forgotten, collective values on the individual sense of self would make a subject for a whole other chapter. They have, since the onset of neoliberalism in the 70s, been replaced globally by a consumer mentality, which now shapes the perceptions of "superior" and "inferior" ways of surviving, making a living and "succeeding" as individuals, collectives, countries and regions of the world.

In psychotherapy, much thought has been given to the individual's place within the family (power) dynamics, for example, is our patient the first, second or middle child; were they, perhaps, adopted and so on, but hardly any to their place in society, both in childhood and as adults, to their social status and how they feel about it. We think of ways of approaching issues regarding race, gender and sexual orientation, but so far we have not done the same with the issue of social class inequality. Our clients are typically middle class or higher who, for the most part, can afford our fees should they wish to invest in psychoanalytic self-exploration. The "lower" classes, on the other hand, often cannot afford our fees, so we are protected from having to look into their social-related concerns and how these concerns may make both them and us feel.

It suffices to say that in many countries, many individual analysts and training institutes offer reduced fees to those who otherwise would not be able to afford them. Furthermore, in recent years, a growing number of psychotherapists have started addressing the uncomfortable subject of the psychological impact of social inequality. In her response to the article by Andrew Samuels "The Activist Client" (2017), the American Relational psychologist, Susan Bodnar, writes that the role of the primary mother figure in attachment must be complemented by the lifelong complex ongoing process of identifications and relations with our cultural objects, may they be economic, social, racial and so on.

> Even at a basic biological level, sociocultural and environmental stress can affect neurological function and give rise to issues we often mistakenly classify as psychopathology rather than what might more accurately be termed the impact of social pathology on individual health. The physical spaces people inhabit influence the development and structure of the psyche.
>
> (Bodnar, 2017: 700)

When I first wrote about it, there was a distinct dearth of psychoanalytic literature on the impact of social environment and status on the sense of self. Furthermore, it seemed to have been considered "un-psychoanalytic" to bring up the subject in psychoanalytic discussions. If, and when, I did bring it up with my British colleagues, a common response would be: "Class doesn't come up in my work". One colleague added, "My patients just *know* that I am upper class." Presumably, this meant that there was nothing to explore. As already said, and in line with neoliberal political directives, other forms of social stratifications and discriminations, for example, race, gender and sexual orientation had, over time, entered the psychoanalytic discourse, but not socioeconomic inequality, which has, along with other unsettling psychosocial and environmental factors, remained outside psychoanalytic thinking as one of the potential causes of trauma.

> As an example of how problematic some views of trauma have become, in a discussion of the denial and dangers of global warming and the nuclear threat, one North American colleague commented that she was taught by her supervisors that such factors in the associations of analytic patients were always to be seen and analysed as displacements from internal conflicts and not dealt with as things in themselves.
>
> (Levine, 2021: 796)

All creatures must find ways to survive in the jungle-maze of power-based conditions and relationships or perish. The "fittest" (in our current materialistic mindset, the richest) do not only survive but flourish and are often rewarded by higher social status than those who struggle. Along with their material possessions, the "fittest" possess (and are mostly perceived as deserving) the power to dominate, shape society and define its moral and ethical values. They can punish those who transgress and reward those who obey. Is this "natural", "normal" and therefore inevitable? In her Nscience talk: "Dangerous Edge: working with the clients with a history of risk", Dr Gwen Adshead (2021) challenges some of the deeply set stereotypes in our collective mind on what is normal in society. "Is it normal for men to be violent? No, it isn't normal!" she asserts. Adshead sees income inequality as a political act of "violence by the state". "Income inequality sets people up to feel small, weak, ashamed and humiliated" (Adshead, 2021).
Or in the words of Wilkinson and Pickett,

> What other people think of us is filtered through our expectations, fears and tensions about where we come in the scale of personal worth. ... a great many aspects of individual preferences and behaviour – such as aesthetic taste, pronunciation, table manners, knowledge of the arts – serve as markers of status, almost as if they were designed to trip and expose the unwary.
>
> (Wilkinson and Pickett, 2018: 19)

Being subjected to violence may induce trauma and shame. This includes violence by the state through income inequality, as Adshead puts it, particularly if it has been experienced and transmitted trans-generationally. Andrew Samuels (2021) explores the political and social roots of personal shame which is underpinned by economic inequality. "Inequality leads to political violence – but is fuelled, in my view, by shame," he says. "Why is there so little equality in our society? Are we guilty of "economic sadism?" Samuels asks.

Shaming can be an effective way of keeping individuals and groups in line with the dominant group's social norms, rules and demands.

Moving Up and Away

In a culture where middle-class values are so prevalent in politics and the media that they tend to be seen as somehow universal, it is assumed that everybody *wants* to be middle class. Wilkinson and Pickett (2009) quote the anthropologist Gillian Evans, who, in her book *Educational Failure and Working Class White Children in Britain* (2006), describes the working-class culture in an East London district and shows how it is expected of children in schools to engage at home in activities that fit with a middle-class life style and which may clash with the way working class parents interact with their children. To an extent, Evans writes: "working class people resist the imposition of education and middle-class values because becoming educated would require them to give up ways of being that they value" (Evans, 2006, quoted in Wilkinson and Pickett, 2009: 115). When a working-class patient of mine expressed the desire to go to university, his parents were angered and dismayed: "What do you wanna do *that* for!?".

To an extent, those who are middle class and those who are not dwell in quite different socioeconomic and cultural universes, but both find themselves subjected to the same, in essence, conservative, self-affirmative system of values which resists change. Sennett and Cobb (1972) explore how this sociocultural attitude requires displays of "badges of ability" as a manifestation and protection of one's sense of personal dignity. In the interviews they conducted for the material for their book, they found that "The calculus of material well-being to which both [the middle class and the working class] subscribe, hinges on an historic assumption that between the world of culture and the realities of life for the masses there is an unbridgeable gulf" (Sennett and Cobb, 1972: 7).

For those who aspire to cross this unbridgeable gulf, acquiring "the right tastes" can become a "badge of ability". The American Psychoanalyst, Elizabeth Corpt (2013) in her paper "Peasant in the Analyst's Chair", explains:

> our taste distinctions are always embedded in complex and meaning-filled relational matrixes expressed through enigmatic or declared messages such as "that's for the likes of them, not for us" or "we don't do that sort of thing here", or "we do it this way, not that".

Taste distinctions help us determine where we belong, and with whom, and provide us with a sense of who we are, are not, and whom we may or may not become. These distinctions also make demands on us; to psychologically define ourselves as we socially declare ourselves. If all goes well, a firming of identity and a sense of social belonging take place.

If all does not go well, integration of one's identity and social position can remain painfully in flux and in some cases, pit wanting against belonging.

(Corpt, 2013: 60)

Secure early attachment relationships can provide foundations for a degree of resilience towards social shame as Corpt expands:

Identifications with one's class become inseparable from one's individual narcissistic vulnerabilities, if one's primary attachment figures and affiliations can provide ways to strongly mitigate against the split (between the class of origin and the class one aspires to belong to) through the promotion of acceptance and pride in one's class affiliation melded with a sense of freedom regarding ambition, one can be inoculated, to some degree, against the trauma of class shame.

(Corpt, 2013: 60)

Inequality and Social Justice

Resentment is a natural response to mistreatment or injustice. It can help one cope with, adjust, make sense of and protect one's self against injustices, says Ruth Buczynski in the 2022 NICABM talks on social trauma. Social resentment can also fuel the desire for "revenge", for restoring a sense of self -worth and gaining "the badge of ability". The Nobel prize novelist, John Updike, in his memoirs *Self-Consciousness* (1989) describes how his deep sadness, shame and pity for his father and grandfather, both educated men but of modest material means, led to his decision to avenge their low social status by becoming famous and rich, and he did. My patient, Sam, of whom I will say a bit more later in this chapter, responded in the opposite way: "Nothing good can ever come out of me because of where I come from!".

Dan Siegel (2022) asks: can resentment best be understood as a call to action or a psychological issue to be addressed through exploring unresolved pain and past experiences? They are not mutually exclusive, he says, but it is very important that as psychotherapists "we do our homework, to be self-aware and aware of social and political history in current circumstance as well as the past, so that we don't reflexively just default to one position or the other". Both can be going on simultaneously, Seigel continues, "depending on whether we're in the same or different demographic group from our client, it could be quite tricky to take something that's being experienced as a resentment, currently for unfair systemic treatment, and to start interpreting it in terms of the personal story" (n.p.).

Which takes us back to situations where, belonging to a typically middle-class profession, we might oversee our working-class clients' social concerns and anxieties and explore them through the lens of personal material. Moreover, we may not recognise that an ongoing state of resentment for the sociocultural value system which undermines some of our clients' sense of self-worth can, over time, accumulate into social trauma.

The unstoppable rise in economic inequality in affluent societies was crudely exposed during the coronavirus pandemic, when many millions of those on the lower income scale had no choice to work from home (if indeed they had a home) or educate their children online: 60,000 children in the UK had no internet at home and 12 million in the USA had no broadband at home (Samuels, 2021). More than 3.8 million children in the UK depended on school meals or went hungry during the lockdown. The notoriously underpaid health workers, who were risking their lives on the front lines in hospitals were offered a pay rise of 1%, while the military received 4%.

Meanwhile, during the pandemic, 5.2 million more people became millionaires (Samuels, 2021).

How does all this *feel*? Seeing this degree of income inequality as "normal" or just a feature of "the real world", demands that those who find themselves among "the weak" must demonstrate that they possess at least the strength to accept "reality" and do what they can to "better themselves", to make their way up the social hierarchy and so on. Any feelings they might have towards this version of reality must be suppressed as an expression of weakness. The unacknowledged (dissociated?) sense of inferiority, the ensuing resentment and shame are kept in check by sociopolitical, cultural and legal measures which encourage obedience and protect the status quo. Thinking about, let alone discussing, the subject too much is branded as "too left", "socialist" or even "communist". Moreover, in the current neoliberal discourse, even the term "social inequality" is sometimes replaced with "social distinction" as, presumably, a less thought-provoking term for the same thing.

"We are in this together", the Conservative party millionaire, and Baronet, the then Chancellor of the Exchequer, George Osbourne, famously proclaimed in 2009, referring to the pay freeze for public sector workers as "a way of protecting their jobs". Presumably, he was attempting to convey the same message to the underprivileged segments of society as in the 90s when Tony Blair famously proclaimed "we are all middle class now". It is of note that while Blair was in power, the rift of inequality became even deeper and wider than it was during the reign of his neoliberal predecessor, Margaret Thatcher.

The reality is that inequality causes real suffering, regardless of how we choose to label such distress. Greater inequality heightens social threat and status anxiety, evoking feelings of shame which feed into our instincts for withdrawal, submission and subordination: when the social pyramid gets higher and steeper and status insecurity increases, there are widespread psychological costs. Status competition and anxiety increase, people become less friendly, less altruistic and more likely to put others down (Wilkinson and Pickett, 2018: 56).

Despite its infrequent mention in the psychoanalytic writings and discussions, the subject of social inequality has made a comeback into the public discourse (if indeed it ever left). The BBC Radio 4 programme "Breaking the Class Ceiling" (February 2020) introduced the term "social racism" and debated whether or not class discrimination should become illegal and given the same treatment as gender, sexual orientation and race discrimination. Together with the experiences of those who did not feel adversely affected by the "class ceiling", the radio programme included testimonies from people who currently experience professional restrictions based on their class of origin. One example was a woman from a working-class North of England (markedly poorer than the South) family background, who worked as an administrator in a London-based glossy magazine. She was university educated and a talented writer, who wished one day to write an article for the magazine she was working for and move up the professional hierarchy. When she showed a piece of her writing to a work-place superior, she was told in no uncertain terms that, yes, she was a good writer but her social background did not permit her to move up from her current professional position: "you realise that we are all posh Londoners here … you don't really fit in …" she was told.

Of note, is the widening divide in life expectancy between the South and the North of the United Kingdom. According to the then figures from the Office for National Statistics, citizens of the affluent South lived on average eight years longer than those in the poorer North (Meikle, 2011).

Corpt (2013) candidly describes her personal struggle to fit in with her middle-class profession, coming from a poor family of Polish emigrants. She refers to her own first analysis, where she found that she had no shared language with her analyst (who came from a higher class than Corpt) to

explore her class related feelings, which persisted silently despite her significant move up the social class ladder.

> I attempted to talk around … my experience of feeling like a have-not.
> That's what I called myself. My analyst was the have, and I the have–not.
> I was functioning at a very high level, and living a middle-class life. Why,
> I wondered, was I persistently and defensively invested in this "have-not"
> identity? On the surface I strove to be a have; to be an analyst like my
> analyst, to make a decent living and to advance professionally. But never,
> in this analysis, had I actually found a way to sit with the real shame and
> feelings of loss about actually deep down, being a have-not. I mean this
> in a non-negotiable, existential, Heideggarian-throwness[3] kind of way; in
> a way that recognizes a very real difference and all that accompanies that
> difference.
>
> (Corpt, 2013: 62–63)

Similarly to that which Corpt describes from the socioeconomic-division
and bias point of view, a piece of research mentioned by Christine Padesky
(2022) shows that, compared to white clients, people of colour want their
therapists to ask about and bring up the issues of race:

> People who are not part of the dominant group really want some discus-
> sion of the impact of race on their life, and also some sense that their
> therapist understands their ethnicity, their culture, their race and some of
> the discrimination that they face … This is a very important element of
> accepting the immensity of the issue and being able to acknowledge the
> hugeness of it – not just in this lifetime, but with the trans-generational
> transmission and the historical imprint of historical trauma and commu-
> nity trauma and slavery.

Referring to Sennett and Cobb's findings, Corpt writes that class relational
injuries come from one's primary identification with a social class of people
who have suffered "power discrepancies, assaults to their dignity, lack
of opportunity or a compromised sense of positive possibilities" (Corpt,
2013: 60).

In the BBC Radio 4 programme, "This Cultural Life" (2022) British actor,
writer and comedian James Corden talks about having to "bully his way up"
to the top of his profession because he was born into a working-class family.
"You are not bred for success. You are not invited to the table," he said.
"The opportunities are everywhere but not for you. … You are not invited
to the ranks if you come from a working-class environment."

Britain remains one of the countries with the sharpest, ever-widening, socioeconomic inequality. Historically, the British working classes suffered immense assaults to their dignity and lack of opportunity, as famously depicted in the work of Charles Dickens. The severe living and working conditions in, the then, newly developing industrial Britain described in his work, notably in his novel *Oliver Twist* (1838), give a very bleak picture of early Victorian Britain, where poverty was seen as a dishonourable state and the poor as "deserving to be poor". This attitude does not seem to have changed much in the contemporary world which we and our clients inhabit together.

If we accept the existence of such a phenomenon as trans-generational trauma, we can assume that the ancestral suffering of the poor, not so long ago in Victorian Britain, may have found its way into the cultural layer of the collective psyche of the neoliberal Britain of today. Can the cultural heritage of its ancestors' traumatic experiences of extreme poverty or enslavement on the one side, and wealth and privilege created by exploitation or enslavement of others on the other, travel through time and reach the current generation's collective and individual sense of self? Here is what Jung says about this:

> There is one ego in the conscious and another made up of unconscious ancestral elements, by the force of which a man who has been fairly himself over a period of years suddenly falls under the sway of an ancestor ... perhaps certain traits belonging to the ancestors get buried away in the mind as complexes, with a life of their own which has never been assimilated into the life of the individual, and then, for some unknown reason these complexes become activated, step out of their obscurity in the folds of the unconscious, and begin to dominate the whole mind ... The complex will be awakened because the situation is one in which the individual is best adapted through this ancestral attitude.
>
> (Jung, 1989: 36–37, 82, quoted in Kimbles, 2014: 24)

Cultural creativity of the British working class came to the fore in the 60s, at the time of world-wide political and cultural (r)evolutionary change. The Beatles, Twiggy, Mary Quant and so on, paved the way onto the "social mobility" track for other exceptionally talented working-class people. However, it seems that in most cases they still needed to be noticed by an interested member of the higher social stratum, "their betters" as the expression goes, whom, like in a novel by Charles Dickens, they were lucky enough to encounter and who made their way up possible.

Michael

Michael is a talented person from a working-class background who has achieved an elevated social position with all that comes with success in an esteemed profession which, in Michael's case, includes a degree of social anxiety. We were exploring the possibility that his anxiety was about "being found wanting" to borrow Corpt's expression, which may originate in his feelings about his working-class roots and a deep-seated concern that he doesn't really belong with the people who were born into the social strata he had earned entry into by his own merit. Contrary to his calm and gentle disposition, Michael frequently had violent dreams with recurring motifs of anxiety. Has he properly learned the rules of his acquired status? Sennett and Cobb (1972) call this "status incongruity" where the person who has achieved a status above "the station of their parents" finds him/her caught in between two worlds and can often feel that something is wrong with him/her. This became clear when, on an occasion at work, Michael was puzzled by his emotional response to a situation where, within the structure of his organization, he needed to ask for something from the organizational body over which he in fact had authority. The image that helped us elucidate and illustrate his sudden sense of anxious, infantilizing dependency on their decision, was that of Oliver Twist asking for more food in the orphanage.

According to van der Kolk (2022), the unintegrated context of past events remains in the nervous system as a "piece of the past". The event Michael described can be thought of as a moment of an emotional flashback of his past experience of being in the world (Levine, 2022). The sustained trauma of living in a marginalized/subordinate social group can be expressed as an emotional implicit memory, not necessarily of an event, but of the experience of being humiliated, devalued or inferior, of being denied dignity (Levine, 2022).

The image of Oliver Twist, an orphan, appeared in another aspect of Michael's story: once he made the decision to go to university and develop a career in a profession that his parents saw as not for "people like us", they reduced the frequency and level of communication with him and his own family. Michael believed that this may have been because his parents were feeling awkward, not fitting into their son's acquired milieu. Meanwhile, they continued to be close to his siblings who remained working class.

Sam

Sam featured in my first paper (Kiehl, 2016) and I will return to him briefly here. Despite his university degree and relative success in a middle-class profession, Sam found it difficult to feel at home among those who were born middle-class. "The moment I open my mouth, people know where I came from," he told me. I asked him once where does he place me on the British social scale. Sam thought about it for a while and said that he saw me as an educated, middle-class person. However, he added, that because of my foreign accent, I do not really belong in the British class system: "In England, people with an accent are seen as classless. You were not born here, so you are classless, you are free!"

Sam's deeply ambivalent sense of self reflected his experience of the culture of his parents and his own bitterly resentful response to it. His unconscious conviction that, whatever he manages to accomplish externally, internally he will forever remain in the same, inferior place, illustrates the powerful impact of social environment on his individual sense of self.

Guided by his talent for arts, Sam applied to an art college. To his surprise, he was invited for an interview. Carrying his portfolio, Sam made a long journey to the end of an underground line and stepped out into a wide tree-lined avenue leading to the college. The momentous scene made him unable to move. The prospect of walking along the long wide avenue to his cherished goal overwhelmed him. He turned back into the underground and went home (Kiehl, 2016).

Sam was unable to separate a sense of personal identity from the social class he so desperately wanted to leave behind (in the underground) and walk freely along the long avenue towards social status and success he desired. There was something he was afraid he would lose, have to disavow, in the new life he was longing for. The frightening gap between the class of Sam's birth and the class he aspired to, and only tentatively managed to reach but not really enter, prevented Sam from completing both the internal and external transitions. Corpt suggests that this mode of operating in the world requires that those exposed to social inequality,

> had to protect themselves from the injuries of class divisions by maintaining a divided self, i.e., a splitting between the domains of love – one's primary attachments and sources of affection (the realm of belonging), and the domains of power – one's function in the world of work (the realm of wanting).
>
> (Corpt, 2013: 60)

Corpt sees this as a relatively common experience among immigrants as well as those who move from one social class to another: they may have to disavow aspects of self that seem not to belong in their new social setting.

This aspect of the trans-generational struggle in response to social inequality has become an important part of my work with clients who did manage to make an external class transition (that Sam had not been able to make completely), but who internally find themselves stuck in a no man's land between the class of their parents that they had externally left behind and the class that they appeared to have successfully entered into. In the language of analytical psychology, the transcendent function (Jung, 1958) had not been activated. I have found that the (in some cases, paralysing) effect of guilt for betraying the world of their parents and the shame and fear at the possibility of being "found out" as not really belonging in the world they have apparently become part of, needs to be identified and made conscious in its own context before these clients can take a step across the chasm of social class divide and begin to make sense of other spheres of their relational experiences, including the transference.

Some Concluding Remarks

Together with rising socioeconomic inequality, the awareness of its impact on the physical and mental health of our species is also rising. The need for help is becoming all too clear. Nevertheless, the governments of the leading world powers choose to spend more and more public funds on wars and weapons, rather than on the ever underfunded health and education needs of their growing population which cannot afford private schools and health care. We, mental health professionals, are faced with the ethical question of how far are we prepared to venture out of the comfortable fold of our middle-class profession and look at the impact that the sociopolitical system, which we are benefitting from, has on the psyche of those whom that system exploits and abuses. It is a difficult task, particularly if we do not believe in the possibility of change in the collective attitude to social inequality, and even more so if we believe that social inequality may have genetic foundations. Wilkinson and Pickett (2018) quote the former British Prime Minister, Boris Johnson expressing this belief in his 2013 "The Margaret Thatcher" lecture where "he articulated the view that economic equality will never be possible because some people are simply too stupid to catch up with the rest of society" (Wilkinson and Pickett, 2018: 151).

However, they add,

[C]rediting differences in intelligence to biology, and [Johnson's] belief that people have a 'natural' endowment of talent, mainly determined by the genes they inherit from their parents, are not new. At least since classical times, there has been a tendency for the rich and powerful to believe – and encourage others to believe – that members of each class in society are made of different stuff. Plato imagined that members of the ruling class had souls made of gold. In the class below them were people with souls of silver and, below them, of bronze or iron. Class and racial prejudices have always been bolstered by beliefs that there are innate differences in ability between groups that explained social position – from philosopher kings at the top to slaves at the bottom. As we now know, however, social classes are not based on genetic differences.

(Wilkinson and Pickett, 2018: 155)

While neoliberalism continues to triumph across the planet making the rich richer while the poor become poorer, it seems less and less possible to imagine a world more equal. Concluding their findings in *The Inner Level*, Wilkinson and Pickett invite us to imagine such a world by taking us back to our distant, long-forgotten collective past:

One of the most important but largely unrecognized features of human social organization is that, for about 95 per cent of the last 200,000–250,000 years of human existence, with brains their current size, human societies have been assertively egalitarian. Although generations of anthropologists have recognized, studied and written about the equality of hunter-gatherer societies, our egalitarian past remains virtually unknown to the public at large, and many people imagine that human nature is irredeemably competitive and self-serving.

(Wilkinson and Pickett, 2018: 121–122)

A confrontation with the deep unconscious bias regarding superiority and inferiority in all of us is essential for understanding the need we share to belong. But also to stand out, to be seen, recognized and respected by others. On the most profound level of the ego-self relationship lays our common yearning to be valued equally, not less than the next person. It is within that yearning that what we call social trauma may arise, develop and secretly inhabit our inner lives.

Notes

1 Nursery rhyme from a XVII century English folk song. Authors are unknown.

2 See: Sennett, R. and Cobb, J. (1972) *The Hidden Injuries of Class*. New York: W.W. Norton.
3 Corpt refers to the early 20th-century German philosopher, Martin Heidegger's idea of being thrown into the world of limitations by time, place, gender, race, class, all already there when we are born.

References

Adshead, G. (2021) *The Dangerous Edge: Working with Clients with a History of Risk*. Therapy Session Masterclass (TMS) Series: Nscience (Available online).

Bodnar, S. (2017) "Hamilton: The 'Activist Client' is no longer an academic exercise", *Psychoanalytic Dialogues*, 27(6): 694–702.

Buczynski, R. (2022) *The Treating Trauma Master Series*. NICABM: National Institute for the Clinical Application of Behavioural Medicine.

Corpt, E.A. (2013) "Peasant in the analyst's chair: Reflections, personal and otherwise, on class and the forming of an analytic identity", *International Journal of Psychoanalytic Self Psychology*, 8: 52–69.

Dickens, C. (1838 [1996]) *Oliver Twist*. Urbana, IL: Project Gutenberg.

Evans, G. (2006) *Educational Failure and Working Class White Children in Britain*. London: Palgrave Macmillan.

Jung, C.G. (1958) *The Transcendent Function*. CW8. Princeton, NJ: Princeton University Press.

Jung, C.G. (1989) *Analytical Psychology: Notes of the Seminar Given in 1925*. Princeton, NJ: Princeton University Press.

Kiehl, E. (2016) "'You were not born here, so you are classless, you are free!' Social class and cultural complex in analysis", *The Journal of Analytical Psychology*, 61(4): 465–480.

Kimbles, S. (2014) *Phantom Narratives: The Unseen Contributions of Culture to Psyche*. Lanham, MD: Rowman & Littlefield.

Levine, H.B. (2021) "Trauma, process and representation", *The International Journal of Psychoanalysis*, 102(4): 794–807.

Levine, P. (2022) *The Treating Trauma Master Series*. NICABM: National Institute for the Clinical Application of Behavioural Medicine.

Malle, L. (Director). (1981) *My Dinner with Andre* [Film]. The Andre Company; Saga Productions Inc.

Meikle, J. (2011) "Life expectancy rises in UK but north-south divide widens", *The Guardian*, 8 June. Available at: www.theguardian.com/society/2011/jun/08/life-expectancy-north-south-divide-widens

Padesky, C. (2022) *The Treating Trauma Master Series*. NICABM: National Institute for the Clinical Application of Behavioural Medicine.

Papadopoulos, R.K. (2021) *Involuntary Dislocation. Home, Trauma, Resilience, and Adversity-Activated Development*. London: Routledge.

Sennett, R. and Cobb, J. (1972) *The Hidden Injuries of Class*. New York: W.W. Norton.

Samuels, A. (2017) "The 'Activist Client': Social responsibility, the political Self, and clinical practice in psychotherapy and psychoanalysis", *Psychoanalytic Dialogues*, 27(6): 678–693.

Samuels, A. (2021) "How equal is 'equal'? Power, privilege, and the shameful shadow of the wounded healer", *Becoming Shameless: Encounters with Humiliation in the Therapeutic Relationship*. Online Conference, 3 July.

Sayer, A. (2005) *The Moral Significance of Class*. Cambridge: Cambridge University Press.

Shawn, W. (1985 [1997]) *Plays*. London: Faber and Faber.

Siegel, D. (2022) *The Treating Trauma Master Series*. NICABM: National Institute for the Clinical Application of Behavioural Medicine.
This Cultural Life (2022) BBC Radio 4, 24 September, 19:15.
Updike, J. (1989) *Self-Consciousness*. New York: Alfred A. Knopf.
van der Kolk, B. (2022) *The Treating Trauma Master Series*. NICABM: National Institute for the Clinical Application of Behavioural Medicine.
Wilkinson, R. and Pickett, K. (2009) *The Spirit Level*. London: Penguin Books Ltd.
Wilkinson, R. and Pickett, K. (2018) *The Inner Level*. London: Penguin Books Ltd.

Chapter 11

New Evolutionary Perspectives Between Trauma and Resilience

Dysregulated and *Con-fused*

Gianluigi Di Cesare and Chiara Caprì

Introduction

According to the latest studies by the World Health Organization (Fusar-Poli et al., 2021), about one billion people, out of a total population of 7.5 billion, are affected by some form of psychological distress or disorder. It is significant that around 50% of these begin around the age of 14 and 75% arise before the age of 24. If we consider that young people – those between the ages of 0 and 25 – account for about 41% of the global population, with a distribution of 25.5% for the 0–14 age group and 15.5% for the 15–24 age group, we can state that mental disorders are a chronic disease of the young. This means that the mental health risk of the younger generations is a real threat to our future. This risk is exacerbated by the fact that young people suffering from mental disorders are also more likely to suffer from physical illnesses and have a higher mortality rate than the general population, which can lead to a reduced life expectancy of 10–20 years (Fusar-Poli et al., 2021). This data clearly indicates the need to increasingly invest in prevention and mental health promotion with programmes and services dedicated to this age group. This is reinforced by the fact that the traditional separation of services for the developmental age group (0–18 years) and those for adults (from 18 years onwards) has been shown its limits; in fact there is a large number of drop-outs from treatment at the moment of transition from one service to the other. This is a time which often coincides with the highest frequency of emerging serious psychiatric pathologies. All these elements have forced the mental health services to rethink their organisation with the aim of building treatment pathways capable of guaranteeing early and continuous treatment. The Prevention and Early Intervention Complex Operative Unit (Unità Operativa Complessa PIP) of the Department of Mental Health of Local Health Agency (Azienda Sanitaria Locale, ASL) Roma 1 was started to respond to the needs of young people aged between 14 and 25, resident in the area covered by this agency. ASL Roma 1 is one

DOI: 10.4324/9781003298076-15

of the three health authorities in the metropolitan area of Rome and includes a total resident population of more than one million people. It is a very large and diversified area that ranges from residential and high-income areas to urban suburbs that are socially compromised, thus shaping a multiplicity of needs. In this area, the population aged between 14 and 25 amounts to approximately 110,000 people who represent the catchment area of the UOC PIP. The UOC PIP has two main operational sites (conventionally named "East" and "West") located in two different municipalities and is currently responsible for more than 1,700 patients, with an influx of about 800 new patients per year. In addition to this, the UOC PIP is also involved with schools in the area, organizing a helpline and participating in class groups and training programmes aimed at teachers and family members reaching approximately 55,000 high school students. It is therefore reasonable to say that the UOC PIP represents not only an important service for early and ongoing intervention, but it also provides a perspective on the actual anthropological, cultural and psychopathological transformations of young people.

In this chapter, we first attempt to examine the ways young people have manifested their suffering in recent years, later suggesting new understandings for them.

Diagnosis in Adolescence: Is it an Impossible Construct?

The problem of diagnosis in psychiatry represents a complex and unresolved topic. The attempt to put an end to the debate between essentialists (illness seen as a morbid entity which exists objectively) and nominalists (diagnosis is simply a theoretical construct) dominated the 20th century, highlighting how the conflict around diagnosis concerns the entire epistemological status of psychiatry (Di Cesare, 2016). The appearance of the Diagnostic and Statistical Manual of Mental Disorders (DSM), starting with the III-R edition, abdicated all nosological pretensions in the name of a nosographic reliability, described as atheoretical, which has certainly not solved the problem, leading instead, over time, to a progressive increase in diagnostic categories. These, in fact, increased from 112 mental disorders identified in the first edition in 1952, to 374 in the fourth edition and over 500 in the latest version, the DSM-5 (American Psychiatric Association [APA], 2013). This increase in categories was aimed at limiting the problem of overlapping and comorbidity of diagnostic evaluations. Moreover, the exponential increase in diagnostic categories did not lead to a diversification of treatments and prognostic developments, revealing the impossibility of a correlation between diagnostic category and nosographic entity (Saraceno and Gallio, 2013). This problem is even more evident in adolescence due to the particular characteristics of this age, linked to the ongoing maturation of the central nervous system (CNS). Furthermore, the high performative power of diagnosis, that is, its ability to make an object real and true by simply naming it (Beneduce, 2013), risks labelling the young patient too quickly with a specific disorder, instead of considering that he is living through a developmental crisis. By doing so, we miss the opportunity to grasp the true meaning of the disorder (Money, 2023). The failure of these classifications to identify aetiological hypotheses capable of explaining the onset of mental disorders, together with neuroscience studies on neurodevelopment, has progressively shifted research towards alternative explanatory models. For this reason, studies aimed at going "beyond" the DSM (Hayes and Hofmann, 2020), privileging the processes that create and maintain problems, rather than describing categories, are increasingly frequent. To these we can add studies that focus on staging, trying to identify not only the overt disorder, but also the "sub-threshold" or "threshold level" disorders (Shah et al., 2020). These studies seem to focus more on the functioning of the psyche than on simple nosographic categories, in analogy with the unitary model proposed by Jung (1907, 1958). Here the emphasis is more on the number of symptoms rather than their intensity or gravity. This is why a qualitative psychological formulation is of more value than a series of overlapping diagnosis.

There have been studies of factor analysis aimed at identifying the primary dimensions to which different disorders can be attributed (Fonagy and Campbell, 2017; Shah et al., 2020). The first results of these studies led to the identification of two dimensions: an internalising one (emotional difficulties and conflicts are developed and experienced within), determining the developmental trajectories leading to anxiety and depressive disorders, and an externalising one (the discomfort becomes evident and disturbs the environment). The latter is capable of identifying the possible development of other categories of disorders such as ADHD, impulse control disorders, substance use and antisocial disorders. Moreover, all these dimensions are strongly related to gender, with females being more prone to internalising disorders and males to externalising ones (Caspi et al., 2014). In fact, in our clinical practice we have observed that girls tend to suffer more from depression or anxiety (internalizing dimension) than boys, who in turn are more prone to addiction (drugs, alcohol, gambling) or anger outbursts thus showing a deficit in the control of impulses (externalizing dimension).

This model of developmental psychopathology was then further expanded to include a third dimension: that of psychotic experiences, namely dissociation, disorganised thinking, bizarre and unusual beliefs, delusions and hallucinations. This dimension would also be implicated in the development of mania, obsessions and compulsions. However, the model was challenged by the discovery that a borderline personality disorder can be equally well predicted both by an externalising as well as an internalising dimension. Children can develop borderline personality disorder either from internalising (high levels of negative affectivity) and externalising (marked difficulty in controlling impulses and behaviour) functioning, leading to interpersonal difficulties, such as inability to build lasting bonds and social isolation. This possible "dual" origin of borderline disorder showed the limits of the previously described factor analysis and opened up further lines of research. Caspi et al.'s study (2014) thus identified, again by means of factor analysis, a single factor (called **p**-factor), of a more general order than the internalising and externalising factors, implicated in all mental disorders. This factor was defined as a general factor of psychopathology. **p**-factor is a general factor defined in later research as a diffuse unpleasant affective state, often identified as neuroticism or negative emotionality (Lahey et al., 2017). Higher **p**-scores were associated with higher functional impairment, greater presence of psychopathology amongst family members, worse developmental backgrounds and more impaired early childhood brain function.

Several attempts have been made (Caspi et al., 2014) to find a correspondence between factorial analysis and the clinical evidence, trying to identify clinical elements that could represent the equivalent of **p**. Alternatively, **p** has been identified with emotional dysregulation, with a deficit in cognitive functions or with a specific disorder of the form and content of thought, but none of these attempts has led to reliable results. More interesting was the attempt to link **p** to traumatic experiences and, in particular, to early relational trauma. Traumatic elements and events seem to be present in almost all patients' histories and, within these experiences, neglect seems to play an important role in determining the clinical severity, early onset and resistance to treatment. Neglect does not seem to produce unambiguous responses, resulting instead in a wide variety of individual responses.

From Diagnosis to Developmental Trajectories: The Role of Trauma Factors

The absence of traumatic experiences in the history of our patients is unusual, as it is unusual for everyone – since life is, from its very beginning, inevitably "traumatizing". This raises the question as to why similar experiences can produce different outcomes while different ones can, almost paradoxically, result in overlapping outcomes.

In order to reflect on this question, we must consider that our body can be described as an open system in which the interaction between genetic, psychological and environmental factors is continuous. Concerning this interaction in open systems, we observe, as mentioned above, that different events can lead to similar results – this is known as the "principle of equifinality". The "principle of multifinality" emphasizes instead how the same event can lead to different results, as its impact is closely dependent on the moment in which it happens, thus determining different effects due to the level of maturation of the central nervous system (CNS).

Our focus then shifts from a clinical description to a developmental history, in trying to identify in it any risk factor and the developmental trajectories for the subject. In this way trauma, understood as a general factor of psychopathology, is inevitably linked to the temporal moment and its duration. As Alessandra Cavalli (2020) argues,

> when trauma occurs in a mind which developmentally has not yet been able to achieve such complex functioning, the work of recovery becomes more complicated, as a young mind has to deal not only with the trauma as such, but also with how the trauma may have impacted on the organisational development of the mind when the trauma occurred, and how the mind might therefore have remained fixed at its developmental level of functioning before the trauma occurred. Development will then be impaired because of the impinging trauma and the incapacity of the mind to integrate it into the self, leaving the self unable to continue its journey of individuation.
>
> (Cavalli, 2020: 793)

The decisive element would then consist in the moment when the initial traumatic event encounters a certain level of maturation of the CNS, thus leading to an alteration of the developmental pathway. In particular, early relational trauma and neglect can impede the construction of epistemic trust[1] (Fonagy et al., 2017) and markedly reduce resilience capacities; the result is a subject weakened by the failure of early relational experiences and more prone to react negatively to adverse events. The fragility caused by neglect or abuse would become manifest even before the actual onset of a proper disorder, showing itself in greater relational difficulty and lower socio-emotional competence (Caretti, Craparo and Schimmenti, 2013).

Abused children show in fact impairment in several areas of activity that require mentalisation skills: they often prefer to play solitary and less symbolic games and do not seem to feel empathy when confronted with other people's distress. Moreover, having little or no ability to recognize emotional expressions, they risk understanding even neutral expressions as hostile, often responding aggressively to situations of normal interaction. This can result in others perceiving them as different and untrustworthy. The consequence is their progressive exclusion from the group, which leads to isolation and increased negative affectivity. The lack of epistemic trust (Fonagy et al., 2017) leads to a state of alarm and epistemic hypervigilance. As a result of this, the subject can either fail to find acceptance within a group, or the opposite, that is, an inappropriate and absolute trust in others that borders on gullibility. In this condition, instead of the normal processes of mentalisation, mechanisms of pseudo- or hypermentalization are activated, resulting in brooding and increasing negative affectivity.

Epistemic trust is thus closely connected with resilience (Kalisch, Müller and Tüscher, 2015), which depends upon the ability to correctly assess events and to continuously monitor the external social environment and internal functioning. The process underlying resilience, guided by top-down processes relating to the evaluation of stressful stimuli (Positive Appraisal Style Theory Of Resilience, or PASTOR), not only allows a positive evaluation of what happens to us, but also allows for a positive reappraisal of any negative experiences and, above all, by maintaining a good degree of flexibility, allows us to adapt to new situations by modifying our usual patterns of functioning. Instead, in the case of a resilience deficit, the individual is incapable of modifying his approach with sufficient flexibility to reach his goal in the presence of environmental changes.

With conditions of epistemic distrust, communication cannot be processed for its emotional meaning, cannot be internalised or "digested" and thus cannot be transformed into new social competence. The process of changing one's own beliefs about the world, as an effect of social interaction and communication, is disrupted or even destroyed.

This inability of the patient to rely on some "epistemic trust", generates rigidity of thinking and this leads to the experience of not "reaching the patient", which can be very frustrating for therapists working with cases of severe neglect or severe relational trauma in childhood. Changes in therapy fail to take place because, although the patient can hear and understand what is being said, the information cannot be considered relevant and cannot be transformed into knowledge for social contexts. The absence of epistemic trust prevents the construction of reliable learning relationships, causes a permanent state of alert, thus determining a generalised social dys-functioning, accompanied by a distressing sense of isolation and loneliness. These constitute the subjective experience of borderline patients and of all those conditions that belong to the post-traumatic area syndromes. As Lara Lagutina (2021) suggests, we could say that "the most painful and devastating impact of early relational trauma is that it leaves the person feeling profoundly alone and unable to trust human connections, in other words, *orphaned*" (Lagutina, 2021: 21).

The Rejected Orphan

It was precisely the image of the orphan that came to mind in encountering Miguel, a 16-year-old boy who had been living in a socio-educational community since he was 12 and who was reported to our Complex Operative Unit for his increasingly oppositional and provocative behaviour, with frequent outbursts of anger. At the first meeting, conducted in the presence of the community operator, he responded in monosyllables, making no eye contact, as if he was completely disinterested or as if he considered any possible interaction useless. Miguel was adopted from another country at the age of 10 by a family that did not actually want him; in fact, they had chosen to adopt his younger brother but, for reasons that were not clear, they had to take Miguel with them too. As soon as they arrived back home, the parents immediately pointed out the boy's behavioural difficulties and entrusted him to social services. Miguel, abandoned by his biological family and then seized from his homeland, immediately experienced a further abandonment as he was relocated even from his new family. If it is true that "the orphan in mythology is often a hero who experiences painful abandonment and rejection, an outcast, profoundly alone and isolated from others" (Lagutina, 2021: 8), it is also true that "while other folklore heroes must leave home in order to reach their goal, the orphan usually doesn't have a home" (Lagutina, 2021: 8) to return to.

In the end, Miguel no longer trusted anyone and was living in a constant state of alarm and hypervigilance, anticipating the possible hostile intentions of others, to which he responded immediately and with powerful emotional intensity. A sudden glance, a change in tone, a simple posture quickly became incontrovertible signs of a risk that threatened psychophysical integrity and from which he could only defend himself with an advance attack. When, however, he judged the environmental situation to be risk-free, Miguel immediately detached himself from it, closing himself off in his own world and relegating his relationship with others to complete disinterest.

In the therapeutic team, this mode of functioning of Miguel activated the image of a frightened and abandoned child, resulting in a countertransferential shared feeling of tenderness and care. Beyond a "sterile jousting" (Jaspers, 1959) between the different possible diagnostic categories, Miguel's story confronted us with a situation in which early traumatic experiences, amplified by later ones, had determined the absence of epistemic trust and an alteration of the entire system, leading to a state of permanent emotional dysregulation.

Emotion regulation in fact, is defined as the set of affective, behavioural and cognitive processes that coordinate the intensity, duration and expression of emotions, in response to internal or external stimuli (Gross, 2007). That is, it concerns the subject's ability to recognise and thus regulate his internal state, implementing functional strategies to reduce (hypoarousal) or increase (hyperarousal) certain emotional tones, to respond in a flexible manner to the requests coming from the environment. Emotional dysregulation, by contrast, consists precisely in a failure of these processes and the attribution of predominantly negative meanings to the emotional and intentional states of others. This activates a response mechanism that is rigid, rapid, intense and lasts much longer than usual. Early relational trauma, by attacking and destroying the processes of emotional attunement between caregiver and child (Tronick, 2007), leaves the latter alone to cope with internal states and challenging external situations, deprived of the regulation mechanisms that can only be generated within a stable and safe primary relationship. The child finds himself left alone to cope with emotional states in the absence of an adult mind capable of progressively challenging them and naming them. The processing of emotional experiences has been damaged and the result is that these emotional states remain chaotic and inaccessible to awareness, leading to alexithymia.

Alexithymia, that is the inability to recognize and then name emotions, is increasing more and more in the young population nowadays. For Miguel, such an inability to name affects exacerbated his tendency to focus on negative, unbearable and unpleasant emotions (Taylor, Bagby and Parker, 1997; Young, Sandman and Craske, 2019). The result is a real alteration at the physiological level with the impairment of the regulation and balancing of the vegetative nervous system (Porges, 2011). As Margaret Wilkinson observed:

> traumatized individuals tend to be hypervigilant about their surroundings as they seek to stay safe and avoid threat. Re-experiencing and/or hyperarousal are forms of dysregulation that involve emotional under-modulation

and indicate a failure of prefrontal inhibition of limbic regions. The cognitive system has failed to manage the underlying emotional overload. These symptoms are "associated with the defensive fight or flight circuitry of the sympathetic nervous system" (Harricharan et al., 2016: 2). In contrast, the dissociative subtype of post-traumatic stress disorder is a form of dysregulation that involves emotional over-modulation mediated by midline prefrontal inhibition of the same limbic region. Such an overly strong control of feelings may be accompanied by symptoms of depersonalization and derealization.

(Wilkinson, 2017: 532)

It is common experience that such dysregulated patients bring to therapy their rage and destructiveness, thus activating counter-responses of anger and intolerance in those who are in charge of their mental care. Helped by the understanding that Miguel's symptoms had a post-traumatic origin, it was then possible for the therapeutic team to manage their counter-transference, so to work better on his personal history and not only on the outcomes of his outbursts.

Sloth and Withdrawal: A New Psychopathological Configuration

Over the last few years, alongside these clinical presentations that could be described as "traditional", others are emerging in which the traumatic element does not seem to be so evident. There are patients, in fact, who do not report traumatic events in an immediate and direct way, on the contrary, their childhood is often described as "happy and safe", lived in families characterised by affective and good enough communicative exchanges. Despite this, they seem to be completely blocked in their own individuative path, lacking curiosity in life and initiative.

This was the case of Francesco, who was 22 years old and had already experienced psychotherapy a few years earlier following some panic attacks. After moving abroad for a semester of study, his symptoms of anxiety had suddenly reappeared, in the form of frequent and sudden panic attacks that, each time, left him breathless and with the fear that he could die. Francesco lived the experience of studying abroad as an imposed duty, to be completed as quickly as possible, without ever opening himself up to the possibility of new experiences in the foreign country. He had no interest in the new city he was living in and no desire to make new friends. "I don't want to make new friends, the ones I have at home are enough for me. Besides, what would be the point of becoming friends with people who will leave and live elsewhere?". During the sessions, which he attended very punctually, he often expressed his inconsolable lament for missing his own city, his home, his family, his friends and his girlfriend. If it were possible, he repeated, he would immediately return to his own room, at home, and would attend the lessons online instead of being here, at university.

In this case, we can argue that his search for meaning and interest in the world, which Panksepp and Davis (2018) called the research system, had been completely deactivated, thus generating a condition devoid of curiosity and desire. Francesco, however, was not only unaware of this situation but he even denied it stating: "No, doctor, it is not true that I am not curious; I am curious about what my friends are doing, where they have spent the evening, ... I AM CURIOUS, but I am not curious about what is *unknown* to me." The unknown, that is, everything that is not familiar or immediately comprehensible, can only evoke disinterest or fear. He seemed to shy away from any change that was not predictable, from anything that was not similar to himself (Schwartz, 2022). The absence of curiosity in the outside world, except for games, light entertainment and social media (Byung-Chul, 2019), led him to develop an indolence where any activity was seen as a task, a chore to be hurriedly completed in order to quickly return to a form of "serenity", understood as the absence of problems or any form of commitment. Francesco is a good example of the growing number of young people who are passively incorporated in the micro-universe provided by the family, from which they find hard to escape. In letting themselves be led by others, they experience an inertia, an inability to move by themselves or act in the absence of external demands (Schwartz, 2022). They experience laziness, idleness, forgetfulness of any personal project (Lancini et al., 2020) and this sadly often slips into suicidal fantasies, driven by boredom and lack of meaning. What these patients have in common is something that can now be seen as a characteristic of our society and is precisely the inability to be in what Eugène Minkowski (1933) called "the black space".[2]

The Claustrophilic Family

Remaining in black space means accepting "not knowing beforehand" (Fordham, 1993) and not understanding (Bion, 1967); it means managing the narcissistic wound, taking the time to construct the ability to wait and not to immediately solve the riddle (Basaglia, 1965). Therefore, being in black space helps meeting the other, and allowing him to meet us. In the case of Francesco, this inability to remain in the "black space" could be found in his stating that he was only interested in what he already knew, or what he could understand immediately and effortlessly. As a consequence, the picture presented by these young people inevitably refers to the question of narcissism, understood as an intolerance to otherness, a xenophobic impulse or a psychic atopy, that is, a hypersensitivity to psychic differences (Mizen, 2022).

This rejection of otherness seems to be one of the most significant features of this epoch, represented in all spheres of life in both inter- and intra-personal dimensions. The negativity of the other is replaced by the positivity of the equal with all the consequences that this entails. "Seeking the equal" invades every sphere of life, today.

> One can go everywhere without ever really experiencing. Information and data are piled up without ever reaching learning. Experiences and excitements are craved, but the subject always remains the same. One accumulates friends and followers without ever really meeting the Other. Social media represents an atrophy of sociality. The all-pervasive digital network and total digital communication preclude the encounter with others, rather they serve to find the equal, those who have the same opinion as us, thus ensuring the progressive narrowing of our horizon of experience. They entangle us in an endless I-node, and ultimately lead to a self-propaganda that indoctrinates us with our own ideas.
>
> (Byung-Chul, 2018: 9–10)

In order to understand the genesis of these new clinical findings, it becomes necessary to look at today's families and the transformation undergone over time in the parent-child relationship. Francesco's family, as well as those of many adolescents, seems to be characterised by a mode we could define as claustrophilic:

> Today's families, beyond their composition, all tend to develop a special relationship with their offspring, historically unprecedented: a claustrophilic bond. Family functions, today, as the place where members think they can find everything they need: exchanges, affection, love, support, confidences, companionship, education, love, leisure … The world seems to have been sucked inside the family and so everyone's horizon has narrowed … The contemporary family lacks a yearning for otherness. The *other* is only made acceptable if he is brought in, made identical to the familiar: it is a dangerous irreducible that must be made domestic. The enigma that every other conveys, is annoying. The exogamic is treated

and purified by bloodless devouring: by assimilation. The children's friends and their boyfriends, the parents of the children's friends become friends, and all must be put in common, made familiar as mirrors that reflect only similarities.

(Pigozzi, 2019: 25, 28–29)

All emotional and affective exchanges must take place within the familiar space. As a consequence of this, the *other* – who poses as an alien, as the representative of an enigmatic strangeness – can be accepted only if he can first be absorbed and digested, transformed into the similar or even identical. We can observe this more frequently in the family dynamics of adolescents, where everything that is alien is either rejected or incorporated, thus limiting identity confrontation.[3] This perpetual drive for repetition of the identical and the search for the similar not only fosters conformism and an absence of curiosity, but also makes it impossible to implement a process of subjectivation. This is understood in the dual sense of making one's own experience subjective and being the subject of it, at the same time (Cahn, 1991; Richard and Wainrib, 2006), because "without the *other* we can neither speak nor think nor undertake paths of subjectivation (no game of truth opens up for us if we do not run the risk of transforming ourselves, altering ourselves, becoming others" (Di Vittorio, 2022: 30).

This family system, moreover, seems to function through the continuous alternation of introjective/projective identifications. When the former predominates, mental and bodily attributes of the others are treated as one's own, as if they belong to the self. "The boundary of the self is extended to include the other, self and other being experienced inside the same skin. Otherness is denied or attacked, and two minds are felt to be one. This could not be described as an identification with the other but a state of psychosomatic identity" (Mizen, 2022: 783). When the latter prevails, fear, pain and dependence are denied and attributed to others. Subjectivity is intolerable and the patient talks about himself as if he were talking about another. One mind has split into two.

This claustrophilic dimension of the claustrophilic family, one in which there are no secrets, where feelings and affects are immediately expressed and shared, is the result of a profound transformation of the educational tasks for the family. If, in the past, the educational task for the family could be summarised as the need to "build a responsible adult", today it can instead be conceptualised as the need to "build a happy person" (Pietropolli Charmet, 2000, 2013). A happy person, in this definition, is a person sheltered from any possible pain, protected from any situation with a potential traumatic impact, from any challenging task of life. Since the concept of trauma, in recent years, has undergone an enormous semantic amplification, which has led it to encompass radically different phenomena under the same term, the unattainable attempt to avoid any trauma could only result in a real "securitarian drive" (Recalcati, 2019). This leads to the family making an over-investment in boundaries that become barriers to be protected at all costs, to avoid any possible irruption of an intolerable otherness and difference. The libidinal investment in borders inevitably shifts into a marked distinction, not only geographical but also in terms of value attribution, between the inside – the place *par excellence* of positivity – and the outside which, due to this contraposition, can only be populated by unknown and dangerous presences.

The claustrophilic family finds its strength in this sharp separation and, in order to ensure its existence, has to pay a high price: the continuous denial of the negative that is projected outside, which favours and reinforces the opposition between inside and outside. The result is that in the inside, deprived of any conflictual element, an apparent harmony is created, a harmony that is inevitably lacking diversity and creativity. Conflict, which clearly signals the inescapable presence of subjective identities that differ from one another, must be eliminated at all costs. The elimination of any conflict between parents and children is, however, a constraint with potentially dramatic consequences for both. The dyad that is therefore established is one where happy children correspond to perfect parents and vice versa. One is the narcissistic guarantor of the other and neither parents nor children can escape the bond without betraying their implicit pact of perfection and happiness. Any sign of sadness or unhappiness must therefore be immediately denied both on the side of the child, who, experiencing it, would disappoint their parents, and on the side of parents, for whom their child unhappiness represents the failure of their strongly pursued project for a happy family. If children are therefore not able (or not allowed, since they have learnt not to disappoint their parents) to express their malaise, parents cannot use it as a signal to open up to doubt and problematisation. Any difficulty, then, must immediately find an external culprit on whom to project its origin or the failure of any immediate solution (Di Cesare and Panaccione, 2021). The result is an army of fragile, resentful and highly sensitive young people, permanently seeking the immediate satisfaction of their needs and incapable of building a healthy self-esteem to face adversity.

How can the process of individuation begin, in these families?

Opening to Individuation

Giving up the personal project means abandoning the individuation process and with it the possibility of constructing an identity that is not conformistically pre-determined. Eliminating transgression and conflict, in exchange for a permanent "pleasantness", protects one from the outside world and from an encounter with the other, keeping the subject in an infantile state and depriving him of the possibility of new experiences.[4] Therefore, there are no longer borders to cross that allow for transformative experiences, but mere thresholds separating almost identical spaces through which one can only glide indolently. The adolescents just do what their parents ask them to do, without straying from the family project and challenging it.

From this point of view, it is extremely interesting to observe the profound transformation the last generations have gone through, which consists of subordinating the encounter with the *other* to the prior reassurance of the existence of a profound similarity. In fact, if in former times common interests were progressively discovered and constructed through dialogue, now the encounter has an absolute priority: the reassuring certainty of sharing interests and passions with those we meet. If not, the meeting should be avoided or not pursued because *a priori* it does not make sense. In this way, true "autistic microcosms" are created: restricted and highly predictable worlds, filled with repetitive and stereotyped activities, interspersed with the refuge of solipsistic fantasies often characterised by grandiosity.[5] In other words, the problem of the *other* is faced asymmetrically as if he were the bearer of a structural and irremediable diversity that condemns him to exclusion or, at best, indifference. The need to make the other similar and thus denying any possible creative difference results in a loss of curiosity on the interpersonal and social level, but also in a reduction in complexity and a flattening on the intrapsychic level.

From Freud onwards, the ego had to abandon any illusion of completeness, accepting instead that it is "not the master in its own house" (Freud, 1917), or rather that it has to coexist with an irreducible internal otherness. The recognition of this otherness and the continuous dialogue with it facilitates psychic growth. It is exactly on the border between the ego and the unconscious that a dialogue becomes fruitful, allowing, in Jungian terms, the process of individuation. We recall that for Jung:

> Individuation is an heroic and often tragic task, the most difficult of all, it involves suffering, a passion of the ego: the ordinary empirical man we once were is burdened with the fate of losing himself in a greater dimension and being robbed of his fancied freedom of will. He suffers, so to speak, from the violence done to him by the self.
>
> (Jung, 1942, para. 233)

Individuation is the process of self-realisation, the discovery and the experience of the meaning and purpose of life; the means by which one finds himself and becomes who he really is, beyond parental projections or societal expectations. This process, for analytical psychology, has as an essential premise, that is acknowledging the presence of the Shadow. The Shadow is understood as the part of us that constantly refers to something we don't want to see inside us, or something that is still unknown to us. It is the dialogue with the Shadow that allows us to begin to individuate and opens us up to desire and growth, thus rejecting the omnipotent fantasy of considering ourselves already complete. Unfortunately, "it would be practically impossible to see one's own shadow, because there would be no one to say how you looked from the outside. There needs to be an onlooker" (von Franz, 1995: 4), an Other who opposes. If even the internal otherness is denied and projected outwards, the creative force that this conflict should stimulate is lost; the result is a weaker subject, undermined in his own ability to desire (since he can only desire what is already known), who is set against a world filled with conscious and unconscious ghosts. The subject, deprived of both relational and intrapsychic otherness, cannot but sink into the self, into a narcissistic illusion that transforms any dialogue into a monologue in which only an echo responds. The subject finds himself in an omnipotent fantasy in which everyone has the same interests or the same problem and so things work out seemingly perfectly (von Franz, 1995).

This dichotomous vision of the world, sharply split between an "inside" experienced as welcoming and safe and an "outside" where dangers and negative judgements predominate, not only excludes any exploratory instinct, but also exposes the subject to dramatic existential failures that spring up, suddenly and violently, when he is forced to leave the family nucleus to face the outside world. The judgement of the others, in fact, does not reflect the one he was used to in his family. The intelligent, sensitive and special boy suddenly discovers that he is no longer so special. Disappointment, in some cases, can be so severe that it results in self-harm to both the body and the Self where both are inadequate to survive the social challenge.

It is exactly this experience of inadequacy and shame that can lead to eating disorders, social withdrawal or, in the worst cases, suicide. This was the case with Giovanni, a 16-year-old boy who, for several years, had increasingly reduced social contact to the point of shutting himself completely in his room. Similarly, in the case of Rosa, who attacked her body through fasting or with continuous acts of self-harm because she couldn't bear the disappointment of not being the perfect girl that, according to her mother's promises, she would definitely have become.

Final Remarks

This developmental block, the fear of growing up, becoming something different coupled with the shame of not being able to meet the parents' grandiose fantasies, results in the impossibility of becoming an adult. As Jung observes:

> An individual is infantile because he has freed himself insufficiently, or not at all, from his childish environment and his adaptation to his parents, with the result that he has a false reaction to the world: on the one hand he reacts as a child towards his parents, always demanding love and immediate emotional rewards, while on the other hand he is so identified with his parents through his close ties with them that he behaves like his father or his mother. He is incapable of living his own life and finding the character that belongs to him.
>
> (Jung, 1912/52, para. 431)

In the new typology of patients we are here considering, trauma consists not so much in neglect phenomena or physical abuse since "nowadays more than ever children represent the fulfillment of life for those who generated them ... it is as if they were there to give value to their father's or mother's existences or to demonstrate their generative power" (Stoppa, 2022: 100). It is extremely challenging and even impossible for the child, and then for the adolescent, to free himself from this excess of expectations, from the projections of the narcissistic needs of his parents. The disappearance of certain rites of passage (such as communion and confirmation for Catholics, for example) results even more in the loss of the child's separative and then individuative process from the family of origin. The increasingly frequent use of the pronoun "we" which we can observe when mothers and fathers talk about their children – implying that they are one mind only – highlights precisely this rejection of any form of separation, thus preventing the child from constructing his autonomous psychic space. The absence of this psychic space keeps the child "safe" in a dimension of concreteness where the Other, in order to exist, must be within continuous and real reach. It also makes it difficult for the child to understand his own desires and so the construction of his identity becomes purely imitative, using the models made available by fashionable trends and amplified by social networks. Fragile and fictitious identities are the result, mutable and constantly in need of external approval. It is an identity permanently in transition (Zoja, 2022), which, moreover, is trapped and unable to become an adult. In this continuous skipping between the various possibilities for an identity, paradoxically, "the stable datum becomes precisely the transition" (Zoja, 2022: 150), meant not only as referring to the sexual identity, but as the continuous postponement of an authentic choice.

Notes

1 For Fonagy, epistemic trust is the trust in the authenticity and personal relevance of interpersonally transmitted knowledge. This kind of trust allows social learning in constant change of social and cultural context and permits individuals to benefit from their (social) environment (cf. Fonagy and Allison, 2014; Fonagy, Luyten and Allison, 2015; Fonagy and Luyten, 2016).
2 Minkowski distinguished subjective space into clear space and black space, the former characterised by distance and improbability, the domain of reason and ideas, the latter by penetration, mystery, depth, even confusion (Ferrari, 2014).
3 "If the element of otherness does not pierce the ego, the risk is to remain trapped, locked in the ego", in Rovatti (2022: 11).
4 "The culture of 'I like' rejects all forms of wounding and shaking. Those, however, who want to completely avoid wounding do not experience anything. The negativity of wounding is intrinsically part of all deep experience, all knowledge. Wounding represents the zero degree of experience. The wound is the opening through which the Other enters. It is also the ear that is held open for the Other. Those who are completely at home within themselves are incapable of listening. The home protects the ego from the intrusion of the Other. The wound shatters the domestic narcissistic interiority. In this way it becomes the door for the entrance of the Other" (Byung-Chul, 2018: 103).
5 It would be interesting, in this regard, to reflect on how this existential mode may be one of the factors that have contributed to the exponential increase in autism spectrum disorder diagnoses. Interest is further amplified by shifting the focus from psychopathology to the world at large. Here, too, fear of risk has produced a progressive increase in procedures, that is, pre-constituted ways of dealing with reality.

References

American Psychiatric Association (2013) *Diagnostic and Statistical Manual of Mental Disorders: DSM-5*, 5th edn. Arlington, VA: American Psychiatric Publishing.
Basaglia, F. (1965) "La distruzione dell'ospedale psichiatrico come luogo di istituzionalizzazione. Mortificazione e libertà dello 'spazio chiuso'", *Annuali di Neurologia e Psichiatria*, LIX, f.1.
Beneduce, R. (2013) *Frontiere dell'Identità e della Memoria. Etnopsichiatria e Migrazioni in un Mondo Creolo*. Milano: Franco Angeli.
Bion, W.R. (1967 [2018]) "Notes on memory and desire", in J. Aguayo and B. Malin (eds) *Wilfred Bion: Los Angeles Seminars and Supervision*. London: Karnac.
Byung-Chul, H. (2018) *The Expulsion of the Other: Society, Perception and Communication Today*. Cambridge, MA: Polity Press.
Byung-Chul, H. (2019) *Good Entertainment: A Deconstruction of the Western Passion Narrative*. Cambridge, MA: MIT Press.
Cahn, R. (1991) *Adolescence et Folie*. Paris: PUF.
Caretti, V., Craparo, G. and Schimmenti, A. (2013) *Memorie Traumatiche e Mentalizzazione: Teoria, Ricerca e Clinica*. Roma: Astrolabio.

Caspi, A., Houts, R.M., Belsky, D.W., Goldman-Mellor, S.J., Harrington, H., Israel, S., Meier, M.H., Ramrakha, S., Shalev, I., Poulton, R. and Moffitt, T.E. (2014) "The p-factor: one general psychopathology factor in the structure of psychiatric disorders?", *Clinical Psychological Science*, 2(2): 119–137.

Cavalli, A. (2020) "Noah's ark: technical and theoretical implications concerning the use of metaphor in the treatment of trauma", *Journal of Analytical Psychology*, 65(5): 788–805.

Di Cesare, G. (2016) "Sull'utilità e il danno della diagnosi", *Rivista di Psicologia Analitica*, 42: 89–102.

Di Cesare, G. and Panaccione, I. (2021) "Erranza del sintomo e crisi identitaria: riflessioni su adolescenza e pandemia", *Psicobiettivo*, XLI(3): 38–58.

Di Vittorio, P. (2022) "Il discorso è una terra straniera", *Aut Aut*, 395: 19–31.

Ferrari, E. (2014) *L'ambiguità del Patire*. Bergamo: Moretti & Vitali.

Fonagy, P. and Allison, E. (2014) "The role of mentalizing and epistemic trust in the therapeutic relationship", *Psychotheraphy*, 51(3): 372–380.

Fonagy, P. and Campbell, C. (2017) "Mentalizing, attachment and epistemic trust: How psychotherapy can promote resilience", *Psychiatria Hungarica*, 32(3): 283–287.

Fonagy, P. and Luyten, P. (2016) "A multilevel perspective on the development of borderline personality disorder", in D. Cicchetti (ed.) *Developmental Psychopathology. Vol. 3: Risk, Disorder, and Adaptation*, 3rd ed. New York: John Wiley & Sons, pp. 726–792.

Fonagy, P., Luyten, P. and Allison, E. (2015) "Epistemic petrification and the restoration of epistemic trust: A new conceptualization of borderline personality disorder and its psychosocial treatment", *Journal of Personality Disorders*, 29(5): 575–609.

Fonagy, P., Luyten, P., Allison, E. and Campbell, C. (2017) "What we have changed our minds about: Part 2. Borderline personality disorder, epistemic trust and the developmental significance of social communication", *Borderline Personality Disorder and Emotion Dysregulation*, 4(9): 9.

Fordham, M., (1993) "On not knowing beforehand", *Journal of Analytical Psychology*, 38: 127–136.

Freud, S. (1917) *A Difficulty in the Path of Psycho-Analysis*, in *SE XVII*. London: Hogarth Press, pp. 135–144.

Fusar-Poli, P., Correll, C.U., Arango, C., Berk, M., Patel, V. and Ioannidis J.P.A. (2021) "Preventive psychiatry: A blueprint for improving the mental health of young people", *World Psychiatry*, 20(2): 200–221.

Gross, J.J. (2007) *Handbook of Emotion Regulation*. New York: Guilford Press.

Harricharan, S., Rabellino, D., Frewen, P.A., Densmore, M., Théberge, J., McKinnon, M.C., Schore, A.N. and Lanius, R.A. (2016) "fMRI functional connectivity of the periaqueductal gray in PTSD and its dissociative subtype", *Brain Behaviour*, 6(12).

Hayes, S.C. and Hofmann, S.G. (2020) *Beyond the DSM Toward a Process-Based Alternative for Diagnosis and Mental Health Treatment*. Oakland, CA: Context Press.

Jaspers, K. (1959 [1997]) *General Psychopathology* (trans. J. Hoening and M.W. Hamilton). Baltimore: Johns Hopkins University Press.

Jung, C.G. (1907) *The Psychology of Dementia Praecox*. CW3. Princeton, NJ: Princeton University Press.

Jung, C.G. (1912/52) *Symbols of Transformation*. CW5. Princeton, NJ: Princeton University Press.

Jung, C.G. (1942) *A Psychological Approach to the Trinity*. CW11. Princeton, NJ: Princeton University Press.

Jung, C.G. (1958) *The Undiscovered Self*. Boston, MA: Little, Brown and Co.

Kalisch, R., Müller M.B. and Tüscher O. (2015) "A conceptual framework for the neurobiological study of resilience", *Behavioral and Brain Science*, 38:e92.

Lagutina, L. (2021) "Meeting the orphan: early relational trauma, synchronicity and the psychoid", *Journal of Analytical Psychology*, 66(1): 5–27.

Lahey, B.B., Krueger, R.F., Rathouz P.J., Waldman I.D. and Zald, D.H. (2017) "A hierarchical causal taxonomy of psychopathology across the life span", *Psychological Bulletin*, 143(2):142–186.

Lancini, M., Cirillo, L., Scodeggio T. and Zanella, T. (2020) *L'adolescente: Psicopatologia e Psicoterapia Evolutiva*. Milano: Raffaello Cortina Editore.

Minkowski, E. (1933 [1968]) *Le Temps Vécu. Études Phénoménologiques et Psychopathologiques*. Neuchâtel: Delachaux & Niestlé.

Mizen, C.S. (2022) "The Self and alien self in psyche and soma", *Journal of Analytical Psychology*, 67(3): 774–795.

Money, L. (2023) "Labels and the Self: identity labels as scaffold", *Journal of Analytical Psychology*, 68(3): 590–609.

Panksepp, J. and Davis, K.L. (2018) *The Emotional Foundations of Personality: A Neurobiological and Evolutionary Approach*. New York: W.W. Norton & Co.

Pietropolli Charmet, G. (2000) *I Nuovi Adolescenti*. Milano: Raffaello Cortina Editore.

Pietropolli Charmet, G. (2013) *La Paura di Essere Brutti*. Milano: Rafferllo Cortina Editore.

Pigozzi, L. (2019) *Adolescenza Zero: Hikikomori, Cutters, ADHD e la Crescita Negata*. Milano: Nottetempo.

Porges, W.S. (2011) *The Polyvagal Theory: Neurophysiological Foundations of Emotions, Attachment, Communication, and Self-Regulation*. New York: W.W. Norton & Co.

Recalcati, M. (2019) *Le Nuove Melanconie. Destini del Desiderio nel Tempo Ipermoderno*. Milano: Raffaello Cortina Editore.

Richard, F. and Wainrib, S. (2006) *La Subjectivation*. Parigi: Dunod.

Rovatti, P.A. (2022) "Intersoggettività, un enigma", *Aut Aut*, 395: 6–18.

Saraceno, B. and Gallio, G. (2013) "Diagnosi, 'common language' e sistemi di valutazione nelle politiche di salute mentale", *Aut Aut*, 357: 21–35.

Schwartz, S.E. (2022) "Narcissism – the refusal of twoness through sexual addiction and pornography", *Journal of Analytical Psychology*, 67(1): 287–305.

Shah, J.L., Scott J., McGorry P.D., Cross S.P.M., Keshavan M.S., Nelson B., Wood S.J., Marwaha S., Yung A.R., Scott E.M., Öngür D., Conus P., Henry C. and Hickie I.B. (2020) "Transdiagnostic clinical staging in youth mental health: A first international consensus statement", *World Psychiatry*, 19(2): 233–242.

Stoppa, F. (2022) 'La sana instabilità della famiglia', *Aut Aut*, 395: 97–109.

Taylor, G.J., Bagby, R.M. and Parker J.D.A. (1997) *Disorders of Affect Regulation: Alexithymia in Medical and Psychiatric Illness*. Cambridge: Cambridge University Press.

Tronick, E.Z. (2007) *The Neurobehavioral and Social-Emotional Development of Infants and Children*. New York: W.W. Norton & Co.

von Franz, M.L. (1995) *Shadow and Evil in Fairy Tales*. Boston, MA: Shambhala.

Wilkinson, M. (2017) "Mind, brain and body. Healing trauma: The way forward", *Journal of Analytical Psychology*, 62(4): 526–543.

Young, K.S., Sandman, C.F. and Craske, M.G. (2019) "Positive and negative emotion regulation in adolescence: Links to anxiety and depression", *Brain Sciences*, 9(4): 76.

Zoja, L. (2022) *Il Declino del Desiderio*. Torino: Einaudi.

Chapter 12

Working with Cultural Trauma

The Archetype of the Wounded Healer in a Multicultural Analytic Couple

Julia Ovchinnikova

In our modern world with emigration and multilingualism fast becoming the norm, there are more and more cross-cultural encounters in the consulting room. They have become quite commonplace and, as a result, we do not always reflect on what kind of unconscious processes have brought the analyst and the patient from different cultures together.

To ease my readers into these uncharted cultural waters, I would like to invite you to think about any of your patients with a different cultural background to yours. Take a minute to reflect on who you were for this person from a cultural perspective. Then please focus on yourselves. Working with this patient did you become more aware of your own culture?

With this cultural frame in mind, let us explore what an analyst from another culture may represent for their patients.

1   *A need to change and an opportunity to discover something new.* An image of a different culture facilitates projections of something other, something foreign. If the projections are frightening and hostile, then a cross-cultural encounter is unlikely. If the projections are more of an opportunity to explore a new realm in one's own personality, then there is an invitation to embark on an inner journey to a faraway land with someone foreign. Jungian analyst Kamala Melik-Akhnazarova (2015) is referring to foreign languages, but I believe we can apply what she says to foreign cultures as well: "to perceive it [the world] differently, to acquaint another facet of it and maybe even – to let oneself become 'another' for a moment, to change, to become open to the "agent of changes" within oneself – and an impulse for transformation is given …" (Melik-Akhnazarova, 2015: 161).

2   *An object of envy.* Another culture could be seen as having desirable resources. Financial stability, powerful leaders, artistic legacy and diversity are just a few examples of these qualities. Magic thinking may be employed when a patient chooses an analyst from other lands with

DOI: 10.4324/9781003298076-16

desirable resources: "Having therapy with that analyst, I'll get the power/ stability/artistic abilities of their country".

It is worth noting that one can witness a new emerging cultural wound in Great Britain. English teenagers and younger schoolchildren, who attend schools with a high diversity of nations, are envious of their classmates who have mixed cultural origins. They say to their parents: "Our food is plain, we don't have enough herbs and spices", "I wish we spoke different languages in our family", "It's a shame I don't have a grandfather coming from a foreign land". They long for something that other cultures have, often leaving their parents feeling bewildered, angry and helpless.

3   *An adopted parent/motherland.* Some people don't feel "at home" in their culture. It is beyond the scope of this chapter to explore the reasons for that feeling so I will just illustrate it with some quotes: "Nature doesn't speak to me here, yet I find it animated in other lands", "All of my girlfriends are from another country", "My partner and close friends are not from here", "My home culture is too individualistic for me and estranged from nature". By choosing an analyst from another culture, some patients unconsciously hope to find a better home for themselves. I observe a similar process with patients who have spent their childhood abroad and have a sense of a different home. Nostalgia for childhood, longing for the paradise of those years and the hope of being understood by someone who has had a similar experience drive them to foreign analysts.

4   *A safe, personal, trauma-free space.* One's home country and mother tongue can be tightly associated with personal trauma. Beverley Costa (2020) proposes that "using a different language from the 'traumatised language' can provide cognitive distance and emotional detachment until the client is ready to tolerate the intensity of feelings" (Costa, 2020: 22). She refers to Bessel van der Kolk (2000) who argues that it may be necessary for a person to gain some emotional distance from the traumatic incident in order to be able to talk about it. We could add that the analyst's "foreign" body and cultural background may similarly represent much-needed distant, safe soothing properties. Cédric Bouët-Willaumez (2021) compares a second language to an antalgic posture, defining this as a subtle and often unconscious rearrangement of a healthy body posture to accommodate an injury. A second language "makes it possible to minimise the pain from an existing wound" (Bouët-Willaumez, 2021: 84). Kamala Melik-Akhnazarova (2015) considers the foreign language (and we can add the foreign culture as well) as

occupying the role of a symbolic Father and believes that "it is highly relevant in cases where there is a constellation of a negative mother complex". We may suggest that a foreign language becomes a representation of the psychic forces that attempt to rescue an ego from annihilation, that give a chance of deliverance from threatening psychic flood, that strive to transcend a deeply rooted trauma of some kind (Melik-Akhnazarova, 2015: 173).

5 *A safe, cultural trauma-free space.* Cultural trauma may have profound psychological consequences for identity formation. It can also become tightly intertwined with personal trauma and become instilled in the early history of the patient (Pavlikova, 2021; Fleischer, 2022). The analyst deals with the collective while working with the individual. Catherine Kaplinsky (2008) believes that "the cultural unconscious is a dynamic field, a living history, connecting simultaneously to both the collective and the personal. Culture influences the way individuation processes are lived out. In turn, individuation processes influence the culture. It follows that identity and culture are entangled" (Kaplinsky, 2008: 192). Challenges associated with cultural trauma could become obstacles to the start of therapy. Some patients look for an analyst from their own culture in the hope of being better understood. They believe that only those who share their own cultural wounds can help them. The opposite is also true, patients may unconsciously choose an analyst from another culture because he or she is unburdened from their cultural traumas.

Cultural Trauma

Before immersing ourselves in an exploration of patients' choices and underlying unconscious processes, we need a working definition of cultural trauma. Jeffrey C. Alexander (in Alexander et al., 2004), has developed the concept of cultural trauma as empirical, suggesting a new meaningful and causal relationship between previously unrelated events, structures, perceptions and actions: "cultural trauma occurs when members of a collectivity feel they have been subjected to a horrendous event that leaves indelible marks upon their group consciousness, marking their memories forever and changing their future identity in fundamental and irrevocable ways" (Alexander et al., 2004: 1). For Alexander, the *representation* of events is more instrumental in trauma creation: "Events are not inherently traumatic. Trauma is a socially mediated attribution" (Alexander, 2012: 13) and these representations and attribution "are believed to have abruptly and harmfully affected collective identity" (Alexander, 2012: 14). Owing to the mediated character of cultural trauma, members of the group could become trauma-tized even if they do not witness a traumatic event. Elena Pourtova consid-ers the concept of time essential to trauma definition: "a traumatic event doesn't last outside, but endlessly continues its existence inside the psyche, not letting wounds heal" (Pourtova, 2021: 6).

Cultural trauma and collective trauma might overlap, but they are not the same. Cultural trauma affects a subset of the population and is experienced as something horrible that happened to *your* people. The group shares a core set of beliefs, patterns of behaviour and values. One of the main mech-anisms of its transmission is through a sense of belonging and group iden-tity. Collective trauma, on the other hand, is a horrific overwhelming event that affects a few cultural groups or society as a whole. Often the two are connected. A recent example is the collective trauma of COVID-19. Yet, certain populations – for example the Chinese – experienced *cultural* trauma within that collective trauma. Cultural trauma, transgenerational and inter-generational trauma may also be connected. However, in cultural trauma the generational aspect is not necessarily present.

Some historical traumas are apparent, others are hidden: "deeply buried, experienced by all and observed by none. It is the most private and most subjective of psychic experiences. Wars, dynasties, social upheavals, con-quests and religions are but the superficial symptoms of a secret psychic attitude unknown even to the individual himself and transmitted by no his-torian" (Kaplinsky, 2008: 189).

D. Kalsched also refers to trauma as "an accumulation of painful emo-tional experiences – mismatches and attachment derailments" (Kalsched, 2013: 59). Building on his ideas, we could add a cumulative aspect to the definition of cultural trauma. It may come as a result not of a single event, but as an accumulation of painful experiences that make representatives of a particular cultural group feel shaken and cracked to the core of their cul-tural identity.

Minority groups are often affected by cumulative cultural trauma. For example, many African American men have been influenced by culturally traumatic events like the Tuskegee study, as highlighted by Alsan and Wanamaker (2018). In that instance, a group of researchers passively mon-itored hundreds of African American men with syphilis to study the disease without ever offering treatment, which was readily available. The over-whelming experience of being watched dying came not after a single event, but long-term medical exploitation and mistreatment.

Representation of a traumatic event is also coloured by cultural com-plexes. Different cultures demand the repression of diverse aspects of the self which has an impact on the ways cultural complexes shape themselves. These repressions are part of what makes up a dynamic and shifting cultural complex which inevitably influences historical change. Historical change, in turn, plays its part in shifting these dynamics: "Major political shifts – historical change – inevitably affect cultural dynamics, 'secret psychic attitude(s)' and shifting shadows" (Kaplinsky, 2008:189).

Catherine Kaplinsky interprets a recurrent dream of an exiled white South African professor, giving a brilliant example of a culturally repressed self. Exploring his dream, the patient says: "All the Black part of me … became inadmissible. I could not allow myself to own the experience with Rosie (a black nursemaid that had been his mother in every sense of the word). The culture of Apartheid, 'the racist shit that was pushed into me' repressed authenticity of the dreamer's self" (Kaplinsky, 2008: 191).

It is important to underline that both personal and collective trauma often release new powerful feelings, whereas cultural trauma is already a narrative. Cultural trauma has been discovered and named. This collects its emotional charge and turns it into something solid, visible – into history, allowing you to also see its positive sides (Loseva and Pourtova, 2021).

Alexander Brodsky (2018) considers the conscious and unconscious aspects of the impact of cultural trauma. At a conscious level, the group may refer to adversity or a hostile environment and suffer from rejection. Unconsciously, the group may go through self-denial as it is unable to change and its members "doomed to remain themselves" (Brodsky, 2018: 32). Both aspects of experiencing trauma are potentially creative and may lead to new developments in personal and collective identity.

Concluding this brief theoretical exploration of the concept of cultural trauma, in the analytic setting, an encounter with cultural trauma is inevitably intertwined with the patient's personal history and traumas, as well as his/her shadow dynamics and the cultural complexes of both participants, which impacts upon the transference and countertransference. "Central to this dynamic is the absorption of cultural attitudes – including that which must be repressed, allowed in or defended against" (Kaplinsky, 2008: 189). Such dynamics nearly always relate to themes of identity and otherness which need to be both kept in mind and addressed in the analytical process.

I propose that *choosing an analyst from another culture is often an unconscious choice of a patient with cultural trauma and cultural wounds*. Sometimes we find it is also a conscious choice as well. Encounters between an analyst and a patient from different cultures can evoke the entire history of cultural complexes and wounds. The unconscious impact of this history finds expression in a specific dynamic in the transference and in the activation of the

Wounded Healer archetype. I shall consider five phases of this dynamic and illustrate them with clinical material.

Similar dynamics can occur in all cases of trauma. My aim here is to highlight the constellation of the Wounded Healer archetype and its application to cultural trauma because it often doesn't get the attention it deserves.

First phase: *an unconscious choice of an analyst from another culture*. The purpose of this choice may be to ease unbearable feelings provoked by trauma and facilitate the start of the therapy. In her 2016 paper Emilija Kiehl, a British analyst of Serbian origin, mentions her patients' words: "You were not born here, so you are classless, you are free!". In the presence of an assumed "trauma-free analyst", patients may feel less ashamed and rejected allowing them to talk more easily about those aspects of their culture that made them feel humiliated (Kiehl, 2016). In my practice, I observe a similar phenomenon. For example, one of my English patients stated: "I hate when I'm asked, 'Where are you from?' Isn't my South London accent good enough? Why do they need to know that I was born in the North? You are lucky, you don't have that problem." Another one spoke along the same lines: "The Northern accent is heavy, rough, crude. I don't like it. But people are so snobby down here (in the South), they judge us by our accent." This was echoed by another patient: "I'm a class traitor. Coming from the North and living in Surrey, what could be more extreme?". Yet it's not always about class. Another English patient chose me over other Jungian analysts because I am from the continent and in that sense closer to C.G. Jung, who was also from the continent. For that patient, the cultural wound of living on an island, which had been exacerbated by the Brexit referendum result, has been a very painful experience and I have been his trauma-free "bridge" to Europe.

A colleague of mine shared her story with me and has given me permission to mention it in this chapter. As a young woman, she moved to London from an Eastern-European country. At one point, she decided she wanted therapy and had narrowed the available options down to five therapists; two of whom spoke her mother tongue. Eventually she chose one of the English therapists. One of the reasons, as she realized later, was her need for a cultural trauma-free space to assist her search for a new identity. She was deeply ashamed of the way she spoke. In her home country, people in academic and quasi-academic circles occupied a higher place in the social hierarchy and they were supposed to have an articulate, sophisticated manner of talking, effortlessly using their vast vocabulary in complex, multi-clause sentences. Although her family related to those circles and she attended one of the best schools in the city, her speech in her mother tongue was inarticulate, albeit rapid, and she was often lost for words. Shame, a sense of cultural dislocation and the confusion of belonging, while not belonging, to the abovementioned privileged circles constituted for her an unpresentable and overwhelming experience of cultural trauma. Speaking in English gave her the chance to build new language patterns, representations of her inner world, a new identity and a new way of expressing herself. Having chosen an English therapist, she reduced the intensity of her cultural shame and was able to start therapy. She also developed a different style of talking: first in English, then in her mother tongue.

Quite often, during the initial stage, we can observe a positive transference where *the analyst is seen as a healer who is free from cultural wounds*. We could also say that the Wounded Healer archetype is split, for when the patient identifies with the "wounded" polarity, the "healer" polarity is projected into the analyst.

I recall here Jung's quote: "it is his own hurt that gives the measure of his power to heal. This, and nothing else, is the meaning of the Greek myth of the wounded physician" (Jung, 1951, para. 239).

The positive side of this idealization of the analyst is the sense of safety for the patient it allows and the lowering of the intensity of his shame to a level that enables the patient to speak about his cultural issues. In my practice, patients often say that they can talk about culturally embarrassing moments because they feel secure in the knowledge that they won't be judged according to their own cultural standards. Although analysts should never judge their patients, especially from a moral or cultural perspective, patients can still project a judgemental, critical attitude into their analysts. Usually, projections related to their own culture are less intense in the presence of a foreign analyst. The analyst is seen as non-biased with respect to standards and traditions of the patient's cultural reference.

Here I would like to give you an illustration of cultural wounds from my own work. Sally, an English woman whose maternal side had its origins in a poor working-class area in the North of England, used to tell me that she felt looked down upon by her neighbours because she had blue Christmas lights around her house. She said that true middle-class people are supposed to have white lights. She felt that she could freely explore her choice of Christmas decorations and her family's past with me because she felt respected. Her sense of dignity did not feel under attack.

Another example is from my work with a Russian patient, Alex, who lives in London now. Although we were born in the same country, he perceived me simultaneously as a person from the same and a different culture. He spent his childhood and youth in an industrial city where most children had only one career option after finishing school: to work in one of the city's factories, but Alex pursued a career in the arts. He felt that only someone from outside the culture of the environment in which he grew up could understand the difficult and, by the metrics of his hometown, shameful nature of his career choice. He saw me as a person free from that tension and humiliation.

Let us now move on to *the second phase*. The analyst isn't perceived as a wound/trauma-free healer for ever. Before long, the cultural perspective exposes the so-called "wounds", making them easily seen. In the patient's eyes, *the analyst turns into an apparent carrier of the Wounded part of the archetype* as the patient now projects his wounded polarity of the archetype into the analyst while at the same time identifying with a culturally superior "healer" aspect himself. The patient now notices the analyst's cultural differences and deficits then treats them as if they are potentially vulnerable spots, for example a lack of competence, moments of appearing lost and confused. What do I mean by deficits here? It might be an accent, grammar mistakes (if an analyst is speaking in his/her second tongue), unfamiliar speech patterns and variations (some of my Russian-speaking patients who come from regions different to mine say: "In my home town we don't speak like that") and gaps in, or lack of knowledge of, historical or cultural traditions such as culturally significant films or bands. Sometimes an analyst from another culture is thought of as a person who lives away from his home, loved ones and who misses them a lot. This all points to being wounded. The power dynamic shifts and the patient can feel more competent. Quite often they can enjoy their sense of competence and are willing to educate their analysts, explaining their cultural traditions or sharing their knowledge.

This shift can be very subtle and hard to notice. One of my English patients used to be very happy about her analysis, finding it deep, meaningful and insightful. We could therefore think of a positive transference as the initial stage of her therapeutic process. One day, as per usual, she started the session with a social question "How are you?". As usual, I replied, "I'm good, thank you. And how are you?". "I'm goo ...", was her unfinished answer. Suddenly she interrupted herself and corrected: "I'm well", she replied and stressed the word "well". Then she added, "Good is an Americanism, we need to use our adverbs properly." Through that interaction she exposed my lack of linguistic competence, her linguistic superiority and her strong identification with the English and the concept of Englishness. It helped to open the door to her mixed cultural background and start exploring it. Her cultural past was not overwhelming for her psyche, so she did not experience trauma, however it was an important part of her wholeness. Neither of her parents were English yet she never thought about the impact of their home cultures on her development. Actually, her father's affection for South African culture was emotionally denied. I also considered this dynamic through the transferential lens: the patient could use language and cultural difference to display a sense of superiority, emerging negative transference and aspects of her shadow. However, if I limited myself just to a transference interpretation, I would overlook the importance of her cross-cultural identity and related pain.

Cross-cultural encounters require a great deal of respect, curiosity and sensitivity towards other cultures. The work might become more difficult at this stage of the analytic process as it reveals, while simultaneously bridging, the cultural gap between the analyst and the patient. As an example, let us think about something that looks the same but actually is different – common terms. Again, I invite my readers to use their imagination. Let us suppose that your patient speaks about "a *friend*". How do you interpret that word? What does it mean to you? And what might it mean if you and your patient are from different cultures?

Henry Abramovitch and Jan Wiener (2017) speak about understanding what can become distorted in translation.

> Translation can hide as much as it reveals. For example, the translator for a Russian supervisee said in English, "Her patient said I feel like your friend". I enquired about the original Russian word and was told, it was *drug*. In Russian, *drug* implies an intense, demanding, enduring relationship that is both exhilarating and exhausting. In Soviet times, your *drug* was the one person one could choose freely. He, or she, often took the place of missing brothers and sisters. The transference implications for me as supervisor are profoundly revised when I understand that the patient is not talking about a "friend" in the English sense, but a *drug* with all its Russian depth. Such experiences sensitized me to try to comprehend the untranslatable.
>
> (Abramovitch and Wiener, 2017: 93)

The discovery of the other pole of the Wounded Healer archetype (deficits and "wounds") at this stage of analysis is experienced ambiguously. On one hand, patients may take pleasure in their sense of competence and expertise. The countertransference is key here: if the patient is acting in such a way as to put the analyst down, this would indicate "the will to power". Yet there is also an opportunity for the patient to actualize an inner healer. On the other hand, it is often taken as premature because it opens up the depth of the patient's cultural traumas, pain and shame, which he/she is not yet ready to face. The threat of being overwhelmed by those feelings may lead to actualization of some defences and quite often the theme of cultural trauma might disappear from the therapeutic field for a while.

The third phase: *a Wounding healer is projected onto the analyst*. Usually, the analyst helps to bring the theme of cultural trauma back to the consulting room by noticing it in the patient's story. The accompanying pain edges towards consciousness, but it is still hard to become fully aware of it. Quite often during this period, the analyst is experienced as someone who causes pain by confronting the patient with reality. The analyst is now wound*ing* (Shalit, 2008). It begs the question whether we are in the realm of a different archetype now such as that of the "victim – perpetrator" (Kalsched, 1996). The wounding polarity could be seen as the perpetrator and, in many cases, is experienced in this way by patients. I would argue that we are still in the presence of the "Wounded healer" archetype. A "Wounding healer" is an aspect of the healer polarity, who treats through pain, raises awareness and leads to integrity through confrontation. A double lens approach could be quite beneficial here: the analyst holds an object-relationship perspective but also offers archetypal amplification. I suppose that to have a culturally sensitive ear and to hear cultural wounds in that dynamic is of paramount importance. I'll explain this with a case example.

John is a mixed-race, middle-aged man whose cultural trauma was an intricate weave of several factors. His mother was of Afro-Caribbean origin, carrying with her historical intergenerational trauma of slavery and oppression. In her personal history she was rejected by the family of her white husband on a racial basis and experienced difficulties in her new European country. The father's relatives were also cold and hostile to John. He developed a sense of inferiority and lack of self-worth. He also adopted a very negative attitude to the male population of his mother's country. John saw Caribbean men as violent, brutal and aggressive. His hatred and anger were very present in the consulting room. When John was 11 years old, his father died. The young boy became trapped searching for his male identity, as he didn't have any good role models. His father was dead, his grandfather was cold, rejecting him, and other Caribbean male relatives were horrible and dangerous. It was an overwhelming experience for him: if not angry, John became frozen. I could hardly see any animation in his personality as his capacity to feel was injured (Kalsched, 1996). His frozen state was a manifestation of a cultural trauma. It was as if his soul was captured in the Caribbean identity he denied and was rejected by his white relatives.

Writing these words, I misspelled the word "Caribbean" three times and didn't pay any attention to the red underline by my computer Word corrector. Perhaps in my countertransference, I also turned a blind eye to half of John's identity.

From the very first session with John, I felt extremely inferior. Each week in my countertransference I expected "to be fired" for being a useless analyst. It didn't happen and at one of the sessions a few months later, he was talking about a big house his family had rented and mentioned that their Eastern-European landlord kept one room shut, in which he kept his own stuff. In the transference, there was an obvious correlation between the landlord's ethnic origin and my own which I could recognise through an object-relationship lens. Looking through a cultural lens helped me to see that the landlord also represented someone from another culture with secrets. I asked John whether he felt that his own other culture kept some secrets? This opened up the theme of his mixed-race origin, the shame and inferiority associated with it and provided me with a better understanding of my initial countertransference reaction. For John, I became a Wounding Healer, an adversary, who made him aware of some of the hidden treasures of his Black part: for example, liveliness and assertiveness kept away in the images of Caribbean people, the painful experience of his ancestors and his cultural identity. The integration process started.

The Jungian analyst Erel Shalit (2008) believes that

> A *Wounding* Healer carries the negative transference of the projected shadow, and also functions as consciousness-raising adversary. We know that the healer must carry his wounds, as does the *wounded* healer, but he must also be able to *inflict* wounds …. This often produces resistance, but resistance is also a way the patient's ego is invigorated in its confrontation with an adversary, with a therapist that interrupts the habitual way of an ego in the grips of repetition-compulsion. This is not the containing but rather the adversary function of the therapist.
>
> (Shalit, 2008: 123)

This process of wounding can happen when there is a well-established alliance, trust and a sense of safety. Usually the first out of the five phases considered here – the choice of a cultural trauma-free therapist – provides a solid base. Shalit continues,

> Naturally, this can only take place if the patient is already well enough contained and held in the therapy situation. In this stage, the patient may

find the therapist aggressive, misunderstanding, lacking in empathy, a martial adversary. This is not the detrimental countertransference acting out of the therapist, but the readiness of the therapist to block the way or burden the patient with what he or she necessarily must carry, within a setting of caring and concern.

(Shalit, 2008: 123)

The fourth phase: *first the analyst becomes a Wounding Healer and then the patient does so*. Why?

For if the patient is to experience fully this archetypal image in a dynamic way, the analyst must show him the way. This can happen only if the analyst first has courage to experience these powerful archetypal contents. The analyst "takes on" the patient's illness or wounds, and also begins to experience more fully the wounded aspect of the archetypal image. This in turn activates his own wounds or vulnerability to illness on a personal level and/or in its connection with the wounded-healer archetypal image.

(Groesbeck, 1975: 131)

The patient wounds the analyst in return. We may see this as revenge and an expression of the patient's rage. But how can this help us to get closer to his cultural wounds? We can also see this as a change in the archetypal dynamic: the patient gets closer to his inner healing powers while the analyst to his cultural wounds. Of course, we may see this dynamic working with any type of trauma. Here, I would like to draw my readers' attention to manifestations of the archetypal dynamic both in the context of cultural traumas and cultural wounds. The analyst gets wounded, and this can help him to become more aware. The patient takes the projection back and experiences himself as capable of wounding, thus getting in touch with his own power and aggression.

While the analyst must get close enough to be involved, activated and aware of his own wounds to catalyse the process (as described), he must also be aware of the dangers of inflation as well as his limitations, including the possibility of his own death and demise. It is precisely the archetypal image of the Wounded Healer that can most help him here. If one "leaves the healing to God", he is much better off. In fact, it was God who brought the illness, and hence knows the cure. Hence, though one must be involved deeply, paradoxically, one must not be over-zealous in trying to cure (Groesbeck, 1975: 133).

The fifth phase: *The analyst and the patient live through their cultural wounds, a Wounding and Wounded Healer.*

This chapter was born out of my analytic journey with Dan. Working with him, I became more and more aware of the dynamic of cultural wounds in analysis. I have chosen the archetypal image of the Wounded Healer to illustrate the cultural dynamic in our therapeutic relationship.

Case Study: Dan

Dan, a man in his fifties, approached me because his midlife crisis had triggered sudden problems at work. Despite having lived all his adult life in London, in South-East England, he had actually been born and brought up in the North and described the prevalent attitude of his home region as "Whatever happens – roll up your sleeves and get the job done". Self-reflection and taking one's own feelings into account were considered to be self-indulgent. The atmosphere in his family was "lethargic ... there was neither support, nor neglect". His overall impression of his place of birth could be expressed as "dull, grey, miserable". He had a northern accent, so while he was getting used to my accent, I was getting used to his. At the beginning of the analysis, he talked about his home culture in a flat tone, distantly – though I got a sense that he had mixed feelings about it. Love, hate and shame were intertwined in that amalgam.

1   *Unconscious choice of cultural trauma-free analyst.*
    Being in the room with me as a person from another culture, Dan wasn't exposed to unnecessary shame. He was certain that I wouldn't judge him for doing therapy instead of "rolling up his sleeves" or being so emotional about the problems at work. The only person in the room who criticized him for that was himself.

    The idealised transference formed from the very beginning of analysis. Despite my age, Dan saw me as "an old wise woman who lived in a hut in the woods". Her hut was full of healing herbs and the woman had gravitas. This made more evident the power and the archetypal features of the transference. I was overtly placed into the role of healer and expert. Dan was Chiron's pupil, he used to say, "I'm learning from you".

    Soon he presented a strange somatic "wound" – a mild, temporary deafness and asked me to speak louder. There were various possible interpretations of the meaning of his symptom: from a reaction towards the stress at work to an unwillingness to hear the truth. I also noticed that his comment made me immediately feel concerned whether my English was clear enough. We were moving towards the next phase in our work with cultural traumas.

2 *Discovering the gaps and wounds of the wise old lady.*

The positive transference started to fade and gave way to questioning the "old lady's wisdom", as if Dan was able to see Chiron's wounds now. I can refer here to C.G. Jung who states: "These opposing forces are at work in the mythical healer himself: the physician who heals wounds is himself the bearer of a wound, a classic example being Chiron" (Jung, 1950, para. 159).

It was interesting to observe that his questioning related just to cultural differences and gaps. For example, on one occasion, Dan asked me if I knew what Roman Catholic churches are like. He was nearly certain that I didn't. Another time, he talked about his children and their choice of secondary school. When he mentioned grammar schools, he added: "you are from a different culture. How could you know what grammar schools are?" His tone of voice and the comments were hardly neutral. There was a taste of his expertise, sometimes also a light contempt. He wanted to find out my deficits, lack of knowledge and moments of confusion to approach our cultural wounds: first mine, then his own. The more gaps in our cultural backgrounds he discovered, the less he needed his "deafness". Soon the symptom had gone completely.

3 *The Wounding Healer.*

The Wounding Healer came in quite an ordinary way. Dan brought a dream about a very unpleasant, tough and selfish man. I suggested thinking about him as an internal figure. He was hurt and felt that I saw him as a narcissistic person, similar to his horrible boss, although I didn't say that at all. I became his consciousness-raising adversary and inflicted not only a personal wound, making him face his shadow, but also reopened an old cultural wound. Being assertive, rough or even worse, aggressive and explosive in communication, was his personal nightmare and a part of his cultural background that he strongly disliked. The situation became more complicated when I used some English words whose meaning he didn't know. In the transference, it put me in the Southern camp and him into the Northern camp, resulting in the re-emergence of his cultural trauma in the room. In some way, the wounding healer opened the possibility for Dan to see and acknowledge his wounds.

4 *"Do you know that word?"*

Dan became more attacking. Quite often I could hear him saying in response to my comments: "That was so perceptive and accurate. It was obvious. So simple. Why didn't I see it?". He made me feel that I was a very good therapist for him, yet he devalued me at the same time. I wondered if he felt the same about himself, questioning his sense of self-worth. He also started checking my understanding of words and phrases, suddenly doubting my mastery of English. There was also the issue of linguistic power: Beverly Costa (2020) assumes that some languages are dominant in discourses and have disproportionate power to influence and, of course, English is one of them. I was observing a power shift in our dynamic: Dan recalled the power that he projected onto me at the beginning of analysis.

In one session, Dan was talking again about his problems at work that nearly ruined his life a year ago. The painful struggle wasn't over yet. However, he lightly called that experience "sour" and I responded, echoing the word: "sour"? He exploded: "Do you not know that word?! Oh, of course, you're speaking in your second language. How could you know?!" It was a blow. I didn't speak my mother tongue with him and was therefore deprived of the eloquence to which I was accustomed. More than that, as in the abovementioned story of my colleague, in my home culture well-educated people also were supposed to deploy an extensive lexicon and "not knowing that word" would be embarrassing. I managed to pull myself together, acknowledged his anger and said, "You feel very angry because I doubted your choice of a word". He wasn't aware of his rage at all and was astonished to hear my comment. After the session, I reflected on his explosion. Unconsciously, Dan chose the multilingual aspect of our analysis as a battlefield and challenged my linguistic agency. Beverly Costa assumes that "language enables us not only to think but also to communicate our decisions, act and impact others. Our linguistic ability is one of the essential skills that helps human beings to move from a disempowered infancy to a productive and creative adulthood where we can make choices and have influence – where we have agency" (Costa, 2020: 12). It was as if he wanted me to feel as diminished and disempowered as he felt at work and in some competitive areas of his life.

Dan also made me think about my loss: speaking a second language in which I could not always be as fluent as I would like. Sometimes I felt tongue-tied, stumbling or primitive in my expressions. In addition, sadly, I had to admit that the process of language attrition had started. Over time, fluency in my mother tongue had faded: it could take time to select the "right" word, and some phrases became a copy of their English equivalents, sounding awkward and incorrect in Russian. I was losing something precious, which was a part of my identity and a connection to home.

The archetypal image of the Wounded Healer was helpful in understanding the dynamics of our process. Groesbeck reminds us that "the analyst 'takes on' the patient's illness or wounds, and also begins to experience more fully the wounded aspect of the archetypal image. This in turn activates his own wounds or vulnerability to illness on a personal level and/or in its connection with the wounded-healer archetypal image" (Groesbeck, 1975: 131). As an analyst, I had to get close enough to my cultural background and vulnerability to catalyse the process. Dan's arrow, similar to Heracles' poisoned arrow that pierced Chiron, helped me to become more aware of my cultural connection and losses. At the same time, Dan experienced himself as capable of wounding, became in touch with his own power and aggression and, later, became able to face these features as an aspect of his Northern English identity.

For the first time, I thought about the cultural aspect of the Greek myth: centaurs were famous for being wild and fierce. Their general character was that of wild, lawless and inhospitable beings, slaves to their animal passions. But the Centaur Chiron, the Wounded Healer, was different in this respect and chose to leave his tribe and live in exile. Did he also suffer from a cultural trauma in addition to being rejected by his mother and accidently wounded by his pupil, Heracles?

5   *"My culture is my love, my shame, my identity"*
A few sessions later, Dan mentioned his own accent. After 30 years of life in London, his accent had softened and Dan worried that he might lose it altogether. He wanted to keep it because it was an important part of his identity. He grew up in a monoculture, yet his adult life was culturally diverse, and he liked its mix: new family members from overseas, his children attending a multinational school, his working-class home area in the past and the middle-class borough in which he resided. The image of his home culture had changed for him. He discovered perseverance, a positive side of competing, as well as the assertiveness inherent in his tough northern character and was thus able to integrate those previously shadow qualities into his personality. He was able to compete now, to set firmer boundaries and exercise better discipline at work and with his children at home. He accepted the diversity of his own nature. "A class traitor" started to turn into "a class integrator" or, in other words, the integrator of the shadow with the Self. It became possible to talk about his deep attachment to his home region, his warm feelings towards the nature and the people there. Dan's eyes filled with tears when he realized that he was ashamed of his love for – and attachment

to – his homeland. He once spent nearly an entire session exploring the character of his home area and his feelings towards it. He said that the right description of the character is "dour" and asked me in a soft voice if I knew that word. I didn't. To my surprise he didn't explain it but picked up his smartphone to use Google dictionary, read the meaning aloud and then briefly considered whether the definition matched his understanding. I was fascinated by its phonetic resemblance to "sour". Was *this* the word he had meant to use last time?

In the following session, while we were still exploring cultural identity, he recalled a term "namby-pamby" as an example of cultural shadow. Once again, he asked me whether I knew what it meant. I didn't. He admitted that he had last heard the phrase 30 years ago. Once again, Dan used Google dictionary to explain the meaning to me. Sorrow entered the consulting room: we both felt the loss of our mother-tongues, the words and phrases that surrounded us before were not in common use anymore. The times had changed, the territory had changed. I would say that each of us was a Wounded Healer and both of us were wounded. I was very curious about his use of Google dictionary. So was he. As if a third person had been invited to join our dyad. Was it a renewed and more competent symbolic Father? I believe it was. However, there was more to it. He could not own the Northern and Southern parts of himself but then he transcended the previous tension of two languages and cultures and created a third – "our" language in the sense that it was the unique language of our analytic encounter. His new united identity was emerging out of what could be culturally and personally acceptable and unacceptable in his internal world.

In Dan's story, cultural unconscious and cultural trauma were very present and created a dynamic field in his psyche and in the consulting room. Cultural trauma influenced his individuation processes and the analysis would have not progressed without addressing it.

Epilogue

An academic or clinical paper is supposed to end with a conclusion. I have chosen an epilogue over a conclusion as a more poetic form that resonates with the psyche.

Below, and with the author's kind permission, I reprint a story told to me by Craig Ashton, a linguist and an author of the book *Excuse Me, I'm a Foreigner*. Craig published his childhood linguistic memories and reflections recently on his telegram channel. His narration not only brilliantly illustrates the cultural chiasm but also explains cultural identity:

"Don't say 'melk', Craig", my mum told me, "Say 'milk'". I was 5, sitting in the kitchen with my mum in Winwick, Northern England.
  "But why, mum? It's melk!"
  "That's incorrect, my dear."

But I was absolutely certain that I'd heard other people speaking like that and it was alright! In Denmark and Holland people say "melk". I was also taught at school about Danelaw, when Danish Vikings took control over the North of England. So, I'm a Viking and I drink melk! In 2001, I went to Exeter and faced the same problem. Out of 1500 students just 2 were from the North: one from Liverpool and the other one from York. All the rest were guys from the South, many from Guildford, with the same upper-middle-class vowels. My vowels were different. Once I asked my new friend a question, "Dya wan' owt from't' shop?" He was very surprised and asked me: "What the hell does it mean 'do you want out from shop'?" "Owt" means "anything" in the North. "Nothing" is "nowt". I guess it is from "aught/naught". In the South you are not understood if you speak like that. Sadly, I had to get rid of "my" cool words.

In England your accent says a lot about you: what social stratum you come from; whether you are well-educated or not; culturally well behaved or not or worth bothering about or not. I'm not complaining here, I don't take it as "snobbery". It's just a function of the society that my people belong to. You can't remove it.

At my first job in the South it became even more apparent. Some people were initially unfriendly towards me. As soon as they learnt that I was an Exeter graduate their attitude to me changed drastically for the better. So, I decided to learn the southern accent. In front of the mirror I imitated a billon times how Hugh Laurie speaks in Jeeves and Wooster. It was an unpleasant process as I felt that I was losing a part of myself. I was about 90% successful. There were a few sounds that I couldn't learn perfectly There was a sound /u:/ that I couldn't change at all. Not because it was completely impossible, I'm able to say "cup" (/kʌp/), "but" (/bʌt/), etc just like a southerner. Yet my brain doesn't allow me to do so. I can't do it for psychological reasons. I feel lots of resistance. *As if it is the ultimate betrayal.* One's voice and one's language are important parts of a person's psyche and culture. They are a part of the soul. You can't remove them without losing your soul.

Cultural traumas can create an invisible background in analysis and be strongly intertwined with a patient's personal history. Not receiving proper attention in analysis, they may not only block the therapeutic process but, also, be an obstacle to individuation, resulting in unnecessary shame. Rejection of one's cultural roots or suffering "cultural cringe" because of trauma may lead to betrayal of the Self. An analyst's culturally sensitive ear and awareness of his own cultural wounds can therefore both facilitate and enhance the analytic process in multicultural encounters.

A shorter version of this paper was presented in October 2022 at the open lectures in ISAP, Zurich.

References

Abramovitch, H. and Wiener, J. (2017) "Supervising away from home: Clinical, cultural and professional challenges", *Journal of Analytical Psychology*, 62(1): 88–106.

Alexander, J.C., Eyerman, R., Giesen, B., Smelser, N.J. and Sztompka, P. (2004) *Cultural Trauma and Collective Identity*. Berkeley, CA: University of California Press.

Alexander, J.C. (2012) *Trauma: A Social Theory*. Cambridge, UK: Polity.

Alsan, M. and Wanamaker, M. (2018) "Tuskegee and the health of black men", *The Quarterly Journal of Economics*, 133(1): 407–455.

Bouët-Willaumez, C. (2021) "Silence, dissonance, and harmony: Integrating the multilingual self", in: A. Zarbafi and S. Wilson (eds) *Mother Tongue and Other Tongues*. Bicester, Oxfordshire: Phoenix Publishing House.

Brodsky, A. (2018) "Creative suppression (towards a methodology of cultural trauma study)", *Philosophy and Culture*, 8: 40–50.

Costa, B. (2020) *Other Tongues: Psychological Therapies in a Multilingual World*. Wyastone Leys, Gwent, UK: PCCS Books.

Fleischer, K. (2022) "At the train station: the Self, suspended in collective trauma. Symbolic analysis with victims of childhood trauma caused by state terrorism", *Journal of Analytical Psychology*, 67(1): 130–144.

Groesbeck, C.J. (1975) "The archetypal image of the Wounded Healer", *Journal of Analytical Psychology*, 20(2): 122–145.

Jung, C.G. (1950) *Psychology and Literature*. CW15. Princeton, NJ: Princeton University Press.

Jung, C.G. (1951) *Fundamental Questions of Psychotherapy*. CW16. Princeton, NJ: Princeton University Press.

Kalsched, D. (1996) *The Inner World of Trauma: Archetypal Defences of the Personal Spirit*. London: Routledge.

Kalsched, D. (2013) *Trauma and the Soul: A Psycho-Spiritual Approach to Human Development and its Interruption*. London: Routledge.

Kaplinsky, C. (2008) "Shifting shadows: Shaping dynamics in the cultural unconscious", *Journal of Analytical Psychology*, 53(2): 189–207.

Kiehl, E. (2016) "'You were not born here, so you are classless, you are free!' Social class and cultural complex in analysis", *Journal of Analytical Psychology*, 61(4): 465–480.

Loseva, M. and Pourtova, E. (2021) "Introduction", *Jungianskij Analiz [Jungian Analysis]*, 3: 3.

Melik-Akhnazarova, K. (2015) "Bridging two realities: A foreign language in an analytic space", in C. Crowther and J. Wiener (eds) *From Tradition to Innovation: Jungian Analysts Working in Different Cultural Settings*. New York: Spring Journals.

Pavlikova, N. (2021) "Collective and individual trauma in the consulting room", *Jungianskij Analiz [Jungian Analysis]*, 3: 18–25.

Pourtova, E. (2021) "There was nothing afterwards. Cultural trauma and its narratives", *Jungianskij Analiz [Jungian Analysis]*, 3: 3–17.

Shalit, E. (2008) *Enemy, Cripple, Beggar: Shadow's in the Hero's Path*. Sheridan, Wyoming: Fisher King Press.

van der Kolk, B. (2000) "Posttraumatic stress disorder and the nature of trauma", *Dialogues in Clinical Neuroscience*, 2(1): 7–22.

Chapter 13

A Jungian Approach to Working with the Trauma of Migrants

Waves, Tempests, Harbours

Giancarlo Costanza

Via viatores quaerit

(Notre Dame – Paris)

Unexpected Sirens

One day, during my time as chief consultant for the Child and Adolescent Mental Health Service (CAMHS) of the Catania National Health Trust, I received a phone call asking if I would be willing to accept for psychotherapy a young English-speaking migrant girl from Africa, who had been through some very traumatic experiences. My first inclination, considering our heavy workload, was to refuse, but the temptation to escape the usual institutional routine prevailed, and I agreed to the first appointment with Sophie.

This decision opened the door to further requests that led me to meet, in quick succession, several young migrants (Sophie, John, Abraham and Ali among them), all coming from Africa and the Maghreb. Then, I also met Akira from China – who had not faced the dangers of crossing the Mediterranean, but had similarly come to Italy in pursuit of a better life. In all these cases, there was a gap between reality and desire, which had led them down a potentially treacherous path.

Their stories, and their storytelling, were dramatic and powerful, making me often feel strongly surprised and, in some way, touched as J. Fenimore Cooper (1821) says in *The Spy*:

> My body is tempered by war burdens,
> my cheek never turned pale for fear,
> but, with your sad tale, go away
> all my forces which were, once, my male pride.
> Gelid trembling caught my body
> and childish pain tears flow uncontrollably
> along those rough tracks left by my wounds.

DOI: 10.4324/9781003298076-17

Maps and Portolans

In a psychotherapeutic pathway – that is potentially transformative – the therapist's interpretative and empathic skills are often challenged by the intense and conflicting wishes of the patients and by their traumatic experiences. Furthermore, the therapist will have to come to terms with the harsh and penetrating dynamics associated with the *Shadow of Power* (Guggenbühl-Craig, 1971) and the ghost of the *Wounded Healer* (Sedgwick, 1994). The Shadow, besides being a hidden genuine psychological force, an archetype with multiple faces, can also produce suicidal or murderous impulses in each of us, as Guggenbühl-Craig warned (1994). When the therapist is not aware of his Shadow, it can cast its net over the therapeutic encounter. However, if the therapist is aware of his own weaknesses, as well as of his own Shadow, he can use them to work more effectively. Quite often, psychotherapists are challenged by these factors, which are stubbornly present in every therapeutic encounter. In this regard, it is useful to recall Adolf Guggenbühl-Craig when he advises to courageously question ourselves on the deep drives that move the actors of any therapy, in order to identify the Shadow and its effects on the therapeutic encounter. He then adds: *"We don't really want to connect with Shadow. Shadow connects with us and our job is to notice and be aware of it. In our dreams, fantasies and feelings Shadow is always there"* (Guggenbühl-Craig, 1994: 72).

In addition, there are inevitable transference and countertransference dynamics, with reciprocal projections in the therapeutic dyad. The therapist needs to continually pay attention to both his and the patient's inner worlds, to the constant exchange between them and to the making of the analytic space.

Indeed, the problem of transference and countertransference appears central. The observations of Paola Cuniberti (2012), who looks at the challenges of analytic work, are remarkable. She recalls Augusto Romano, who points out the particularity of Jungian therapeutic practice which: "is modelled on a co-presence of adhesion and distance, of sympathetic participation, of reconstruction and restitution of the discourse that is interwoven between the ego and the unconscious, in which the patient is seen as having the right to reject and correct the interpretation" (Romano, 2004, in Cuniberti, 2012: 46). In this way, Romano suggests a sort of inner nomadism that allows both parties real and deep communication.

According to Gaetano Benedetti (personal communication, 1984), we can define the therapeutic relationship as "a reciprocal act of faith, hope and charity" necessary to deal with the storms of the unconscious, the persistent ambushes of the Shadow and the interlacing of wounds between patient and therapist. While the patient undoubtedly asks the therapist to take care of his wounds, the therapist himself must not be distracted by his own wounds and should be able to learn from the patient.

Empathy is necessary, but not the layman's empathy, which can be seen as merely resulting from the activity of mirror neurons, nor the empathy offered by the constant and unstoppable functioning of our "default mode network" – a network of interacting brain regions that is active when a person is not focused on the outside world as observed with fMRI (Jang et al., 2011). Instead, empathy should come from the therapist's ability to get in touch with the patient's states of mind, to be aware of his own countertransference[1] and to manage boundaries in a flexible way. In short, it is only through the profound questioning of one's own preconceptions and potential, as well as through the ability to use different perspectives (Bion, 1962), that we can confront the Other in a productive way, and activate the *heroism of survival* (Mendelsohn, 2017). This is the capacity to stay alive in the face of life's difficulties, as Ulysses did, in Homer's Odyssey. This contrasts with Achille's *heroism of death*, which had the aim of reaching κλέος – that is, fame and glory. Even if the former is an ideal goal of the therapeutic encounter, it is not always possible for the therapist to empathize with the patient, for example, when the patient is wounded by psychopathic and/or psychotic functioning, it can be extremely difficult for the therapist to empathize (Hare, 1993; Guggenbühl-Craig, 1999).

Here C.G. Jung comes to our rescue: "What I am waiting for is a new revelation from within, one that enables us to see behind the disorganised fragments of infantilism, in which the true image is manifested, a vision that is constructive" (McGuire and Hull, 1977: 223). In this way, Jung suggests that the analytical space is set up as a safe place, where different ways of looking at life can find expression; it can be seen as a harbour after endless storms, a place for a thousand new beginnings for life, an unbreakable and protective *temenos* (Guggenbühl-Craig, 2000).

However, the therapist must be aware of the risk of potentially being harmful to the patient if he fails to meet him in the depth of his wounds. We can imagine the therapist as being caught between Scylla and Charybdis, where Ulysses had to sacrifice some of his fellow travellers to continue his journey. Giving up his unrealistic desires and expectations was the price he had to pay. Like Ulysses, the therapist has to give up his own expectations of being a sort of magic healer, a safe and perfect haven for the patient's needs.

As Dora Kalff puts it: "My aim, however, is to find a new access to the healing qualities of the Self … a connection with the numinous or a contact with inner meaning and happiness", and she adds: "I also think of Jung who said that the moment we are with the client we must forget everything we have learned in order to be open to his needs" (in Aite, 1989).

Shipwrecks

The difficulties outlined above acquire unforeseen power when the therapist is not able to meet the patient on a deeper level, or when they do not share the same reference points. The multitude of people migrating to our countries, carrying with them knowledge, values and faiths different from our own, brings several challenges to our work. They usually come from distant countries, which were once thriving places, but, over time, have been tragically plundered of their natural and geological resources, forcing their citizens to fight for the right to a decent life. They have paid the price for modernity, dramatically losing their points of reference and then finding themselves thrown into new systems of relationships and values, experiencing marginalisation, pain and death.

Authors belonging to former colonial and now migrant populations, such as Abdelmalek Sayad, Ahmed Boubeker and Abdellali Hajjat (Sayad, Boubeker and Hajjat, 2013) have been able to grasp the dynamics and sufferings (as well as the potential) present in the migrant phenomenon. The work of Sayad, who achieved academic success in France with his work with the famed sociologist Pierre Bourdieu, helps us better understand the migrant experience, exploring the unfortunately common transformation of illusion into *dis*illusion. In his posthumous book *La Double Absence* (Sayad, 1999), he delineated the concept of "double absence" in order to describe the migrants' feeling of absence from both their homeland as well as their new land, focusing attention on the migrant's ἀτοπία, as he is trapped in a hybrid position – out of place in both systems that define his non-existence (Palidda, 2002). The migrant is no longer recognized in his society of origin and not yet (or ever) in his society of arrival.

Above all, young migrants, disillusioned and demotivated by the living conditions in their homelands, are strongly attracted by the promise of goods, healthcare and economic security, accompanied by the hope of becoming "lords" of their new "kingdom". The so-called "migrant mirage" (Palidda, 2002), meaning the fantasy they create of a new and better world, can be seen as a way to transform their material and existential conditions. He who abandons his own world to pursue the *djinn*[2] of change is at risk of madness and finds himself travelling backwards along the dangerous road portrayed by Joseph Conrad in the *Heart of Darkness* (1899).

The following clinical vignettes are inevitably fragmentary, since they mirror the experience I had in the encounters with the patients I met at

CAMHS. In doing such work, the usual reassuring procedures of the first interview (e.g., the "ritual" of the anamnesis) are doomed to failure owing to the impossibility of obtaining precise information. In fact, often even dates of birth are not accurate but just "assigned" in order to allow bureaucratic existence status (tax code, health card, identity documents, etc.), almost in a metaphorical repetition of the Conradian *blank space*, a sort of no man's land where everything is possible, even the transformation of objective data.

In the analytic encounter, we must be aware that any attempt to understand an Other, that is a stranger to us, has its limits. It is not possible to know everything about the other, so we must be content with our imperfect knowledge, proceeding with caution and humility (Gladwell, 2019).

In my encounters with the young migrants, I could witness the presence of what Kalsched calls "anti-life forces" (Kalsched, personal communication, 2021), capable of deviously and tenaciously attacking one's inner world. These forces were evident in all the migrants whom I met in my work. They were my fellow travellers and their stories reminded me of Fairbairn's (1952) *internal saboteur*. To cope with these *internal saboteurs*, we are required to summon all our energies, to resist not being overwhelmed, to help our patients see that they are victims and not perpetrators but that, at the same time, they are activating their anger and hatred in their inner world,

Figure 13.1 "Horizon", Francesco Finocchiaro

becoming their own merciless attackers. The analyst's ability to stay with the patients' terrible rage helps create a shared space where words, emotions and gaze come together to build a foundation for new directions.

In such an endeavour, it sometimes helps that my patients had no knowledge of the social reality of Catania nor of my *Persona* (the Jungian archetype of mediation between the Ego and outer world) as this facilitated an encounter free of psycho-social presumptions. Emiljia Kiehl succinctly describes these dynamics in her work, cleverly focusing on the unconscious impact that differences in culture and social class have on the clinical encounter and how awareness of this can open space in the analytical relationship (Kiehl, 2016).

The Castaways

The first patient I met was Sophie, who was 16 years old (or so she said). She had arrived in Catania after a very risky and difficult journey, having crossed Africa using many means of transportation from Central Africa to Libya. She had then boarded a rubber dinghy, and for a long time was at the mercy of the waves. At the end of her journey, she was so dehydrated that she had to be evacuated, in treacherous weather conditions, by a Navy helicopter and admitted to a hospital in Catania, first into an intensive care unit and then into an ordinary ward. From there, once her physical condition had stabilised, she was placed in a migrant community and referred to me for psychological support.

She was tall, good-looking, despite her extreme thinness, with an absent or, at best, half-smile, but she immediately opened up when she realized that she could talk in English, a language more familiar to her. After completing the bureaucratic formalities, we briefly discussed some contractual aspects. We scheduled appointments for the following weeks and I invited her to use a *booklet* to mark her reflections, questions and dreams. In subsequent meetings, in which she always arrived a little late, we talked about the experiences she had endured, the distances she had covered and why she had chosen such a dangerous and difficult path for her life considering her high-level tribal affiliation with high economic status.

She tried to gloss over all this at first and reported her first dream in a fragmented, hesitant way, with at times a shrill voice: "I am a gazelle, I walk in my herd … Suddenly I realize that someone is a carnivore, he bites another gazelle like me and I run away". Then, she began to cry and explained the dramas that had led to her sudden and secret departure, telling me that she had been sexually abused by her father. Sophie recalled the dramatic escape from her homeland; the repeated abuse suffered at the hands of the soldiers she met at countless checkpoints, the long wait in Libya and then the stormy sea crossing of which she only remembers her fear, exhaustion, proximity to death and the transfer by helicopter. Over time, other dreams arrived, which were told in a progressively firmer and more confident voice, as she was improving physically (she gained weight) as well psychologically (her mood improved, although her sleep-wake cycle remained unbalanced for a long time): "A little girl, she is lost in the dark desert… from hidden holes appear carnivorous animals that repeatedly try to bite her …", "Water everywhere, I feel as if I were drowning … a pipe, a tunnel, full of water that goes, gets lost … I don't know why, I am afraid".

I didn't offer interpretations to these dreams, which tell of early trauma and inner dangerous forces. While listening to them, I tried to avoid sudden movements of my body, being aware of her state of high alert, a sort of inner fear that warned that I too could be a danger to her integrity, her body and soul. I remained emotionally present, listening with a calm, breathing rhythm that was slowly imitated by her, thus changing the atmosphere in the room. By doing this, I offered her some containment of her unthinkable fear.

Afterwards, she recounted a dream that suggested the possibility of being saved: "Among the waves, a raft appears, a boat … on board there is a strange elephant [with an obelisk on his back] that looks at me and, sucking up water, makes the sea less terrible". In this dream, the chance of rescue appeared via an animal familiar to her – the elephant. This image of an elephant with an Egyptian obelisque on its back might even recall the coat of arms of Catania, thus embodying a positive image of therapy and of her new life in the city.

Often, upon entering the consulting room, she was surprised to see that I was there for her, and she wondered why. Over time, there was an overall improvement – her confidence increased, and she seemed more at peace with herself. She stopped seeing herself as guilty for the trauma that she had suffered, especially her father's sexual abuse, from which she feared she had been infected with HIV. In Africa there is a belief that a virgin's blood can cure HIV infection, and this was why her father had raped her. This belief is an important factor in the increase in rapes and HIV-positivity amongst girls in certain parts of Africa (Meel, 2003). We arranged an HIV test for her, which fortunately came back negative.

We took our time. Occasionally, I could hear Sophie becoming suddenly irate and switching to her mother-tongue, punctuated with harsh, menacing sounds and snake-like sibilants, accompanied by incomprehensible words which, although eloquent, were delivered with hurt and aggressive looks.

I stayed with her, sitting in front of her, and resumed, after her critical outbursts, by speaking in our shared adopted tongue (English), a common linguistic space, which was also a metaphor for this reassuring therapeutic space. We spoke of her previous life, of the psychic death she had experienced countless times in the repeated abuse. We talked of the threat to her physical life during her sea crossing and her time in hospital, when the doctors thought she wouldn't survive. In my encounter with Sophie I was reminded of that which James Hillman said in his dialogue with Sonu Shamdasani: "To see clearly, we need the rigour of death... we cannot live authentically if we do not encounter death" (Hillman and Shamdasani, 2013: 33).

During our work together, Sophie was able to get a school diploma, which meant she could move to the north of Italy and enter another community where there was a good possibility of work for her. At our last meeting, she greeted me and told me that she was torn about the transfer to the north, because she was afraid of experiencing further alienation. She was worried about this new migration, even if it was planned and desired. I asked her if she had any new dreams to share before leaving. She told me, in a quiet voice: "They are opening a park for animals which were formerly captives in cages... a gazelle is freed and moves, although she has signs of a wound on her legs, she manages to run... she is afraid to enter the new herd, but in the middle of the park there is a platform, inside there are rangers watching everything... sure that nothing bad can happen". I invited her to interpret the dream, which I hoped would help her to acknowledge the beginnings of trust and security. She smiled, said goodbye and quietly left.

Letting her go was an experience rich in conflicting emotions: on the one hand there was happiness and satisfaction with the positive changes I could observe in her inner world, on the other, there was the feeling similar to the experience of a parent whose child leaves home to somewhere far away, a feeling heightened by the realisation that meeting again would be almost impossible. Our work together was built on shared trust and empathy. It was very important that I was able to respectfully wait for her, to not be overwhelmed by her aggression which threatened both of us. I tried to strengthen her pro-life forces while challenged by her internal saboteur.

Abraham came to me shortly after Sophie. He was from Central Africa and seemed to be about 16 years old. He had crossed the Sicily Channel from Libya with his slightly older brother. Terrible events befell him: while he was on the raft, the boatmen tried to rape a girl. He and his brother tried to protect her so the boatmen threw both his brother and the girl into the stormy sea, killing them and then savagely beat Abraham.

When he arrived in Sicily, traumatised, he managed to report what had happened during the sea journey, which led to the arrest of the smugglers. He was then transferred to a community for young migrants, where I met him. Abraham came to our first meeting with two requests: the first was to get better, to overcome "survivor's shame" (Levi and Mujcic, 2017) with its dysthymic aspects (sleep and appetite disorders), the second was to find the courage to tell his mother and sisters, who had remained in his homeland, about the catastrophe that had happened. We then scheduled a series of meetings for the following three months.

The constancy of my presence was initially experienced as something strange, unusual for him. As had occurred with Sophie, Abraham too was surprised to find that I was regularly waiting for him to come to our sessions. He had difficulty in remembering dreams, which were few and distressing in the beginning. They told of dark presences, of aggressors who wanted to strike his family, of the impossibility of talking to his brother and finding his way back home: "Suddenly a masked man enters our home and kills everybody with a short sword, there's blood everywhere" ... "Terrible and fierce animals move around my home, roaring all the time" ... "I am lost, walking around in a desert, I don't know how to reach my family. My brother's phone is off, I can't speak with him". As our sessions continued, his dreams calmed down and we were able to find a turning point in one dream where there was a disturbing reunion of the inhabitants of his village, which then turned into a party.

There was a rapid improvement in his psychosomatic symptoms and a progressive improvement in his dysthymic problems. He was then able to telephone his mother to recount the succession of events, sobbing about the drama he had endured (it was his brother who had pressed him to leave Libya, where Abraham was in a good position). Finally, he began to understand that he was not to blame and that he was also a victim and decided to stay in Italy if he could find regular work. He finished his studies in Sicily and now works in northern Italy. Working with Abraham was difficult, owing to his self blame for the tragic events of the journey, his gaze would often search out mine trying to see if in my eyes there was reproach for his "faults". My constant presence, which was experienced as something "funny" – but internally recorded as friendly – helped to contain and share his grief, allowing him to manage his fears. As Kalsched suggests, "if we want to heal from trauma, we'll have to find ways around them ... to give them up. We'll have to drop the story, written by our defences ... to find alternative interpretations of life" (Kalsched, personal communication, 2021).

Ali was 17 years old, when he came to Italy from the Maghreb. Unusually, the story of his journey to Sicily did not involve any dangers or dramas. Ali told me that he had got to know Italy through the Italian television channels and so decided that his life there would be better than the one at home, where he had a very large family that paid little attention to his needs and requirements.

However, despite this apparently simple story, Ali was not able to respect the rules of community life, which resulted in problems with educators as well as with other fellow residents. His impulsiveness and pantoclastic outbursts of anger could be understood as a cry for help. Although he had said that he watched Italian television, Ali insisted that he could only speak his own language and so I always met him with the help of a cultural mediator.

Throughout the therapy, despite the prescribed drug therapy (the correct intake of which I always doubted), I never noticed any change in his behaviour or relational patterns, which were always marked by surliness, latent aggression and a defiant attitude towards all adults. Moreover, Ali strongly refused to take orders from female educators, whom he considered inferior and impure because they wore inappropriate clothes.[3] This was linked to religious and cultural factors, however I think a deeper reason was the relationship between Ali and his mother. She was not "good enough for him" (Winnicott, 1958), as she had been unable to make him feel welcome in the family and instead played a part in his expulsion from it. Perhaps this dynamic explained the activation of violent feelings against his self, which were also projected onto the outer world especially women.

A real therapeutic relationship was never established between the two of us. I always felt there was a distance between Ali and myself (probably not helped by the presence of the cultural mediator) and also that his request for help was fake. What is more, I had a perception of him as having a deserted soul, a poor and cold inner world, in which there was no interest in transforming himself and being really helped at a deeper level.

When looking at him, hearing his voice and noticing his gaze, I could feel Kurtz's words ("The horror, the horror"), from Conrad's *Heart of Darkness*, resonating inside me. Furthermore, I experienced the disconsolate sensation of having nothing to offer him, as Ali had been taken by the *djinn* of easy gain and freedom to get what he wanted.[4]

He stopped our sessions and, as the outbursts and aggressive behaviour persisted, was then transferred to a specialized community.

John is the fourth of my castaways, who was also supposed to be 16 years old. He came from Eastern Africa, where he lived alone, having lost both parents. He had been living with his Christian grandmother (although he was Muslim) and a brother. He spent about seven months in Libya, where he worked as a waiter in semi-slavery conditions for an Egyptian family, which he fled as the political situation deteriorated in Libya.

During our first encounter, John recounted his birth, which had been marked by a "magical" event. He was told that his mother's pregnancy had lasted thirteen months (sic!), and that it ended only with the intervention of an elderly *marabout*, a Muslim holy man, who died once he was born.

He asked me for help with his depression, accompanied by suicidal thoughts, but also for pantoclastic outbursts of anger and his difficulty with physical contact, especially with women. We arranged a series of appointments that lasted for over a year.

From the very first meeting, what impressed me most was his powerful physicality, his beaming smile (which appeared more often as we got to know each other), the great effort he made to relate to others (educators, therapist, teachers) and his ability to go from using shared English to an increasingly fluent Italian. He expressed a desire to stay in Italy, to acquire citizenship and enlist in the Army. To achieve these goals, he wanted to learn the language properly and go to school to reach a level of education consistent with his plans.

A core of sadness, despair and anger appeared at times during the therapeutic work, often caused by the memory of his grandmother and his orphanhood. In contrast to other migrants, he was alone in Sicily and not connected to family networks. Moreover, his family was so poor that they could not be reached by telephone or through social networks, due to the absence of telephone lines. Thus, he only managed to contact his grandmother and brother a few times and with great difficulty.

Occasionally dreams appeared: "my aunt (actually a kind of sorceress) lays me down on the table and cuts off my legs". When I asked him what he thought about this dream, he immediately replied "I don't know", then became pensive and added, with a sad voice, that he thought he didn't deserve the prize and the cost of the journey to Italy. Inside himself there had always been, and still was, an inner voice repeating that he wasn't a good boy, that he deserved only "bad things". At one of the worst moments in therapy, when despair had gripped him again, he cried continuously for days, as the bad weather we were having reminded him of the extreme poverty he had experienced at home (the house had an inadequate roof and the rain inevitably flooded in, washing their few poor possessions away). However, he was also able to overcome his despair and guilt. He dreamt: "I met a dangerous dog that barks and seems to want to attack me in order to devour me, but I manage to find food that turns it into a cat that meows and lets me pet it". This dream suggests that the ferocity of the attacks of his sadistic superego was somewhat calmed by the containment provided by the therapy.

Time, the good work of the educators, the acceptance of his life in Sicily and the therapeutic containment seemed to support his journey, to activate the possibility of modifying disharmonious functioning patterns and self-attacks. Destruction and fear were finally transformed into relationship, nourishment, warmth and movement.

During the therapy, I could feel the need to protect John, which was probably in tune with the need to protect the poor and lost inner parts of myself. When he had to prepare for his meeting with the Government Commission for International Protection to evaluate the extension of his permit to stay, it was hard for him to remember the past, which was marked by pain and despair. He declared,

> I am afraid to go back to Africa because I do not want to return to my old life of slavery ... I have had to sacrifice my life for everything that would have happened to me ... I had to escape from Libya, go by sea, maybe it could be the end of my suffering and uneasy life ... I have no place to go and I have no choice in life, the only choice is death ... Look at me now in Italy. I never thought I would be alive to write my story ... it's a miracle for me and I thank God ... when I remember what I went through during these years I cry deep in my heart, please forgive me! I can't tell you everything about me because it makes me suffer and bleed in my heart ... I want to live in Italy forever because I believe that Italy will give me a good and better education ... and Italy will be proud of me in the future.

Currently, John continues his life in the south of Italy, where he studies and expresses himself in a fluent and rich Italian (far superior to many of my native patients!). Sometimes he has disheartening moments which he then overcomes, and his characteristic beaming smile reappears. He is now more able to project himself into his "Italian" future.

Akira, unlike the others, did not arrive on overcrowded barges or by crossing dangerous seas – her shipwreck was not far away from her family but occurred, paradoxically, *in* her family. She was a 13-year-old Chinese girl who had lived in China with her grandparents since her earliest childhood, while her parents moved to Italy, working in a firm owned by a relative.

In recent years, Akira had seen her parents no more than 15 days a year. Before coming to Italy, she had been attending school in China and had built a good network of friendships there. She was well placed emotionally within her grandparents' family, which itself was part of a solid extended family network. Suddenly, and for no apparent reason, this balance was broken, and Akira was called to Sicily, without any negotiation or confrontation.

By the time she came to me, she had been in a town in the south of Italy for six months and had been placed in a class mainly composed of Italians, but which also included two Indian boys and another Chinese girl of the same age, whom she befriended. Akira found herself lost in a sea of loneliness, helped only by the regular use of a mobile phone, which meant she could keep in touch with her friends and family in her Chinese hometown.

She was sad, defensive and almost emotionless, her gaze fluctuating between bewilderment and feeling lost. She nervously jumped from one thing to another. Her state of anxiety was such that she managed to break through the usual resistance of migrants (which is especially strong for the Chinese community) to contact the Italian mental health services (D'Anna et al., 2022).

Silence characterised her, not only in her contact with me but also with her family and classmates, with the exception of her Chinese classmate, whom she relied on, although with caution.

Attempts to enter dialogue with her through her aunt, who spoke good Italian, or through a mother-tongue mediator, failed miserably thus leaving us in gloomy silence, accompanied by desolate looks. I experienced helplessness and felt the impossibility of making real contact with her. Suddenly, one afternoon, Akira's gaze fell on my plants, which I cherish and which accompany my clinical work with their erupting flowers, their fragrances but also occasional problems related to the presence/absence of water or to attacks by aggressive and dangerous insects. They embody a natural constant metaphor of the passing of life, of seasons and the need to care for the living.

But there is another peculiarity here: among the plants I have partially hidden small toy figures (e.g. a giraffe with a rotating neck, a GI Joe-type soldier, an ankylosaurus and a damaged Catwoman without legs). They catch the attention of my patients, but they usually don't find the courage to touch or take them.

One day, Akira looked at me and then shifted her gaze onto the toys. She slowly touched them, looked at them and then placed them on the table outside the protection/hiding place of the plants. We stood like this for a while, then she put them back in their original place and went away. In the following sessions, the toys featured more and more, becoming progressively involved in a story of group meetings, in a shared exploration of the "forest", from which they would cautiously emerge. The muscular Soldier would carry the legless Catwoman on his shoulders up to the Lego bricks fortress inside which they could find shelter. Afterwards, the fortress became a place with open access so that Catwoman would be able to ride around on GI Joe's shoulders while either the giraffe or the ankylosaur would watch. As our encounters came to an end, Akira built, with the chassis of a small car, a kind of wheelchair on which Catwoman could move "autonomously" in the playground.

In the meantime, the school had informed me of significant improvements in her relationships with other classmates and teachers. What is more, Akira had started to learn Italian.

Although there have been no other meetings, I continue to receive reassuring communications from her school about her progress. I see our therapeutic relationship as a shipwreck without waves, resolved without shared words but with an excellent use of the available materials. We shared a kind of original and modified sandplay, an "unconscious" instrument of transformation, as is widely used in dyads and groups around the world (Pattis Zoja, 2011). Even if no real conversation happened, with the exception of a few shared words, a mobile translation application helped us, together with a game of meaningful glances inside this sandplay-like setting.

There are many different approaches to sandplay, particularly in relation to the use of interpretation. In my experience with Akira, where using words felt difficult and a potential trap, I chose to let Akira's inner world emerge and express itself while being a silent but active companion, just like the Soldier transporting the disabled Catwoman. I think that my choice made it possible for her to finally experience her inner autonomy, the same thing that happened when Catwoman became able to move around in her wheelchair.

Waves and Surf

The meetings I had with my castaways often had positive outcomes, but I think it is necessary to examine the internal dynamics. Those in the helping professions can easily succumb to the seduction of the bipolar patient-healer (or wounded-healer) archetype (Guggenbühl-Craig, 1971), where the danger is that, if the therapist identifies with the "healer" pole of the wounded-healer archetype, they may force the patient to identify with being, and staying, "wounded" or sick.[5] To help the patient, the analyst must be able to "show him the way" (Groesbeck, 1975) by experiencing both poles of the wounded-healer archetype and its personal ramifications, becoming a guide and a catalyst for the patient's "inner healer" (Groesbeck, 1975). This means also accepting the patient's aggressive statements such as "You are rigid" or "You don't listen to me" as Ali once said – and he was right about this, as I was listening to the interpreter.

For most of the dramatic experiences and traumas lived through by my castaway patients, I was able to find common ground, as I managed to see them not only as suffering fragments of another continent but also as unknown resources for my own world. They had fragile wings which were, however, capable of resisting the insult of the Sun.

For Akira, the plants and toys in the therapeutic space provided vital momentum. They offered pathways, a fortress in which she felt accepted and from which she could start again. She was able to move from a position of defending herself to finding a courageous independence, while being aware of her limitations, expressed in a symbolic way by the legless Catwoman in her wheelchair.

For Ali, things went wrong owing to the language barrier and, most of all, to the distance which increased due to the presence of an unreliable interpreter. In fact, the translator's work increased my fears of not being trusted. I was afraid of being betrayed rather than translated.

Somehow his demands were not properly met, allowing the undertow to stall his progress, turning him back into a castaway far from my shore.

Landings

Eventually, we all ended up on a shore which was very different from that at the start of our journey. Both my patients and I changed: in the therapeutic encounter, we were able to experience the transformative power of a psychodynamic setting, despite coming from different cultures, and found ourselves travelling through labyrinths, balanced between near and far, separation and interpenetration, affectively charged answers and unshared interpretations.

They were unconscious travellers of a transformative process that changed us all, leaving us "marked" by the process (Zinkin, 1974), echoing the splendid and icastic statement by Luciano Perez:

The way Jung put it was that of the discovery of the inner Imago. Recognizing the features and splendour of this Imago on a face is no longer wandering around in a vain external search for the inaccessible, but understanding that this Imago is first present in myself, that it is this inner presence that makes me recognize it outside.

(Perez, 2003: 97)

Figure 13.2 "Vertical", Francesco Finocchiaro

When we meet others in need of help, the only chance to help them recognize their inner strength and beauty comes from our own ability to first find strength and beauty inside ourselves.

I found, among my books, a phrase in Latin which I think perfectly describes the core of our work – and with this phrase this journey comes to an end:

Factum mutat facientem

Notes

1 To understand the extreme difficulty hidden behind these banal terms, I consider this quote from C.G. Jung's letter to S. Spielrein to be exhaustive: "My mind has reached rock bottom. I, who have had to represent a firm tower for many weak people, am the weakest of all" (Covington and Wharton, 2003).
2 Lit.: "spirit, genius" – but the term belongs to a vast semantic area to which matrix (janna), foetus (janin), garden (jenena), paradise (jennat), madness (jnoun) belong, however the plural of djinn generates junan, madness.
3 There would be much to discuss about the necessary training for the operators of such facilities: certainly, elements of anthropology, ethnopsychiatry and religion should be known.
4 In fact, he had quickly and skilfully become part of an Italo-Arab drug-dealing organisation.

5 See Harold Searles when talks about using the patient to carry the weight of all the severe psychopathology in the whole relationship in "Psychoanalytic therapy with the borderline adult: some principles concerning technique" (1978), and in "The patient as therapist to his analyst" (1999).

References

Aite, P. (1989) "Alcune domande a Dora Kalff", *Rivista di Psicologia Analitica*, 38/39: 17–28.

Bion, W.R. (1962) *Learning from Experience*. London: William Heinemann.

Conrad, J. (1899) *Heart of Darkness*. Urbana, IL: Project Gutenberg.

Covington, C. and Wharton, B. (2003) *Sabina Spielrein. Forgotten Pioneer of Psychoanalysis*. New York: Brunner-Routledge.

Cuniberti, P. (2012) "Tecnica, soggettività dell'analista, empatia nella relazione analitica", *L'Ombra*, N.83 of *Il Tridente* series, Moretti & Vitali.

D'Anna, G., Zorzetto, S., Del Matto, L., Costanzo, G., Kalke, T., Ricca, V. and Cardamone, G. (2022) "Il primo contatto con i Servizi di Salute Mentale in una città multietnica: differenze diagnostiche e terapeutiche nella popolazione di Prato", *Rivista di Psichiatria*, 57(4): 173–183.

Fairbairn, W.R.D. (1952) *Psychoanalytic Studies of the Personality*. London: Routledge.

Fenimore Cooper, J. (1821) *The Spy*. Urbana, IL: Project Gutenberg.

Gladwell, M. (2019) *Talking to Strangers: What We Should Know About People We Don't Know*. Boston: Little, Brown and Company.

Groesbeck, C.J. (1975) "The archetypal image of the wounded healer", *Journal of Analytical Psychology*, 20(2): 122–145.

Guggenbühl-Craig, A. (1971) *Power in the Helping Professions*. Washington, DC: Spring Publications.

Guggenbühl-Craig, A. (1994) "Eyes in the night country", *Psychological Perspectives*, 30(1): 70–82.

Guggenbühl-Craig, A. (1999) *The Emptied Souls*. Washington, DC: Spring Publications.

Guggenbühl-Craig, A. (2000) *Quando il Temenos è Infranto: Abusi del Terapeutca e Rispetto del Paziente*. Bergamo: Moretti & Vitali.

Hare, D.R. (1993) *Without Conscience: The Disturbing World of the Psychopaths Among Us*. New York: Guilford Press.

Hillman, J. and Shamdasani, S. (2013) *Lament of the Dead. Psychology After Jung's Red Book*. New York: W.W. Norton & Co.

Jang, J.H., Jung, W.H., Kang, D.H., Byun, M.S., Kwon, S.J., Choi, C.H. and Kwon, J.S. (2011) "Increased default mode network connectivity associated with meditation", *Neuroscience Letters*, 487(3): 358–362.

Kalsched, D. (2021, October 9) *Life and Anti-life Forces in the Inner World of Trauma Survivors*. Lecture at AIPA.

Kiehl, E. (2016) "You were not born here, so you are classless, you are free! Social class and cultural complex in analysis", *Journal of Analytical Psychology*, 61(4): 465–480.

Levi, F. and Mujcic, E. (2017) *Primo Levi in Bosnia. Il Paradosso della Vergogna del Sopravvissuto*. Forlí: Una Città Editore.

McGuire, W. and Hull, R.F.C. (1977) *C.G. Jung Speaking. Interviews and Encounters*. Princeton, NJ: Princeton University Press.

Meel, B.L. (2003) "The myth of child rape as a cure for HIV/AIDS in Transkei: a case report", *Medicine, Science, and the Law*, 43(1): 85–88.

Mendelsohn, D. (2017) *An Odyssey. A Father, a Son, and an Epic*. New York: HarperCollins Publishing.

Palidda, S. (2002) "Introduction", in A. Sayad, *La Doppia Assenza. Dalle Illusione Dell'Emigrato alle Sofferenze Dell'Immigrato* (trans. D. Borca and R. Kirchmayr). Milano: Raffaello Cortina Editore.

Pattis Zoja, E. (2011) *Sandplay Therapy in Vulnerable Communities. A Jungian Approach.* London: Routledge.

Perez, L. (2003) "Homo viator", in F. Donfrancesco (ed.) *Figure della Devozione*. Bergamo: Moretti & Vitali.

Sayad, A. (1999) *La Double Absence*. Paris: Seuil.

Sayad, A., Boubeker, A. and Hajjat, A. (2013) *Per Una Teoria Postcoloniale delle Migrazioni.* G. Avallone and S. Torre (eds) Il Carrubo Editore.

Searles, H.F. (1978) "Psychoanalytic therapy with the borderline adult: Some principles concerning technique", in J.F. Masterson (ed.) *New Perspectives on Psychotherapy of the Borderline Adult*. New York: Brunner Mazel, pp. 41–65.

Searles, H.F. (1999) "The patient as a therapist to his analyst", in *Countertransference and Related Subjects: Selected Papers*. Madison, CT: International Universities Press, pp. 380–459.

Sedgwick, D. (1994) *The Wounded Healer. Countertransference from a Jungian Perspective.* London: Routledge.

Winnicott, D.W. (1958) *Collected Papers. Through Paediatrics to Psychoanalysis*. London: Tavistock Publications.

Zinkin, L. (1974) "Flexibility in analytic technique", in M. Fordham, R. Gordon, J. Hubback and K. Lambert (eds.) *Technique in Jungian Analysis*. London: Routledge.

Part IV

Poetic and Creative Methods

Chapter 14

Myths, Trauma and the Neurobiological Psyche

Roberta Perri

Introduction

Traditional Western thinking is usually based on a split between spirit and matter, but neuroscience has revolutionized this view with regard to human functioning. Neuroscientific studies have revealed the extent to which the laws of matter determine the form and functions, that we acquire during the evolutionary process, which govern our growth, both as an individual and as a species. Even the development of complex behaviours which may be considered to have a spiritual component, such as ethical and moral choices or sensitivity to beauty and harmony, follow the structure and functions of neuronal circuits (Changeux, 2008). Freedom of choice is a capacity, acquired through the refinement of behavioural patterns, which concerns flexibility, complexity, diversification and differentiation of responses to the surrounding environment. Interestingly, ancient Western thought is related to mythic narratives, in which early cognitive attitudes were confronted with unitary ideas of a living cosmos where human beings are just one of the phenomena of creation. The relationship between myth and science has been widely debated including the hypothesis that both emerged as a result of the human need to explain the origin and functioning of our physical world (Segal, 2009). Accordingly, ancient myths functioned like science did in later times. These myths observed natural phenomena and explained them in a conceptual framework in which deities were seen as personifications of natural phenomena and their actions as metaphors for natural processes. Myths cover a broad range of topics, ranging from geological to atmospheric events, from astronomical phenomena to laws governing the human individual and society. They lay the foundations for rituals providing the ancients with a means to interact with the divine forces of nature in similar ways as modern applied science (Segal, 2009). There are opposing views to the idea that myths are precursors to science. For Lévy-Bruhl (1926), myths represent attempts to re-establish a mystical communion with the natural

DOI: 10.4324/9781003298076-19

world through magical thought processes; in contrast, science aims to understand the workings of the natural world and master them (Segal, 2009). However, the topics covered by myths undoubtedly concern the same realities observable in every epoch and the phenomena described are the same as those that engage contemporary researchers. The overlap between myth and science had already been acknowledged in the Middle Ages, when Ovid's Metamorphoses was considered a natural sciences compendium (Barchiesi, 2005). Since his poem centres its narrative on the human body and its transformations in response to traumatic events, it can be seen as underlining the commonalities between modern science and myth. Ovid observed the precariousness of human beings who are at the mercy of a menacing world (Barchiesi, 2005). Ovid's insights arise from the analysis of mythical events in which trauma powerfully impacts the body and robs the traumatized person of his identity. The worldwide bestseller, *The Body Keeps the Score* (van der Kolk, 2014), provides years of neuroscientific research on the consequences of traumatic events on mind and body. Surprisingly, when meeting trauma stories either through the mythical perspective or through a contemporary scientific lens, we find that we are observing the same phenomena. Several features of the events narrated by Ovid in his *Metamorphoses* strongly coincide with the hallmarks of the modern definition (according to neurophysiology) of traumatic experiences, especially those related to interpersonal relationships. Examples include the randomness of violent acts, which Ovid attributed to the arbitrariness of the gods, but also the protagonists' fragility when isolated from their family or social contexts. Moreover, in the Ovidian poem, we see the deepest effects of traumatic experiences in individuals with developing identities such as adolescents, who are the most common characters in the poem (Segal, 2005). Furthermore, Ovid recounts the effects that trauma can have on the psyche using descriptions which are very similar to those currently employed to define symptoms in severely traumatized subjects. These include the alienation of the ego from the self and the social environment also the annihilation of the psyche, both of which leave the body to tell the story of what happened. Ovidian accounts are surprisingly modern in describing how trauma is not confined to a moment or a specific situation in the past. As neuroscience informs us, trauma is the imprint left in the brain and body by that event.

Daphne

Many a one courted her; she hated all wooers; not able to endure, and quite unacquainted with man, she traverses the solitary parts of the woods, and she cares not what Hymen, what love, or what marriage means. Many a time did her father say, "My daughter, thou owest me a son-in-law"; many a time did her father say, "My daughter, thou owest me grandchildren." She, utterly abhorring the nuptial torch, as though a crime, has her beauteous face covered with the blush of modesty; and clinging to her father's neck, with caressing arms, she says, "Allow me, my dearest father, to enjoy perpetual virginity; her father, in times, bygone, granted this to Diana." He indeed complied. But that very beauty forbids thee to be what thou wishest, and the charms of thy person are an impediment to thy desires.

(Ovid's Metamorphoses, book I, 1893, vv. 478–489)

Peneus, the river-father, expects a son-in-law and grandchildren from his daughter Daphne. Having no male children, he appears more concerned with the fulfilment of his desire for grandchildren than his own daughter's wishes (Silvestri, 2015). However, Daphne, opposing the life chosen for her by her father, decides to follow a different path modelled on the behaviour of Diana, the goddess of virginity, forests, wild animals and hunting. Daphne is an extremely feminine young woman, but instead of submitting to her father's will, she sees becoming a follower of Diana as the best way to define her own identity. For Diana, virginity and purity represent an individual choice, even for an immature girl. Diana, as a deity, already knows who she wants to be and what she wants to do. In Callimachus' Hymn to Diana, the dialogue between Zeus and his daughter is very similar to the one depicted by Ovid between Daphne and Peneus (Barchiesi, 2005). Diana asks to keep her virginity and also for a bow and arrow to be a hunter and live in the woods. At the same time, she is also the patroness of childbirth (Frazer, 1925) and her Greek version, Artemis, is the personification of the moon (Graves, 1955). Thus, Diana symbolically embraces the full development of female potential with all her roles.

In contrast to Diana's story, Daphne's similar request for virginity marks the beginning of a tragedy (Barchiesi, 2005). Her choice to dedicate her femininity to a goddess leads her to ignore another god, the god of love. From this point of view, Peneus' words are prophetic: his daughter must consider the different aspects of her nature because, unlike a divinity, she cannot take a one-way path without facing consequences. Why does Daphne make such an irrevocable choice? Where does Daphne's reluctance to romantic encounters come from, especially as she's at an age that should be physiologically open to discovering sex? Such a definitive choice closely resembles the functioning of a rigid defence – and we know that rigidity is a characteristic of the aftermath of trauma (van der Kolk, 2014). We cannot establish the causes for such a defence against a sexuality that should be open to desire, but we can make a few hypotheses following some Ovidian suggestions.

The theme of the virginal body as an object of male desire exposed to the constant danger of early violation runs through the entire Ovidian poem. Here, the poet describes scenes of erotic contemplation in which the male imagination is aroused by the innocence and demureness of the maiden (Segal, 2005). Diana herself was a victim of the concupiscent gaze of a mortal, when Actaeon violated her intimacy just by spying on her (Barchiesi, 2005). In this case, Daphne becomes the object of the desire of a god (Apollo), Diana's twin brother, which introduces an incestuous atmosphere, a dimension more explicitly touched upon in other Ovidian episodes (Barchiesi, 2005). Incest is a particularly offensive category of abuse for which Roman law stipulated that expiatory sacrifices had to be offered to Diana, the goddess of fertility for women and for animals, to prevent famine (Frazer, 1925). Within this framework, we can consider the hypothesis that Daphne's intolerant contempt for her suitors may be motivated by some past traumatic experience. Indeed, Ovid describes Daphne's reaction to her father's demands with the words blush and shame ("has her beauteous face covered with the blush of modesty" Latin "pulchra verecundo suffunditur ora rubore") which convey a strong emotional tone. Thus, the poet gives us an insight into the clinical neurophysiology of emotions. In fact, redness (Latin "rubore") reveals the arousal of the autonomic nervous system in the presence of a problematic and distressing trigger. Physiologically, redness is due to the dilation of capillaries that carry blood to the skin, a consequence of the peripheral action of catecholamines that primarily mediate bodily responses to distress and promote defensive or aggressive behaviours (Gilbert, 2017). In the central nervous system, norepinephrine appears to influence the arousal of primary emotions such as fear and anger. In addition, interactions between noradrenergic activity and serotonin are involved in the onset of secondary emotions such as shame and guilt (Terbeck et al., 2016). Shame, which usually accompanies blushing, is a very painful feeling, often activated by the gaze of others, it induces inhibition, a tendency to social withdrawal and intense somatic reactions. It arises in social contexts where relationships are based primarily on dynamics of dominance and interpersonal competition (Gilbert, 2017). The emergence of feelings of shame often occurs in early childhood during problematic relational episodes (Schore, 2003). However, in persistently traumatizing relational contexts, shame evolves into dysfunctional feelings with an inability to act, confusion and feelings of estrangement. In more extreme cases, it can also lead to a desire to permanently disappear. The most severe manifestations can be found in victims of child abuse, usually coupled with feelings of weakness and humiliation (van der Kolk, 2014).

In the case of Daphne, her strong refusal of intimate relationships with men suggests the existence of defences against painful feelings evoked by intimacy. However, at this point in the Ovidian narrative, these claims might seem like a misleading clinical hypothesis. Daphne is an inexperienced adolescent, at the age when human beings' biological potential awakens powerfully. Perhaps Daphne's choice to follow Diana's path could be interpreted as an attempt to achieve psychological maturity. We could argue that her choice of celibacy is a protection which buys her time until she is ready to be intimate with men. Indeed, contradictory feelings of fear and strong sexual urges are typical at this age. Moreover, Diana is the protector of girls' chastity until marriage (Graves, 1955), representing the traditional overcoming of the virginal condition. Typically, adolescence is characterized by changes in cognitive abilities and in social interactions, in order to gain independence and "adult skills". Observation and imitation of familiar and loyal role models is a learning behaviour that humans and other mammals use to survive and to learn how to behave according to social norms from an early age. In an interpersonal relational context, humans acquire social skills using imitation more efficiently than through individual trial and error (Leblanc and Ramirez, 2020). Therefore, imitating Diana could be a way for Daphne to develop skills that could then be applied in the sentimental field. What is more, as a divine model, Diana symbolizes the epitome of that which a young woman can achieve, and so she ends up representing the highest example of individualization, free from any external conditioning. Alternatively, if Daphne had chosen Diana's path because she was driven primarily by the effects of an early violation of her psychic integrity, this would represent a rigid and primitive defence, such as the denial of her own sexuality. Instead, this myth tells us of a tragedy resulting from the sudden intrusion of a real or perceived danger into an immature psyche.

Swifter than the light wind she flies, and she stops not at these words of his, as he calls her back: "O Nymph, daughter of Peneus, stay, I entreat thee! I am not an enemy following thee. In this way the lamb flies from; thus the dove flies from the eagle with trembling wing; in this way each creature flies from its enemy: love is the cause of my following thee. ... run more leisurely, I entreat thee, and restrain thy flight; I myself will follow more leisurely. And yet, inquire whom thou dost please; ... The Delphian

land, Claros and Tenedos, palace pays service to me. Jupiter is my sire; ..."
The daughter of Peneus flies from him, about to say still more, with timid
step, and together with him she leaves his unfinished address.

(Ovid's s, book I, 1893, vv. 502–526)

Keeping in mind current research on the consequences of trauma, the
hypothesis that young Daphne experienced early traumatic event(s) in her
encounter with men is supported by the progression of the Ovidian tale.
Although, as readers, we can't bear witness to any past traumatic event,
Daphne's sudden reaction to Apollo's attentions alerts us to such an eventu-
ality. Indeed, Ovid recounts the events triggered by Daphne's encounter
with Apollo, which is marked, from the outset, by Daphne trying to escape,
even though Apollo approaches her gently and tries not to frighten her.
However, Daphne perceives the god's concupiscent gaze as the unmistaka-
ble sign of sexual desire, which immediately turns into a danger signal and
triggers a series of chain reactions, eventually leading to tragedy. Suddenly,
the narrative takes on a relentless pace from this event to the fatal outcome,
transporting us from the heat of the initial reaction to a threatening place.
As if in a hunting scene, Daphne finds herself becoming the prey pursued
by a predator, arousing in the two protagonists beastly behaviours instead
of divine ones. Poetic insight masterfully penetrates the neurobiology of the
human psyche, which is eternally aspiring for the divine sphere but remains
trapped in its animal nature, bringing to mind Jung's warning: "too much of
the animal distorts civilised men, too much civilisation makes us sick animals" (Jung, 1917, para. 32). From now on, the automatic reactions of this
escape behaviour pattern will override Daphne's desire to achieve freedom
through becoming like a Goddess. In describing the phenomenology of
Daphne's reactions, the poet's attentive gaze powerfully presents us with
what we now understand to be the neurophysiology of survival reactions to
threats, rooted in primitive ways of coping with the world.

The Neuroscientific Scenery

Throughout our evolutionary history, advantageous behaviours have been
gradually selected in the development of our neuronal networks and brain
systems. Phylogenetically more evolved behaviours overlap with older and
less evolved ones. MacLean (1985) recognized three basic systems in the
human brain, corresponding to different evolutionary levels of development of brain structures. The earliest evolutionary level is the *reptilian brain*,
capable of providing a set of behavioural repertoires for reproductive strategies based primarily on individual competition and strongly linked to brain

arousal systems. A second evolutionary level, the *limbic brain* (common to birds and mammals), promotes caring and nurturing behaviours and provides the emotional patterns necessary for prosocial and attachment repertoires. The third evolutionary level is the *neo-mammalian brain*, where our capacities for symbolic representation reside, as well as planning, prediction and linguistic communication. In the course of evolutionary history, archaic mechanisms are progressively enriched and incorporated into later, more sophisticated forms, but they remain most effective under certain conditions and are activated automatically. In these situations, the interconnection between systems, which guarantees harmonious functioning between structures belonging to different evolutionary levels, can be partially or completely deactivated. The presence of real or potential dangers and the perception of the seriousness of a threat are the key variables for the activation of specific, ready-to-use automatic behaviours aimed at satisfying the degree of urgency of the situation.

The functional complexity of our responses reflects the complex anatomical organisation of our brain. Specialised, parallel and segregated network circuits, first evolved from the basic sensory-analytic and motor-executive functions of all living organisms, are integrated into the large cortical (analysis/execution)-thalamic, (sensory)-striatal and (motor)-cortical circuits (Fricchione and Beach, 2019). Other interconnected structures and circuits are dedicated to different functions, such as attribution of value and salience to environmental cues; processing of visceral interoceptive information (relevant to the individual's metabolic state), motivation and learning. At the centre of this organisation is the limbic system. The limbic cortex represents a central node in the regulation of the autonomic responses of the organism, controlling limbic and extra-limbic subcortical structures (such as the amygdala, hypothalamus, ventral tegmental areas, sympathetic and parasympathetic autonomic nervous systems), which are responsible for the central regulation of basic life functions (respiratory, cardiovascular, hormonal, musculoskeletal) through direct and indirect connections with effector organs (Smith, Ahern and Lane, 2019). Together with the hippocampal structures central to learning, this integrative machine can incorporate multiple sources of information to adapt existing behavioural responses or learn new ones (Amiez and Procyk, 2019). The cingulate cortex performs the function of integrating and organising datasets from inside (interoceptive system) and outside (somatosensory system) the body and, equipped with extensive interconnections with the neocortical areas, transmits the preprocessed information to the prefrontal regions. This process allows information to come back enriched by further levels of analysis to determine behavioural policies (Fricchione and Beach, 2019). Thus, the cingulate cortex plays a central role in emotional awareness, making sense of bodily sensations (Smith, Ahern and Lane, 2019), body ownership, agency and discrimination between self and other (Tsakiris, Prabhu and Haggard, 2006). The relationships among structures within the limbic system and with extra limbic areas are complex, sometimes redundant, with multiple simultaneous functions or with the same function but different purposes. With such complexity, top-down and down-top information can circulate in a repeated and spiral fashion accepting enrichments and corrections simultaneously. The final products are adaptive responses finely tuned to the demands of the environment (segregated functioning) and, at the same time, the implementation of necessary behavioural changes based on environmental effects (integrated functioning).

Under normal conditions, the continuous flow of information and integration, from the farthest peripheries of the body, via the cingulate cortex to the prefrontal cortical areas, enables the highest and finest coordination for complex environmental demands. The prefrontal cortex is organised into specialised areas. The ventromedial prefrontal cortex has the function of understanding cognitive states, thoughts and intentions of others, as well as one's own affective states, emotions and feelings. The orbitofrontal cortex, focused instead on the evaluation of stimuli in terms of rewards, contributes to maintaining motivation. Endowed with many recurrent collateral connections underlying auto-associative synaptic plasticity, the orbitofrontal cortex is characterised by a rapid update on changes in the situation. The dorsolateral prefrontal cortex performs executive control for the planning of unconsolidated routines and sequential actions, integrating them into purposeful behaviour and providing logical-rational resources for completing complex and rapidly changing cognitive tasks. Focused attention, attentional shifting, working memory, abstraction, stimulus categorisation, problem solving, inhibition and control of interfering stimuli all depend on these prefrontal areas and allow for the continuous updating of behavioural strategies, particularly important in social interactions and in the modulation and regulation of emotions (Mitchell, 2011). The activity of the prefrontal areas must be continuously supplemented by limbic processing of bodily and external changes in order to allow the best adaptive responses. However, in emergency situations, the undoubted advantage of integrated functioning, which underlies human reflexivity, flexibility and creativity, might become a hindrance to a quick response. In such situations, the limbic system must function rapidly, and limbic structures must be activated independently of each other to promote rapid responses to danger, even to the exclusion of full awareness. Intense emotions such as fear, sadness, and anger significantly reduce prefrontal lobe activities and increase activation of emotion-related brain areas to start schematic behaviours (van der Kolk, 2014). Typically, the activation of alert behavioural modes ends as soon as the danger is over, and at the same time, the integrated functioning resumes. By contrast, when environmental conditions are consistently characterized by danger, as in the case of long-term abusive relationships, behavioural alerting modalities become prevalent and the related neurophysiological aspects, rather than being temporary, become permanent. In traumatized people, this efficient dissociative modality becomes dysfunctional and responsible for a systematic fragmentation of the differentiated behavioural responses.

Exposure to continuous traumatic conditions, such as childhood abuse, results in chronic elevation of hormones and neurotransmitters related to arousal states, which in turn induces functional and structural neuroana-tomical alterations (Xiao et al., 2022). Examples of this are hyper/overacti-vation of the cingulate cortex, insula or amygdala; hypoactivation and/or volumetric reduction of hippocampal structures together with impaired functioning and/or thinning of prefrontal cortical areas. One of the many consequences this produces is alteration of the individual's warning systems in the event of danger. In traumatised individuals, hippocampal deficits dis-turb the formation and reprocessing of autobiographical memories and reduce behavioural flexibility due to the inability to distinguish between past and present (van der Kolk, 2014). They also seem to play a key role in the rapid transition to a state of alertness due to the formation of social engrams consisting of the association between negative emotions and behavioural responses (Leblanc and Ramirez, 2020). In trauma victims, the amygdala (responsible for integrating vegetative and hormonal components of emotional responses) reacts with alarm to trauma-related stimuli even years after the event(s) alongside abnormal activation of the insula (the cen-tre that integrates and interprets input from internal organs) (van der Kolk, 2014). The hyperactivity of alerting systems pushes an individual toward an emergency set-up that results in the constant exclusion of brain areas responsible for enriching awareness of one's emotional experience. This becomes a vicious circle in which limbic structures are constantly separated from the modulatory and regulatory effects of the higher centres.

Phylogenetically, the prefrontal regions are the most recent brain acquisi-tion and the last to complete ontogenetic development. Although steady development of cognitive and executive abilities continues into adulthood, structural and neurophysiological changes in prefrontal areas and related regions appear to reach a plateau during adolescence (Kolk and Rakic, 2022). These brain regions are particularly vulnerable to alterations. Their development can be arrested by prolonged exposure to adverse experiences in childhood and adolescence. In victims of prolonged trauma, the inhibition of the functioning and development of prefrontal areas and related regions results in social relational deficits plus behavioural rigidity. This, in turn, prevents the further development of appropriate skills to establish healthy relationships, exposing them to repetitive trauma and the inability to escape from traumatic environments.

The Metamorphosis

This articulated neuroscientific picture, summarized and simplified above, is effectively condensed in Daphne's sudden flight from Apollo's behavioural disposition. Such a disposition, which we can imagine as characterized by a sense of freedom and agency, is the result of the harmonious integration of efficient hunting strategies, perseverance to achieve rewarding goals and deliberate decision-making based on a critical evaluation of environmental cues. By contrast, Daphne does not reflect, evaluate or have alternatives and demonstrates only her urgent need to escape from the grasp of the hunter. From this point on, the poet forces us to watch a rapid and stark unfolding of various emergency behaviours, each triggered by perceived danger and hope for safety. The detailed description of the hunting scene drags us into the depths of our defence apparatus, rooted in the most archaic animal core, in which only feelings of terror and perception of danger reside. Continuing the narrative, Ovid's words reveal a detailed picture of the behavioural phenomenology and underlying neurophysiological changes resulting from the enactment of well-established mechanisms that protect an organism either from injury, physical and psychological pain or death.

> But the youthful God has not patience any longer to waste his blandishments; and as has seen the are in the open field, and the one by the speed of his legs pursues his prey, the other seeks her safety; … and is now just at her back as she flies, and is breathing upon her hair scattered upon her neck. Her strength being now spent, she grows pale, and being quite faint, with the fatigue of so swift a flight, looking upon the waters of Peneus, she says, 'Give me, my father, thy aid, destroy that form, by which I have pleased too much, ….' Hardly had she ended her prayer, when a heavy torpor seizes her limbs; and her soft breasts are covered with a thin bark. Her hair grows into green leaves, her arms into branches; her feet, the

moment before so swift, adhere by sluggish roots; a leafy canopy over-spreads her features; her elegance alone remains in her. This, too, Phoebus admires, and placing his right hand upon the stock, he perceives that the breast still throbs beneath the new bark; ... he gives kisses to the wood, and yet the wood shrinks from his kisses. To her the God said: 'But since thou canst not be my wife, at least thou shalt be my tree; my hair, my lyre, my quiver shall always have thee, oh laurel!'... the laurel nodded assent with its new-made boughs, and seemed to shake its top just like a head.

(Ovid's Metamorphoses, book I, 1893, vv. 530–567)

Having recognized the danger, the limbic system takes over from the neo-cortical areas and selects the defence behaviours most appropriate to the internal and external circumstances. The effector organs are the ultimate targets of the limbic system: the musculoskeletal system for motor responses and the viscera for adaptations of the metabolic state, the latter implemented through the action of the autonomic nervous system (ANS). The ANS is organized into three subsystems: the myelinated component of the para-sympathetic; the sympathetic portion and the unmyelinated motor compo-nent of the parasympathetic. The first two subsystems are only present in mammals whilst the third one is also found in reptiles. The circuits are dynamically designed to promote adaptive responses to different contexts, schematically summarized into the Safe/Social-Engagement-System and the Defence-System (Porges, 2007; Gilbert, 2017). In a safe environment, vagal myelin system activity uses inhibiting sympathetic responses (involved in attack and escape behaviours), lowering heart rate and blood pressure and establishing optimal homeostatic conditions for tissue oxygenation (the cortex is highly oxygen-dependent). In addition, there is an inhibition of stress and inflammatory responses. The functioning of the ambiguous nucleus of the vagus is integrated with that of the truncus-brain nuclei that innervate the facial musculature to regulate gaze direction, facial expres-sion, willingness to listen and prosody. All these are involved in social rela-tionships activated in safe environments and are linked to body states that favour rest, recovery and growth. In phylogenetically more evolved systems, the visceral myelinated vagal component functions by blocking or unlock-ing phylogenetically older components. In unsafe environments, its activity is reduced to favour the activation of both the sympathetic (related to active defences) and the parasympathetic systems, inducing slower heart and res-piratory rates and hypotension. The result of this latter regulation is fearless immobilization and analgesia, useful for defensive behaviours and, in phylogenetically older species, for reproductive conducts (Porges, 2007).

The different motor and autonomic patterns fostered by the ANS correspond to specific subjective experiences. In the absence of threats and in a reassuring situation, subjects are usually less attentive to potential dangers, less sensitive to alarms, and receptive to positive reinforcing stimuli and bio-social incentives promoting cooperation, sharing and evaluation of self and others' values. The activation of the reward system allows relaxation and restorative sleep, pushes toward active learning, hedonic and affective attachment behaviours. In this context, behavioural flexibility and modulation of activities (such as running, jumping, playing) are encouraged which can then be applied in different areas (from attachment to sexual behaviour). This contrasts with the behavioural rigidity of the blocking and defensive suppression in unsafe conditions (Gilbert, 2017). When the safety-sociality-attachment system is switched off, people are under the control of two different subsystems. The mammalian "fight-or-flight" system is activated first, which allows for a large amount of energy to be mobilized in states of arousal, as well as stimulation to action, anxiety and aggression. When this system is not sufficient to resolve the threatening situation, the very last resort is activated: the reptilian brain that causes temporary paralysis or "freezing". This strategy is a survival reaction used by a trapped animal, where the underlying neurovegetative state remains ready to resume escape if the opportunity arises. The corresponding cognitive state is numbness: if the animal (or man) is killed while frozen to the spot, there won't be any pain or terror during death. Another form of freezing is demobilization, a form of camouflage, which involves weakness, fainting, muscle relaxation and a drop in blood pressure where there is a complete shutdown and the animal (man) appears dead to the world. Both freezing and fainting routines are short-term reactions and (as in a predatory context) can be quickly interrupted by a successful defence. When conditions of safety are restored, the social system is quickly re-established. However, in persistently unsafe social contexts, chronic exposure to aggressive individuals may temporarily or indefinitely impair the subject's physical-biological and cognitive well-being. When there is neglect or abusive relationships, attitudes are shaped by the perception of danger and self-blame. Under these conditions, the ability for self-care does not develop and instead behaviours such as subterfuge, contempt, rejection and shame appear along with involuntary subordination and marginalization. Sexual behaviour also becomes constrained in a rigid rejection mode, different from safe conduct centred on modes of attraction and desirability (Gilbert, 2017).

Daphne's behaviour can be read as a description of what happens when we suddenly find ourselves in a situation evoking a familiar danger. In the sudden presence of a young man full of desire, the exploratory attitude of the girl is not applied in the field of romantic relationship with curiosity and a search for closeness, instead he is perceived as a significant danger, triggering the defence system and the prompt activation of the fight-flight system. When these systems are forcefully activated, they trigger feelings of terror and panic (van der Kolk, 2014). However, active defences (fight and flight) do not help Daphne to become safe. Pale and exhausted, she became lost, and this activated the defence system towards immobilization. The neurophysiology of freezing is effectively depicted by the progressive stiffening into a life form devoid of mobility but still seeking salvation. We can see this in the myth when Daphne transforms herself into a tree – under the cold and rigid bark Apollo could feel the accelerated beating of Daphne's terrified heart and the wood repelling his kisses. In this way, Daphne managed to successfully avoid being raped; her signs of surrender calmed Apollo, who did not rage at the tree. Sadly, this solution also didn't help Daphne to permanently become safe. In fact, Apollo takes possession of her by becoming the owner of the tree (which he named Laurel) into which she was transformed and forcing her to live with him forever. Henceforth, Daphne is rooted in the soil of chronic relational trauma and its severe consequences. In this soil, the ancient reptilian brain appears as the main source of basic life behaviours, meaning that the young girl abdicates all active defence and survives in a death-like state in the hands of her predator.

Immobilization has been observed in chronic trauma cases, as opposed to panic and rage in survivors of more recent trauma, and is more likely to occur when escape is unthinkable, as in the case of children abused by aggressive and violent parents (van der Kolk, 2014). Daphne's tragic mutation seems to reflect the radical changes in the cognitive-behavioural and neurovegetative patterns responsible for apathetic and deep depressive states, characterized by feelings of helplessness and failure in the face of adversity. These patterns are designed to inhibit perception of environmental input and therefore suppress reactions to an aggressive, dominant conspecific. Psychomotor retardation, attention deficit, learning, memory, appetite and sleep disorders are part of the cognitive-neurovegetative corollary to apathic-depressive states. At the same time, feelings of depersonalization, psychic death, loneliness and incommunicability dominate the subjective experience. The most devastating effect of this condition is the inability to feel oneself real and to experience curiosity about others. Furthermore, emotional, affective or sexual intimacy is avoided and a semblance of it is obtained through immobilization, chronic sensory deafferentation to the point of loss of pain perception. In these cases, only an internal sense of emptiness and death remains (van der Kolk, 2014). Daphne's transformation into plant life can be seen as the perfect metaphorical representation of victims' experiences of severe and prolonged relational trauma. Furthermore, metamorphosis can be re-interpreted using current neuroimaging data which document how dramatic adaptations are caused and maintained by real functional and structural changes in the brain. Brain areas which receive signals from the viscera, crucial for the regulation of basic bodily functions and sense of self, are chronically silenced whilst language areas are disconnected and deactivated whenever victims encounter situations similar to their traumatic experiences.

The Metamorphosis in the Service of Hope

The connections between the narrated facts and clinical neuroscientific data give us a picture not much different from what we, as analysts, can observe in our work with relational trauma victims. If Daphne were our patient, at the emergence of feelings of shame, fear and panic we would hypothesise a trauma in her history. The activation of automatic avoidance in sentimental relationships would indicate to us the traumatic relational area, while the isolation of the girl who closes herself in her defences, with a lack of reactivity and apathy, would be indicators of the trauma severity. The metamorphosis into a plant perfectly symbolizes the difficulty of approaching such a patient, who remains locked in the unthinkability of her traumatic experiences. So far Ovid, using the mythic canvas, has been very precise in describing the anatomy of relational violence. Therefore, we should be cautious about considering this image a literary *topos* suitable for effective poetic solution. Ovid himself recounts various metamorphoses as the result of unbearable trauma such as the transformation of the human form into stone (Niobe) or water (Arethusa) or an animal (Arachne, Io). It seems as if the type or the form of metamorphosis has a specific meaning, symbolically alluding to different traumatic outcomes. For Daphne, we can ask ourselves why was she transformed into a plant and not a stone? In both cases, humanity is lost. Yet completely different semantic areas are evoked: the stone alludes to something immutable and final; a stone can only break down in geological time, which is not compatible with human time. The plant, on the other hand, refers to the cyclical transformations of the plant world, maintaining a link to the hope of rebirth. Eliade (1948) noted that many tales and fables revolve around the mythical motifs of the transformation of a human being into a plant. Here, usually a maiden emerges from a miraculous fruit or she is killed and transformed into a flower or a tree, from the fruits of which, the maiden can be reborn. In all cases, the transformation of the maiden into a plant is the consequence of dramatic events. Yet the maiden's life continues in its new form.

The meaning of these transformations could thus indicate a protective strategy in which the vital core of living beings waits for the right conditions to be reborn. Indeed, plant life represents the symbolic framework, par excellence, of the mythical ideas of death and resurrection and of the regenerative renewing capacities of life (Eliade, 1948). Thus, Daphne now finds herself in a place related to the idea of waiting for new possibilities for rebirth. For Daphne, this place is the laurel, a sacred plant in Greco-Roman mythology symbolizing wisdom and glory. Laurel wreaths encircled winners' foreheads in Delphic games, and it was also the highest honour for a poet to become a poet laureate (*laurus nobilis*), a morally noble person, fine of mind and intellect. The connection between laurel and poetry conveys the insight that rebirth (and a new life) can take place through the flourishing of words. Poetry brings man closer to the heights of human expression, that is, to the divine sphere.

The impossibility to tell relational trauma, especially childhood trauma, is related to both the overwhelming effect of the traumatic experience on the psyche and the lack of mirroring in the traumatizing environment. Abusive parents are, at best, blind to their destructive power and, at worst, consciously denying the crime perpetrated. The victims are thus condemned to live in lonely silence and their symptoms remain the only clues to what has happened in their life. In these conditions, giving meaning to victims' feelings is impossible and dangerous as the truth remains under the surveillance of protective functions that limit and kill the possibility to think (Ogden, 2016). However, in the depths of the psyche, the incessant search for truth survives and, like a plant that during winter waits for the warmth and sunshine of spring to be reborn, victims wait for words that can restore meaning to their lives (Ogden, 2016). Strumia (2014) helps us to recognize the healing power of poetic words by suggesting that poetry seizes, with a sudden insight, the mental image as it emerges from the psychic depths and offers it to the mind as material for further conscious use. Indeed, the prophetesses of Apollo, in search of momentary inspiration, ate and sprinkled themselves with laurel before prophesying (Frazer, 1925). We can thus imagine that Ovid left us waiting for the first bud, the instant in which a word of truth re-emerges from the psyche's depths. By outlining the transition from a plant's vegetative state to the emergence of the hidden truth with the use of poetic words, the myth seems to emphasize a possible natural law regulating both the workings of human psychic reality and the springtime rebirth of vegetation.

The Ways of Truth

> I am on the patio of a house. I am serene, but I see a distant wolf. I approach the house slowly, without any sudden movements, but there is another wolf near the door. I know that the only way to save myself is to touch this door, I run, but the wolf blocks me, I manage to reach the door and he whispers: 'You are safe for now, but sooner or later you will get distracted, and I will be here waiting for you'.

Julie, a severely depressed 32-year-old woman, brought this dream to me after about a year of therapy. Since childhood, she suffered from insomnia, anger outbursts and oppositional behaviour, which were never understood by her family and for which she was often blamed. Julie clearly remembered when, at the age of 11, she started to be abused by her grandfather. She recounted this dream with the feeling that it was a premonitory dream. In the course of the session, the memory emerged of when, at the age of 4 or 5, Julie witnessed her grandfather molesting her older sister while she continued to play without apparently noticing anything. Julie realized that through this dream the truth behind her symptoms could finally emerge. Together, Julie and I interpreted the distant wolf as her grandfather molesting her sister while she had to remain cautious with her movements in order not to be seen by him, to stay safe. The wolf in front of the door was understood as her grandfather who would later molest her too. The feeling of premonition conveyed by the dream was understood as the unconscious understanding for the young Julie – witnessing her sister being abused – that sooner or later she will be another victim of the grandfather/wolf.

In Julie's case, the images of the dream bore witness to her experience as a child, when confronted with the unspeakable.

There are many ways in which "the unthought known" (Bollas, 2017) can find words over the course of life or therapy. Ovid seems to point us to another universal law of the human psyche which Hillman (1975) calls the "poetic function of the mind" similar to Jung's transcendent function (1958). Poetry allows the mind to grasp inconceivable aspects of individual or collective human experience when they first emerge in the form of fleeting insights (Strumia, 2014). Then, through poetry, the mind can imagine and process these images further. Usually, victims of trauma encounter enormous difficulties in finding comfort in others; their defences against memory triggers and undermines their ability to communicate about traumatic experiences and hinders the possibility of finding solace in support. However, when the victim finds a person able to welcome the signs of his trauma, they can initiate a rebirth process. In this framework, the link between Daphne-laurel and the poet could represent the need for the presence of a sensitive human being, to whom we can entrust the re-emergence of painful experiences from the unconscious. The poet/analyst/sensitive-other is able to capture such fragments and return them to the victim after carefully stripping them of their (re)traumatizing power, making them finally thinkable, and thus laying the foundation for the healing process. Paraphrasing Winnicott (1974), poets can grasp new truths with their intuitive sensations, and they can offer them to consciousness to initiate the strenuous psychological work of (re)appropriating unconsciously lived facts into transformative experiences.

One final aspect of the Ovidian narrative deserves our attention. Daphne begs her father to let her be transformed into a plant, thus facing the metamorphosis consciously. We have noted that under the effect of trauma, dissociative mental mechanisms prevail and automatisms guide action more than intentional choices. However, it seems that the integrated mental activity in Daphne's functioning is still working and intentionality is also put at the service of the best survival strategy. At the poet's suggestion, we may ask whether this conscious choice, though dictated by the extreme severity of the danger, allowed for her own safeguarding of a possible future recovery. We might infer that a conscious acceptance of the inevitability of the situation allowed Daphne to rely on an automatic strategy to shut down thought functions and, thus, protect herself from destructive pain. This represents an extreme attempt at resistance where Daphne effectively protected herself and avoided Apollo's violence. In fact, in response to Daphne's metamorphosis, Apollo lost both his fury and his own violence. Such fury was the result of the frustration of his automatic predatory behaviour, which had not necessarily been triggered by Cupid's spell, but might have been the response behaviour to the blind flight of the nymph. Finally, Apollo, by electing Daphne-laurel as the plant symbol of the god, abandons unreflective fury and effectively lays the foundations for the symbolisation process necessary for rebirth.

Final Considerations

At the end of this proposed reading of myth through the lens of (neuro) science, one might ask whether the overlaps between mythic intuition, the poet's ability to observe and the modern clinical vision stem exclusively from a *post-hoc* "neuroscientification". However, we should keep in mind the Jungian idea that mythic fantasies, images and narratives represent nothing more than a mental expression of psychological processes in perfect continuity between somatic and mental processes from which representations and thoughts emerge (Jung, 1946). Indeed, in Jung's view, all human cultural products come from the same unconscious psychological functioning in order to perform symbolic functions. This process is necessary for the evolution of both the individual and the collective psyche. Thus, this suggested continuity between myth and science is possible because of the creative processes that characterize the development of the human psyche. In this framework, myths could represent the first emergence of the intuition of human functioning and science could represent the subsequent conscious reworking of it. It has been suggested that creative experience itself, rooted in biology, enables innovative experiences capable of penetrating to a very deep biological level in such a way that the very expression of matter is altered (Changeux, 2008). Within this framework, the growth in consciousness which we witness in the transition from myth to science, fits fully into the grand fresco of natural evolution.

References

Amiez, C. and Procyk, E. (2019) "Midcingulate somatomotor and autonomic functions", *Handbook of Clinical Neurology*, 166: 53–71.

Barchiesi, A. (2005) *Ovidio – Metamorfosi. Vol I*. Milano: Mondadori.

Bollas, C. (2017) *The Shadow of the Object. Psychoanalysis of the Unthought Known*. London: Routledge.

Changeux, J.P. (2008) *Du Vrai, Du Beau, Du Bien. Une Nouvelle Approche Neuronale*. Paris: Odile Jacob Publishing.

Eliade, M. (1948) *Traité d'Histoire des Religions*. Paris: Payot.

Frazer, J. (1925) *The Golden Bough*. New York: Macmillan Company.

Fricchione, G. and Beach, S. (2019) "Cingulate-basal ganglia-thalamo-cortical aspects of catatonia and implications for treatment", *Handbook of Clinical Neurology*, 166: 223–252.

Gilbert, P. (2017) *Human Nature and Suffering*. London: Routledge.

Graves, R. (1955) *The Greek Myths*. London: Penguin Books.

Hillman, J. (1975) *Re-Visioning Psychology*. New York: Harper & Row.

Jung, C.G. (1917) *Two Essays in Analytical Psychology*. CW7. Princeton, NJ: Princeton University Press.

Jung, C.G. (1946) *The Psychology of the Transference*. CW16. Princeton, NJ: Princeton University Press.

Jung, C.G. (1958) *The Transcendent Function*. CW8. Princeton, NJ: Princeton University.

Kolk, S.M. and Rakic, P. (2022) "Development of prefrontal cortex", *Neuropsychopharmacology*, 47(1): 41–57.

Leblanc, H. and Ramirez, S. (2020) "Linking social cognition to learning and memory", *Journal of Neurosciences*, 40(46): 8782–8798.

Lévy-Bruhl, L. (1926 [1966]) *How Natives Think*. New York: Washington Square Press.

MacLean, P.D. (1985) "Brain evolution relating to family, play and the separation call", *Archives of General Psychiatry*, 42(4): 405–417.

Mitchell, D.G.V. (2011) "The nexus between decision making and emotion regulation: a review of convergent neurocognitive substrates", *Behavioural Brain Research*, 217(1): 215–231.

Ovid (1893 [2007]) *Metamorphoses* (trans. H.T. Riley). Urbana, IL: Project Gutenberg.

Ogden, T.H. (2016) *Reclaiming Unlived Life. Experiences in Psychoanalysis*. London: Routledge.

Porges, S.W. (2007) "The polyvagal perspective", *Biological Psychology*, 74(2): 116–143.

Segal, C. (2005) "Il corpo e l'io nelle metamorfosi di Ovidio", in A. Barchiesi (ed.) *Ovidio – Metamorfosi. Vol I*. Milano: Mondadori.

Segal, R.A. (2009) "Myth and science: Their varying relationships", *Religion Compass*, 3(2): 337–358.

Schore, A.N. (2003) *Affect Regulation and the Repair of the Self*. New York: W.W. Norton.

Silvestri, D. (2015) "Di padri e madri, di figli e figlie e di altro ancora nell'opera di Ovidio", in S. Cardone, G. Carugno and A. Colangelo (eds.) *Generazioni a Confronto nell'Opera di Ovidio*. Sulmona: Rotary Club, pp. 25–43.

Smith, R., Ahern, G.L. and Lane, R.D. (2019) "The role of anterior and midcingulate cortex in emotional awareness: a domain-general processing perspective", *Handbook of Clinical Neurology*, 166: 89–101.

Strumia, F. (2014) "L'emergenza del verso. Note di analisi della poesia", *Rivista di Psicologia Analitica. Nuova serie*, 89(37): 111–128.

Terbeck, S., Savulescu, J., Chesterman, L.P. and Cowen, P.J. (2016) "Noradrenaline effects on social behaviour, intergroup relations, and moral decisions", *Neuroscience & Biobehavioral Reviews*, 66: 54–60.

Tsakiris, M., Prabhu, G. and Haggard, P. (2006) "Having a body versus moving your body: How agency structures body ownership", *Consciousness and Cognition*, 15(2): 423–432.

van der Kolk, B. (2014) *The Body Keeps the Score: Brain, Mind and Body in the Healing of Trauma*. London: Penguin Books.

Winnicott, D.W. (1974) "Fear of breakdown", in C. Winnicott, R. Shepherd and M. Davis (eds) *Psychoanalytic Explorations*. Cambridge, MA: Harvard University Press, pp. 87–95.

Xiao, S., Yang, Z., Su, T., Gong, J., Huang, L. and Wang, Y. (2022) 'Functional and structural brain abnormalities in posttraumatic stress disorder: A Multimodal Meta-Analysis of Neuroimaging Studies', *Journal of Psychiatric Research*, 155: 153–162.

Chapter 15

The Role of Memory and Creativity in the Healing Process of Trauma

Eduardo Carvallo

Introduction

Traditionally, the development of the psyche has been seen as a linear and evolutionary process in which, step by step, the internal resources that guarantee self-regulation are activated, reinforced, and enriched. James M. Baldwin (1924–1987), Jean Piaget (1896–1980), Sigmund Freud (1856–1939) and Carl G. Jung (1875–1961) were pioneers in the study of the developmental processes of the psyche. Following their ideas, we have discovered the importance of the conditions that frame the interactions between our natural psychological predisposition and our environment. But, and this is a huge "but", this situation is not the same for everyone.

Day after day, we witness, or are informed of, terrible experiences that many people have to suffer: forced displacement, kidnappings, slavery, sexual abuse, natural disasters, accidents, loss of family members due to unnatural causes and other violent scenarios. Many of these situations represent a clash between the resources we have to deal with the event and the impact of the violence of being in contact with something we are unprepared for, which may be experienced as diabolical, destructive and overwhelming. These events, which our psyche is unprepared to assimilate, become trauma.

In trauma, there is a rupture in the natural development of the human psyche, giving rise to adaptive responses that often affect its self-regulating capacity. Pierre Janet defined psychological trauma as

> the result of exposure to an unavoidable stressful event that overwhelms the person's coping mechanisms. When people are too overwhelmed by their emotions, memories cannot be transformed into neutral narrative experiences. Terror becomes a memory phobia that prevents integration (synthesis) of the traumatic event and fragments traumatic memories away from ordinary consciousness, leaving them organized into visual perceptions, somatic preoccupations, and behavioural reactions.
>
> (Janet, 1919/25: 251)

DOI: 10.4324/9781003298076-20

This definition contains the essential elements of the concept of psychological trauma. One is faced with a situation of psychological threat from which one cannot escape and for which one's normal resources are not effective; that is, one cannot cope with it in a way that can make it disappear, nor can one flee. In many ways, the psyche activates defensive mechanisms in order to control the pain associated with trauma, such as dissociation and inhibition of the regular mechanisms of memory.

Joseph LeDoux has investigated the effects on the brain of experiences in which intense fear is present and his conclusions shed light on the behavioural expressions that we find in people who have endured traumatic events:

> The brain has a very effective system for learning in dangerous situations, this implies that sometimes we learn things that we do not want to remember implicitly, as in the case of certain traumas. In traumatic situations the amygdala registers the situation, but the hippocampus does not. The hippocampus is very sensitive to hormonal changes resulting from stress. These hormones reach the hippocampus and prevent it from memorizing properly. Thus, we have very little memory of what happened. These same hormones reach the amygdala and allow it to memorize everything in detail. Faced with the same situation, a strong unconscious memory and a weak conscious memory come into play.
>
> (LeDoux, 1996: 48)

The lack of memory about the traumatic event is related to the intense emotional experience that accompanies it. Some of the consequences of this interference with the memory of the traumatic event are distorted versions or inadequate evaluations of oneself, the environment and life itself. The biggest impact is not the traumatic event itself, but the fact that you create a worldview about yourself and what you expect people to do to you, around that traumatic event.

At the same time,

> Children are particularly prone to dissociate in traumatic experiences, and consequently people with a history of past trauma, especially sexual abuse, are more susceptible to elevated arousal, paralysis, and retraumatization after exposure to even a nonspecifically traumatic stimulus … Individuals who actively dissociate at the time the trauma occurs are more likely to develop subsequent PTSD symptoms than those who do not dissociate … Persistent and chronic dissociation makes humans prone to become paralyzed, or dissociate, to a wide range of stimuli that may be associated with the threatening situation.
>
> (van der Kolk et al., 1985: 321)

This is why responses to trauma are often accompanied by chronic suffering and the sensation of living trapped in an exhausting whirlpool which swallows up the hope of building a meaningful life and deeply effects the image that we have built about ourselves. It can generate a sense of strangeness towards ourselves.

Often, we can identify the wound that the trauma has left in a person without any prior clinical experience. In children, we can find combinations of an evasive attitude, deep sadness, aggressive and oppositionist behaviour or, on the contrary, extreme compliance and shyness. In adults, this spectrum ranges from the timid and fearful person, who believes that he will never achieve his goals (or that he is not worthy enough to reach them), to one with psychopathic traits who believes that he has paid more than enough for all the suffering he has experienced during his life and that the world owes him.

The traumatic event has a profound impact on the developmental processes of our psyche, including our emotional dynamics and instinctive world: sleep, hunger-satiety, aggressiveness, sexuality, creativity and the capacity to reflect. We cannot change the traumatic event and its consequences, but we can reframe it and see it from another perspective which allows us to "understand" the event in a way that allows us to assimilate it.

Approaching the Experience of Trauma

It is not easy to approach the experience of trauma. The psyche of traumatized people develops defensive mechanisms which attempt to avoid the pain associated with the traumatic situation (the experience itself or any associations that trigger memories about it). It is not easy for anyone – including psychotherapists – to hold the emotions that arise when we are exposed to stories in which we dive into images related with "strong experiences". This is why it is not easy to accompany people who carry painful traumatic situations. We really do not know in which instant the reactivation of the pain can sting us.

Two of the psyche's main defensive mechanisms involved in trauma are *repression* and *dissociation*. The reconstruction of biographical memory (in individual cases) or historical memory (in collective cases), and the incorporation of aspects of the experience that had to be denied or repressed, makes it possible to rethink the experience in a new way in which the natural mechanisms of assimilation and elaboration of the event can be activated.

Jung included creativity in his catalogue of fundamental instincts (Jung, 1936). From his perspective, creativity is rooted in the Self and is nourished by its regulatory, constructive and healing dynamics which allow and promote the structuring and evolution of the psyche.

Creativity has a special place within Jungian thinking with regard to mobilizing the psyche. Painting, carving and writing were Jung's natural ways for balancing and dancing with his psyche. He incorporated Lowenfeld's use of Sand-play as a clinical tool in his work (1954). It was in this natural world that techniques such as active imagination arose. This is our clinical playground – enriched by later post-Jungian contributions on work with the body – in which we find the instruments for analytic work as Jungian analysts.

Research by neuroscientists – amongst whom we can mention Nobel prize winner Roger Sperry – has demonstrated that the process of creativity bridges our two brain hemispheres and promotes movement in paralysed psyches. During the creative process, diverse functions and cerebral structures can be aligned in an integrative way through complex dynamics (Sperry, 1980: 201). Rafael Lopez-Pedraza, the Jungian analyst who was a cofounder (together with Hillman, Berry, Guggenbühl-Craig and Heron) of Archetypal Psychology, emphasized that we have to look for a psychopathological story wherever we find any sign of the psyche's paralysis or lack of "plasticity and gracefulness".[1]

I would now like to share two clinical vignettes in which we can notice phenomena associated with trauma, such as dissociation and paralysis, their manifestations and possible ways of making clinical interventions.

Unlocking the Psyche: A Close Look at Expressive Sandwork

Before sharing the first vignette, I would like to say a few words about the Expressive Sandwork technique (ES). ES was developed as a response to work with vulnerable groups. Its founder, Eva Pattis Zoja, a Jungian analyst, was challenged with the call to attend to victims of an earthquake that occurred in China in 2008. At that time, she was training a group of trainee Jungian analysts in Sand-play technique. She decided to help the group form a team which could help the child victims of the natural disaster.

The clinical setting proposed consisted of a circle of sand trays, each one of which was allotted to a child who would be supported by a facilitator. The figures and other elements, used to represent the symbolic situation that each child wanted in his sand tray, were located in the centre of the circle. The entire process was conducted in silence. After eight sessions, the facilitators started to recognize objective changes from the initial behaviour and symptoms that the group of children presented. The experience seemed to restore the self-regulatory function of the psyche through the process of playing and representing the traumatic situation they had endured. The containing function of the facilitator (and the group itself) helped to build a safe and protected space in which the children felt confident to open themselves to the experience and allow the intrapsychic dynamics to do their restorative job. I myself learned the technique in 2012, and each time I have used it with a traumatized group of children, I have been surprised by the results achieved during the process.

First Clinical Vignette

J.G. is a 6-year-old boy who was part of a group of children from a foster home in Colombia who participated in a process of Expressive Sandwork (ES). He was separated from his parents when he was three-and-a-half years old due to domestic violence and child negligence. Since his admission to the foster home, he has presented intermittently with symptoms such as: difficulty with sleeping and frequent nightmares, aggressiveness towards caregivers and other children, difficulty with respecting boundaries, unexpected mood swings and onychophagia. He had visible scars from a hot water burn on his back and his left arm.

About seven months before starting the therapeutic process, J.G.'s custodial team requested an evaluation due to an exacerbation of symptoms when the potential parents interested in adopting him suspended the process. One month later, J.G. entered an ES group, in which he shared his experience along with other children who also had difficulty containing anxiety (expressed in different ways) and/or respecting boundaries.

At the beginning of the therapeutic process, J.G. was very disorganized. In many sessions, he filled the sandbox with lots of items that he placed in a compulsive and chaotic manner. Frequently, he interfered with the work of other children who were doing their sandwork near him. Repeatedly, he had to be reprimanded for not having a respectful attitude towards the work of others and this generated angry reactions in him.

After three months of sessions twice a week, he began to be more discriminating in his choice of sandbox figures and concentrated more on the activity he was carrying out in his assigned box. He began to establish eye contact with his accompanying-facilitator, to whom he began to describe what the characters he had chosen represented and what was going on between them. Initially, the dynamics between the figures (human figures and wild animals or human figures of different gender) regularly ended in conflicts that he represented with violent clashes between the figures accompanied by the spilling of large amounts of sand outside the box. Gradually, he stopped incorporating the animal figures and the interaction between the human figures became "cordial".

Then J.G. began to show more enthusiasm when he had a session, he became more respectful of the other children's space and was able to focus on his assigned space. The interaction between the figures he chose for his sandbox began to be mutually supportive in the execution of daily activities such as cooking or cleaning the designated spaces of houses or rooms. He began to incorporate figures of babies and children who were cared for by figures representing adults.

For J.G., the changes observed in the box were also visible in his daily life. He began to show himself as a gentler child and was now more able to tolerate boundaries and frustration. He slept peacefully and his mood swings practically disappeared.

During the last three months of the process, which lasted six months in total, with sessions twice a week, J.G. used figures representing nature (trees and other types of vegetation, rocks, rivers) with which he composed harmonious and balanced landscapes in a mandalic structure. The interaction with his caregivers changed significantly with frequent expressions of affection towards them. Moreover, he began to show protective attitudes towards the younger children in the institution.

What we know about J.G.'s personal history could be described as cumulative trauma (Khan, 1963: 301). Trauma of this kind occurs over an extended period of time in which the child lives in an environment consisting of features such as a lack of affection, physical abuse, aggressiveness and emotional neglect. In such situations of chronic or extreme threat, the usual active defense mechanisms (fight-flight) are often ineffective. The reason this instinctual response fails to appear is connected to the lack of autonomy and resources that most of the children have. The child cannot rely on interactions with significant adults that allow him to consolidate an image of a worthy self. What is more, the psyche's development is interfered with by high levels of anxiety which the child has no resources to contain.

Through the work with ES, the child starts to experience the possibility of playing and expressing himself in a space which is both protected and protective. The figure of the facilitator carries with it the projection of a respectful and protective adult, that can teach the child with gentle manners the importance of boundaries which, simultaneously, allows natural and fluid self-expression. The facilitator acts as an auxiliary ego to the child. Using a metaphor from neuroscience, we can see the facilitator as an external auxiliary cortex that helps, through the process of inquiry, to direct and bring into the child's consciousness aspects of his experience (just as mother does with her small child). In the traumatized child, such experiences had to be denied, set aside or repressed in order for him to be accepted in meaningful relationships with others. The therapeutic relationship that we are considering here, facilitates the integration of an experience that has been dissociated from consciousness and so allows for the establishment of new, more adaptive neural connections.

In our experience as Jungian analysts, we meet many processes that start – as they did for J.G. – with chaotic manifestations of the inner dynamics of the child. We may associate these manifestations with the alchemical symbol of the *massa confusa*, which often reveals expressions of aggressiveness and destructive scenes, but with elements and figures that can become more clearly identified. This can be seen as a movement from chaos to polarization, the first step toward differentiation and the building of our internal world.

We can become aware of the importance of recognizing the shifts in the nature of the figures and interactions that the child demonstrates through the therapeutic process. This allows us to follow the changes in the emotional experience of the child during the process. The swings between aggressive and gentle interactions reveal internal mechanisms that help to contain anxiety and aggressiveness. Furthermore, it is important to observe the choice of human figures instead of wild animals which bear witness to this internal movement. Kalsched points out that initial sandtray and art therapy imagery of traumatized patients is often archetypal in nature, indicating the difficulty to process, at a personal level, the dynamics and memories related with the traumatic situation (Kalsched, 2013).

Often, it was possible to see reflected in the sandbox that which was happening in J.G.'s developmental process: the mirroring of what was going on in the sandbox in his daily interactions, as well as the emergence of a caring attitude towards others. This can be associated with the self-caring function of the Self that we can observe even in very young children when they are exposed to situations in which they notice individuals who are in worse situations than themselves.

In many of his writings, Jung wrote about the significance of the symbol of the mandala (Jung, 1963). He considered that this symbol has the power of an integrative and organizational image. For Jung, this understanding of the mandala came from his own experience with this symbol during his military service during WWI. He repeatedly drew mandalas in his Black Books (Jung, 2020), which are described in his Red Book (Jung, 2009). Quite often, we can see that psychic processes end with the building of mandalic structures in the sandbox. Again and again, we experience this fact with fascination and the deep emotions that arise when we are witness to the presence of the Self.

Images and Art Therapy in the Treatment of Trauma

Second Clinical Vignette

L.C. is a young 23-year-old woman who began her therapeutic process six years ago after being kidnapped and raped. She was brought by her parents to my office only a few days after her release, having been in captivity for two days.

She arrived in a self-absorbed state. She had a lost, faraway look and difficulties in sustaining eye contact. Her voice was very faint – almost a whisper. She tried to mutter something and started crying intensely, hugging her mother very tightly, hiding her face, looking like a little girl searching for protection. This image of a little broken girl, in the body of a young and healthy women, touched me deeply. I tried to imagine what she must have gone through, the feelings of terror and vulnerability that she had recently endured. On meeting her parents, I also wondered how I would respond in the same situation. As on other occasions when I received victims of the degradation of Society in the country in which I live, I felt the rage and sense of injustice for the vulnerable generated by the inefficiency of governmental authorities.

Her parents commented that, since returning home, she had not wanted to get out of their bed, that she had slept in an agitated state for very short periods of time and had asked to be accompanied at all times. She was silent nearly all the time, answering questions with monosyllables and could barely eat even small portions of food. She cried frequently in an explosive, desperate and disconsolate manner. I was told that she was abducted after a tennis lesson at a court near her house. The same day she was kidnapped, the criminals contacted her father demanding a ransom for her release, which was delivered two days later. She was abandoned on the outskirts of the city. The kidnappers called the family to pinpoint her location.

Her parents found her wandering along a road, looking dazed, wearing the same tennis clothes she had on the day of the kidnapping, but which were now dirty. As soon as she recognized their car, she threw herself on it, crying frantically. From that moment on, she has maintained the same "closed" attitude, not wanting to talk about what happened. The terrible sense of her suffering, the injustice and the mindless violence made me think about the quality of evil in human beings. I perceived her as being dissociated and regressed. She was in a state of shock. She was extremely fragile, and at that initial moment of her assessment, as a psychiatrist, I considered the option of hospitalization to avoid the possibility of a psychotic crisis, or worse, suicide.

After talking with her parents, we agreed that the best option was to give L.C. the opportunity to stay home and start a psychotherapeutic process. Owing to her high level of anxiety and insomnia that can affect the self-regulatory function of the psyche, I decided to prescribe anxiolytics and sleeping pills during this initial phase of her process, which needed to be administered under supervision.

The first stage of this process lasted approximately two weeks, during which we met on a daily basis. During the first week, the parents participated in the sessions and the conversation revolved around how everyone's life had changed. They were all in a constant state of vigilance with a profound sense of vulnerability. The father looked anxious with much pent-up anger. The mother was sad, but very attentive and wanting to stay close to L.C., whom she hugged for long periods of time. L.C. remained silent.

As in other cases of rape, my thoughts flew from the analytical consideration of the psychic dynamics present in both L.C. and her parents, to my own images and emotions related to how unfair it is to be abducted by criminals who act heartlessly, and often are not punished for their terrible actions. I think these situations represent huge challenges to us as psychotherapists. We need to be able to process our conflicting feelings in order to be emotionally present for our clients who are having to deal with their traumatic experience alone.

During the second week, her mother accompanied her during the sessions. L.C. remained isolated and silent. The conversation was limited to the mother informing me about her sleep, feeding and behaviour patterns at home. She answered my questions in monosyllables and without making eye contact. During the sessions, the mother and I would talk, in front of her, about how terrible it is to feel one's own vulnerability and to lose confidence in feeling protected. Initially she refused any connection with anyone other than her parents but, on my recommendation, her best friend visited her. When she saw her, she threw herself on top of her crying, saying: "It was horrible, it was horrible".

From the third week onwards, L.C. began to enter the sessions alone, while her mother waited for her outside. Owing to her difficulty in finding a way to express herself, I handed her some sheets of white paper and coloured pens and invited her to use them in any way she liked. Gradually, she began to draw. Initially her strokes were short and slow. Lacking energy, she could draw for only very shorts periods of time.

I would ask her very superficial questions about different topics, looking for small talk. Her mother informed me that she still asked to sleep with them in their bed and spent the night restless, waking up several times, startled. I asked her about going back to school. She answered by shaking her head without saying a word. At the time the rape occurred, L.C. studied in a Catholic school, run by nuns, which was only for female students. She had always stood out as a very good student, attentive to her academic obligations and loved by her classmates. The director and school psychologist were aware of the situation and had agreed to support the process as much as necessary.

At the end of the third week, she came to the session accompanied by her best friend and at the end of the session she commented that she wanted to try to return to classes. Closing the session, she commented to me: "I don't remember anything". I knew she was talking about the abduction and that she was making great efforts to move away from the paralysis that she had been consumed by since the trauma. She began to attend classes and we started to see each other every other day. I always handed her the sheets of paper and coloured pens. She would automatically draw lines while answering me with monosyllables or short sentences to the questions I asked about her daily life.

I was in regular contact with the school psychologist who reported that she was withdrawn and taciturn. The change she had undergone was evident. However, she maintained contact with those who had always been her closest friends. Little by little, she joined the school sports activities (she was a member of the swimming team), and maintained her academic performance, although she was distracted and not very interested in the classes.

During this period, I sensed the enormous suffering that L.C. was going through. I understood that her psyche was making desperate efforts to put things back in order, while she remained in a maelstrom of thoughts and images. I wondered what could have happened during those two days she was held captive, the horror of being trapped in a strange place in the hands of criminals. I felt a deep compassion for her pain and a deep rage towards the rapists and the political system in which we were living, where we have lost the fundamental securities for day-to-day living. I reflected on the unexpected turn our lives can take from one moment to the next and felt powerless. One moment she was a joyful, self-assured, confident young woman with plans for the future, then the next she had become a container of suffering, confined in a continuous present full of questions and uncertainty. I knew we were both committed to a long, slow process.

Little by little, she agreed to invite her closest friends to her house, although she refused any invitation to leave home. As she was not ready to go to her high school graduation celebration, her parents planned a family trip to meet some close cousins at the beach instead. There, L.C. could take part in marine activities which she had always liked. As her anxiety was still present in high to moderate levels, I decided to add a low-dose antidepressant to the medication she had been on since the beginning. I knew that would help her to avoid the frequent peaks of anxiety and to maintain her in a more "familiar" and stable emotional state, and from there, monitor how she was feeling. I intuited that she would receive this as another expression of my concern about her. I explained to her how this medication, which she would only take on a temporary basis, could help her to have enough strength to deal with what she was going through. It acted as a new resource with which she could defend herself.

After returning from the trip to the beach, I found L.C. a little more upbeat. She told me that she had felt very close to her cousins and that she had started sleeping alone. She had enjoyed the days by the sea and the beach sports. Her mother commented to me, with deep sadness, that she hadn't seen L.C. smiling, not even once. It was as if something had died inside her. Inevitably, the image of the broken girl appeared again in front of me, and also my thoughts returned to wondering whether there was anything to gain from these situations or whether they are just meaningless expressions of the evil and darkness in human souls.

She began the process of entering the College School of Arts, which had been her fantasy for many years. A driver was assigned to pick her up and drop her off at the end of classes. We changed the frequency of the sessions and started seeing each other twice a week. I thought that beginning this new experience in her life could work as a natural container and that I was sending a trustful message about her progress. We talked about medication, her eating, sleeping and level of distress. Although she still kept her gaze fixed on the coloured strokes as she drew, she would occasionally look up and make eye contact for a little longer. During the sessions of this period, we talked about different artists and styles of artistic expression. I didn't venture to use tools of creative expression like writing or Sand-play, because I didn't yet know what L.C. might be dealing with internally.

During the first year of her art studies, I asked her to bring me some of the exercises she was working on in the different subjects she was taking. We talked about the colours she was using, the brush strokes and the images that were appearing. I was feeling optimistic about her progress but was concerned that she was still "kidnapped" by the traumatic event.

One afternoon, she called me because she was very upset and asked to see me that same day. I felt her urgency and asked myself why, for the first time, she wanted to bring her session forward. What had happened that made her ask for this meeting? As well as feeling her anxiety, I also recognized that this perhaps indicated that she was feeling in some way sustained by the psychotherapy process and more trusting of me. When she arrived, she showed me a picture that she had painted in class. It was a drawing in very dark colours. There were no defined images, but in the middle of what I perceived as an atmosphere of confinement or a whirlpool, two threatening figures appeared. She let me know, pointing to the figures, while crying, that this was something from "what had happened last year". It was the first time she had made reference to her kidnapping since we had started seeing each other.

I felt that, in her despair, she was trying to reach the painful core of her wound and I felt for her struggle. I pointed out to her how, in "our inner world", there are things that can affect us profoundly and that we need to get to know them little by little. I talked to her about the importance of continuing to work with the images as a way to build the bridge to her inner world. Although I trusted in the strength that she had gained to cope with her painful emotions, I did not want to take her pain for granted and asked her about whether she wanted to increase her medication. She replied that she thought she could manage. I read this as an acknowledgement of the resources she had.

In addition to the images that she was bringing, I also asked her to start paying attention to the images that appeared in her dreams. For a long time, she insisted that she did not remember any dream images. As time went by, L.C. came out of the emotional paralysis in which she had found herself, she became more animated in relation to subjects related to her career such as art exhibitions, visits to museums, lectures by some artists and courses on techniques that her university did not offer. It was as if, little by little, she was recovering something of what the terrible experience – of which she had not yet spoken – had taken away.

After a few months, she called me again. This time she was very distressed and asked me for an urgent session. During our meeting, she informed me that, in her dreams, she had recognized a man's voice that she associated with her captivity. She felt terrified and completely vulnerable. I felt her fear and recognized my own struggle with what was happening. On one hand, I knew that what was taking place was very important to her healing process, on the other, I myself felt afraid about what images and memories may appear and how I would react or feel towards them. I knew it would not be easy to share with her the trauma she had experienced, the re-appearance of which felt very close. I told her about how gradually her psyche was beginning to show her very important elements, even if they were disturbing. I let her see how much time had passed and how she had been able to respect the time she needed for these images to emerge, which – for some reason – she had now started to see.

She began a new period of waking up startled and going to her parents' bed with some frequency. I began to invite her to paint the images that were emerging. Intuitively, I asked her to assign bright colours to them (yellow, deep greens, electric blues) and to try to avoid dark colours. Gradually she was able to begin to talk about the sense of threat, vulnerability and the terror she felt in the face of these internal characters. Very slowly, as the characters started to make their appearance, we were able to begin to talk. First, about the emotions that were activated as the images emerged from her inner world, and then gradually she became able to talk about the images themselves: their evil presence, their threatening attitude, their primitive and aggressive essence, representatives of a dark and shadowy world.

She began to have some associations to the feelings she experienced during her captivity. Other images started to arise: the dark, dank, awful-smelling room. Other feelings surfaced: the sense of panic, the despair, the thought that she would never see her parents again, the persistent anxiety that every time the door was opened, she was going to be killed. All this brought with it the experience of hopelessness, vulnerability, absolute loneliness and helplessness. We sustained this dynamic for about one year. Each time, I could see the interaction between the images she had drawn and that which was emerging from L.C.'s emotional world. I had an intuition that there was something else "floating" in the background. Something terrible that had not yet been seen or talked about.

It took another year for what was at the bottom of that dark, hazy cloud to finally emerge. One day she arrived unannounced at my office, broken down, crying uncontrollably and overwhelmed. She gave me the impression that she was in a psychotic state of mind. She kept repeating in desperation: "He raped me, he raped me". Initially, in the midst of this confusion, chaos and despair, I thought that something terrible had happened to her again. I soon realized that the horrible content that had been trapped by the repression of her memory, had finally emerged, with all its emotional charge together with the reverberations of what had transpired.

It was a long and painful session. In the midst of her crying, she described to me in detail what had happened. How the door had opened and one of the men, who had kept her in captivity, had entered. She remembered the smell of alcohol, his lewd attitude, the disgust at the touch of his skin, the gasps, the pain, the deepest despair she had ever felt and the wish to die. After what seemed to her an eternity of being trapped in the deepest disgust and revulsion, she felt that something inside her had died. She felt so alone. I could feel her despair, her loneliness, her fear, as well as my rage, my powerlessness and my own horror. I had to contain a strong impulse to hug her, and instead tried to accompany her with just my silent presence, which was overwhelmed with compassion. This all poured out of her like vomit, in the midst of her despair and agitated sobs. She then lay curled up, weeping silently. Deep inside me, I knew that the worst was over. I called her parents to pick her up to take her home and we arranged to meet the next day.

The next session, she arrived with an elusive look on her face, as if she was embarrassed. I told her that she had been very brave and that the worst was over. From now on, we had to start picking up where she had left off more than three years ago. Intuitively, I asked her to draw a mandala. She lost herself in the peace and calm of the exercise. The next year was accompanied by writing and mandala drawing with which we closed each session. We would talk or write about many dark features of her experience: human evil, the shadow, destiny and death. She talked about her fear of not being able to have a partner or a family of her own. She felt vulnerable and "strange".

In many sessions, she would express her rage about what had happened to her. She would declare: "Why me?" … in which I could recognize some envy towards those whom she described as "nothing has touched them", and also some perverse fantasies of damaging others as revenge for her "unfair experience". Sometimes I felt I was carrying, unjustly, her anger, and needed to point out this dynamic as I was concerned about how frequently traumatized people can become some kind of bitter angry tyrant. In her process, there were opportunities for us to talk about these shadow aspects of her psyche, of our psyche.

We needed many hours to put things in their rightful place, to separate and differentiate what she had experienced from what could be a future life with a different "energetic charge". It took time to rediscover her capacity to dream, to fantasize, to allow herself to connect with her passions and desires. In parallel, she became able to express her anger, her rage, hate and feelings of an unfair destiny.

It has been a hard and complex road which we have shared in the conscious rebuilding of a new floor for her to stand on. She stopped all medication some time ago, and the nightmares are no longer present. Today, she is in a romantic relationship with an old friend who reappeared in her life. She has started to explore her sexuality with this partner and to project her future fantasies of sharing her life with another person she can trust. She has continued to work with mandalas which, in her words, are her tools for self-regulation.

In addition to the therapeutic tools mentioned in this chapter, now there are new ones, such as Eye Movement Desensitization and Reprocessing (EMDR) and other therapy techniques focused on movement and body, that have proved effective. In my experience, finding the right combination of different techniques and the timing for them, reflects psychotherapy as an art. I would like to add that not all my work has such good outcomes as that of L.C. Despite our best efforts, many of the therapeutic processes we embark on are interrupted before we can see any change or they are unable to move the patient from the paralysis the traumatic event has caused.

The treatment of traumatized people is fraught with difficulty, because although a part of their psyche fights to engage in life, the dissociative complex caused by the traumatic event maintains a strong gravitational pull that tends to swallow all the good intentions directed at healing the trauma. This is at the core of the suffering: an apparent never-ending struggle between the reasonable desire to move on and the complex that keeps the person feeling either a helpless victim or transforms them into an angry tyrant who can tear their relationships and opportunities for life into pieces. By contrast, there are also many resilient people who seem to be able to get over the crippling aspect of the trauma and find a way to continue their path relatively quickly. From them, there is still much that we need to learn about this theme.

Note

1 Lopez-Pedraza R., personal communication (1999).

References

Janet, P. (1919/25) *Psychological Healing*. New York: Macmillan.
Jung, C.G. (1936) *Psychological Factors Determining Human Behaviour*. CW8. Princeton, NJ: Princeton University Press.
Jung, C.G. (1963) *Memories, Dreams, Reflections*. A. Jaffé (ed.) New York: Random House.
Jung, C.G. (2009) *The Red Book: Liber Novus*. S. Shamdasani (ed.) New York: W.W. Norton.
Jung, C.G. (2020) *The Black Books of C.G. Jung (1913–1932)*. S. Shamdasani (ed.) New York: W.W. Norton.
Kalsched, D. (2013) *Trauma and the Soul*. New York: Routledge.
Khan, M.M.R. (1963) "The concept of cumulative trauma", *The Psychoanalytic Study of the Child*, 18: 286–306.

LeDoux, J. (1996) *The Emotional Brain*. New York: Simon & Schuster.

Sperry, R. (1980) "Mind-brain interaction: mentalism, yes; dualism, no", *Neuroscience*, 5(2): 195–206.

van der Kolk, B., Greenberg, M., Boyd, H. and Krystal, H. (1985) "Inescapable shock, neurotransmitters and addiction to trauma: towards a psychobiology of post traumatic stress disorder", *Biological Psychiatry*, 20(3): 314–325.

Chapter 16

Understanding Trauma and Mourning from the Knowledge of the Heart

Heyong Shen

We have always lived with trauma and suffering, but without effective mourning there will be no recovery. What is more, many do not know what this means.

The Covid-19 pandemic has caused colossal damage. Approximately 555 million people have been infected and over 6 million have died. It has impacted all our lives, has damaged the world economy and undermined our physical and mental wellbeing. The ongoing crisis in Ukraine, Gaza and the shadow of further war poses a greater threat to the entire world. More trauma and suffering seem inevitable.

Here, I offer an Oriental approach to treating trauma, based on both Jungian analysis and Chinese "Psychology of the Heart". I will explore symbolic images related to this quest and try to reveal the meaning of trauma, suffering and mourning.

Jung and the Knowledge of the Heart

Jungian psychology is deeply rooted in C.G. Jung's own experience of trauma and suffering, not only personal but collective. He lived through the times of the first and second world wars. His connection to mourning, and his reflections on it, are well charted in *Lament of the Dead: Psychology After Jung's Red Book* by James Hillman and Sonu Shamdasani (2013). Jung referred to the work of the Red Book and his own confrontation with the unconscious as the most difficult experiment of his life. Such a process was not only for his own personal trauma, but also for the sake of humanity, for the psychological wounds of mankind after the world war. Jung called himself a wounded healer, his struggle was on behalf of depth psychotherapy and for the healing of the psyche and the soul.

As we know, while working on the Red Book, Jung descended into the Spirit of the Depths, which was the most demanding self-experiment for him and required extreme ascetic practice. But for what purpose? One of his

DOI: 10.4324/9781003298076-21

aims was to try to find the knowledge of the heart and the meaning of the soul. In his later years, Jung frequently reflected upon the dangers to the world. He warned: "The world hangs by a thin thread, and that thread is the human soul".[1] One of the primary goals of Jung's psychology is to search for the soul, to find the path to healing trauma and to facilitate individuation. Jung valued the work of Meyrink (1921), whose ideas influenced the naming of the Red Book: "it is called the Cinnabar book because, according to an ancient belief in China, that red is the colour of the garments of those who have reached the highest stage of perfection and stayed behind on earth for the salvation of mankind" (Jung, 2009: 212).

Jung agreed with Richard Wilhelm that in the wisdom of Chinese culture there lies the medicine and healing of trauma for modern Europe. As Jung opined:

> Wilhelm's life-work is of such immense importance to me because it clarified and confirmed so much that I had been seeking, striving for, thinking, and doing in my efforts to alleviate the psychic sufferings of Europeans. It was a tremendous experience for me to hear through him, in clear language, things I had dimly divined in the confusion of our European unconscious. Indeed, I feel myself so very much enriched by him that it seems to me as if I had received more from him than from any other man.
>
> (Jung, 1957, para. 96)

In his letter to Wilhelm, Jung wrote: "Fate seems to have apportioned to us the role of two piers which support the bridge between East and West" (Jung, 1973: 66). From my perspective, the knowledge of the Heart, relates to the experience of the Soul and this communication between East and West.

Jung started his *Liber Primus* with "The Way of What is to Come", describing his encounter with the spirit of the depths. His journey of self-discovery was traumatic: "The spirit of the depths forced me to speak to my soul, to call upon her as a living and self-existing being" (Jung, 2009: 232). Jung found a way to rediscover and communicate once more with his soul. How could he do that? He spoke to his soul with his heart and found that "there is a knowledge of the heart that gives deeper insight" (Jung, 2009: 233). As he described in the *Black Books*: "I gave you my heart … my soul, speak to me!" (Jung, 2020: 687). When Jung asked his soul: "How? And do you speak the truth?" His soul replied: "I have your heart. That's how. I feel with you, I am united with you" (Jung, 2020: 688). This "Knowledge of the Heart" is the calling from both the spirit of the depths and the soul; as Jung proclaimed: "Where in my soul do I shelter you? In my heart? Should my heart be your shrine, your holy of holies? So choose your place. I have accepted you" (Jung, 2009: 308).

In his later years, C.G. Jung tried to introduce a new method, which he called the "intuitive method" or, in other words, how to use the heart. As he said in his last Eranos Lecture (in 1951): "Outward hearing should not penetrate further than the ear; the intellect should not seek to lead a separate existence, thus the soul can become empty and absorb the whole world. It is Tao that fills this emptiness" (Jung, 1951a, para. 923). Jung continued: "If you have insight, says Chuang-tzu, 'you use your inner eye, your inner ear, to pierce to the heart of things, and have no need of intellectual knowledge.' This is obviously an allusion to the absolute knowledge of the unconscious and to the presence in the microcosm of macrocosmic events" (Jung, 1951a, para. 923). Jung described this new method as a means of yielding measurable results and, at the same time, provide an insight into the psychic nature of synchronicity. Jung explained: "I therefore turned my attention first of all to the intuitive technique for *grasping the total situation* which is so characteristic of China, namely the *I Ching* or *Book of Changes*" (Jung, 1952, para. 863). As I understand, through this new method, Jung wanted to put the knowledge of the heart into practice.

There is one hexagram in the I Ching (Wilhelm and Baynes, 1967: 541) especially related to the intuitive method described by Jung, this is hexagram 31, translated as "Influence" by Richard Wilhelm. The meaning of this hexagram is provided by this Chinese character, which means "touching by the Heart":

The upper part is "touching all" (with also a symbolic meaning of wound and trauma), and the lower part is the heart (container and healer). As the I Ching says:

> The Xian hexagram means 'gan' (heartfelt influence), heaven and earth have such heartfelt influence and all things take shape and come into being. The sage has such heartfelt influence on the hearts of humans, and the world attains peace and rest. If we contemplate the out-going of such heartfelt influences, we can know the nature of heaven and earth and all beings.
> (Wilhelm and Baynes, 1967: 541)

The Image and Meaning of Trauma Suffering and Mourning

As Jung advised in the Red Book: "If you go to thinking, take your heart with you" (Jung, 2009: 230). Let's take a look at the Chinese character for thought and thinking:

It is composed of two parts; the upper part is a symbol of the head or brain and the lower part is the symbol of the heart. For thinking about the truth, we need both and for beyond, the third level of meaning, we need the transcendent function.

There is one Chinese character that expresses both trauma and suffering (nan):

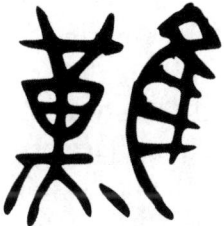

The image is related to a bird. It can be combined with "ku" as "ku-nan" (suffering, distress) or combined with "zai" as "zai-nan" (disaster, injury). The original meaning of "nan" is "huan" (injury, disease); its old form is:

which has the meaning of a split, broken or even lost heart.

In ancient times, the image of nan was combined with the image of the heart:

This reminds me of hexagram 36 of the I Ching: "Ming I", Darkening of the Light:

The meaning of Ming I is "at such a moment, it is appropriate to persevere in the right way in difficulty" (Huisheng, 2008: 204–209). Just as the image suggests, the sun sinking into the earth symbolizes the darkening of the light. It alludes to a man who is yielding and obedient in appearance but virtuous and brilliant inside. In this way, he can overcome great disasters (Huisheng, 2008). Six in the fourth place of the hexagram means: "he penetrates the left side of the belly, that is, he finds out the inner most sentiment of the heart". Wilhelm explained the meaning of the image: "Thus does the superior man live with the great mass, he veils his light, yet still shines" (Wilhelm and Baynes, 1967: 332).

The Chinese character of "dao" is the key word for "mourning":

Its basic meaning is grief and fear. From the image, we can distil the meaning of mourning: a special use of the heart, the transcendent nature of the heart.

There are two Chinese terms related to the meaning of mourning, "ai-dao" (grief and mourning), and "dao-nian" (mourning and memorial) from the image of nian (memorial):

We can see the meaning of this combination of the presented heart, its moment and timing, namely, bring the heart with you.

Jung studied the I Ching and Chinese characters. He once described them as "readable archetypes" (Young, 2011: 9). The images can help us understand, but more importantly, they convey the way or thread of doing things; through practice, we can reach the meaning.

In Chinese culture, there is the "Ching Ming Festival" (around 5 April each year), when graves are attended to and special offerings are made to the dead. On 5 April 2020, I was invited to give a public lecture on: *Facing Suffering, Compassion and Transformation*. It was organized by Tong Jun, who is the most influential psychoanalyst in Wuhan, China. I started with the following:

> We all know that an epidemic has resulted in so many people losing their lives; most of them owing to respiratory failure, without the company of family members, dying alone, without a farewell ceremony. How many people have been heartbroken and how many families have been shattered; leaving a loneliness and pain that the survivors cannot express, leaving behind the trauma and suffering we have to face alone? We need to mourn, we need to entrust ourselves to the care of our mourning.

From a Kleinian perspective, Loewald (1962: 493) said: "Mourning involves not only the gradual, piecemeal relinquishment of the lost object, but also the internalization, the appropriation of aspects of this object." It's a very good explanation. However, from my understanding, mourning, may look like the "gradual and piece-by-piece abandonment of the lost object", but not really. In mourning there is a sense of "missing", a sense of longing or yearning for someone or something that is absent. This is the meaning of Dao-Nian in Chinese; it not only "includes the internalization and absorption of aspects of this object", but perhaps also encompasses a kind of

transformation, turning grief into strength and self-knowledge. This is precisely what the "compassion" and "transformation" referred to below
are about.

In 2006, we set up a project named Garden of the Heart & Soul in Chinese
orphanages, which used Jungian psychology, Sand-play Therapy and the
Psychology of the Heart to support the psychological development of
orphans. This was later expanded in 2008 to help victims of earthquakes
and natural disasters. Many people refer to our work as healing by "Ci-bei"
(loving-grief-compassion therapy). We started the "Garden of the Heart &
Soul online" on January 26, 2020 and focused our work on people affected
by the Covid-19 pandemic.

Here are the Chinese characters for "Ci-bei":

Both take the symbol of the heart as their core. For Ci, it is a picture of
growing (increasing) above an image of heart and has a basic meaning of
love. The character of Bei combines "no" and the heart and has the meaning of "not the heart", or a lost heart. If we integrate Ci and Bei as "Ci-bei",
we get "heart to heart", "hold and contain love and grief together within
the container". This is at the core of the work of the Garden of the Heart &
Soul. A new meaning emerges and we have the opportunity to experience
the transcendent function and compassion.

The "512 Wenchuan Earth Quake" which happened in 2008 in China was
a great tragedy in human history. The Chinese Federation of Analytical
Psychology and Sand-play Therapy organized volunteers to go to Wenchuan
at the first week of the earthquake to provide psychological relief, to set up
seven workstations of the "Garden of the Heart & Soul" using Sand-play

Therapy, Jungian therapy and Psychology of the Heart to help the survivors and other victims. The work was truly arduous, both physically and emotionally; people there desperately needed help.

Our work and practice, based on analytical psychology and Chinese culture, can be divided into three stages:

First, with the image and meaning of Ci-bei, "contain love and grief together within the container", we built an effective relationship: a contained, free and protected space to re-establish and increase the victims' sense of reality and safety.

Second, with the image and meaning of Ci-bei, "from heart to heart", we tried to enhance the therapeutic containment by active listening with the heart:

(the Chinese character of "listening", combined with the ear, growing, intuitive, and the heart).

Then we used Sand-play, music and painting, embodied dream work and archetypal psychodrama to work with the clients individually and in groups.

Finally, we offered sustained psychological support, using the psychology of the heart, employing the principles of Ci-bei, and "Gan-ying":

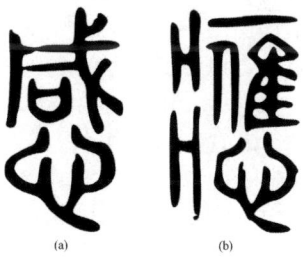

(a)   (b)

(touching by the heart, and responding from the heart) which represent the healing and transformative function of the cultural archetypes (Dayu for Naming and Initiating; Shennong for Taming and Nurturing; and Fuxi for Timing and Transforming).

In the first period of our work, from the Sand-play Therapy, we can see the process and images of how the victims expressed their trauma, their wounded feelings of chaos, suffering and helplessness. And then, in the next period, after several weeks or months, through the Sand-play we can see, they were touched by the heart. An image of an angel emerged with figures of the heart, and the healing process happened in the Garden of the Heart & Soul.

Healing and Transformation, Psychology of the Heart

The Chinese name for psychology, "Xin-Li-Xue", is similar to "Heart-ology" and contains a special meaning: "learning the truth of the heart".

The heart, in both image and meaning, is at the centre of Chinese culture and philosophy. When Confucius was asked to use just one word to represent his whole teaching and thought, he gave the character of "shu" (forgiveness, benevolence):

The image of the character conveys the meaning of "the same heart" or "following the heart". As Mencius says: "To fully develop the kindness of the heart is to understand human nature" (Zhi Meng, 1999: 291). The Taoist tradition has beautiful images for the "empty heart" and related significant metaphors, for example, the story of "Fasting of the heart" by Chuang-tzu, which C.G. Jung quoted from and referred to several times (e.g., Wilhelm and Jung, 1929). Chinese Zen Buddhism has, as its original name in Chinese, the "Heart Sect" (Xin-zhong) which continues the line of the fundamental teaching of "heart to heart" and "enlightening of the heart nature", which is closely related to knowledge of the heart. Even the Chinese character for "culture", as well as for civilization, has the image of the heart as its core.

I took the Psychology of the Heart and the Heart of Jungian Analysis as the theme for my Fay Lectures in 2018. This theme has lived in me for over 30 years. I also used this topic for the Fulbright in residence-scholar lectures (1996–1997), and for the Eranos lectures (1997/2007/2019). I consider them as part of my continued exploration of the "knowledge of the heart", and the "intuitive method" following Jung.

Take the Chinese image of therapy and healing for example. The keyword of therapy in Chinese is zhi:

The left part of zhi is the image of water and the right part is an image of built-up earth. This Chinese character originally utilized the image and meaning of "dealing with water" (preventing a flood by controlling water). The image fits with the Chinese five elements theory, too much water (yin) may cause diseases and using earth (yang) can defend water or make (yin and yang) balance. In the Chinese language system, medical and psychological therapy (cure and treatment), management, scholarship and politics all take the image and meaning of controlling and containing water – they are all related to how to deal with "water". This of course also resonates with the importance of the paradigm of containment in therapy in the West.

Based on the Psychology of the Heart, we take the image of "healing" in Chinese combined with the image of therapy together to further explore the "knowledge of the heart" and the "intuitive method" left by Jung.

The original image of the Chinese character for "healing" is "Boat on the Heart":

which is such a beautiful image. It is combined of four parts together: 1, canoe or boat; 2, making (constructing) or fitting; 3, flowing water; and 4, (the lowest part) the Heart.

Today in museums, we can see canoes that are around 9,000 years old made by ancient people. Making or constructing a canoe or boat involves creating an empty space with a piece of wood. This empty space requires equilibrium in the philosophical sense (*zhong*), as well as in the physical sense. This resonates with how the creation of an empty space might be viewed from the standpoint of psychotherapy.

Considering the images in the Chinese character for "healing", "a boat resting upon the heart", we can see a new meaning of the symbol for "water" in therapy. There is a new kind of relationship between boat and water, in comparison with using earth to defend against water. Without enough water, a boat cannot move; without deep water, a big boat cannot go further. We can find, in these images, inspiration for our work in Jungian analysis and depth psychotherapy.

Of course, we should always also keep in mind that water can be dangerous: the unconscious can indeed be dangerous. This idea can also be seen in the "abysmal" hexagram of the *I Ching*: The double Kan (abysmal) trigram symbolizes danger after danger. I learned from my own personal Jungian analysis that to face the unconscious, or to do therapy at the level of the unconscious, is almost like embarking in a small boat in order to fish in the sea. I believe that with this metaphor, Jung was telling us to prepare the container well and to keep in mind that the deep water (the unconscious) can be dangerous.

So, if we combine the Chinese character for "healing" (a boat or canoe resting upon the heart) with the character for "therapy" (defence against water with built-up earth), we arrive at a new situation: the meaning of the knowledge of the heart and the intuitive method, not only involves defence but also allows us to "ride the waves" and "sail".

In ancient China, there is a character "yu":

for both "defence" and "riding". As an old Chinese proverb says: "Boat supporting/benefitting the world". When doing therapy as Jungian analysts

and depth psychotherapists, we should remember this image and its meaning and find or construct the "boat resting upon the heart" with our patients.
I am also mindful of the old Chinese saying which recommends how the
therapy should proceed: Heaven/God using you as boat, as oar and as rower.

In *Aion: Researches into the Phenomenology of the Self* (1951b), Jung used
the image of water as it appeared in the Tao: "For this reason the ancients
often compared the symbol to water, a case in point being Tao, where yang
and yin are united. Tao is the 'valley spirit,' the winding course of a river"
(Jung, 1951b, para. 281). Jung continued:

> The undiscovered vein within us is a living part of the psyche; classical
> Chinese philosophy names this interior way "Tao" and likens it to a flow
> of water that moves irresistibly towards its goal. To rest in Tao means
> fulfilment, wholeness, one's destination reached, one's mission done; the
> beginning, end, and perfect realization of the meaning of existence innate
> in all things. Personality is Tao.
>
> (Jung, 1934, para. 323)

Dora Kalff, student of C.G. Jung and founder of Sand-play Therapy, made
this conclusion after she described the image of water in the 29th hexagram
of the I Ching: "Remember this in Sand-play. And remember that when we
do succeed with the work of bringing about the inner harmony that defines
a personality, we speak of grace" (Kalff, 1980: 140).

The image of the I Ching's Kan hexagram expresses the idea that "the
heart's ailment also requires the heart's remedy". When Dora Kalff established Sand-play Therapy, she took the diagram of Chou Tun Yi, which is
also called the "Tai Chi Diagram" as the philosophical foundation for her
methodology. As she says: "While studying Chinese thought, I came across
a diagram that seems to correspond to our viewpoint. It is the diagram of
Chou Tun Yi, a philosopher of the Sung period, who lived around the year
1000 ce" (Kalff, 1980: 10). Taiji is Tao. Jung said in *Memories, Dreams,
Reflections*: "The question of the unity which must compensate this diversity led me directly to the Chinese concept of Tao … It was only after I had
reached the central point in my thinking and in my researches, namely, the
concept of the self, that I once more found my way back to the world"
(Jung, 1963: 208). Dora Kalff took the "Diagram of the Supreme Ultimate"
as the main methodology for Sand-play Therapy. She connected the concept
of the "Supreme Ultimate" to the Self and its unfolding, into the polarity of
Yin and Yang, to the manifestation of the Self as a basis for healthy ego
development and healing.

Conclusion

The origination of psychology is deeply connected to the inscription over the ancient Greek temple at Delphi: "Know thyself". But how can this be achieved? When I was there, facing the omphalos, I realized that it is through the profound depths of suffering and the expansive realms of knowledge that lies the way to know one's self, to acquire self-knowledge and the knowledge of the heart.

The images of Chinese characters and I Ching hexagrams for trauma and mourning convey the inspiration for our understanding and clinical practice. Both trauma (nan, Huan-Nan) and mourning (Dao-Nian), not only describe the symbolic meaning of suffering, but are related to the core element of the heart and convey the intimation for healing. This is also a manifestation of the principle of the 16-characters heart Sutra in Chinese culture, which Jung referred to as the transcendent function. Its essence, through mourning, achieves the transformation of trauma. Therefore, Jung's knowledge of the heart, his intuitive method (the method of using the heart) and the psychology of the heart can offer us many insights and guidance. As Jung said in the Red Book: "But how can I attain the knowledge of the heart? You can attain this knowledge only by living your life to the full" (Jung, 2009: 233).

This is my understanding of the knowledge of the heart and the meaning of trauma: suffering and mourning.

Note

1 First published in *Time Magazine* and then in the *Houston Post*, 16 September 1957. It was then recorded by Gerhard Wehr in *An Illustrated Biography of C.G. Jung* (1989: 438–439).

References

Huisheng, Fu (2008) *I Ching: The Zhou Book of Changes*. Changsha: Hunan People's Publishing House.

Hillman, J. and Shamdasani, S. (2013) *Lament of the Dead: Psychology After Jung's Red Book*. New York: W.W. Norton & Co.

Jung, C.G. (1934) *Development of Personality*. CW17. Princeton, NJ: Princeton University Press.

Jung, C.G. (1951a) *On Synchronicity*. CW8. Princeton, NJ: Princeton University Press.

Jung, C.G. (1951b) *Aion: Researches into the Phenomenology of the Self*. CW9/2. Princeton, NJ: Princeton University Press.

Jung, C.G. (1952) *Synchronicity: An Acausal Connecting Principle.* CW8. Princeton, NJ: Princeton University Press.

Jung, C.G. (1957) *Richard Wilhelm: In Memoriam.* CW15. Princeton, NJ: Princeton University Press.

Jung, C.G. (1963) *Memories, Dreams, Reflections.* A. Jaffé (ed.) (trans. R. Winston and C. Winston). New York: Random House.

Jung, C.G. (1973) *Letters, Vol. 1: 1906–1950.* G. Adler (ed.) (trans. R.F.C. Hull). Princeton, NJ: Princeton University Press.

Jung, C.G. (2009) *The Red Book: Liber Novus.* S. Shamdasani (ed.) (trans. M. Kyburz, J. Peck and S. Shamdasani). New York: W.W. Norton & Co.

Jung, C.G. (2020) *The Black Books 1913–1932: Notebooks of Transformation.* S. Shamdasani (ed.), (trans. M. Liebscher, J. Peck and S. Shamdasani). New York: W.W. Norton & Co.

Kalff, D. (1980 [2012]) *Sandplay: A Psychotherapeutic Approach to the Psyche.* Cloverdale, CA: Temenos Press.

Loewald, H.W. (1962) "Internalization, separation, mourning and the super-ego", *The Psychoanalytic Quarterly*, 31(4): 483–504.

Meng, Zhi (1999) *Gaozhi (Part A).* Changsha: Hunan People's Publishing House.

Meyrink, G. (1921) *The White Dominican.* Sawtry, UK: Dedalus Limited.

Wehr, G. (1989) *An Illustrated Biography of C.G. Jung.* Boston: Shambhala.

Wilhelm, R. and Baynes, C.F. (1967) *The I Ching or Book of Changes.* Princeton, NJ: Princeton University Press.

Wilhelm, R. and Jung, C.G. (1929 [1972]) *The Secret of the Golden Flower: A Chinese Book of Life.* (trans. R. Wilhelm). London: Routledge.

Young, W.K. (2011) *Jung on Synchronicity and Yijing: A Critical Approach.* Newcastle-upon-Tyne: Cambridge Scholars Publishing.

Name Index

Pages followed by "n" refer to notes.

Subject Index

Pages followed by "n" refer to notes.

class discrimination 218
claustrophilic family 236, 238–239
clustered feeling-states 16
clusters: of information 17; of memories 17
compassion 24, 30, 42, 46, 70, 84, 177, 313, 317, 325–326
compensation 36, 129, 171
complex: autonomous 13, 20, 22, 25, 30, 31n6, 128, 161, 184, 189; collective 36; cultural 17, 249–250; trauma-related 120, 122, 139, 153, 161–162, 179, 293; traumatic 148; autonomous 13, 20, 22, 25, 30–31, 128, 161, 184, 189
confusion of languages 86
consciousness 13, 17–18, 24–25, 28–29, 31n12, 43, 56n2, 81, 87–89, 91, 93, 110, 113, 120, 128, 132, 144–146, 175, 184–188, 198, 216, 248, 255–256, 259, 301–302, 304, 310
CONSPEC 19
containing function 98, 169, 308
containment 51, 97, 161, 165, 168, 174, 271, 276, 327, 329
conversion 139, 142, 144; symptoms 155, 157–158
corpus callosum 149
cortex: cingulate 291–293; limbic 291; prefrontal 149, 292
countertransference 24, 27, 61, 63, 68, 71–72, 74–75, 85–86, 88–89, 91–92, 107, 142–143, 156, 171–172, 176–177, 179, 200, 250, 254, 256–257, 266; somatic 88
countertransferential experience 83–84
COVID-19 83, 193, 249, 320, 326
creativity 29, 55, 130, 174, 176, 220, 239, 292, 304, 306–307
cross-cultural encounter 246, 254
cryptomnesia 14, 22, 31n2
Cuckoldry 165
cultural wounds 248, 250, 252, 255, 257–259, 264
Cupid 174, 177, 301

death drive 149, 175
death instinct 164–165, 175
defence(s): mechanisms 61, 68, 147; primitive 128, 147, 289; of the Self 38, 171
defensive mechanism 134, 176, 305–306
deficits in representation and symbolization 62
depersonalization 121, 127, 131, 142–145, 151, 156–157, 169, 235, 297
depression 128, 167, 197–198, 211, 229, 275
derealization 84, 121, 127, 131, 142–145, 151, 156–157, 235
developmental process(es) 93, 96, 304, 310; of our psyche 306
developmental psychopathology 230
diagnosis 83–84, 120–123, 126, 130, 142–143, 178, 228–230

Diagnostic and Statistical Manual of Mental Disorders (DSM) 119–122, 140–141, 144, 154, 165, 228–229
Diagram of the Supreme Ultimate 331
discrimination 213, 218–219, 292
disorganized attachment 190
dissociability 31n12; of the psyche 15, 87
dissociation 22–23, 37–39, 43–46, 56n3, 65, 84, 86, 96, 109, 131–133, 139–158, 161, 184–191, 200, 212, 230, 305–307; post-traumatic 149; vicarious 156
dissociative: defences 37, 40, 45, 54, 92, 130; fugue 156; multiplicity 144–145; phenomena 121, 131, 139, 145, 148, 150–151, 157–158, 188; states 156, 190
Dissociative Identity Disorder (DID) 132, 139, 144–146, 153, 157
domestic violence 308
domination 46, 164, 180
doppelgänger 74–75
double absence 268
dream: big dream 111, 113; creating a path 25; daydreams 178; ego 43, 54; images 49, 71, 315; non-dream 65; premonitory 300; recurrent 164, 250; re-living the trauma 150; symbolically significant 102

early bodily experience 24, 63
ego complex 31n5, 88, 128, 134, 185
ego-destructive superego 161
ego-syntonic aggression 162
embodied: cognition 88; disperceptive phenomena 84; simulation 90
emergent process 91
emotion: as dynamic energy of the psyche 39; regulation 234; schema(s) 17–18, 31n7; vehement, vs. feelings 40, 56n2, 188
emotional: attunement of emotional states 90; dysregulation 230, 234; instability 82–83; shared emotional tone 16; tone 13, 288
enactment 38–39, 47–54, 92, 105, 143, 170–171, 294
endogenous opioids 150
envy 104, 172, 212, 246, 317
epistemic: distrust 232; trust 126, 232, 234, 243n1
Eros 174–175, 177–179, 181
eroticized: complex 166; countertransference 176–177, 179; transference 171, 176–177, 179, 181; trauma 161
evil 42–45, 48–49, 56n1, 66–67, 194–195, 312, 314, 316–317
evolutionary level 290–291
Expressive Sandwork (ES) 307–308
exteroceptive aspects 87
Eye Movement Desensitization and Reprocessing (EMDR) 318

Printed in the United States
by Baker & Taylor Publisher Services